101 751 056 3

D1576464

ONE WEEK

THE FUTURE OF LABOUR LAW

All over the world a different kind of labour law is in the process of formation; in Gramsci's phrase, this is an interregnum when the old is dying and the new is struggling to be born. This book, to which an internationally distinguished group of scholars has contributed, examines the future of labour law from a wide variety of perspectives. Issues covered include the ideology of New Labour law; the employment relationship; the public/private divide; termination of employment; equality law; corporate governance; collective bargaining; workers' participation; strikes; international labour standards; the role of EU law; the EU Charter of Fundamental Rights; labour law and development in Southern Africa; and the impact of globalisation. The essays are written in honour of the outstanding labour lawyer Professor Sir Bob Hepple QC, who has contributed to so many areas of this dynamic field.

The Future of Labour Law
Liber Amicorum Bob Hepple QC

Edited by

CATHERINE BARNARD, SIMON DEAKIN

and

GILLIAN S MORRIS

·HART·
PUBLISHING

OXFORD AND PORTLAND OREGON
2004

Published in North America (US and Canada) by
Hart Publishing
c/o International Specialized Book Services
5804 NE Hassalo Street
Portland, Oregon
97213-3644
USA

Hart Publishing is a specialist legal publisher based in
Oxford, England. To order further copies of this book or to request a list of other
publications please write to:

Hart Publishing, Salters Boatyard, Folly Bridge,
Abingdon Rd, Oxford, OX1 4LB
Telephone: +44 (0)1865 245533 Fax: +44 (0)1865 794882
email: mail@hartpub.co.uk
WEBSITE: http//:www.hartpub.co.uk

British Library Cataloguing in Publication Data
Data Available

ISBN 1-84113-404-X (hardback)

Typeset by Olympus Infotech Pvt Ltd, India in Sabon 10/12 pt
Printed and bound in Great Britain by
MPG Books Ltd, Bodmin, Cornwall

List of Contributors

Steven Anderman is Professor of Law at the University of Essex.

Catherine Barnard is a Fellow of Trinity College; University Senior Lecturer in Law at Cambridge, and Jean Monnet Chair of European Union Law.

Brian Bercusson is Professor of Law at King's College, London.

William Brown is Master of Darwin College and Montague Burton Professor of Industrial Relations at the University of Cambridge.

Breen Creighton is a Partner of Corrs, Chambers, Westgarth in Melbourne, Victoria, and a Professorial Fellow of the Faculty of Law, University of Melbourne.

Paul Davies is Cassel Professor of Commercial Law at the London School of Economics and Political Science and a Deputy Chairman of the Central Arbitration Committee.

Simon Deakin is Robert Monks Professor of Corporate Governance and a Fellow of Peterhouse at the University of Cambridge.

Keith Ewing is Professor of Public Law at King's College, London.

Sandra Fredman is Professor of Law and Fellow of Exeter College at the University of Oxford and a barrister at Old Square Chambers.

Mark Freedland is Professor of Employment Law and Fellow of St John's College at the University of Oxford.

Evance Kalula is Professor of Employment and Social Security Law at the University of Cape Town.

Gillian S Morris is a former Professor of Law, now Professor Associate, at Brunel University, a barrister at Matrix Chambers, London, and a Deputy Chairman of the Central Arbitration Committee.

Paul O'Higgins is Honorary Professor of Law at Trinity College, Dublin, and Emeritus Professor of Law at King's College, London.

Sarah Oxenbridge is an officer of the Advisory, Conciliation and Arbitration Service, London, and a former Senior Research Associate of the Department of Applied Economics, University of Cambridge.

Silvana Sciarra is Professor of Law at the University of Florence.

Manfred Weiss is Professor of Law at the Institute for Labour Law, Johann-Wolfgang Goethe University, Frankfurt-am-Main.

Abbreviations

ACAS	Advisory, Conciliation and Arbitration Service
CAC	Central Arbitration Committee
CBI	Confederation of British Industry
CEACR	ILO Committee of Experts on the Application of Conventions and Recommendations
CEEP	European Centre of Enterprises with Public Participation and of Enterprises of General Economic Interest
CFA	Committee on Freedom of Association
CRE	Commission for Racial Equality
ECHR	European Convention on Human Rights
ECJ	European Court of Justice
EPZ	Export Processing Zones
ETUC	European Trade Union Confederation
EWC	European Works Council
GMP	guaranteed minimum pension
HRM	human resource management
ILC	International Labour Conference
ILO	International Labour Organisation
ILS	international labour standards
ITF	International Transport Workers Federation
NAP	national action plan
OMC	open method of coordination
PFA	ILO Principles of Freedom of Association
PFI	private finance initiative
SADC	Southern Africa Development Community
SERPS	State Earnings-Related Pension Scheme
TNC	transnational corporation
TUC	Trades Union Congress
TULR(C)A 1992	Trade Union and Labour Relations (Consolidation) Act 1992
TUPE	Transfer of Undertakings (Protection of Employment) Regulations 1981 (SI 1981/1794)
UNICE	Union of Industrial and Employers' Confederations of Europe

Preface

This book is dedicated to our great friend and colleague, Bob Hepple, who has taught and inspired us to follow in his trail-blazing footsteps, and to aspire to his own standards of creativity and intellectual rigour, in the dynamic field of labour law. There are many others who would want to thank Bob Hepple for his support and friendship. The editors decided that instead of a collection of diverse contributions, it would be a more fitting tribute to elaborate on the theme of the future of labour law, on which Bob published a seminal article in the *Industrial Law Journal* in December 1995. The constraints of space, and the need to preserve this coherent theme, have meant that we have not been able to invite contributions from everyone who would have wished to join this tribute.

Bob Hepple was born on 11 August 1934, in a South Africa beset by racial bigotry. By his own account, two experiences in his early youth shaped the course of his life. The first was when, at the age of 12, his mother took him to see the horrifying documentary films about the Nazi death camps, in which two of his Jewish maternal ancestors had perished. This demonstrated in graphic terms where anti-semitism and racism could lead. The second occurred a few weeks later, when his aunt took him to the shanty towns near Johannesburg, with their open sewers, hessian and corrugated iron shacks, and ill-clad children suffering from malnutrition. These experiences motivated what was to become his life-long struggle for equality and democracy. Bob's own family, too, inspired him to fight for social justice. His paternal grandfather, a patternmaker who had fled unemployment in England, was a branch secretary of the Amalgamated Society of Engineers, blacklisted for leading a strike. He and his wife, a Johannesburg pioneer and suffragette, were founding members in 1910 of the South African Labour Party, of which Bob's father, Alex Hepple, was later to become Leader. Both Bob's parents gave up their business careers to struggle for unity between black and white South Africans in pursuit of a democratic socialist society. In doing so, they faced hatred and violence from their fellow white South Africans.

Bob entered the University of the Witwatersrand in 1952. At the age of 18, he was arrested, spent a night in prison and several weeks on trial, because he was one of a group of students who had entered the Southwestern Township without the necessary permit to participate in a concert which was in fact the cover for a political meeting. From then on, he became a target for police raids and surveillance. Bob was also active in student politics, becoming President of the Students' Representative

Council, and was threatened with expulsion for his part in protests against racial segregation by the authorities of the University's Great Hall. In 1954 he represented the National Union of South African Students at an international students' congress in Moscow, an occasion which aroused his international awareness.

Bob graduated in law with distinction in 1957. He had simultaneously completed articles of clerkship, and practised first as an attorney and then spent three years as a lecturer in law at Wits, assigned by the Dean to teach property law, negotiable instruments and obligations, subjects in which he thought Bob's political views could be insulated. Bob's first writings were on the 'safe' subjects of the Roman-Dutch law of sales of goods and company signatures on negotiable instruments, although he was permitted to write a heavily-censored piece on economic and racial legislation in Keeton's series on the Laws and Constitutions of the British Commonwealth.

By this time Bob was deeply involved in the multi-racial South African Congress of Trade Unions (SACTU), as co-editor of their newspaper *Workers' Unity* and voluntary legal adviser. The organisation operated in the shadows of legality, its leaders being frequently arrested and banned. During the state of emergency, declared after the Sharpeville massacre in 1960, Bob was given the gigantic task of managing the affairs of SACTU following the arrest of virtually all of its activists. Bob gave up his lectureship so as to have greater freedom to undertake this work. He joined the Johannesburg Bar in January 1962.

Bob soon found himself defending *pro amico* in political trials. In his autobiography, Nelson Mandela recalls that he was 'ably assisted' by Bob during his trial in 1962 for incitement to strike against the establishment of an apartheid republic. Bob also began to specialise in what was called 'industrial law', a system which provided conciliation and arbitration but excluded most black workers. In addition there was an 'underground' life, in which he helped to hide and support outlawed black leaders. This culminated with his arrest at Rivonia, the secret headquarters which the police uncovered, on 11 July 1963. After three months' interrogation under physical and psychological pressure in solitary confinement, Bob was brought before the Supreme Court with Mandela and others on charges which carried the death penalty. The defence lawyers launched an attack on the indictment. When it was quashed, the State Prosecutor announced that the charges against Bob were being withdrawn but he would be compelled to testify as a state witness. He was released from custody.

Bob was not prepared to testify against the accused. Refusing to do so would have brought imprisonment, and he chose instead to flee the country, with his then wife, Shirley, in dramatic circumstances via Bechuanaland Protectorate (Botswana) and Tanzania to England. They could not take their infant children, Brenda and Paul, on this hazardous journey, but were later reunited with them in England. Bob was immediately placed under banning orders by the South African government, lifted only 27 years' later, in February 1990, the day after Mandela was released from prison.

Bob arrived in Britain in December 1963. As a citizen of South Africa, then outside the Commonwealth, he had no right of entry. Bob was granted asylum initially for seven days, then indefinitely, with the support of Ben Birnberg, a pioneer civil liberties solicitor. On the basis of his British grandparentage he was granted British citizenship in 1966.

Bob decided to pursue an academic career. With the help of Ken Polack, Colin Turpin and Charles Feinstein, three former South Africans in Cambridge, he found a place at Clare College. After two years' study he obtained a first-class postgraduate degree in English Law. During his second year, Bob was obliged to pursue advanced research. His choice of subject was prompted by an experience soon after his arrival in Britain. He was invited to address a trade union branch at a London bus depot on behalf of the anti-apartheid movement. The branch pledged their support for black trade unionists in South Africa, but then went on, as the very next item of business, to approve a motion opposing the introduction of 'coloured' bus staff in London! The similarities with the attitudes of white South African workers led Bob both to become involved in community relations and the anti-discrimination movement and also to propose to the Law Faculty that his dissertation should be on racial discrimination and the law. He was taken on one side and told that this was unsuitable because there was 'no law' on the subject. Only Paul O'Higgins, who was then teaching administrative law and labour law in Cambridge, expressed enthusiasm and supervised the research which led to *Race, Jobs and the Law in Britain* (1968, 2nd edn 1970), the first book of its kind. Bob also received help and encouragement from Otto Kahn-Freund, with whom he later wrote the influential Fabian booklet on *Laws Against Strikes* (1972). Bill Wedderburn, whose seminal work *The Worker and the Law* was first published in 1965, was a further important source of support and inspiration.

After graduating, Bob had a short spell (1966–68) as a Lecturer in the Department of Law in the University of Nottingham. Labour law was not in the curriculum. Bob was, however, encouraged by Professor John Smith to develop case law teaching of tort, and this led, in collaboration with Martin Matthews, to *Tort: Cases and Materials* (1974), an attempt to break free from the traditional constraints of law teaching in Britain at the time by adopting a socio-legal and contextual approach. In 1968 Bob returned to the Cambridge Law Faculty as an Assistant Lecturer and then Lecturer, and became a Fellow of Clare College. Again, tort was one of Bob's teaching subjects, and he was asked by Glanville Williams to collaborate with him on a tort textbook based on work he himself had left unfinished some years earlier. The result was *Foundations of the Law of Tort* (1976), to which Bob added chapters on the effect of insurance and social security. Bob also taught administrative law, then at an exciting turning point.

He collaborated with Stanley de Smith and David Williams in writing (under Lord Hailsham's watchful eye) the administrative law title in the fourth edition of *Halsbury's Laws of England*.

Bob's primary interest, however, remained labour law. He shared the teaching of labour law with Paul O'Higgins, and this led to a number of collaborative projects. These included editing the newly-established Sweet and Maxwell's *Encyclopedia of Labour Relations Law*, whose innovative introduction on individual employment law was also published as a separate monograph, in later editions under the title of *Employment Law*. Other projects included the first full-scale study of the law and practice of public employment in the United Kingdom, as part of a project sponsored by the University of Michigan, and a *Bibliography of the Literature on British and Irish Labour Law* (1975) together with a companion volume (1981). From 1969 onwards, Bob and Paul also began to build up a group of young labour law researchers in Cambridge. These included Breen Creighton, Patrick Elias, Julian Fulbrook, Brian Napier, Brian Bercusson, Bill Rees, Bob McCreadie, Sonia Mackay, Jonathan Kitchen, Naomi Wayne, Gillian Howard, Gillian Morris, Susan Dawe, Phillipa Watson, Carole Whicher, Cathy Tailby, John Hendy and Keith Ewing. Several of them went on to pursue full-time academic careers in the subject and have contributed to this book. Many of their dissertations found their way into the Mansell Studies on Social and Labour Law which Bob and Paul established. Bob also became the first editor of the *Industrial Law Journal* in 1972 (successor to the *Bulletin of the Industrial Law Society* first edited by Mark Freedland), a role that he handed over to Paul Davies in 1977. In this period he established close links with Steven Anderman and William Brown at Warwick University.

In 1976 Bob accepted a personal chair in Comparative Social and Labour Law at the University of Kent at Canterbury, where he taught on a multi-disciplinary Industrial Relations course. However, he soon decided to take a different path. In 1975 Bob had become a part-time chairman of industrial tribunals, having completed a pupillage in 1972 and undertaken some practice in the tribunals. In 1977 the opportunity arose to become a full-time industrial tribunal chairman, based in Kent. His five-year experience in this role made Bob critical of the way the tribunals had come to operate. He welcomed, therefore, the opportunity to chair the Justice Committee which made some radical proposals for reform of the tribunals in 1986, only some of which were implemented.

Bob continued, while a full-time chairman, to teach part-time at Canterbury and to chair the Social Science Research Council's Monitoring of Labour Legislation Panel, which commissioned a number of important studies. He also found time to embark on a comparative project in 1978 with Ole Hasselbalch, Antoine Jacobs, Jean-Claude Javillier, Thilo Ramm, Bruno Veneziani and Eliane Vogel-Polsky, explaining the origins of, and the relationships between, the labour laws of nine European countries from the beginning of the industrial revolution until 1945. This led, after eight years' intensive collaborative work, to the monumental book *The Making of Labour Law in Europe*. Bob also continued to pursue other comparative work. He had met Silvana Sciarra and Bruno Veneziani in 1972, and this began a long and fruitful collaboration. In 1979 Bob first met Manfred Weiss. In later years he and Manfred collaborated in many ways, including in Laszlo Nagy's comparative labour law seminars in Szeged which brought students from Central and Eastern Europe into contact with the outside world even before the fall of the Berlin Wall. From the time of the United Kingdom's accession to the European Communities, Bob became involved in committees of experts appointed by the European Commission. The most important of these was on the first Acquired Rights Directive. He also wrote commissioned reports on the application of EC law in the United Kingdom (leading to later successful infringement proceedings), on the revision of the Acquired Rights Directive, on legal consequences of cross-border mergers, and on transfer of rights in supplementary pension schemes. Bob's idea of a system of fundamental rights in the European Community was later taken up, with Roger Blanpain, Silvana Sciarra and Manfred Weiss, in their pamphlet on Fundamental Social Rights (1996), which bore some fruit in the EU Charter of Fundamental Rights adopted at Nice in December 2000.

In 1982 Bob returned to university life. He was appointed Professor of English Law at University College London, while continuing as a part-time chairman of tribunals. Bob's teaching activities at UCL included developing an undergraduate course on aspects of anti-discrimination law and a Master's level course on International and Comparative Labour Law. He was joined on the latter course by three former Cambridge research students, Brian Bercusson, Brian Napier and Keith Ewing, and by Sandra Fredman, with whom, from 1986 onwards, Bob collaborated on the monograph on Great Britain for Roger Blanpain's *International Encyclopedia for Labour Law and Industrial Relations*. As well as returning to the field of equality law as an academic (including a WG Hart Workshop run with Erika Szyszczak in 1990) Bob also engaged in the pursuit of equality in practical ways. He was a member of the Commission for Racial Equality from 1986 to 1990, a member of the Runnymede Commission on the Future of Multi-Ethnic Britain from 1998 to 2000, and became Chair of the European Roma Rights Center in 2002. From 1965 onwards he collaborated with Anthony Lester (Lord Lester of Herne Hill QC), and witnessed many of the ideas in his academic writings on discrimination helping to shape the Sex Discrimination Bill 1975 and the Race Relations Bills of 1976 and 2000. At Lord Lester's instigation, they wrote a paper before the 1997 General Election proposing a review of anti-discrimination legislation which had become fragmented, outdated and unduly complex. After the election they had a meeting with the Home Secretary, Jack Straw, who said that the government could not undertake a review, but he supported them in securing funding from the Nuffield Foundation and Joseph Rowntree Charitable Trust. The resulting *Report of the Independent Review of the Enforcement of UK Anti-Discrimination* Legislation (1999–2000), which Bob produced together with his wife Mary Coussey and Tufyal Choudhury, led to Lord Lester's Equality Bill which passed through all its stages in the House of Lords and was supported by 246 members of the Commons in 2003.

In 1989 Bob became Dean and Head of the Department of Laws at UCL and became a leader in the field of legal education. He was Chair of the Committee of Heads of University Law Schools, and Chair of the Quality Assurance Agency's Law Benchmarking group. From 1994 to 1999 he served as a member of the Lord Chancellor's Advisory Committee on Legal Education and Conduct (ACLEC). Lord Steyn, the chairman of ACLEC, asked him to undertake the drafting of the First Report on Legal Education and Training (1996). The Report aimed to prepare the system of legal education and training for the changing market for legal services in England and Wales, but even its rather limited proposals were too much for the vested interests in the legal profession to stomach and not many of its recommendations were followed. Bob was equally frustrated by the work of ACLEC's under-resourced successor, the Legal Services Consultative Panel, declining reappointment after two years' service.

In February 1990 the orders imposed by the South African government preventing Bob from returning to South Africa were lifted. Bob immediately received an invitation to address the annual Labour Law Conference in Durban, at which he made contact with a new generation of labour lawyers, including Halton Cheadle, Clive Thompson and Martin Brassey, who had creatively used labour and human rights law in the dying years of apartheid as a form of 'politics by other means'. The University of the Witwatersrand, which had publicly disowned Bob in 1963, conferred on him an Honorary Doctorate of Laws in 1996, and he returned to lecture there on several occasions. Bob also became an Honorary Professor at the University of Cape Town, where Evance Kalula had built up a thriving Labour Law Unit in the School of Law. In 1990, Bob drafted a Labour Code for the newly independent Namibia, and in 1994 he was appointed, with Manfred Weiss, as an ILO expert on the Ministerial Task Force which drafted a new Labour Relations Act for South Africa, so enabling him to apply for the benefit of the country of his birth some of the lessons he had learnt from three decades in Europe.

In 1993, the Fellows of Bob's old College invited him to return as Master. Two years later he was appointed to an established Chair of Law in the Cambridge Faculty, and shared the teaching of the undergraduate Labour Law course, and also an LLM course on civil and social rights in the EU, with Catherine Barnard and Simon Deakin. He reached the mandatory retiring age in 2001, whereupon he became Emeritus Professor. He retired as Master of Clare College in 2003. However, this is a retirement only in the most nominal sense, one which will afford Bob greater opportunity to pursue the multitude of research and other activities in which he is enthusiastically engaged. His constant flow of creative energy is amply reflected by the award of a Leverhulme Emeritus Fellowship, and a role as senior partner in a Nuffield New Career Fellowship. Bob is continuing the limited practice at the Bar that he has maintained since 1972, now at Blackstone Chambers; he was appointed Queen's Counsel (Hon), and became a Bencher of Gray's Inn in 1996. In 2000 Bob was invited to chair a working group of the Nuffield Council on Bioethics on *Genes and Human Behaviour: The Ethical Context*, a topic which will undoubtedly have serious long-term implications not least in the fields of equality and employment. In January 2003 he became Chairman of the Nuffield Council on Bioethics, and he was elected a Fellow of the British Academy in July 2003. He was knighted for services to legal studies in the New Year's Honours 2004.

The activities of this highly distinguished and most generous scholar will continue to inspire the contributors to this volume and labour lawyers throughout the world as they struggle to forge the future of labour law in a rapidly changing world.

The Editors

Contents

The Future of Labour Law: Introduction

CATHERINE BARNARD, SIMON DEAKIN AND GILLIAN S MORRIS

T HE ESSAYS COLLECTED in this book were first presented at a workshop on 'The Future of Labour Law' which was held in the Faculty of Law of the University of Cambridge on 11–12 July 2003. The workshop was held in honour of Bob Hepple on the occasion of his retirement from the Mastership of Clare College, Cambridge, but it was not intended to, and did not, take the form of a 'Festschrift' in which contributions principally addressed Bob's work as a labour lawyer. Instead, the intention of Bob himself and of the organisers of the conference was for a workshop which would reflect upon the many changes which are currently taking place within labour law — some would say, besetting it — and to assess its future development.

As a number of the chapters point out, this type of critical reflection on the state of labour law is a genre to which Bob Hepple himself has made many significant contributions. In particular, his essay 'The Future of Labour Law', published in the *Industrial Law Journal* in 1995,[1] provided the starting point for the project which led to this book. In that far-ranging analysis, he argued that the labour law of the future would be constructed on 'the great ideals of social justice, equality and human rights, to which all democrats subscribe,' and which 'are powerful symbols in defence against public and private power'. In the labour law context, these values found expression in the laws which, for most of the twentieth century, had protected trade union autonomy against the encroachments of both employers and the state. However, he argued that, under current circumstances, 'an alternative labour law cannot be constructed out of nostalgia for those values' and presciently suggested that 'while we have not reached the "end," we are in what Gramsci might have described as an "interregnum" in which the "old is dying, and the new cannot be born"'.[2]

---

[1] 'The Future of Labour Law' (1995) 24 *ILJ* 303.
[2] *Ibid* at 305. The reference to Gramsci is to *Prison Notebooks*, edited with an introduction by J Butigieg, translated by J Butigieg and A Callari (New York, Columbia University Press, 1992) vol I.

That realistic appraisal of the prospects for revival very well sums up the state of today's debate. The prospects are certainly no clearer, and the challenges if anything greater, than they were a decade ago. Part of the reason for that lies in political developments. As Sandra Fredman explains in Chapter 1, the 'New Labour' government elected to office in the United Kingdom in 1997 has adopted a 'Third Way' philosophy which clearly breaks with the social democratic tradition which nourished labour law in the developed economies and in particular in Western Europe for most of the past century. As Fredman argues, the 'Third Way' is difficult to classify. It contains many progressive elements and in some respects can be seen as simply the latest in a long line of attempts by left-leaning political movements to reconcile social values with the ever-present reality of a market economy. There is, however, a sense in which the Third Way's ostensible rejection of neoliberalism, the dominant ideology of the Thatcher and Major years, is no more than skin-deep. The fundamental tenets of neoliberal economic policy are not to be questioned, and this has led to a casual association of the public interest with the *business* interest. As a result, measures with the potential to bring about a realignment of the balance of power between labour and management, such as the national minimum wage and the new procedures for trade union recognition, have been hedged about with exceptions and limitations which are the price to be paid for the reluctant acquiescence of employer groups. Against this background, the terminology of the Third Way has become so debased that it is now essential, Fredman suggests, for labour law to abandon it, if it is to free itself from the shackles of neoliberalism.

The contradictions of the Third Way are also apparent in the law relating to industrial action, the subject of Keith Ewing's Chapter 2. A central plank of New Labour's labour law policy has been its refusal to abandon the highly restrictive and rigid regime of industrial action legislation introduced by Conservative governments of the 1980s and 1990s. As Ewing argues, this flatly contradicts the traditional labour law justification for the right to strike, namely that it underpins the process of voluntary collective bargaining. Yet it is also possible to see how the discourse of human rights, which the New Labour government has done much to encourage, could form the basis for a new settlement in strike law. Ewing's chapter considers the implications of viewing the right to strike as a *human right*. This would imply a right which vested in individuals and not simply in collective entities; which would no longer be parasitic on collective bargaining; and which it would be the responsibility of the state to uphold, implying far-reaching changes to the wider body of employment and social security law. While the main inspiration for this model so far lies in international instruments and in the constitutions of other national systems rather than in UK human rights law, its importance as a basis for the future development of the law should not be overlooked.

William Brown and Sarah Oxenbridge in Chapter 3 place discussion of the reform of collective labour law in context by explaining the social and economic background to the changes of the past 25 years. Their analysis is sobering: there is little prospect of a revival in traditional forms of countervailing power. Strikes are only effective when the scope of union power corresponds to the extent of competition in the relevant product market; the deregulation and, increasingly, globalisation of product markets make it difficult for many unions to offer a credible threat to employers. Instead, to achieve legitimacy, unions have been required to demonstrate, through 'partnership' agreements, their contribution to the competitiveness of firms. This is a process which can lead to disenchantment, as many 'partnership' agreements are no more than a front for the reassertion of employer power. But with legislative encouragement, the goal of labour-management cooperation could be made a meaningful one. In the view of Brown and Oxenbridge, a return to the legislative framework of 1906 would be largely pointless; but reforms aimed at upholding the role of unions as channels for consultation, enforcers of workers' legal rights, and potential defenders of the unorganised, could see them reclaim their historic mission as instruments of social citizenship.

It is perhaps not surprising that the current government has retained the Conservative laws governing industrial action; their intention to do so was clear in advance. It is more surprising that many of the proposals for the reform and modernisation of the economy which were put forward by prominent Third Way thinkers such as Anthony Giddens and Will Hutton have also fallen by the wayside since 1997. The field of corporate governance, highlighted by Hutton in his book *The State We're In*[3] in 1995, provides a good example of this. Simon Deakin's Chapter 4 shows how the government-sponsored Company Law Review, concluded in 2001, failed to address the negative consequences for workers and unions of restructurings carried out in the name of shareholder value. Some good might come out of restructuring if efficiency gains were translated into greater security of income for the ultimate beneficiaries of pension schemes, who are after all the millions of workers who regularly pay into them. However, changes to pensions law have encouraged employers to begin winding up final salary pension schemes, thereby transferring the considerable risk of stock market instability on to employees. What progress there has been in the corporate governance area has largely occurred as a result of the campaign, spearheaded by the TUC, to involve unions in the processes of shareholder activism. This is a movement which the government could encourage by legislating to clarify the social responsibilities of corporate boards and fund managers.

---

[3] London, Jonathan Cape, 1995.

The difficulties facing labour law are not simply the result of legislative failure. In the field of termination of employment, common law conceptions of the unqualified nature of employers' property rights continue to shape the law. Steve Anderman in Chapter 5 shows how this can account for a number of other puzzling doctrinal developments, such as the courts' reluctance to give up the unilateral theory of contract termination, the restrictive interpretations which they have accorded to the right to receive redundancy compensation, and their unwillingness to set a high bar for employers when formulating the statutory test of fairness in dismissal. The approach of the British courts contrasts sharply with that of their Continental counterparts, who have been willing to accept and where necessary extend statutory controls on managerial prerogative. In an echo of the corporate governance debate, Anderman suggests that this is, in part, the result of a civilian conception of the enterprise which views the firm as a cooperative endeavour involving multiple interests, and not simply as the property of the shareholders. One possible route to reform of British law, he suggests, lies in the adoption of the Continental European model of *collective* consultation over *individual* dismissals, a mechanism which recognises the legitimate interests of employee representatives in the exercise of managerial power.

Paul Davies and Mark Freedland in Chapter 6 address a related area of labour law in which reform is urgently required, namely the legal definition of the employment relationship. This has long been regarded as a conceptual morass. In addition, the courts have been criticised for their willingness to allow the application of protective statutes to be determined by highly abstract arguments about the meaning of legal concepts, such as 'mutuality of obligation.' Since 1999, the government has had the power to clarify the personal scope of employment legislation by delegated legislation, but has shown a decreasing willingness to do so. According to Davies and Freedland, the issue of personal scope cannot be addressed by looking only at the definition of the 'employee' or 'worker'; it is necessary to consider also the conceptualisation of the employing entity, and, in addition, the law's understanding of the nature of the relationship between the worker and the employer. This requires labour lawyers to enter unfamiliar territory, such as the law relating to corporate groups. These issues are further complicated, in the authors' view, by changes in the social character of employment, including greater use of outsourcing by employers and the rise of human resource management techniques and their individualising tendencies. While a new paradigm of the employment relationship may be said to be emerging in response to these developments, its features are not yet completely clear.

Gillian Morris in Chapter 7 addresses a further issue in respect of which considerations of policy are closely bound up with conceptual analyses, namely the future of the public-private divide in labour law. The boundary between the public and private sectors has been blurred by outsourcing, the introduction of market-like mechanisms into the public services, and the growing use of private finance to support public sector infrastructure projects. Her analysis contends that, notwithstanding these developments, the state continues to have a distinctive position as an employer which requires a distinctive conceptual response. Considerations of democratic accountability and the potential for the abuse of governmental power, as well as a 'functional' view of the tasks and responsibilities of workers performing public services, caution against applying labour law rules on a uniform basis to public and private sector alike. From this point of view, the restriction of the remedy of judicial review within the employment field, on the grounds that the employment of public-sector workers normally raises 'private law' issues, has not been helpful. There is no sign that the unprincipled approach of the courts is likely to end soon, even though it has produced discontinuities and anomalies in the treatment of different groups.

The chapters we have reviewed to this point all focus on the United Kingdom. What of the European and wider global context? In his 1995 ILJ paper, Bob Hepple warned that 'the future of labour law will not be determined … by dependence on endless social progress through the European Union'.[4] The complexity and contradictions of the European project as far as labour law is concerned are brought out in Brian Bercusson's Chapter 8. This consists of a close examination of the work of the Convention on the Future of Europe during 2002–03, in particular as it related to the EU Charter of Fundamental Rights, proclaimed at the Nice summit in 2000. Where the Charter crucially placed social and economic rights on an equal footing with civil and political rights, the Convention attempted to downgrade social rights by reducing them to a 'programmatic' status. As a result, there was a danger that the draft Constitution of the EU would not adequately reflect the values inherent in social rights. Whatever the political fate of this particular attempt to arrive at a European constitutional settlement may turn out to be, it is essential, Bercusson suggests, that the Member States of the EU undertake to respect the fundamental rights of labour which are guaranteed by the EU Charter.

Silvana Sciarra in Chapter 9 looks at the implications for the discipline of labour law of one of the most important developments in the system of European-level governance in recent years, the technique of the 'open method of coordination' (OMC). In contrast to traditional forms of harmonization, the OMC appears to be a radically decentred form of rule-making in which Member States are given considerable leeway to choose their own path in achieving general goals of economic and social policy. At the same time, OMC provides opportunities for mutual learning between the various

---

[4] Above n 1, at 304.

actors involved in the process of policy formulation and application. From this perspective, it represents a new stage in the evolution of labour law, which has the potential to facilitate the adaptation of traditional regulatory instruments to changing labour market conditions. For labour lawyers, it offers the prospect of interdisciplinary collaboration of the kind which can help to reinvigorate the field.

In Chapter 10, Catherine Barnard considers the future of European equality law. She argues that it is the idea of citizenship which increasingly provides the basis for the application of equal rights to the disadvantaged in EC law, and that citizenship implies, in turn, a specific conception of social inclusion based on solidarity. Solidarity has a particular meaning here which refers to the steps which need to be taken by both public and private decision-makers to ensure the integration of the individual into the community to which he or she has the opportunity to contribute. The principle can be seen at work in the case law of the European Court of Justice on the rights of migrants; here, the ECJ has moved beyond a traditional discrimination test to focus on the removal of obstacles to economic participation. It is particularly significant that in its most recent decisions, the ECJ has moved beyond approaches based on 'negative integration' to impose positive obligations upon Member States. Expressed in these terms, the 'solidarity' principle has the potential to reorientate the debate over social inclusion at both national and transnational level, shifting the law beyond a narrow focus on existing categories of equal treatment.

Manfred Weiss's Chapter 11 looks at the progress made at EU level towards the recognition of a distinctive European model of worker participation. After the passage in the 1970s of the Directives on information and consultation in the context of collective redundancies and transfers of undertakings, there was a deadlock over further measures which was only broken by the passage of the European Works Councils Directive in 1994. The innovative structural features of this Directive — in particular, its encouragement of negotiation in preference to imposed solutions — were in large part responsible for its adoption, and have since shaped its implementation. Weiss regards this as a success, noting that while European Works Councils (EWCs) are far from comprehensive and have limited powers, they have instituted a learning process which has helped to legitimate and extend worker participation. It is therefore appropriate that many of the features of the EWC model should have been incorporated into the more recent Directives on the European company and information and consultation over national-level employment issues. Notwithstanding some significant weaknesses in the drafting of these measures, Weiss argues that they mark a significant turning point: systems which until now have depended on adversarial structures of employment relations will in future have to adapt to an institutional model based on social partnership and cooperation.

Breen Creighton in Chapter 12 addresses the current state of the system for setting and enforcing international labour standards. Focusing on the work of the International Labour Organisation, he suggests that the system is in crisis. Few of the Conventions and Recommendations recently adopted by the ILO have made any substantive contribution to the existing corpus of standards, while many of the older ones are obsolescent or obsolete. Ratification rates are low and falling, and the ILO's machinery is ill-equipped to deal with problems of non-compliance. More generally, Creighton suggests, the ILO is failing to rise to the challenges posed by globalisation, the ascendancy of neoliberalism, and the emergence of rival sources of international standards, such as the EU. There are, nevertheless, ways in which this organisational crisis can be addressed. These include the promotion of core standards (as in the 1998 Declaration of Fundamental Rights and Principles), making more use of the flexible Recommendation route in preference to Conventions, and streamlining the machinery of supervision of standards. But there is a hard road to travel, he concludes, if international labour standards are to fulfil the hopes invested in them as a mechanism for social and economic progress.

In Chapter 13, Evance Kalula locates the global debate concerning the relationship beween labour standards and economic development in the highly concrete context of the recent experience of southern Africa. In this region, the harmonisation of labour law is seen as a priority for encouraging economic growth of the kind which is needed to deal with high levels of poverty and a large informal economy. But these very same factors also require innovative approaches to regulation to be considered. Kalula argues that an approach based on social rights, exemplified by the core-standards approach of the ILO, provides a useful starting point. The constitutionalisation of social rights in Lesotho, Namibia and South Africa is therefore to be welcomed. In addition, what he calls 'surrogate corporatism,' a distinctive model of social dialogue addressing a wide range of issues of social and economic policy, can be seen as addressing the need for a 'socially conscious' form of labour market regulation. By these means, the traditional southern African paradigm of labour law imposed from the outside, with systems 'borrowing and bending' in response to external pressure, can, he argues, be transcended.

The collection concludes with Chapter 14 by Paul O'Higgins, provocatively entitled, in particular for a book concerned with the *future* of labour law, 'The End of Labour Law as We Have Known It?' He argues that for most of the twentieth century, labour law was the product of a balance of power between labour and capital, mediated by governments. This balance of power has broken down for a number of reasons. Within national systems, economic changes have eroded former loyalties and solidarities upon which the strength of organised labour depended. Internationally, the collapse of the Soviet Union has removed a source of pressure on

Western governments to maintain welfare state regimes. The emergence of the USA as the sole world superpower has coincided with the rise in influence of a neoconservative political creed which is virulently anti-labour and opposed to the settlement which underlay the welfare state. The USA uses its political influence to press for international trade rules which suit its interests, while at the same time undermining the role of the ILO and the United Nations more generally. O'Higgins identifies in the World Social Forum, meeting in Porto Alegre in Brazil for the past few years, the beginnings of a movement which could unite non-governmental organisations and global labour interests in opposition to the current form of globalisation; but this movement has not yet achieved a significant readjustment of the balance of power in favour of labour.

If this is an uncomfortable note on which to end, that may not be inappropriate. Nobody should expect the future of labour law to be any different from its past; as Bob Hepple wrote in 1995, it will inevitably be 'the outcome of processes of conflict between different social groups and competing ideologies.'[5] The intellectual task of reconstruction facing the current generation of labour lawyers is in every way as formidable as that undertaken by the very first 'social jurists' in Western Europe a century ago. If the work presented here succeeds in aiding to some degree that process of reconstruction, it will have proved worthy of its objective in honouring the inspiring career of Bob Hepple.

[5] *Ibid* at 305.

1

The Ideology of New Labour Law

SANDRA FREDMAN*

INTRODUCTION

T HE NEOLIBERAL POLICY of the Thatcher and Major regimes propelled labour law in an entirely new direction, clearly mapped and unflinchingly realised. In pursuing an individualistic free market ideology, hostile to state intervention or regulation, neoliberalism deliberately distanced itself from its social democratic predecessor, with its emphasis on an interventionist state and collectivism. New Labour claims to have struck out along a 'Third Way.' It is neither hostage to an untrammelled free market nor overwhelmed by a 'stultifying' welfare state. It subscribes to neither unbridled individualism nor conformist egalitarianism. Is this a coherent philosophy, and has it been consistently delivered in the form of labour law?

The aim of this chapter is to provide a critical appraisal of Third Way ideology. Marx and Engels famously defined ideology as the means which the ruling class has as its disposal to justify the reality of domination.[1] Ideology in this sense connotes a system of ideas which has power to justify and convince: to justify the policies of the ruling group, and to convince the people of its truth.[2]

This chapter begins with an attempt to sketch out the main contours of the Third Way. The second part considers the extent to which New Labour ideology reflects Third Way principles in the labour law field, while the third part contrasts this approach with the extent to which Third Way principles are reflected in the EU social model. In the last part, I turn to a more detailed examination of labour laws themselves, focusing on collective labour law.

* I am very grateful to Keith Ewing, Bob Hepple, Bill Wedderburn, Stuart Hall and participants in the colloquium for their comments on earlier drafts. The errors are all my own.
[1] K Marx and F Engels, *The German Ideology* (New York, International Publishers, 1970) 64.
[2] I will not, of course, enter into the complex theoretical debates within Marxism on the relationship of the superstructure to the base.

I conclude that the new challenges facing labour law require transformative solutions, a project to which Third Way principles can make a valuable contribution. However, Third Way terminology itself creates a risk that, in distancing itself from social democracy, too great a measure of neoliberalism is injected into the policy framework. As New Labour labour law demonstrates all too dishearteningly, behind the Third Way rhetoric, neoliberalism has, by stealth, become the dominant ideology, relegating social democracy to the minor partner. Transformative labour law, instead of attempting to find a 'Third Way,' should be located firmly within a framework which confidently rejects neoliberalism and aims to enrich and develop the social democratic tradition. This in turn is part of a renewed debate about the meaning of social democracy itself, taking forward the valuable contributions of eminent labour lawyers over the decades.[3] Many aspects of the Third Way are vibrant outgrowths of social democracy and can play an important part in the renewed debate. A transformative labour law belongs within the dynamic of social democratic debate, drawing on Third Way principles without accepting that a 'Third Way' is ultimately necessary.

THE RHETORIC OF THE THIRD WAY

The Third Way is espoused in many different ways, not all of them comprehensive or internally consistent. I have nevertheless attempted to extract common themes from various modern proponents, and to present the ideology in a coherent form. The following four principles emerged as the salient distinguishing characteristics: (i) the facilitative state; (ii) civic responsibility; (iii) equality of opportunity; and (iv) community and democracy. These issues are all framed against the background imperatives of globalisation and the move to a service economy. Each of these will be discussed in turn. I do not address the Third Way claim to novelty; except to note that many of the arguments presented as new have strong links to earlier liberal-democratic theories.

The Facilitative State

The Third Way has consciously distanced itself from the powerful market-centred ideology of neoliberalism, with its elevation of the free

---

[3] See O Kahn Freund, 'Labour Law' in Ginsberg (ed), *Law and Opinion in England in the Twentieth Century* (Stevens, London, 1959) 224; HA Clegg, 'Pluralism in Industrial Relations' [1975] *BJIR* 309; A Fox, *Beyond Contract* (London, Faber, 1974); Lord Wedderburn, *Labour Law and Freedom* (London, Lawrence and Wishart, 1995); B Hepple, 'The Future of Labour Law' (1995) *ILJ* 303; K Ewing, 'Democratic Socialism and Labour Law' (1995) *ILJ* 103.

market and its corresponding hostility to the state. But it has also emphasised its divergence from the traditional social democratic model, which it regards as giving the state an overbearing and stultifying role in society. Hence, Third Way authors argue for a new balance between the state and civil society. The aim is to reinvigorate the public domain and the positive role of the state, while at the same time retaining sufficient space for free enterprise and creativity. As Tony Blair argued in his 1998 Fabian pamphlet, *The Third Way: New Politics for a New Century*: 'Liberals asserted the primacy of individual liberty in the market economy; social democrats promoted social justice with the state as its main agent. There is no necessary conflict between the two, accepting as we now do that state power is one means to achieve our goals.'[4]

Central to this balance is a reconstructed notion of individual autonomy. The neoliberal conception of the individual as a free market agent required only formal equality before the law. Inequality in outcome was explained as the natural and proper result of individual choice within the market. By contrast, the Third Way recognises that unequal outcomes are frequently a result of absence of choice, due to differential endowment both of natural talents and of social assets. Real freedom of choice requires active state intervention, a politics of empowerment.[5] Thus state action, far from stultifying, is a precondition for individual autonomy.

This approach in turn has implications for the role of the free market. The aim is to counter both the hegemony of the state and that of markets. Markets must be regulated, but not substituted for by the state.[6] Business is essential to the creation of wealth, and must not be stultified. But markets are limited in their ability to create the human capital they require, and their tendency towards monopoly must be limited. Thus the 'good society,' according to Giddens, requires a competitive market economy:

> a source not only of economic development, but of individual freedom, for markets in principle allow free choices to be made by producers and consumers. But the market has socially damaging traits … . Market mechanisms cannot substitute either for political and democratic rights or for the mechanisms of civil society.[7]

---

[4] T Blair, *The Third Way: New Politics for a New Century* (London, Fabian, Polity Press, 1998) 2.
[5] D Held, 'Inequalities of Power, Problems of Democracy' in D Miliband (ed), *Reinventing the Left* (London, Polity Press, 1994) 47.
[6] A Giddens, *Where Now for New Labour* (London, Fabian Society, Polity Press, 2002) 35; 50–53.
[7] *Ibid* at 37.

Civic Responsibility

Also central to the philosophy of the Third Way is the notion of responsibility. Thus Giddens maintains, 'One might suggest as a prime motto for the new politics, no rights without responsibilities.'[8] Here too, the new ideology attempts to define a Third Way which is distinct from both old left and new right.[9] Thus, countering right-wing accusations that the welfare state is no more than a nanny state, generating dependency, the Third Way stresses that individuals should take primary responsibility for themselves and their children. While the state should provide the basic opportunities for all, it is up to individuals to make the best use of these. Policies should therefore harness self-interest for the public good.[10]

The stress on personal responsibility has had important policy implications. Benefits and entitlements are, it is repeatedly stressed, conditional on correlative responsibilities in the recipient. Thus, according to the 1998 Welfare Green Paper:

> Our ambition is nothing less than a change of culture among benefit claimants, employers and public servants — with rights and responsibilities on all sides .... It is the government's responsibility to promote work opportunities and to help people take advantage of them. It is the responsibility of those who can take them up to do so.[11]

Similarly, *Preventing Social Exclusion*, the 2001 Report of the Social Exclusion Unit, stresses that government has taken 'a 'rights and responsibilities' approach that makes government help available, but requires a contribution from the individual and the community. So, under the New Deal, benefits can be withdrawn if people do not take up opportunities; Educational Maintenance Allowances are conditional on attendance and performance; Individual Learning Accounts match a contribution from the individual; and new funding for neighbourhoods is conditional on community involvement.[12]

At the same time, the Third Way uses the notion of responsibility to distance itself from the neoliberal conception of the autonomous individual as one who is free to pursue his or her own rational self-interest.

---

[8] A Giddens, *The Third Way and its Critics* (London, Polity Press, 2000) 65.
[9] Blair, above n 4, at 4.
[10] See, eg F Field, *Stakeholder Welfare* (London, Institute for Economic Affairs, 1997); C Oppenheim, 'Enabling Participation? New Labour's Welfare to Work Policies' in S White (ed), *New Labour: The Progressive Future?* (New York, Palgrave, 2001) 78.
[11] Green Paper, *New Ambitions for our Country: A New Contract for Welfare* (Cm 3805, 1998) 24, 31.
[12] *Preventing Social Exclusion*, the 2001 Report of the Social Exclusion Unit (London, Cabinet Office, 2001) 8.

Instead, it stresses the responsibility of individuals to one another and to the community as a whole, whether through bearing a fair share of taxes to ensure opportunities for all, caring for the environment, or participation in democratic and other civic structures.[13]

It is the extent of this responsibility which differs as between different authors. For Giddens, responsibility entails that 'people should not only take from the wider community, but give back to it too.'[14] For Vandenbroucke, a 'responsibility-sensitive' conception of social democracy goes much deeper.[15] It focuses not just on the responsibility of citizens, but also on that of the state to provide relevant opportunities and to intervene where differential market reward is not a true reflection of personal responsibility and effort. At the same time, it stresses the social obligations of the rich and powerful, rather than engaging in 'easy rhetoric about the moral responsibilities of the poor and the powerless.'[16]

For Hutton, it is this latter notion of responsibility which sets the European social democratic tradition apart from the neoliberalism of the USA. Property should not be seen as an absolute right, but a privilege, conferring reciprocal obligations:

> Those who hold and own property are members of society, and society has a public dimension to which necessarily they must contribute as the quid pro quo for the privilege of exercising property rights.[17]

Thus 'property is not a right or a simple network of private contracts; rather it is a concession, made by the society of which it is part, that has to be continually earned and deserved.'[18]

This has crucially important implications for the type of society we aspire to. Instead of the rhetoric of 'burdens on business,' the responsibilities of business are stressed. Progressive taxation is a civic responsibility, not an unnecessary imposition, and employees' rights should not be seen as favours or surrenders on the part of business. Similarly, the corporation should be responsible not merely to its shareholders but to its workers, its customers and the community within which it lives. Thus Hutton's approach directly challenges the crude 'filter down' theory, implicit but rarely articulated in so much policy-making in Britain, that the interests of business are the interests of all, and therefore that freedom for business is automatically in the interests of all parts of society.

---

[13] S White, 'The Ambiguities of the Third Way' in White (ed), above n 10, at 5.

[14] A Giddens, *The Third Way and its Critics* (London, Polity Press, 2000) 165.

[15] F Vandenbroucke, 'European Social Democracy and the Third Way' in White (ed), above n 10, at 170–71.

[16] Vandenbroucke, *ibid*, quoting T Wright, *Socialism, Old and New* (London, Routledge, 1996) 147.

[17] W Hutton, *The World We're In* (Abacus, 2002) 63.

[18] *Ibid* at 84.

Equality

Equality is a pivotal principle for the Third Way, and here too an attempt is made to differentiate the Third Way from its two principal rivals. Like the social democrats, the Third Way emphasises that market outcomes left to themselves are unfair and inegalitarian.[19] This entails a rejection of the neoliberal view of equality as equal treatment regardless of differences in physical or social assets. Drawing expressly on Sen's concept of social capability, the Third Way recognises that equality should refer also to the capability of individuals to make effective use of material goods and choices formally available to them.[20]

However, Third Way proponents are also keen to distance themselves from socialist egalitarianism, which they characterise as aiming at 'equality as sameness.' Thus, Walzer argues, the attempt to achieve equality as sameness requires 'endless tyrannical interventions in ordinary life'.[21] Similarly, Hutton rejects any view that a social contract should require the redistribution of resources exactly equally.[22]

Instead, Third Way theorists emphasise equality of opportunity. 'We favour true equality' writes Tony Blair, 'equal worth and equal opportunity, not an equality of outcome focused on incomes alone.'[23] Equal opportunity frequently means more than the removal of demand-side obstacles. In addition, it requires the provision of strategic goods, such as education, child-care and income, which make it possible for individuals to utilise available opportunities.[24] Equality of opportunity fits well with all of the main tenets described so far. It underpins individual responsibility, since it encourages incentives and entrepreneurship. It reinforces the Third Way notion of individual autonomy, making space for lifestyle choices, pluralism and diversity. [25] Finally, it fortifies the Third Way conception of the state as a facilitator rather than a guarantor of outcomes, underscoring the reciprocal obligations of the state and individual.[26]

There remains, however, a deep-seated tension between equality of opportunity and equality of outcomes, which is reflected in the differing emphases of Third Way theorists. All accept that the emphasis on equality of opportunity still presumes some redistribution. People for whom

[19] Giddens, above n 6, at 39.
[20] A Sen, *Inequality Re-examined* (Oxford, Oxford University Press, 1992) 40–41; see also Sen in *Development as Freedom* (Oxford, Oxford University Press, 1999).
[21] M Walzer, 'Pluralism and Social Democracy' *Dissent* (Winter 1998) 47–53 at 50.
[22] Hutton, above n 17, at 89.
[23] T Blair, *The Courage of our Convictions* (London, Fabian Society, 2002) 2.
[24] White, above n 13, at 4.
[25] Giddens, above n 14, at 86.
[26] On equality as a value see B Hepple, 'Social Values and European Law' (1995) 48 *Current LP* 391.

opportunities will necessarily be limited should not be denied the chance to lead fulfilling lives; and it is important to prevent inequality being passed down through the generations.[27] However, for many Third Way theorists, such redistribution is peripheral. Instead of 'social spending' with its redistributive connotations, the Third Way state should concentrate on 'social investment,' creating opportunities through education, training and other measures. On this view, social spending (on welfare) makes some better off at the cost of others. Social investment, however, makes everyone better off and is therefore the preferable mode[28].

Others challenge the attempt to draw a rigid line between equality of opportunity and equality of outcomes. Thus, Vandenbroucke accepts that equality is not uniformity, and that there should always be space for the different outcomes that result from personal choice. However, outcomes are not just dependent on personal choice but also on luck, both in respect of original talents, and of the prevailing market for particular skills.[29] There should therefore be an important role for measures which do not just provide opportunities, but specifically correct unequal outcomes resulting from bad luck or a lesser endowment of original talents. Similarly, Hutton argues that the state should ensure that 'risks and rewards are not allocated by chance and market forces; rather their final balance is settled by an activist state.'[30]

In addition, it is argued that the distinction between social investment and social provision should not be over-estimated.[31] Measures (such as education and training) which prevent social exclusion, cannot fully substitute for measures (such as unemployment benefit) which protect individuals who are in fact excluded.[32] To present social investment in contrast to redistribution raises the suspicion that equal opportunities is no more than a pretext for real retrenchment of welfare provisions and social security.[33] It also buys into the neoliberal assumption that any costs associated with equality are an unnecessary burden, rather than a positive aspect of responsible citizenship and the responsible state.

Also fiercely debated is whether equal opportunities entails narrowing inequalities across society, or merely 'lifting the floor.' Proponents of the latter argue that once measures are in place to improve the standard of living for those at the bottom, an open and meritocratic society ensures that inequalities which arise are legitimate. Their opponents respond that, even

---

[27] Giddens, above n 14, at 89.
[28] Vandenbroucke, above n 15, at 167.
[29] *Ibid* at 171.
[30] Hutton, above n 17, at 57.
[31] J Hills, 'Does a Focus on Social Exclusion Change the Policy Response' in J Hills *et al* (eds), *Understanding Social Exclusion* (Oxford, Oxford University Press, 2001) 233.
[32] Hills in Hills *et al*, above n 31, at 232.
[33] Vandenbroucke, above n 15, at 167.

with an absolute improvement in living standards for those at the bottom, equal opportunity is impossible if large gaps remain between the poorest and the richest.[34] Redistributive policies, therefore, remain essential.

Community and Democracy

Third Way theorists, like their social democratic counterparts, emphatically reject the neoliberal characterisation of the individual as a rational maximiser of self-interest. Instead, people are viewed as essentially social. Thus, argues Hutton, 'human beings depend for their humanity on association, and this requires that they participate in a collective consciousness and shared belief system that allows them to empathise with the conditions of others.'[35] This is a precondition of liberty, rather than an obstacle, as the neoliberals would argue. Individuals can only avoid the anonymity and alienation of the modern market economy if there is strong social solidarity and a powerful collective conscience.[36] 'Individuals ... exercise freedom precisely through their membership of groups, communities and cultures.'[37]

The emphasis on community is reflected in the rhetoric of active citizenship, social capital and social inclusion.[38] Social capital aims to nurture human relationships within a community and to refurbish civil society through democratic renewal.[39] It is a paradigmatic Third Way concept, using a free market metaphor to underscore the importance of investment in social growth for the benefit of the community as a whole. Combating social exclusion[40] is its correlative in policy terms. Thus, according to the Social Exclusion Policy Unit, high levels of exclusion impose costs, not just on the individual but on the community as a whole, leading to 'reduced social cohesion as different areas, generations and minority ethnic communities are divided by radically different life chances; higher crime and fear of crime, for which social exclusion is a key driver ... and reduced mobility.'[41] This has led to a 'joined up approach' to combating social exclusion, including policies for health, education, social services and community regeneration.[42] Social inclusion has also been seen to be a key driver, or

[34] A Harvey, 'Social Justice' in A Harvey (ed), *Transforming Britain* (London, Fabian Society, 2001) 11.
[35] Hutton, above n 17, at 87.
[36] *Ibid* at 91.
[37] Giddens, above n 14, at 88.
[38] *Ibid* at 104.
[39] Oppenheim, above n 10, at 78.
[40] Burchardt, Le Grand and Piachaud in Hills *et al* (ed), above n 31, at 29.
[41] *Preventing Social Exclusion*, the 2001 Report of the Social Exclusion Unit, at 24–25.
[42] *Ibid.*

even a substitute, for the principle of equality, giving a more powerful rationale than that of equality of opportunity.[43]

With community comes a strong emphasis on democracy. Third Way theorists stress the importance of participation, not just in formal politics, but in all levels of decision-making. The notion of the 'stakeholder' society, and the importance of consultation with stakeholders has been a central principle in policy formation, with government emphasising the need to work in partnership with key stakeholders. With this goes an encouragement of the development of civic associations, representative bodies to mediate between the individual and the state.

Although this is a natural space to locate trade unions, little mention is made of trade unions by proponents of the British Third Way. Moreover, in its attempt to avoid the charge of corporatism, New Labour has refused to set up tripartite institutions comparable to the National Economic Development Council, which was abolished in 1992.[44] This can be contrasted with a more European version of participation, which tends towards the institutionalisation of such consultative structures. Most importantly, it contrasts with the EU, which, through 'social dialogue,' has delegated real legislative power to the social partners on social policy matters at the highest level.

Nevertheless, as Ewing shows, partnership has been more than just a catchword for New Labour.[45] In fact, trade unions have been incorporated by New Labour into a wide range of decision-making forums. These range from the virtually tripartite Low Pay Commission, to the Better Regulation Task Force, to the joint CBI/TUC Working Group on Productivity, sponsored by the Treasury. There is also a network of less formal links. Ewing sees this partnership role as an opportunity for trade unions to exercise influence in areas which collective bargaining could not reach, 'reaffirming the mutual dependency of political action, collective bargaining, and regulatory legislation as techniques for promoting the interests of people at work'.[46]

While stakeholder participation is an important revitalising element of Third Way democracy, it has several difficulties which should not be overlooked. First, little attention is paid to the process of selecting 'stakeholders' to be represented in these consultations. The choice of those whose voices will be listened to is therefore vulnerable to bias and partisanship. Even

---

[43] H Collins, 'Discrimination, Equality and Social Inclusion' (2003) 66 *Modern Law Review* 16.
[44] See further P Davies and M Freedland, *Labour Legislation and Public Policy* (Oxford, Oxford University Press, 1993) 142–43.
[45] KD Ewing, 'The Continuing Role of Trade Unions in Labour Law' 11th Annual Labour Law Conference, April 2003.
[46] *Ibid* at 33.

where there is a commitment to transparency, the process tends to favour organised and vocal groups. Secondly, once consultations have taken place, real decision-making continues to be made behind closed doors, so that the influence of the consultation on the actual decision-making is not clear. This is true both domestically and at EU level, where, although the results of social dialogue are binding, the process of decision-making within social dialogue is not made public. Finally, in the domestic context, the use of regulations rather than primary legislation to implement much EU policy has allowed Parliament to be sidestepped, with 'consultation' substituted for proper parliamentary debate. The result has been that the appearance of transparency in fact masks the real and often overwhelming influence of big business. In particular, as Ewing notes, 'the voice of organised labour has been greatly diluted ... The business voice has a disproportionate influence on the policy of the party leadership on a range of issues.'[47]

NEW LABOUR AND THE THIRD WAY

Challenges

Labour law faces many new challenges. A changing labour market requires new conceptions of the notion of the worker. The flexible labour market has melted the boundary between employment and unemployment, with job insecurity elevated into a market asset. The frontier between paid work and the home is challenged by the entry of women into the labour market. Globalisation threatens to prioritise competition, undercutting basic social rights; and the role of the state is undermined by increasingly mobile corporate capital. Technological change means that knowledge resources are a crucial future asset; and there are significant demographic changes such as ageing, low birth rate and immigration.

   These changes not only create new challenges for the traditional British social democratic response, based on collective laissez-faire,[48] but also show up some of its long-standing weaknesses.[49] Trade unions have traditionally catered for those in work, to the exclusion of those out of work; and it is only relatively recently that trade unions have focused their efforts on marginal workers, women, minorities, disabled people and older

---

[47] *Ibid.*
[48] Kahn Freund, *Labour and the Law* (Davies and Freedland (eds)) (3rd edn, Oxford, Oxford University Press, 1983); P Davies and M Freedland, *Labour Legislation and Public Policy* (1993) ch 1.
[49] Lord Wedderburn of Charlton, 'Laws about Strikes' in W McCarthy (ed), *Legal Intervention in Industrial Relations* (Oxford, Blackwell, 1992) 147–49; Davies and Freedland, above n 48, at 641–48.

people. In addition, because it eschews positive collective rights,[50] collective laissez-faire is dependent on industrial might, and therefore, on full employment. It was this weakness which was exploited to the full by the neoliberal regimes of Thatcher and Major, engineering high levels of unemployment in order to undercut trade union strength.

It is clear, therefore, that labour law needs a fundamental re-evaluation if it is to continue to have a transformative effect. It needs to move beyond the formal labour market, and address the increasingly fluid boundaries between work and family, employment and unemployment, and different types of worker.[51] It cannot continue to assume autonomy from other branches of the law, and in particular, from welfare and family law. Equality must be couched not only in terms of countervailing power of workers and employers, but also in respect of heterogeneous parts of the labour force and the broader society. In facing the challenge of globalisation, it is crucial to create a framework of social rights to counterbalance the hegemony of free trade ideology. At the same time, as Wedderburn rightly warns, the effectiveness of the law in bringing about social change should not be over-estimated.[52] This points to the importance of ensuring that labour law is facilitative of collective bargaining and social dialogue, rather than simply providing for individual rights. In this way too, the 'extravagant individualism'[53] of the common law is avoided.

The Rhetoric of New Labour

To what extent has New Labour set labour law in the direction plotted by the Third Way? This section examines New Labour rhetoric, as set out in its policy documents, and in particular, in its blueprint for labour law, the 1998 White Paper *Fairness at Work*. Third Way principles are clearly discernable in all. At the same time, Third Way terminology frequently conceals a strong implicit attachment to neoliberal tenets. That this should be possible is in part due to flaws in Third Way ideology itself. It should to be stressed, too, that New Labour ideology (like all ideologies) is not consistent, nor is it consistently applied. Many of the actions of New Labour are driven by political considerations and only justified retrospectively.

---

[50] As much because of the hostility of the judiciary as for any point of principle. Hence, Wedderburn characterises it as exclusion of the judiciary rather than abstentionism: B Wedderburn, *The Worker and the Law* (London, Harmondsworth, 1986) 20.
[51] K Klare, 'Horizons of Transformative Labour Law' in J Conaghan, R M Fischl and K Klare (eds), *Labour Law in an Era of Globalization* (Oxford, Oxford University Press, 2002) 28–29.
[52] B Wedderburn, 'Common Law, Labour Law, Global Law' in B Hepple (ed), *Social and Labour Rights in a Global Context* (Cambridge, Cambridge University Press, 2002) 23–25.
[53] *Ibid* at 35.

Given the need for labour law to create a wider focus than simply those in work, it is important, in assessing New Labour's approach, to look beyond formal labour law. The National Minimum Wage cannot be assessed in isolation from the Working Families Tax Credit; family friendly policies must be seen to include the national child-care strategy; and measures on job security need to take in the New Deal programme. Equality measures need to be considered together with income redistribution measures and policies on social exclusion. Formal measures on participation, such as the statutory recognition procedure, must be seen in the context of the increased role of trade unions in the political and regulatory process.

The Facilitative State

Fairness at Work sets out as its major policy goal the creation of a balance between fairness and efficiency. This reflects a Third Way characterisation of the state as facilitating fairness while respecting free enterprise. However, there are two striking demonstrations of the use of Third Way rhetoric to disguise continued adherence to neoliberal principles. First, New Labour buys into one of the most powerful neoliberal rhetorical victories, which is to portray the neoliberal state as non-interventionist. In fact, the neoliberal state is highly regulatory: to prevent collectivism flourishing naturally within the free market, the Thatcher and Major regimes intervened heavily in order to restrict trade unions, simultaneously claiming to roll back the boundaries of the state. Similarly, *Fairness at Work* portrays heavy-handed intervention as absence of regulation. Thus, in defending the retention of repressive neoliberal strike laws, the Prime Minister claims that 'even with the changes we propose, Britain will have the most lightly regulated labour market of any leading economy in the world.'[54]

Secondly, the neoliberal assumption that business profitability represents the public interest is unchallenged. The state's role in establishing fair standards is justified on the grounds that fairness is good for business, rather than by confidently asserting this as an essential part of state responsibility. The most pressing concern is to rebut the accusation that employment protection imposes burdens on business. Thus, although *Fairness at Work* notes that 'collective representation ... can be the best method of ensuring that employees are treated fairly'[55], most attention is paid to its role in achieving important business objectives. 'Representatives who are respected by other employees can help employers to explain the company's circumstances and the need for change.'[56] Similarly, the reduction

---

[54] White Paper, *Fairness at Work* (1998), Foreword by the Prime Minister.
[55] *Ibid* at para 4.2.
[56] *Ibid* at para 4.3.

in the qualification period for unfair dismissal rights is not promoted as giving employees greater job security but as facilitating labour mobility. With a shorter qualification period, 'employees would be less inhibited about changing jobs and thereby losing their protection, which should help to promote a more flexible labour market.'[57]

Similarly, in respect of family friendly measures, lip-service is paid to the need for parents to have time to create a supportive home for their children. The emphasis remains on business needs: for employers to have as large a number of people to draw from as possible, for workers to be able to concentrate on their jobs without worrying about their children, for companies to retain staff in whom they have invested.

Thus, fairness is downgraded from an end in itself, to a means to achieve efficiency: 'Unless minimum rights are established, effective relationships in companies cannot prosper.'[58] This in turn makes it easy to argue that whenever employee rights create a net cost to business, they cannot be justified.

Responsibility

In stressing that rights must be matched with responsibilities,[59] *Fairness at Work* appears to reflect the Third Way emphasis on civic responsibility. However, on closer inspection, it can be seen that the White Paper characterises responsibility largely in terms of the responsibility of workers, with little or no attention paid to the responsibilities of businesses: 'In offering new rights, we will demand that employees in return accept their responsibilities to cooperate with employers.'[60] Similarly under the New Deal, the right to benefit is matched by the responsibility to seek work or undergo training. The correlative, however, is that those who do not succeed in finding work are seen to be responsible for their failure — a disturbing return to older notions about the undeserving poor.[61]

It is true that some new responsibilities are placed on employers. However, these duties are not explained in terms of mutual responsibility. Instead, they are portrayed as beneficial to business, and indeed are shaped in order as far as possible to minimise business responsibilities. For example, the duty to recognise trade unions certainly imposes a new responsibility on employers. Nevertheless, it is largely shaped to meet business objectives. Thus, the duty is not considered 'appropriate' for businesses with fewer than 20 employees, even though this excludes

[57] *Ibid* at para 3.9.
[58] *Ibid*, para 1.9.
[59] *Ibid*, Foreword, and para 2.15.
[60] *Ibid* at para 2.15.
[61] A Harvey, 'Social Justice' in A Harvey (ed), *Transforming Britain: Labour's Second Term* (Fabian, 2001) 8.

nearly 4.5 million workers, 20 per cent of all workers.[62] Similarly, because 'employers must and will be free to organise their business in the way they choose,'[63] the bargaining unit is determined in part according to the need for effective management. Finally, 'to deter unwarranted attempts to obtain recognition,' new applications for recognition cannot be considered for three years after an earlier application has been determined.

Thus, New Labour ideology is a considerable distance away from the rich notion of civic responsibility espoused in Third Way literature, and in particular, from Hutton's robust assertion of corporate responsibility. The result of this skewed notion of responsibility is that fairness is quickly transmuted into minimum rights. From the statement 'it cannot be just to deny British citizens basic canons of fairness,' Tony Blair in his Foreword to *Fairness at Work* quickly moves to the assertion that the proposal is to create a 'very minimum infrastructure of decency and fairness.'[64]

Equal Opportunities

New Labour has pursued a wide-ranging equality agenda, which, consistently with the Third Way equality principle, focuses on the provision of equality of opportunity instead of relying on the provision of benefits.[65] Thus, social exclusion is characterised as a lack of access to opportunities[66] rather than as poverty per se, so that attention is directed to social mechanisms that produce or sustain poverty.[67] This shift is captured by the 1999 Department of Social Security Paper, *Opportunity Now*, which aims to 'tackle the causes of poverty and social exclusion, not just the symptoms; create a fairer society in which everyone has the opportunity to achieve their full potential; and invest in individuals and communities to equip them to take control of their lives.'[68] As a result, in tackling social exclusion, 'investment in opportunity is a priority.'[69] In *Fairness at Work* itself, equality of opportunity is dealt with by devoting a chapter to family friendly rights, including the National Child-care Strategy, the Working Families Tax Credit and the National Minimum Wage. The equal opportunities agenda has been supplemented by important new initiatives on training.

However, equal opportunities are to be achieved with the minimum of social investment. For example, in the implementation of the EU Parental Leave Directive, costs are minimised wherever possible. Parental leave is

---

[62] *Review of the Employment Relations Act 1999* (DTI, 2002) para 2.2.
[63] *Ibid* at para 4.18.
[64] *Fairness at Work*, Foreword.
[65] DSS, *New Ambitions for our Country: A New Contract for Welfare* (Cm 3805, 1998) 20.
[66] Barry in Hills *et al*, above n 31, at 19.
[67] Giddens, above n 14, at 104.
[68] DSS, *Opportunity for All: Tackling Poverty and Social Exclusion* (Cm 4445, 1999) 161.
[69] *Preventing Social Exclusion*, the 2001 Report of the Social Exclusion Unit, 7.

unpaid; it is restricted to employees who have been employed for a year or more; and only parents with children under five are eligible. Even more blatantly, the employer is entitled to postpone the period of parental leave if it considers that the operation of the business would be unduly disrupted.[70]

Similarly, while lip-service is paid to the value of flexibility as a family friendly measure, in practice, every attempt is made to minimise social investment. This has been seen by the grudging implementation of the Part-Time Workers Directive and the Fixed Term Workers Directive. It is seen again in the most recent right to request flexible working, found in the Employment Act 2002. On the face of it, this is an adventurous new equal opportunities measure. But far from being required to invest any resources at all in the provision of this opportunity, the employer is permitted to refuse the request for as many as eight different business-related reasons, including additional costs; detrimental effect on quality, performance, or ability to meet customer demand; and inability to re-organise work among existing staff or recruit additional staff.[71]

As well as emptying equal opportunities of its social investment content, New Labour clearly sees equality as a matter of 'lifting the floor' rather than narrowing inequalities across society. Thus, the National Minimum Wage has raised the floor, but no equalising measures have been introduced elsewhere in the system, such as extension of the results of collective bargaining, or fair Wages requirements in government contracts. The only measures capable of narrowing differentials are the equal pay for equal work provisions. But their effects are increasingly limited by the need to find a comparator within the same employment when enterprises are fragmenting due to contracting out. New Labour has determinedly resisted all claims to broaden the scope of comparison.[72] Instead, it has introduced a similarly restricted comparison when implementing the Part-Time and Fixed Term Workers Directives. This failure to address inequalities across society has meant that Britain has now a larger gap between rich and poor than any other Western European society.

One area of heightened activity has been that of discrimination law. An important new contribution to equality was made by the Race Relations (Amendment) Act 2000, which imposes a positive duty on public authorities to promote racial equality. This could certainly be viewed as a Third Way model: it sees the state as under a responsibility to take positive steps to achieve equality in all its activities.

---

[70] Maternity and Parental Leave Regulations 1999 (SI 1999/3312), para 13, Sch 2 para 6(b).
[71] Employment Act 2002, s 47 inserting Part 8A in the Employment Rights Act 1996.
[72] C-320/00 *Lawrence v Regent Office* [2002] IRLR 822, ECJ; C-256/01 *Allonby v Accrington and Rossendale College* [2004] 1 CMLR 35; 2003 WL 100626. See Opinion of Advocate General.

However, the agenda has recently shifted decisively away from equality of opportunity. Consultation documents on implementation of the EU Directive requiring legislation on age, religion and sexual orientation make little mention of equality of opportunity, still less of social investment. Instead, the catchword is now diversity; and diversity is presented emphatically as a business asset. As the 2001 White Paper, aptly named *Towards Equality and Diversity*, put it: 'Equality is about recognising and getting the right people for the job ... A diverse workforce can give [employers] a competitive edge in meeting the demands of a broad customer base ... It may be able to establish new clients for the business, and help to reach a wider market.'[73] Although there is clearly a real business case for equality,[74] this has come to dominate the agenda.[75] It therefore comes as no surprise that the implementing legislation is as narrow and limited as the Directive would permit.[76]

Community and Democracy

A key theme of *Fairness at Work* is the notion of partnership, which on its face appears to promote Third Way ideals of community. However, on closer inspection, partnership in fact denotes little more than cooperation by employees with employers. This is because partnership is proposed as a substitute for conflict. 'This White Paper' asserts the Prime Minister, 'is part of the government's programme to replace the notion of conflict between employees with the promotion of partnership.'

Absence of conflict between employees and employers can only be premised on the twin assumptions that employers' interests are synonymous with the public interest, and that all share equally in the profits of the business, even if only by the 'trickle down' theory that profitability creates and sustains jobs which in turn benefit workers. These are pure neoliberal assumptions, and their discordance with reality is particularly highlighted by the fact that companies in the United Kingdom are accountable to their shareholders rather than to other stakeholders such as employees or the broader community. Ironically, it was the Conservatives in 1980 who imposed a duty on company directors to have regard to the interests of employees as well as the interests of shareholders.[77] But the emphasis has shifted decisively away from even this weak and somewhat ambiguous

---

[73] Cabinet Office, *Towards Equality and Diversity: Implementing the Employment and Race Directives* (consultation document) (London, 2001) Preface [18].

[74] See B Hepple, M Coussey and T Choudhury, *Equality: A New Framework* (Oxford, Hart, 2000) Annex 1.

[75] For a critique see S Fredman, *The Future of Equality in Great Britain* (EOC, 2002).

[76] On age discrimination, see S Fredman, 'The Age of Equality' and B Hepple, 'Age Discrimination in Employment' in S Fredman and S Spencer (eds), *Age as an Equality Issue* (Oxford, Hart, 2003).

[77] Companies Act 1985, s 309.

provision. The Company Law Review,[78] appointed to see company law into the twenty-first century, considered that there were only two alternative views of the duties of directors to groups apart from shareholders. A view based on 'enlightened shareholder value' endorses the directors' overriding duty to shareholders, but requires directors to take a longer term view of shareholder interests by building up relationships of trust with other groups, such as suppliers and employees. On a 'pluralist' view, by contrast, a company is required to serve 'a wider range of interests, not subordinate to, or as a means of achieving, shareholder value, but as valid in their own right.'[79] Although the pluralist view is far from the most radical model, equating as it does employees with external interests such as suppliers or customers, it was decisively rejected. Moreover, the statutory duty on directors to have regard to the interests of employees was considered to be so uncertain in its effect as to warrant repeal. Instead, the 'enlightened shareholder value' should be expressed through a statement of general duties of directors, which include no more than that directors should take into account, so far as practical, 'the company's need to foster its business relationships, including those with its employees and suppliers and customers.'[80] As Wedderburn comments, employees are reduced to suppliers of labour, alongside other suppliers of goods and services, breaching the fundamental principle that labour is not a commodity. Such a foundation for company law, he argues, 'denies fundamental human decencies and makes a mockery of talk of "partnership." '[81]

Collins has argued that this reconfiguration of partnership as cooperation is in fact the essence of the Third Way ideology.[82] For Third Way theorists, he argues, the 'number one problem' is to improve competitiveness of business, and the Third Way response is regulation to promote competitiveness. Partnership at work is therefore endorsed only in order to improve the competitiveness of the business. The corollary, for Collins, is to 'diminish the importance attached to distributive values and ideals of workers' rights.' [83] This is, however, so narrow a view of Third Way principles as to amount to no more than modified neoliberalism. Collins makes no attempt to explain why he regards improving competitiveness as the key Third Way aim. By totally eschewing the importance of redistributive issues, he either assumes that fairness is a natural result of improved competitiveness, or that fairness does not matter. As outlined above, Third Way principles in

---

[78] DTI, *Modern Company Law for a Competitive Economy: The Strategic Framework* (URN 99/654, 1999); *Developing the Framework* (URN 00/656, 2000); *Final Report* (URN 01/943, 2001).
[79] DTI (1999), above n 78, at paras 5.1.12–5.1.16.
[80] DTI (2001), above n 78, vol II at 412.
[81] Lord Wedderburn, 'Employee Partnership and Company Law' (1992) 31 *ILJ* 99 at 112.
[82] H Collins, 'Is There a Third Way in Labour Law?' in Giddens (ed), *The Global Third Way Debate* (Polity, 2001) 300–14.
[83] *Ibid,* at 302.

fact address a far richer agenda, which include corporate responsibility, equality and democratic participation as values in themselves.

In fact, as has been recently argued, the partnership notion gains its persuasiveness because it conflates two different issues: partnership in production, and partnership in the distribution of income.[84] There are clear benefits from close cooperation in production, in raising productivity, generating and diffusing information and ideas, and encouraging innovation and flexible responses. But this should not obscure the inevitable conflicts of interests between workers and employers over the distribution of income. To acknowledge different interests, does not, however, make peaceful resolution impossible, as New Labour would have us believe. Instead, as has been forcefully argued, 'The basis for real partnership is consequently not so much asserting that there are no differences of interests, but rather, in creating ways of finding acceptable solutions to differences.'[85] It is, however, questionable whether the vocabulary of partnership is appropriately applied to collective bargaining, where it entails an easily exploited risk of substituting cooperation for genuine compromise.

Third Way principles of community and democracy are advanced through new provisions on statutory recognition, representation and consultation. But this is tempered by the continuing focus on individual choice. It is acknowledged that individual contracts of employment 'are not always agreements between equal partners' and that 'collective representation of individuals at work can be the best method of ensuring that employees are treated fairly.'[86] However, the key principle remains that of individual choice: 'The rights of the individual, whether exercised on their own or with others, [are] a matter of their choice.'[87]

THE THIRD WAY EUROPEAN STYLE

The EU perspective on the Third Way provides an important contrast with that of New Labour. The rapidly developing 'European Social Model' is supported by policy statements resonant with Third Way ideology. This has been particularly evident in the earlier focus on quality of work, and currently on quality of industrial relations in the 2000–2006 social policy agenda.[88] It should be noted that the rhetoric has not necessarily

---

[84] K Ewing and J Hendy (eds), *A Charter of Workers' Rights* (Institute of Employment Rights, 2002) 14.
[85] *Ibid* at 16.
[86] *Fairness at Work*, above n 54, at para 4.2.
[87] *Ibid*, Foreword and see para 4.2.
[88] Commission of the European Communities, *Social Policy Agenda* (COM (2000) 379 final) para 1.2; and see 'Mid-Term Review' para 3.3.

been matched by corresponding policies or legal instruments, and it is certainly true that the long political process of achieving practical policy can drift some distance from the rhetoric. However, as part of the contribution towards a critical analysis of ideology, this section focuses on the rhetoric. This section examines the four key notions set out above, namely, the role of the state, civic responsibility, equal opportunities and community and democracy.

The Relationship of the State and the Market: Modernising the European Social Model

The major impetus behind the development at EU level of a social dimension was the perceived need to create a buffer against the neoliberal tendencies of a free trade zone. At the same time, EU social policy seeks to move beyond the welfare state, to 'modernise the European social model.' True to Third Way principles, the modernised European Social Model aims at a genuine synthesis between state and market. This entails strengthening the role of social policy, not just as social transfer, but as a 'productive factor,'[89] an essential contribution to the economy. Social expenditure on health and education represents 'an investment in human resources with positive economic effects.'[90] Similarly, pensions and social security support better quality in employment, with consequent economic benefits.

But, crucially, this is not a one-way process. Social policy should promote productivity and efficiency; but at the same time economic policy should promote social objectives. Thus, the focus on job creation is accompanied by an equally important stress on improving the quality of jobs; and competitiveness is put side by side with the need for a high level of social protection and good social services.[91] 'Well targeted social protection is essential for adapting the economy to change and providing for an efficient and well-trained labour force.' But just as importantly, 'raising the employment rate will underpin the sustainability of the financing of social protection systems.'[92] At the same time, the development of fundamental social rights is seen as an end in itself, a 'key component of an equitable society and respect for human dignity',[93] rather than simply a means to a more competitive economy.

This gives the state an active role in addressing the central challenges of modern industrial relations. This role can be direct, through the provision of

---

[89] *Ibid* at para 1.2.
[90] *Ibid* at para 1.2.
[91] *Ibid* at para 3.1.
[92] *Ibid* at para 1.2.
[93] *Ibid* at para 4.2.4.

social assets such as transport or care services. But it is also facilitative, particularly in fostering social dialogue to deal with issues which collective bargaining on its own is unable to address.[94] Thus, social dialogue should be fostered to create new mechanisms to facilitate transitions between employment and unemployment, work and family life, and work and retirement.[95] Particularly important too is the need to create a new synthesis in respect of training and competence-building, which constitute the crucial bridge between mobility and job security. The new skills and competences by which mobile workers reach a sufficient level of security require shared investment by companies, workers and public authorities.[96]

It is arguable, of course, that this is an optimistic view of the power of the state to have an influence over increasingly mobile capital.[97] The power of capital over the machinery of state is clearly reflected in the extent to which the ideals articulated here are diluted in their legislative translation.[98] This is particularly strikingly illustrated when comparing the outcome of the worker participation measures in the European Company Statute with the ideals which originally informed the proposals.[99] But the very fact that the ideals continue to be articulated gives room for some optimism. The EU itself has the potential to combine the strengths of national governments in order to provide some counterweight to the power of capital, and the slow but consistent growth of the social dimension to the EU demonstrates the possibilities. Even in its highly dilute form, the worker participation measures in the European Company Statute still operate to shore up the best practice of EU Member States in the face of a threat of a race to the bottom. As Davies argues, without some measures on participation, 'the agreement to the SE project of Member States with advanced national participation regimes could not be obtained.'[100]

Civic Responsibility

The notion of civic responsibility found in EU rhetoric is perhaps the sharpest distinguishing feature from New Labour ideology. While New

---

[94] European Commission D-G for Employment and Social Affairs, *Report of the High Level Group on Industrial Relations and Change in the EU* (European Communities, January 2002) (henceforth *IR Report*) ch 1.

[95] Such as portable social rights (transferable between companies); or rights decoupled from the employment relationship and linked to citizenship.

[96] *IR Report*, above n 94, at 18.

[97] See P Ireland 'Company Law and the Myth of Shareholder Ownership' (1999) 62 Modern Law Review 32.

[98] See in particular Council Directive 2002/86/EC supplementing the Statute for a European Company (Council Regulation 2157/2001 EC).

[99] *Ibid* and see particularly P Davies, 'Workers on the Board of the European Company?' (2003) 32 *Industrial Law Journal* 75.

[100] *Ibid* at 96.

Labour focuses on individual responsibility, ignoring corporate and even state responsibility, civic responsibility in EU policy documents is represented in a richer and more encompassing sense. A key objective is to:

> develop shared responsibility between business and employees regarding a range of factors, including employability, mobility, modernisation and improvement of employment relationships, in the development of procedures for consultation and information and the creation of tools to prevent and mediate conflicts.[101]

Civic responsibility translates, too, into the pivotal notion of solidarity, which means mutual dependence and a sense of togetherness, but has richer connotations in its original French. Unknown and alien to British rhetoric, 'solidarity' is sufficiently central to EU ideology to function as the title to Chapter IV of the EU Charter of Fundamental Rights. It is striking, too, that solidarity embraces responsibilities both of employers and the state. Thus, the Solidarity Chapter includes not just a range of work-based rights, but also duties of the state towards its citizens, in the form of social security, health-care and environmental and consumer protection. This recognition of the interdependence of rights within and outside of the workplace is an important step towards a transformative vision of labour law.

This is spelt out in more detail in the 2002 *Report of the High Level Group on Industrial Relations and Change in the EU*.[102] Whereas *Fairness at Work* uses the concept of partnership primarily to connote cooperation by workers and their representatives with management, the document stresses mutual responsibility. 'Managing change in a socially responsible way is a key challenge for Europe. Both sides of industry have a responsibility. They are both partners and actors in the process of change.'[103] Particular stress is placed on the 'emergence of a new corporate culture based on social responsibility',[104] including the responsibility to invest more in human capital, environment and relations with stakeholders.[105]

A rich concept of responsibility is also applied to the tripartite level of industrial relations, through the concept of 'social concertation.' While bargaining is substituted by a process of deliberation, this is not envisaged as merely a way of persuading labour to comply with state or employer initiated policies. Instead, deliberation requires parties to 'explain, give reasons and take responsibility for their decisions and strategies to each other, to

---

[101] *Social Policy Agenda*, above n 88, at para 4.1.
[102] *IR Report*, above n 94.
[103] *Ibid* at 39.
[104] *Ibid* at 30.
[105] *Ibid* at 26.

their rank and file, and to the general public.'[106] This gives all participants the opportunity to shape and reshape their identity and preferences:

> Probably, the most interesting property of concertation lies in the possibility that interest organisations such as trade unions and employers' associations redefine the content of their self-interested strategies in a 'public regarding' way. They must be prepared to assume a wider responsibility that goes far beyond the partial interests that are usually expressed through collective bargaining.[107]

Although there is a risk that the public interest could still be conflated with business interests, there remains a strong signal that employers need to look beyond their self-interest.

Equal Opportunities

Equal opportunities is a further consistent theme of the Social Policy Agenda. This is demonstrated in the stress on investing in education, training and life-long learning, and the focus on social inclusion through 'more and better opportunities for vulnerable groups, including those with disabilities, ethnic groups and new immigrants.'[108] The aim of gender equality is characterised as an equal opportunity issue: to promote full participation of women in all aspects of society.

But equal opportunities is also closely allied with a notion of fairness of result. Thus the 2003 Mid-Term Review strongly emphasises that the quality of jobs themselves must improve as a precondition for further reductions in the age, gender and skill-related gaps. Those in jobs that do not offer training and career development or job security are at high risk of unemployment and social exclusion.[109] It also focuses on distributive outcomes, particularly the distribution between the income of the top and bottom 20 per cent of the economy. This focus leads it to give as much emphasis to social protection as it does to social investment.

Community and Democracy

Notions of community are repeatedly stressed within EU policy documents, translating into the policy of mainstreaming social inclusion.[110] Even more

---

[106] *Ibid* at 27.
[107] *Ibid* at 27.
[108] *Social Policy Agenda*, above n 88, at para 4.2.
[109] (COM(2003) 312 final) para 3.2.1.
[110] *Social Policy Agenda*, above n 88, at para 4.3.

important for our purposes is the stress on democracy through the pivotal role of the social partners.[111] Social dialogue at all levels is seen as promoting both competitiveness and solidarity, and balancing flexibility and security.[112]

The 2002 *Industrial Relations Report* is particularly interesting in its Third Way vision of industrial relations, particularly the wholehearted endorsement of collective bargaining as both a democratic process and a force for social cohesion. Thus the Report emphasises:

> the enduring importance of collective bargaining ... 'the royal way' of determining wages, working hours and the employment conditions of workers. Through their joint authorship of the rules, negotiating parties accept joint responsibility for the implementation and renewal of rules always taking into account the need for further social cohesion as well as competitiveness of European enterprises.[113]

At the same time, collective bargaining should not be limited to the bipartite process between management and labour. It:

> works better when embedded in a process of social dialogue. Social dialogue can be defined as a process, in which actors inform each other of their intentions and capacities, elaborate information provided to them, and clarify and explain their assumptions and expectations. This is not the same as bargaining, but provides a setting for more efficient bargaining by helping to separate the digestion of facts, problems and possible solutions from negotiating feasible courses of action and the distribution of costs and benefits.[114]

The report also stresses that, given the inevitable processes of decentralisation, proper structures of representation, consultation and information at workplace and enterprise levels are particularly important. But coordination at higher levels is also necessary to prevent undercutting, facilitate mobility and ensure investment in training and other collective goods. Thus the challenge is to combine coordination at sectoral level with flexibility at enterprise level.

Equally important is the stress on tripartism as an essential part of democracy and social cohesion. The state is envisaged as playing an important facilitative role, both in coordinating and in providing social assets. This has been put into practice through the direct involvement of European social partners in decision-making on social policy through EU social dialogue. In addition, participation is envisaged as extending beyond

---

[111] *Ibid* at para 3.1.
[112] *Ibid* at para 4.3.
[113] *IR Report,* above n 94, at 24.
[114] *Ibid* at 25.

trade unions and the state to include other civic associations. In this way, the traditional exclusiveness of unions can be counteracted.[115] This is particularly important for issues such as the reconciliation of work and family, social inclusion, immigration, non-discrimination and ageing, all of which require 'more interactions between the traditional social partners and civil society actors engaged in innovative civil dialogue.'[116]

NEW LABOUR LAWS: NEW LEFT TURNING RIGHT?

The urgent need for transformation of labour law is widely accepted. Labour law needs to bridge the gap between those in work and those out of work, to create flexibility as well as security, to cater for workers with little industrial strength as well as those with collective power, and to assert the importance of social rights in the face of competitive pressures caused by globalisation. Although few theorists address labour law directly, Third Way ideology provides a rich conceptual resource to create a transformative labour law, provided it is interpreted as building on social democratic foundations in order to mould new solutions to new challenges.

To what extent has New Labour drawn on these resources to create a transformative labour law? This section examines collective labour law, because the influence of ideology is sharpest in this context.

Industrial Action

The most striking aspect of the record of New Labour law is what it has not done. There is still no right to strike in domestic law, and New Labour has refused to do anything but tinker with the worst excesses of neoliberal strike laws. Its only substantial offering is the provision of protection against dismissal during the first eight weeks of a lawful strike.[117] Even the rhetoric has changed very little. Like its neoliberal predecessor, New Labour justifies restrictions on the basis that they enhance democracy within trade unions.

Certainly, Third Way ideology would promote democracy and with it the requirement for majority support in a ballot. However, the democratic justification, as used in both the Tory and New Labour rhetoric, has never rung true.[118] In fact, the strike laws, far from promoting democracy,

---

[115] *Ibid* at 28.
[116] *Ibid* at 28.
[117] Trade Union and Labour Relations (Consolidation) Act (TULRCC)A) 1992, s 238A.
[118] S Fredman, 'The New Rights: Labour Law and Ideology in the Thatcher Years' (1992) 12 *Oxford Journal of Legal Studies* 244.

frequently scupper it. The case-law is a litany of attempts by employers to halt strikes which have achieved majority support, but are declared unlawful because of a technical breach.[119] New Labour's half-hearted changes often have the contrary effect.[120] Nor is there any democratic justification for retaining restrictions on unions' powers to exclude or discipline members for refusing to take industrial action,[121] nor for the continued adherence, with minor revisions, to burdensome notice provisions,[122] which simply give the employer a better opportunity to minimise the effect of the strike. The employer's power to seek an injunction belies any suggestion that this is a promotion of democratic participation, which would give such a power only to the aggrieved member.

The restrictive measures are also justified on the grounds that they promote responsible trade unions. However, the responsibility of the trade union is in no sense matched by corresponding rights. Industrial action is still almost invariably a breach of contract; and the protection against dismissal[123] is in no way equivalent to a right to strike. It expires after eight weeks of dispute and is in any event an intensely individualised and juridified right, requiring individual workers to take their case to a tribunal, and attracting far weaker remedies than those available to employers.

Nor is there any significant sense in which employers are required to act responsibly in return. There is no linkage between restrictions on strikes and the duty to bargain, as would be the case in other European jurisdictions, such as Germany. Even in its own terms, it is intensely one-sided. Employers do not have any responsibility equivalent to the notice requirements imposed on unions, nor are they required to follow any democratic or other procedures in their management of the strike.

The reason why these laws can be maintained by a 'Third Way' government is because Third Way ideology assumes that there are only two kinds of state: the interventionist nanny state of social democracy, and the non-interventionist night-watchman state of neoliberalism. Restrictive state intervention does not appear on the radar. It is this which permits Tony Blair to present these laws in terms of a lightly regulated labour market. For Third Way theorists properly to deal with these measures, it is necessary to place more emphasis on state and corporate responsibility with the correlative guarantees of social rights at both the collective and individual levels.

---

[119] *London Underground v NUR* [1996] ICR 170; *Blackpool and Fylde College v NATFHE* [1994] ICR 648; *RMT v London Underground* [2001] IRLR 228, see (2001) 30 ILJ 206; *RMT v Midland Mainline* [2001] IRLR 813; *P v NAS/UWT* [2003] IRLR 307, HL.
[120] *National Union of Rail, Maritime and Transport Workers v London Underground Ltd and Ors* 2001 WL 98068 CA, [2001] IRLR 228.
[121] TULR(C)A 1992, ss 64–64.
[122] *Ibid* ss 226A, 231A, 234A.
[123] *Ibid* ss 237–39.

Recognition

The statutory right to trade union recognition[124] has been the flagship of New Labour labour law. On the face of it, it is a paradigm Third Way offering. It balances state intervention with free enterprise, 'designed to balance the desire of a workforce to have a union bargain collectively on their behalf with the need for effective management.'[125] It advances democracy, basing statutory recognition on majority voting,[126] and imposes mutual obligations on employer and employee.

The government claims that the procedure is working well,[127] and TUC evidence suggests that it has provided the incentive for thousands of voluntary agreements.[128] By 31 December 2002, the Central Arbitration Committee had received 236 applications, and made 52 recognition awards.[129] An important positive feature has been the use of the CAC rather than courts or tribunals.

However, the statutory recognition procedure reflects at best a partial commitment to Third Way values. In fact, Third Way rhetoric is frequently used to produce neoliberal solutions. Most striking is the way in which the democratic rationale is used to justify imposing a series of hurdles which, far from reinforcing democracy, can combine to obstruct the basic principle of majority support.

The clearest demonstration of this paradoxical use of democracy is that majority support in a ballot is not considered sufficient. In addition, there must be support from at least 40 per cent of all the workers in the bargaining unit.[130] This means that an abstention counts as a vote against, whereas, of course, it cannot be inferred that those who do not vote do not support recognition.[131] The government points out there has only been one CAC-ordered ballot in which the union has gained a simple majority but lost on the 40 per cent requirement. However, this extra requirement has a much wider impact. In particular, a number of employers offering voluntary recognition ballots have insisted on using the 40 per cent criterion as well as majority support criteria.[132] In addition, unions may well be deterred from proceeding with a ballot, even if there is a chance of a majority, if they cannot be certain of support by 40 per cent of the

---

[124] TULR(C)A 1992, s 70A, Sch A1.
[125] *Review of the Employment Relations Act 1999* (DTI, 2002) para 2.2.
[126] *Ibid.*
[127] *Ibid* at para 2.4.
[128] TUC, *Review of the Employment Relations Act 1999: TUC Response* (TUC briefing document, 3 June 2003) para 1.4 (henceforth *ERA Review*).
[129] *Ibid* at para 2.5.
[130] TULR(C)A 1992, Sch A1, para 29(2).
[131] TUC, *Modern Rights for Modern Workplaces (2002)* para 80.
[132] *ERA Review,* above n 128, at para 1.19.

bargaining unit. A misjudgement on this score means three years of waiting for another chance.[133]

How then does the government justify imposing a balloting requirement which is so much stiffer than that generally recognised as sufficient to give democratic legitimacy to an election result? The answer is that the government is not really concerned with the democratic rationale, which is to assure the electorate itself of the legitimacy of representatives. Instead, New Labour regards the main function of the ballot as that of convincing the employer. Thus, the 2002 Review states:

> The 40 per cent threshold was introduced to ensure that a 'yes' vote would be a clear demonstration to employers and others of positive worker support for recognition. Employers cannot therefore argue that recognition was awarded simply on the basis of an unrepresentative ballot in which a minority of eligible workers voted.[134]

Similarly, 'the 40 per cent balloting threshold has worked — as intended — to demonstrate strong evidence of positive support for recognition. This has greatly contributed to employer acceptance of ballot results.'[135] Underlying this is the assumption that the procedure is an imposition on employers, rather than deriving from their civic responsibility.

Similarly, the CAC is required to call a ballot even if over 50 per cent of the bargaining unit are already union members, if it is satisfied that a ballot is in the interests of good industrial relations or where there is evidence that union members do not in fact want the union to bargain on their behalf.[136] This paragraph was inserted at the request of the CBI during the passage of the Bill. By the end of 2002, the CAC had ordered seven ballots in these circumstances,[137] of which the union lost three, despite having over 50 per cent membership, or substantial support shown in a petition.[138] In some cases this was because of redundancies or dismissals, in others because of heavy employer campaigning and intimidation and use of delaying tactics.

Nor are there sufficient measures to ensure that both sides have equal opportunities to succeed in the ballot. Not only is the union hampered by lack of recourse to industrial action, there is also insufficient protection for freedom of association or against victimisation.[139] Particularly problematic

---

[133] *Ibid* at para 1.20.
[134] *Ibid* at para 2.26.
[135] *Ibid* at 14.
[136] TULR(C)A 1992, Sch A1, para 22(3).
[137] *ERA Review*, above n 128, at 14.
[138] TUR1/ 34,54,57,82, 164, 169, 2000–2.
[139] TULR(C)A 1992, Sch 1A, para 156.

is that the union has no right of access to the workplace for electioneering until the CAC has ordered a ballot. This means that an employer has unfettered access to the workforce, while the union is limited to meetings out of hours and off the premises. The TUC has evidence of intimidatory and misleading materials used in recent campaigns by employers.

This is scarcely mitigated by the most recent proposal, which is to permit earlier access,[140] but only in the form of the distribution of written union material by a qualified independent person.[141] Yet the essence of democracy is to permit face to face discussion, as well as giving the union the opportunity to counter employer arguments.[142] The government's justification for this suggests, paradoxically, that the danger lies in intimidation by the union. 'Thereby, the workers who are the subject of an application can be informed by the union about an issue which closely involves them, while withholding their individual identities from the union.'[143] Far from a commitment to Third Way ideals of democracy and civic responsibility, these provisions suggest a continuing adherence to the notion that the employer's power, derived from property ownership, is purely private power.

Similarly, statutory recognition only entitles a union to collective bargaining on pay, hours and holidays.[144] Third Way principles of democracy, community and civic responsibility would entail a far wider remit, extending at the very least to training, pensions and equality, all of which the government has refused to countenance. Belying any Third Way commitment to a facilitative state, New Labour seems intent on reflecting norms, rather than setting new parameters. Thus, the refusal to include pensions is based on the argument that at present most recognition agreements do not include pensions.[145] Similarly, any commitment to equal opportunities through social investment is belied by the refusal to include equality or training, despite substantial TUC evidence of the productive benefits of including training in the bargaining framework.

Consultation[146]

The new EU Directive on Information and Consultation[147] has much potential for introducing a measure of Third Way values into the collective arena in the United Kingdom — provided, of course, they are allied to a

---

[140] From the time when the application is declared admissible.
[141] *ERA Review,* above n 128, at para 2.48.
[142] *Ibid* at para 1.28.
[143] *Ibid* at para 2.48.
[144] TULR(C)A 1992, Sch 1A, para 2(3).
[145] *ERA Review,* above n 128, at para 2.56.
[146] See also Weiss, chapter 11 and Brown and Oxerbridge, Chapter 3 above.
[147] Directive 2002/14/EC of 11 March 2002.

corresponding development in respect of industrial action and collective bargaining. The Directive reflects Third Way attempts to create a synthesis between free enterprise and an active facilitative state, with a focus on democratic participation. Hence, the aims are to improve the flexibility of work and to maintain security; to facilitate employee access to training while increasing employees' availability for change; and to increase competitiveness while promoting employee involvement in the operation and future of the undertaking.[148]

These aims receive concrete expression in two main features, both of which could be potentially transformative. First, the Directive widens the scope of consultation well beyond the traditional subjects of collective industrial relations in Britain. Representatives have a right to information and consultation on 'the situation, structure and probable development of employment within the undertaking,' as well as on decisions likely to lead to substantial changes in work organisation or in contractual relations.[149] This is backed up by a right to information on the recent and probable development of the undertaking's activities and economic situation. Secondly, the right is given to every worker in an undertaking with at least 50 workers, thus extending consultation well beyond workplaces with established trade unions or other consultative mechanisms. It is for these reasons that the TUC has identified the adoption of the EU Employee Consultation Directive as a 'real strategic breakthrough, with major implications for patterns of employee representation and trade union organising strategies in the UK'.[150]

However, the extent to which it can deliver a robust form of Third Way values depends on the ways in which the concepts of consultation and worker representation are filtered through the UK ideological prism. The UK government made sure to dilute central principles during the legislative stage, the most important being the limitation to larger undertakings,[151] and the right to delay applying the legislation to firms with less than 150 employees to March 2008. The result, as Patricia Hewitt, Secretary of State for Trade and Industry, proudly announced in the government consultation paper, was that once fully implemented, the Directive will only apply to 1 per cent of companies in the United Kingdom (benefiting 75 per cent of their employees).[152]

A key test of government's commitment to Third Way principles concerns choice of representatives. It is crucial that trade union representatives

---

[148] *Ibid*, Preamble.
[149] *Ibid*, Art 4(2).
[150] Mark Hall, *EU Directive on Information and Consultation: How Will it Affect Employment Relations in the UK?* (discussion document, 12 July 2002).
[151] DTI, *High Performance Workplaces: The Role of Employee Involvement in a Modern Economy* (July 2002) para 5.4.
[152] *Ibid.*

be fully incorporated, and, in their absence, that employee representatives emerge who are independent, democratically accountable and sufficiently well trained to provide proper representation. This needs to go well beyond the response of the previous administration,[153] which was to create weak, non-independent and non-democratic consultees.[154] Also key is the range of subject matter included in consultation.[155] It is crucial too that consultation takes place at a time when decisions are still fluid; requiring a commitment by New Labour to go well beyond current provisions on redundancy consultation,[156] which in effect transmute the right to be consulted into a right merely to be informed.

At present, however, there is little evidence that the government intends to make use of the opportunity to facilitate Third Way principles. In the 2002 consultation paper, Patricia Hewitt is anxious to reassure employers:

> Information and consultation is not joint decision-making or an extension of collective bargaining. Management continues to be responsible for making the ultimate decisions in the business, but in making those decisions it needs to have seriously engaged with its workforce.[157]

CONCLUSION: THE VOCABULARY OF TRANSFORMATION — SOCIAL DEMOCRACY REVIVED

The new challenges facing labour law require transformative solutions. The four principles which I have attributed to Third Way ideology can make a valuable contribution to achieving new structures based on a positive facilitative state; civic responsibility with a focus on corporate and state responsibility; social investment in equal opportunity; and collectivism based on a rich commitment to democracy and community.

However, the experience of New Labour shows that these principles are easily corrupted. Although this is in large measure due to lack of whole-hearted commitment to Third Way principles, it also reveals a danger in Third Way vocabulary itself. In carving out a 'third way,' this school of thought has put as much effort into distancing itself from social democracy as from neoliberalism. This has been achieved by a distorted view of both

---

[153] *Commission v UK* [1994] ICR 664.
[154] Where trade unions are recognised, they have precedence: TULR(C)A 1992, s 188(1B).
[155] Directive 2002/14/EC, Art 4(4)(e); Transnational Information and Consultation of Employees Regulations 1999 (SI 1999/3323) ('TICE') Sch, para 8(2).
[156] *R v British Coal, ex parte Vardy* [1993] ICR 720, *Griffin v South West Water* [1995] IRLR 15; *MSF v Refuge Assurance plc* [2002] IRLR 324; *Middlesbrough BC v TGWU* [2002] IRLR 332.
[157] *High Performance Workplaces,* above n 151, at para 1.8.

alternatives, and one which derives from neoliberalism itself. Third Way theorists caricature social democracy by portraying the state as suffocating and interventionist and equality as conformist. Likewise, the portrayal of the minimal neoliberal state is a pure neoliberal distortion: our experience during the Thatcher and Major years left no doubt of the heavy-handed interventionism of the neoliberal state in a wide range of areas, from industrial relations to 'family values' and the treatment of homosexuality, to the centralisation of powers over key issues such as education.

Social democracy is itself a political philosophy in need of development to face modern challenges. Its central objective is to reconcile the operation of the market with the redistribution of resources and the provision of public goods.[158] It too places a central value on democracy,[159] and stresses the responsibility of both capital and labour in pursuing public values.[160] These are clearly the natural roots of much of Third Way thinking. But Third Way terminology propels its adherents to distance themselves from social democracy. Hence, New Labour has been able, in the name of the Third Way, to inject so large a measure of neoliberalism into its labour law framework — so much so that Stuart Hall has characterised New Labour's project as the 'transformism' of social democracy into a variant of free market neoliberalism.[161]

Before New Labour came into power in 1997, Bob Hepple asked the question: 'What then is to replace the fractured ideology of pluralism without losing its core values of equality, social justice and freedom of association?'[162] His critique of both pluralism and the language of human and social rights continues to shape the debate, and it is here that transformative labour law should be growing.

Labour law needs to free itself from its neoliberal shackles, if it is to be genuinely transformative. The four principles I have outlined above are valuable contributions to modernising social democracy, but Third Way terminology has outlived its purpose.

---

[158] C Crouch, 'A Third Way in Industrial Relations?' in S White (ed), *New Labour: The Progressive Future?* (New York, Palgrave, 2001) 96.
[159] See eg R Miliband, *Parliamentary Socialism* (George Allen & Unwin, London 1961) at 13.
[160] See, eg HJ Laski, *Grammar of Politics* (1925) esp ch 5.
[161] Stuart Hall 'New Labour's Double-Shuffle' in *Soundings* Issue 24, August 2003.
[162] Hepple, above n 3, at 317.

2

Laws Against Strikes Revisited

KEITH EWING

INTRODUCTION

IT IS OVER 30 years since Kahn Freund and Hepple wrote their seminal
pamphlet on *Laws against Strikes*. A great deal has happened since, but
the law is no less controversial today than it was then.[1] The legislation
in force at the time the pamphlet was published was repealed in 1974 and
replaced with a much more liberal regime. This in turn was the subject of an
extraordinary battle between the courts and Parliament in the course of
which it became necessary for the House of Lords to teach the Court of
Appeal a number of lessons in constitutional law.[2] The legislation of 1974
has in due course been the subject of gradual revision, with a number of
procedural and substantive restraints on the right to strike introduced over
the period of 18 years from 1979 to 1997, first under the governments of
Mrs Thatcher, and then Mr Major. These restrictions brought the United
Kingdom into conflict with a number of international agencies, notably the
ILO and the Council of Europe.[3] Since 1997 some of these restrictions have
been modified, but in essence they remain in place, to the great irritation of
trade unionists. The aim of this chapter is to re-examine the right to strike
in the context of these changing circumstances, but in the context also of
the growth of the human rights movement in Britain and elsewhere since
the early 1970s. The key question considered in the pages that follow is the
contribution which the human rights movement can make to the debate
about laws against strikes.

---

[1] See T Novitz, *International and European Protection of the Right to Strike* (Oxford, Oxford
University Press, 2003) for an outstanding account of contemporary issues.
[2] *Duport Steels Ltd v Sirs* [1980] ICR 161.
[3] See S Mills, 'The International Labour Organisation, the United Kingdom and Freedom of
Association: An Annual Cycle of Condemnation' [1997] *EHRLR* 35.

THE CHANGING CONTEXT

The levels of strike activity in recent years have fallen to their lowest for over a hundred years. The number of working days lost in 1998 was a mere 282,000, compared to the 14,077,000 at the time of *Laws against Strikes* in 1972. It is true that strike activity has tended to increase in the public sector in more recent years, and the figures will be inflated by the national firefighters' dispute in 2002 and 2003. But even so, the number of working days lost in the first 10 months of 2002 was only a quarter of that experienced during each of the years of Thatcher government. Yet it is not only in the United Kingdom that we find evidence of strike levels in decline. The same is true of most countries in the developed world from Europe to North America to Australasia. This is despite the great changes that are taking place in these countries with sometimes severe implications for jobs and pensions, and despite the fact that in many countries in recent years it would be possible to identify a major dispute of some importance.[4] There are doubtless a number of reasons for these changes, though many of these are speculative only. We can point to rising living standards and the ubiquity of the mortgage; more stable economic circumstances and the ending of inflation; the fall in trade union membership and the number of trade union members; and the provision of alternative ways to resolve disputes. We can also point to the fall in collective bargaining activity; the loss of the habit of striking; the changing nature of sanctions used by workers; globalisation and the distance of workers from the source of decision-making; and the impact of the law.

The last is perhaps the most difficult to account for, in view of the widely-held belief that law is not an effective way of dealing with industrial action. This is a view that is reinforced by the experience of the Industrial Relations Act 1971 when the social power of organised labour helped to produce a change in the law and the removal of legal restraints. The ability of trade unions by defiance to remove these laws seemed to vindicate the extraordinarily propitious words of Kahn Freund and Hepple who wrote that 'it is virtually impossible to isolate the effect of the law from that of an infinite number of other social variables,' and that 'what legislatures and courts can do to change the habits of people in industrial relations must in democratic societies always and everywhere be limited.'[5] According to Davies and Freedland, governments had 'wholly underestimated the resistance to law that would arise,' and failed to recognise that they were 'challenging a

---

[4] See KD Ewing and BW Napier, 'The Wapping Dispute and Labour Law' [1986] *CLJ* 285; J Fudge and H Glasbeek, 'Alberta Nurses v A Contemptuous Supreme Court of Canada' (1992) 4(1) *Constitutional Forum* 1; and G Orr, 'Conspiracy on the Waterfront' (1998) 11 *AJLL* 159.
[5] O Kahn Freund and B Hepple, *Laws against Strikes* (London, Fabian Society, 1972) 60.

way of life.'[6] But that was a long time and many disputes ago. Since Kahn Freund and Hepple wrote their pamphlet, we have had the miners' strike,[7] Wapping and the Liverpool dockers, to name but three *causes célèbres*. In all of these disputes the law played a crucial part in delivering a crushing defeat to the unions. It may well be that changing social forces were largely or partly responsible for the outcomes in these disputes. But it is difficult to resist the conclusion that the law also played a part, even if the law in these circumstances was brutally administered. It would indeed be possible to go further and say that these disputes changed our understanding about the power of the state and the role of the law. Neither is to be underestimated when there is a determination on the part of the former to use the latter.

A notable political success of this time was the ability of the government to project onto the strikers the charge that, by their conduct in standing against organised authority, they had 'place[d] themselves outside the democratic tradition'.[8] It had previously been assumed that such a charge might restrain those who would 'lay aside' 'respect for the freedom to strike,' given 'the standards and principles of a democratic society'.[9] Perhaps as a result of these different considerations, there is little talk today about laws against strikes being ineffective, as revealed by the folly of Betteshanger, when more than a thousand striking Kent miners were prosecuted during the Second World War.[10] Trade unionists today are fully aware of the law's force and quite anxious to comply with it. Labour injunctions are greeted with dismay rather than defiance. Talk is of proceeding in an orderly way to the court building in Strasbourg rather than in vast numbers to the streets of London. While it may be true that the social context of modern industrial relations makes the use of the strike much less likely, the law has played a part in containing industrial action in circumstances where workers have been pushed to the wall. Yet strikes still happen, as we continue to be reminded by the recent action by railway workers, local government workers and firefighters. Happily, we can only speculate about what would have happened if the government had successfully carried out its threat to have the action of the firefighters stopped by injunction on the ground that it involved a malicious breach of contract presenting a threat to life and property.[11]

---

[6] PL Davies and MR Freedland, *Labour Legislation and Public Policy* (Oxford, Oxford University Press, 1993) 350.

[7] See the collection in (1984) 16 *ILJ* 145 (articles by P Wallington, KD Ewing, R Benedictus, J Mesher and WM Rees).

[8] Kahn-Freund and Hepple, above n 5, at 60.

[9] *Ibid*.

[10] See *Report of the Royal Commission on Trade Unions and Employers' Associations 1965–1968* (Cmnd 3623, 1968) App 7. See also, N Stammers, *Civil Liberties in Britain During the Second World War* (London, Croom Helm, 1983) ch 7.

[11] Trade Union and Labour Relations (Consolidation) Act (TULR(C)A) 1992, s 240.

CLASSICAL FUNCTION OF THE RIGHT TO STRIKE

In *Laws against Strikes*, Kahn Freund and Hepple address the rationale of the right to strike. There they consider whether the strike is a political or economic freedom, and concentrate their inquiry 'on the strike as an economic weapon in industrial relations,' that is to say 'an industrial sanction, as a means of enforcing a right or a demand for an improved right.'[12] In this they are at one with many trade unionists in both the private and public sectors, by whom the right to strike is seen as a cornerstone of the free collective bargaining process. This function of the right to strike has attracted judicial notice, most clearly in Lord Wright's well known dictum that 'the right of workmen to strike is an essential element in the principle of collective bargaining'[13] though it has been slightly extended in more recent litigation.[14] Apart from judicial notice of the classical purpose of the strike at common law, this same function of the strike is also clearly reflected in the concept of a trade dispute in British law, stretching back to the Trade Disputes Act 1906 and beyond. Under the current law, immunity from legal liability is extended only to disputes between workers and their employer which relates wholly or mainly to terms and conditions of employment, or similar matters.[15] So there would be no legal protection for a strike designed to protest against government policy or the policies of a foreign government. There would certainly be no protection for workers who took industrial action to protest about a war, or the invasion of another country.[16] Indeed, it is a striking feature of labour law — not only in the United Kingdom — that it has singularly failed to provide effective protection for the right to strike.

Historically, the right to strike thus was seen essentially as a right which was parasitic upon the process of collective bargaining, a tactic to be used to press bargaining demands or to ensure that agreements were honoured. In this sense the right to strike is a secondary right which is exercised as part of a larger process in which the primary right is the right to engage in

---

[12] Kahn Freund and Hepple, above n 5, at 6.

[13] *Crofter Hand Woven Harris Tweed v Veitch* [1942] AC 435. It is true, however, that at common law strikes for wider social purposes have also been accepted by the courts, most obviously where the Musicians' Union in 1958 were permitted to boycott workplaces which operated a colour bar. But this is exceptional (at least for English law) and was permitted by the court as a way of promoting the union's policy of opposition to racial discrimination (*Scala Ballroom (Wolverhampton) Ltd v Ratcliffe* [1958] 3 All ER 220).

[14] In *Re P* [2003] UKHL 8, Lord Bingham wrote of strikes applying to 'employment related disputes between employers and employees' (para 4).

[15] TULR(C)A 1992, s 244.

[16] During the invasion of Iraq, a number of British train drivers refused to handle war materials and there were suggestions in the Australian press that Australian trade unionists would impose a ban on war material, though these were swiftly denounced. For a discussion of the limits of British law, see D Brodie, 'Political Strikes' in W Finnie, C Himsworth and N Walker (eds), *Edinburgh Essays in Public Law* (Edinburgh, Edinburgh University Press, 1991) 215.

collective bargaining. Nowhere is this more marked than in the first international treaty formally to protect the right to strike. In the Council of Europe's Social Charter of 18 October 1961, the right to strike appears in a paragraph which bears the title 'Right to Bargain Collectively.'[17] In the context of this rationale of the right to strike, it is or has become very difficult (if not impossible in practice) to resist the imposition of limits and restrictions that appear superficially persuasive and rational.[18] For example, if collective agreements are legally binding for a fixed term and contain a procedure for the resolution of disputes about the operation of the agreement, there may be no need for a right to strike, at least during the period of the collective agreement. So we find in a large number of countries, from Canada and the USA to Germany and Sweden, systems of labour law in which the strike as a weapon in collective bargaining is displaced by other dispute resolution procedures. In some countries it is thus accepted that the right to strike is a right that can be traded or withdrawn for other forms of dispute resolution.[19] Similarly, if employment conditions are settled by conciliation and arbitration in state tribunals, it is hard to argue against the contention that there is no need for a right to strike.[20] No collective bargaining: no need for bargaining sanctions.

If the rationale of the right to strike is that it is a weapon in collective bargaining, it has also become difficult (if not impossible in practice) to resist confining the strike to the parties involved in the dispute. It has also been difficult to resist attempts to restrict its scope and impact by prohibiting various forms of secondary or sympathy action. This is not to agree with such restrictions, rather to acknowledge their superficial attraction.[21] If the strike is a sanction in collective bargaining between A and B, why is there a need for action against C who is not a party to the dispute? This is the question that was asked with some incredulity by the Court of Appeal in the 1970s as it went about undoing the will of Parliament as expressed in the Trade Union and Labour Relations Act 1974 (as amended).[22] But not

---

[17] See also EU Charter of Fundamental Rights 2000, Art 28, on which see B Bercusson, 'A European Agenda?' in KD Ewing (ed), *Employment Rights at Work* (London, Institute of Employment Rights, 2001) 169–72.

[18] Though it is to be noted that the scope of Art 6(4) was extended by the Hoge Raad in *N V Dutch Railways v Transport Unions FNV, FSV and CNV* (1988) 6 ILLR 3.

[19] See respectively, DD Carter *et al*, 'Canada' in R Blanpain, *International Encyclopaedia for Labour Law and Industrial Relations* (Deventer, Kluwer, 2001) vol 4, 340–42; M Weiss and M Schmidt, 'Germany' in Blanpain (ed), *ibid* (2000), vol 6, 154, 170; A Adlercreutz, 'Sweden' in Blanpain (ed), *ibid* (1998), vol 13, 188 *et seq*; and A Goldman and RH White, 'United States of America' in Blanpain (ed), *ibid* (2002), vol 14, 389.

[20] See B Creighton and A Stewart, *Labour Law* (3rd edn, Sydney, Federation Press, 2000) 381–82.

[21] On secondary action, see P Germanotta, *Protecting Worker Solidarity Action: A Critique of International Labour Law* (London, Institute of Employment Rights/Global Labour Institute, 2002).

[22] See *Express Newspapers v McShane* [1979] ICR 210; *Associated Newspapers v Wade* [1979] ICR 664; *Duport Steel v Sirs*, above n 2.

only does it become easy to justify certain substantive restraints on the taking of strike action, procedural restrictions also become much easier to defend. This may apply particularly where the right to strike is to be seen only as a 'collective right' of the trade union rather than a right vested in individual workers. These procedural restrictions include most notably an obligation to ballot workers before a strike is called. If workers are called out by the union over a wage demand, should they not be consulted first to see whether they are prepared to take action for a matter about which they may disapprove? It is not easy to resist the argument that where a union is negotiating on behalf of a group of workers and prepared to reinforce its demand by resort to the ultimate sanction, the union should do so only with a mandate from those whose collective rights it proposes to mobilise.

THE RIGHT TO STRIKE AS A HUMAN RIGHT

One of the most significant developments in legal scholarship in recent years has been the growing interest in human rights and with it the colonisation of much of the legal system by human rights lawyers. It has long been recognised that 'workers' rights are human rights', even though 'the human rights movement and the labor movement run on tracks that are sometimes parallel and rarely meet.'[23] Apart from the European Social Charter of 18 October 1961 to which reference has already been made, trade union and labour rights are recognised in a number of other international human rights treaties.[24] These include most notably ILO Conventions 87 and 98, but also the International Covenant on Economic, Social and Cultural Rights of 1966, as well as the Council of Europe's Revised Social Charter of 1996. Until fairly recently, labour lawyers in the United Kingdom have nevertheless tended to avoid the language of human rights, and indeed have been generally reluctant to cast the claims of labour in the mould of rights at all.[25] Trade unionists, however, are now using the

---

[23] VA Leary, 'The Paradox of Workers' Rights as Human Rights' in LA Compa and SF Diamond (eds), *Human Rights, Labor Rights and International Trade* (Philadelphia, University of Pennsylvania Press, 1996) 22.

[24] For an argument that the right to strike is not a human right, see AF Utz, 'Is the Right to Strike a Human Right?' (1987) 65 *Washington University Law Quarterly* 732.

[25] But see P O'Higgins, 'International Standards and British Labour Law' in R Lewis (ed), *Labour Law in Britain* (Oxford, Blackwell, 1986) where in relation to the Social Charter of 1961, he wrote: 'In the United Kingdom there is no right to strike, only a series of limited immunities that in certain circumstances prevent claims from being brought against trade unions or the organisers of strikes. While there may be debate about the respective merits of a system of immunities as against a legal right to strike, Britain is bound by international treaty to give effect to a right to strike. Such a right would imply a definition of the line to be drawn between unlawful and lawful strikes, and a ban on action taken by employers to penalise workers who exercise their legal right to strike' (585).

rhetoric of rights and the rhetoric of human rights powerfully to reinforce their claims, with the new General Secretary of the TUC referring to the right to strike as a 'human right'[26] in his first public speech following his appointment. There are thus reasons to suppose that the parallel tracks are beginning to converge, with the key question being what difference this will make to the substance of the rights being asserted.

The answer to that question will depend to some extent on the nature of the human rights principles which are being appealed to in order to displace or complement the classical analysis of the right to strike. These are the principles which apply with varying degrees of certainty to human rights recognised by human rights treaties. It is to be acknowledged, however, that human rights law is an evolving and dynamic discipline, and there are very few clear and unequivocal human rights principles or human rights 'rights'. But with that qualification there are a number of recognisable principles, which will have a number of different implications for the right to strike, as they will for other rights. They include the following:

(1) Human rights are rights of individuals (which may also vest in legal persons), though they may be rights of individuals which can only be exercised collectively.

(2) Human rights are universal in the sense that they apply equally to everyone, regardless of who they are, where they are, or what they do.

(3) Human rights are inalienable, in the sense that they cannot be abrogated by the State or by individuals themselves.

(4) Human rights are indivisible in the sense that one reinforces the others, and in the sense that all are important, though an inner core are more important than the others.

(5) Human rights are often unequivocal and not the permitted subject of derogations: Some human rights may have to yield to other compelling rights or interests.

(6) Human rights are rights which the state must not only avoid restraining, but the exercise of which the state must make possible.

Returning to the foregoing question, one response would be to say that the whole matter is sheer sophistry. The classical right is the human right, and that is the end of the matter. But that clearly will not do, for it begs a number of questions, not the least of which are the following: whose right is it that is under discussion? and why should it be limited to collective bargaining and perhaps even conflicts of interest arising in the course of the collective

[26] B Barber, 'The Future of Trade Unionism' (10 June 2003) (www.tuc.org.uk).

bargaining process? There are thus different perceptions of human rights, based on conceptions of individual rights on the one hand and collective rights on the other.[27] So far as the right to strike is concerned, the former means that individuals are the bearers of the right which they exercise together in any particular case. Some of the implications of this are considered below. The latter means that the union is the bearer of the right which it exercises in any particular case on behalf of its members. As a collective right it may be sold by the union, and it may not be possible to exercise the right without the authority of the union. In modern times the idea of a human right being vested in a legal person or other organisation is a solecism, though it is a solecism that is openly recognised in the principle that human rights vest in corporations just as they vest in individuals.[28] Although the trend seems unmistakably in the direction of the individual conception,[29] these rival conceptions are nevertheless acknowledged in international and regional treaties, as well as in new national constitutions.[30] But none sits on the fence quite so ostentatiously as the EU Charter of Fundamental Rights. This refers in Article 28 to 'workers and employers' on the one hand, *or* 'their respective organisations' on the other hand, as having the 'right' in 'cases of conflicts of interest, to take collective action to defend their interests, including strike action'.

IMPLICATIONS OF THE RIGHT TO STRIKE AS A HUMAN RIGHT

The assertion that the right to strike is a human right has three key implications. The first is that, as already suggested, it is a right vested principally in individuals. This reflects the Council of Europe's Social Charter, which Kahn Freund and Hepple observe 'has been defined as a right of individuals, not as a right of unions'.[31] This is 'despite its connection with collective bargaining'.[32] But it does not follow from this that there should be no recognition of the rights of the organisation as well. The right of the individual could be rendered pointless if the union could be restrained or sued for organising or supporting industrial action. So there must be protection

---

[27] See the excellent discussion in Novitz, above n 1, at 275–78. See also Lord Wedderburn of Charlton, 'Laws About Strikes' in W McCarthy (ed), *Legal Intervention in Industrial Relations* (Oxford, Blackwell, 1992) ch 4.

[28] For a discussion of this issue, see M Smyth, *Business and the Human Rights Act 1998* (Bristol, Jordans, 2000) esp 22–23.

[29] See, eg Slovenia ('Employees have the right to strike') and South Africa ('Every worker has the right ... to strike').

[30] Notably Poland where 'Trade unions shall have the right to organise workers' strikes.'

[31] Above n 5, at 17.

[32] *Ibid.*

of the union as a consequence of protecting the worker. Indeed, the fact that the right is vested in the individual does not exclude the possibility that it may also vest in the union as well. The parallel would be the right to freedom of association in the (European Convertion on Human Rights) which confers rights on both the individual worker and the trade union so that acts of anti-union discrimination can be a breach of both, even if British labour law refuses to acknowledge the collective right.[33] It is also the case that the right to strike under ILO Convention 87 is one that vests in both the worker and the union, with the Freedom of Association Committee taking the view that 'the right to strike is one of the essential means through which workers and their organisations may promote and defend their economic interests.'[34] This creating of a right of individuals and organisations by the ILO supervisory bodies is all the more striking for the fact that it has been carved from an Article which deals with the rights of 'workers' organisations.'[35]

The second implication of the right to strike as a human right is that it is a primary rather than a secondary right, and as such is released from its dependence on collective bargaining, important not only because of the decline in the level of collective bargaining activity. As we have seen, under classical analysis the right to strike is a secondary right, secondary to the primary right to engage in collective bargaining. As a human right, however, this one-dimensional connexion is severed (as it is in the case of the ILO's recognition of the right to strike with its locus in Convention 87 (freedom of association and the right to organise) rather than Convention 98 (right to organise and collective bargaining)).[36] To say that the right to strike is severed from its dependence on collective bargaining is not to say that the right to strike is unrelated to collective bargaining. But it does mean that its role in relation to collective bargaining is only one of the purposes which the right serves, even though it may continue to be the main purpose in practice. The human rights lawyer will see the right to strike as having a wider purpose than the labour lawyer, as relating not only to the exercise of power in the workplace but also the exercise of power in the wider political community. To transfer the locus of the right to strike from the arena of labour law to the arena of human rights is thus significantly to change the nature of the right. It is for the workers who bear the right — and not the

---

[33] *Wilson and Palmer v United Kingdom* [2002] IRLR 128.

[34] Complaint against the USA presented by the AFL-CIO, Committee on Freedom of Association, Report No 278, Case No 1543, para 92 (complaint relating to the *Mackay Radio* doctrine in which the US Supreme Court effectively allowed employers permanently to replace strikers who are protected from dismissal: *NLRB v Mackay Radio & Telegraph Co*, 304 US 333 (1938)).

[35] ILO Convention 87, Art 3.

[36] On the right to strike and the ILO, see B Gernigon, A Odero and H Guido, 'ILO Principles Concerning the Right to Strike' (1998) 137 *Int Lab Rev* 441.

state — to determine the purposes for which it will be used, though as we shall see the state may have an interest in protecting those affected by a strike.

The third implication of the right to strike as a human right relates to the obligation of the state, which is to ensure that there are no legal impediments when it is exercised. This would mean that the individual worker would not be subjected to restraints or penalties when taking strike action. So the exercise of a human right would not constitute a breach of contract,[37] the protection against dismissal would extend beyond eight weeks, and those exercising the right would not be subject to permanent replacement. There would be no liability in tort for those trade union officials who called the action, and no liability for the trade union which coordinated and organised the action. Those who exercised what is a human right would not be subject to other forms of discrimination as a result, for example in the way in which state welfare benefits are allocated. But one question with the right to strike as a right which vests principally in individuals is whether it implies a right not to strike, that is to say whether an individual could not be required to take part in a strike against his or her wishes. This is a question raised by the right not to join a trade union which has been read into the freedom of association and right to organise provisions of both the ECHR and the Social Charter. Yet neither the Social Rights Committee of the Council of Europe nor the supervisory bodies of the ILO have been prepared to conclude that the individual right to strike implies an individual right not to strike. Indeed, quite the reverse can be implied from the findings of these bodies that the restrictions in British law on the right of trade unions to discipline or expel strike-breakers violate respectively the Social Charter of 1961 and ILO Convention 87.[38]

THE RIGHT TO STRIKE TO PROMOTE AND PROTECT HUMAN RIGHTS

A human rights perspective on the right to strike introduces an additional matter to the inquiry, which also leads to an even wider view of its scope.

---

[37] On which see P Elias, 'The Strike and Breach of Contract: A Reassessment' in KD Ewing, CA Gearty and BA Hepple (eds), *Human Rights and Labour Law: Essays for Paul O'Higgins* (London, Mansell, 1994) ch 11.

[38] But if the positive right to strike were to imply the negative right not to strike, questions would then arise about the right not to be expelled from a trade union for exercising this right. To deny the right of the trade union to expel in these circumstances would violate the right to freedom of association of the trade union and its members which must include the right not to associate with people whose conduct they find offensive. See *Cheall v APEX* [1983] 2 AC 180; but compare *NALGO v United Kingdom*, Application 21386/93 (European Commission of Human Rights).

Not only is the exercise of the right to strike itself the exercise of a human right, but the right may be exercised to protect or promote other human rights. Indeed, many of the great right to strike cases in the courts are recognisable as human rights cases in this latter sense, even if not expressed as such. But although it ought perhaps not to be necessary, the use of the strike in this way reinforces the respect that the right to strike should attract in the legal system. These human rights may include the right to freedom of conscience (by refusing to undertake duties which offend the conscientious beliefs of the worker). They may include the right to freedom of expression (as a way of communicating support or opposition to a particular course of action whether by government or the employer). They may also include the right to freedom of association (by refusing to work with people whose views are offensive or who are not members of the same trade union). There are a number of well-known cases in the law reports which illustrate specifically each of these points, including respectively *BBC v Hearn*[39] (refusing to participate in the broadcast of the FA Cup Final to South Africa), *Express Newspapers v Keys*[40] (protesting about anti-union laws to be introduced by the government) and *Rookes v Barnard*[41] (refusal to work with a non-unionist). In these cases the strike is simply the means of giving effect to another human right: one human right to protect another.

A variation on the theme of the right to strike to support other human rights extends the role of the strike as an instrument for the protection of human rights. Thus, the human rights which the strike is seeking to promote may not only relate to civil and political rights of the kind identified in the previous paragraph. There is also the possibility of strike action to promote economic and social rights to be found in international human rights treaties. These include the right to a decent wage (which according to the Social Rights Committee of the Council of Europe should be at least 60 per cent of the national average male wage).[42] There is the possibility too of strike action being undertaken to promote the right to safe and healthy working conditions, and the right to bargain collectively. This is not to say that all industrial action is about promoting as well as exercising a human right: it may be difficult to say that all strikes are designed to promote human rights when the working conditions of the workers in question exceed the minimum standards anticipated by international treaties (though this is not to say that such action should not be protected). But where national law and practice fall short of these obligations, it is hard to deny that a strike to raise the standards

---

[39] [1977] ICR 686, approved by Lord Hoffman in *Re P*, above n 14.
[40] [1980] IRLR 247.
[41] [1964] AC 1129.
[42] Council of Europe, *European Social Charter: Committee of Independent Experts, Conclusions XIV-2* (1999), vol 1, 49–54.

of some workers to these international minimum requirements is a strike designed to promote and establish human rights. This applies all the more so where the requirement in question is binding on a particular government which may recently have been found in breach. In the absence of any obligation in legislation or elsewhere on the part of an employer to give effect to these obligations, the strike may be the only weapon available to workers seeking to secure the protection of the human rights which their government is obliged but failing to implement.

In addition to the foregoing human rights purposes of industrial action, there is yet another dimension. The human rights which the strike is designed to protect and establish may not be the human rights of the strikers themselves, but the human rights of third parties. One group of workers may strike to secure the reinstatement of another dismissed because of his trade union activities; another group of workers may boycott a particular workplace because it operates racist practices; while yet another may take action in support of workers trying to secure recognition rights from their employer.[43] What we have here is the possibility of both primary action on the one hand and sympathy or secondary action on the other hand to protect the human rights of third parties. Indeed, those whose human rights the action is designed to promote may not be resident or based in the jurisdiction but may be involved in their own dispute in another part of the world, a dispute which may be with employers or governments. Yet human rights are universal and the ILO Constitution at least urges us all to respect the human rights of everyone.[44] A classic example is the action of the broadcasting unions in refusing to broadcast the 1977 Cup Final to South Africa during the apartheid era.[45] Another is the action of the International Transport Workers' Federation in seeking to ensure that the terms and conditions of seafarers in ships flying flags of convenience are consistent with minimum human rights standards.[46] But it might include a boycott or other action against a multi-national corporation renowned for its poor labour standards in breach of ILO human rights principles, and perhaps as a result in breach of its own corporate code. In some of these cases the action may be taken to protect human rights even though the workers themselves may not be formally engaged in a dispute.

[43] See respectively *Taff Vale Railway Co Ltd v ASRS* [1901] AC 426; *Scala Ballroom v Ratcliffe*, above n 13; and *DC Thomson and Co Ltd v Deakin* [1952] 1 Ch 646. See also *JT Stratford and Son Ltd v Lindley* [1965] AC 269 (recognition dispute).
[44] ILO Constitution: 'the failure of any nation to adopt humane conditions of labour is an obstacle in the way of other nations which desire to improve the conditions in their own countries' (Preamble).
[45] *BBC v Hearn*, above n 39.
[46] See *NWL Ltd v Woods* [1979] ICR 867; *Universe Tankships of Monrovia v ITF* [1983] 1 AC 366; *Merkur Island Shipping Corporation v Laughton* [1983] 2 AC 570.

RESTRICTIONS ON THE RIGHT TO STRIKE

The recognition of the right to strike as a human right compels us to see it in the widest of senses as a substantive right in its own terms, but also to recognise its potential as a device for promoting, securing and protecting other human rights. But it does not follow that the right to strike should be unlimited, though to see the right to strike as a human right means that any restriction must be justified by those who would impose restrictions on strong and compelling grounds. Classical labour law typically introduces a number of contested restraints. The first relates to the purpose of the action. A strike may be rendered unlawful because it is designed to promote a political cause, demonstrate solidarity with others, or promote objectives such as the recognition of the trade union for the purposes of collective bargaining. But as a primary right and as a human right, it would be difficult to anticipate any restriction of such conduct as a general rule, though there may be circumstances where particular strikes falling into these categories might be prohibited because of the impact on the rights of others.[47] But the same may be true of primary action, so that nothing turns upon the purpose or nature of the action being pursued. If the right to strike is a human right, workers must be free to determine the causes they will promote by using it, just in the same way that we do not censor the purposes that may be promoted by the exercise of the right to freedom of assembly.[48] People are free to exercise their human right to peaceful assembly by marching through the streets to demonstrate their opposition to the invasion of another country or anti-trade union legislation. Why should they not also be free to exercise their human right to strike to promote the same ends by staying at home, in order to reinforce the protest? It is not for the state to determine the causes which may be promoted in this way.

The second contested constraint of classical labour law relates to the peace obligation during the life of a collective agreement. This entails the right to strike being rendered unlawful by an agreement between the trade union and the employer, the agreement perhaps being a legally enforceable contract between the union and the employer. Typically, any worker who exercises his or her right in such circumstances will have no protection from employer sanctions taken against him or her, even though he or she is the 'absent third party'[49] to the agreement. In some systems, the peace obligation will be

---

[47] See below.
[48] *Plattform 'Arzte Fur Das Leben' v Austria* (1988) 13 EHRR 204: 'A demonstration may annoy or give offence to persons opposed to the ideas or claims that it is seeking to promote' (210). Moreover, 'Genuine, effective freedom of peaceful assembly cannot, therefore, be reduced to a mere duty on the part of the State not to interfere' (*ibid*).
[49] *St Anne Nackawic Pulp and Paper Co v CPWU, Local 219* [1986] 1 SCR 704, Estey J, at 717.

imposed by the legislature,[50] and in other cases it will be implied by the courts as a term for the compulsory settlement of disputes.[51] But if the right to strike is a human right, and an inalienable human right at that, it is not clear how it can be waived by or as a result of a contract or an agreement. This is an issue which has given rise to some controversy under the ECHR, where the Court has accepted that some rights may be defeated by contracts, but that others may not be.[52] Yet, although the idea of a human right being dependent on the power of contract renders the notion of human rights rather hollow, that is a concern that rings even more loudly in the present context. For here we are not talking about the right being abrogated by a contract to which the individual is a party, but a contract to abrogate the right to strike made by the trade union and the employer. The individual may not have approved the agreement, and may not have approved this particular term of the agreement. Indeed, the individual may be opposed to the agreement. Even if a human right can be waived by contract, it is rather stretching matters to say that it may be waived by the terms of a contract between two third parties.

The third contested constraint of classical labour law relates to the duty of the trade union to ballot its members before calling on them to take part in a strike. The individual will be free to strike if a majority vote in favour of the strike, but will not be free to do so otherwise. This entails the exercise of the individual's right to strike being conditional upon the wishes of hundreds or thousands of other people, and is like saying that there is a human right but only if its exercise has been approved in any particular case by others. It would be difficult to contemplate circumstances where it would be considered acceptable to make the exercise of any other human right conditional on the wishes of others. Imagine if the right to freedom of expression were conditional upon the newspaper proprietor having to seek the views of his or her shareholders voting in a secret ballot. The objections to the right to strike being conditional on a ballot are clearly more pressing where the ballot obligation is imposed by the state (as in the United Kingdom) by legislation, rather than by the trade union through the contract of membership.[53] In the latter case it might be argued that there is no objection to the bearers of a right agreeing between themselves about the circumstances in which they will exercise it. But if human rights are inalienable,

---

[50] See A Adlercruetz, 'Sweden' in R Blanpain (ed), *International Encyclopaedia of Labour Law and Industrial Relations* (1998), vol 13, 189; and M Weiss and M Schmidt, 'Germany' in Blanpain (ed), *ibid* (2000), vol 6, 154.

[51] See *Teamsters v Therein* (1960) 22 DLR (2d) 1, and *McGavin Toastmaster v Ainscough* (1975) 54 DLR (3d) 1.

[52] See G Morris, 'Fundamental Rights: Exclusion by Agreement?' (2001) 30 *ILJ* 49.

[53] The objections are all the more pressing still where the ballot rules are drafted in such a way as to defeat the democratic wishes of those being balloted: see S Fredman, 'The New Rights: Labour Law and Ideology in the Thatcher Years' (1992) 12 *OJLS* 24.

even this causes difficulties for reasons described above, and means that the agreement could be binding only so long as workers agree to be bound. There is certainly no possibility of that agreement being enforced by a third party, and no question of such a requirement being imposed by the state.

THE RIGHT TO STRIKE AS A THREAT TO HUMAN RIGHTS

If the classical restraints on the right to strike seem difficult to justify from a human rights perspective, what about other restraints? There are few human rights which are unequivocal, and there will be circumstances where the exercise of one right collides with other rights. The exercise of one person's right to freedom of expression may violate another's right to privacy.[54] In the case of the right to strike, there are a number of human rights that might be affected as a result of its exercise. These include the right to property (in the case of private sector disputes), though it has been pointed out that the right to property is of doubtful status as a human right, and that it is not clear what is protected by the rubric.[55] But it is expressly protected by the ECHR, and for the sake of argument it might be taken to include the right to own property, the right to use property and the right freely to dispose of property.[56] Although this is probably the most significant human right which typically will be affected by a strike, there are others. In *Express Newspapers Ltd v McShane*, Lord Scarman drew attention to trade disputes which put at risk 'such fundamental rights as the right of the public to be informed and the freedom of the press.'[57] In the same case Lord Salmon raised questions about industrial action threatening the right to life itself when in emotional terms he said that: 'quite recently patients in the Charing Cross Hospital being treated for cancer were brought near to death because industrial action had been taken to prevent fuel from being brought into the hospital.'[58] There is also the right to freedom of association where the strike is to force the removal of a worker who is not a member of the union,[59] and the right to education in the case of a teachers' strike.[60]

When human rights collide in this way, it is necessary to appeal to principle to help to resolve the conflict and to allocate priorities between competing

---

[54] See *Douglas v Hello!* [2001] QB 967.
[55] P Sieghart, *The Lawful Rights of Mankind* (Oxford, Oxford University Press, 1986) 130–32.
[56] For a good discussion, see A Mowbray, *Cases and Materials on the European Convention on Human Rights* (London, Butterworths, 2001) ch 16.
[57] [1980] ICR 42, at 65.
[58] *Ibid* at 60.
[59] *Quinn v Leathem* [1901] AC 495; *Hodges v Webb* [1920] 2 Ch 70; *White v Riley* [1921] 1 Ch 1; *Reynolds v Shipping Federation* [1924] 1 Ch 28; *Rookes v Barnard* [1964] AC 1129.
[60] *Re L* [2003] UKHL 9. See esp para 26 (Lord Bingham of Cornhill).

claims. Usually it means that the human rights of one person can be restrained in order to protect the human rights of another. This is a typical ground for restriction. It means that the right to freedom of expression can be restrained to protect the right to a fair trial of one person or the right to privacy of another.[61] The tool that is usually used for this purpose is the principle of proportionality. Applied to the right to strike, this would mean that limits can be imposed when (a) the use of the strike is a disproportionate way of achieving certain objectives, or (b) where the use of the strike has a disproportionate effect on the rights of others. So far as (a) is concerned, the use of the strike may be disproportionate because there are other ways of resolving a dispute which have not been used, such as conciliation and arbitration in the case of working conditions, or litigation in the case of an unfair dismissal. So far as (b) is concerned, this arises where the exercise of the right to strike has or is likely to have devastating consequences, perhaps 'to the employer or to third parties or the public and perhaps the nation itself'.[62] But there can be no question of any particular form of industrial action being regarded as disproportionate simply because of the nature of the action in question. Secondary or sympathy action, for example, may cause only limited harm to persons other than those engaged in a dispute and may involve less intrusion on the rights of others than primary action by key groups of workers. Action could be disproportionate only because of its effect not because of its form.

The problem with proportionality is that it is potentially a way of reinstating controls on the right to strike which are inconsistent with the notion of the right to strike as a human right. It could be a way, for example, of reinstating the peace obligation as a mandatory precondition of strike action. The rationale for this would be that before you violate my right to the peaceful enjoyment of my possessions, you must exhaust any procedures for the peaceful pursuit of your claim and the settlement of the dispute. It is a way, also, of reinstating controls on secondary action on the ground that it is a disproportionate escalation and extension of the dispute. There was something in this in the decisions of the Court of Appeal in the late 1970s where, struggling with concepts such as remoteness and the impact of the action, they were effectively saying that the extension of disputes in these ways was disproportionate. So while there might be a right to strike drafted in wide and general terms, the effect of the doctrine of proportionality is that in practice there would be some kind of judicial censor who would have to be satisfied in every case before the right to strike was exercised. No one schooled in the common law could be sanguine about a right to

[61] See, respectively, *Attorney General v Punch Ltd* [2002] UKHL 50 and *Venables v News Group Newspapers* [2001] Fam 430.
[62] See *NWL Ltd v Woods* [1979] ICR 867, at 881–82 (Lord Diplock). See also *Express Newspapers Ltd v McShane* [1980] ICR 42, at 65 (Lord Scarman).

strike subject to permissible limitations on the ground of proportionality, particularly in light of the claim that it confers 'almost unlimited' discretionary powers on the part of the courts 'in specifying the law on industrial action.'[63] Given the licence that English procedural law gives the courts, this is a matter of more than passing concern.

PROPORTIONALITY IN PERSPECTIVE

These concerns are reinforced by judicial developments under the Canadian Charter of Rights on the one hand,[64] and the European Convention on Human Rights on the other. So far as the latter is concerned, in *RMT v London Underground Ltd*[65] Robert Walker LJ held that the notice and balloting rules before industrial action were neither 'oppressive nor disproportionate.'[66] This was despite a recognition in the same case that the effect of the 1999 amendments to the law were to make the union's task in complying with the notice rules 'more onerous.'[67] Even more recently, in *UNISON v United Kingdom*,[68] the Strasbourg Court rejected a challenge to an injunction banning a strike designed to ensure that private companies observe public sector collective agreements when managing national health service hospitals. It is true that there are questions about the extent to which the right to strike is protected by the ECHR.[69] Nevertheless, the Court appeared to have little difficulty in concluding in the circumstances that the economic interests of the employer weighed more heavily than the trade union's interest in protecting its members. It also held that the restraints imposed in this case were a 'proportionate measure' and 'necessary in a democratic society for the protection of the rights of others, namely UCLH.'[70] But in so holding the Court did not appear to find it necessary even to specify in any detail

---

[63] Weiss and Schmidt, above n 50, at 170. On proportionality generally, see P Sales and B Hooper, 'Proportionality and the Form of Law' (2003) 119 *LQR* 426.

[64] See especially the judgments of Dickson CJC in the labour trilogy in the 1980s where he held that the right to freedom of association included the right to strike, but that limits could be imposed by way of banning strikes in essential services, imposing a temporary ban on public sector strikes as a weapon against inflation, and banning strikes by slaughterhouse workers to safeguard the interests of third parties who would be affected by the strike (in this case the farmers supplying the livestock). See TJ Christian and KD Ewing, 'Labouring under the Canadian Constitution' (1988) 17 *ILJ* 73. See now *Dunmore v Ontario* (2002) 207 DLR (4th) 193.

[65] [2001] IRLR 228.

[66] *Ibid* at 235.

[67] *Ibid* at 237. The amendments were made by the Employment Relations Act 1999, s 4 and Sch 3.

[68] [2002] IRLR 497.

[69] For a full account, see J Hendy, 'The Human Rights Act, Article 11 and the Right to Strike' [1998] *EHRLR* 582.

[70] At 502.

the nature of the loss to the employer, or to explore ways in which it would be open to the employer to minimise the problems caused by the strike. The margin of appreciation was such that such analysis was unnecessary.

Yet for all that the doctrine of proportionality is not a friend of workers in a dispute, the same Court has shown that the doctrine need not be a threat to workers either. In the jurisprudence of the Court we find a distinction in the cases where it is being asked to lift restraints on the right to strike on the one hand, and cases where it is being asked to impose restraints in order to protect another right on the other. There are two cases where the Court has been asked to rule that strikes imposed a disproportionate burden on the human rights of others: in one of these cases the right to peaceful enjoyment of possessions, and in the other the right to freedom of association.[71] In both cases the applications were rejected. In the first, the Court dismissed claims from the employer based on the effect the action was having on his business. In the view of the Court, the facts complained of were 'not the product of an exercise of governmental authority, but they concerned exclusively relationships of a contractual nature between private individuals, namely his suppliers or deliverers'.[72] According to the Court the repercussions of trade union action to stop deliveries to the applicant's restaurant 'were not such as to bring Article 1 of Protocol No 1 into play.' The second case was decided the same way but on different grounds. Here, the complainant was transferred to another location when his colleagues would not work with him because he was no longer a member of their union. There was no breach of Article 11 where the transfer was not conditional on the applicant rejoining the union, in circumstances where his 'working conditions' would not have been made 'significantly less favourable' by the transfer.[73]

Human rights treaties thus do not appear readily to require restraints on the right to strike to protect property or other rights. This is not to say that on different facts these cases might not have been decided differently. It is also the case that although it does not require restraints on the right to strike, the ECHR does permit such restraints to be imposed, with the Court equally reluctant to challenge these restraints on the ground of proportionality. One solution to the possible danger of the right to strike being swallowed by its exceptions is provided by the precedent of Article 8 of the International Covenant on Economic, Social and Cultural Rights. This provides that

---

[71] *Gustafsson v Sweden* (1996) 22 EHRR 409; *Sibson v United Kingdom* (1993) 17 EHRR 193. On the former see T Novitz (1997) 26 *ILJ* 79.
[72] *Gustafsson*, above n 71, at 451. It is a matter of regret that the Court did not respond directly to the suggestion of the Swedish government that a trade union boycott of an employer 'was comparable to a consumer boycott instituted against a private company. Yet customers should be free to take such measures without the State incurring liability, even if the boycott led to bankruptcy of the company' (450).
[73] At 207.

the state parties to the Covenant undertake to ensure the right to strike, 'provided that it is exercised in conformity with the laws of the particular country.' This last provision would be an obvious worry, and would appear to render any protection of the right to strike tautologous. The position is retrieved, however, by Article 8(3) which provides that:

> Nothing in this Article shall authorise State Parties to the International Labour Organisation Convention of 1948 concerning Freedom of Association and Protection of the Right to Organise to take legislative measures which would prejudice, or apply the law in such a manner as would prejudice, the guarantees provided for in that Convention.[74]

Although the supervisory bodies have read a right to strike into ILO Convention 87, they have done so with remarkably few permissible constraints. The recognition by the ILO supervisory bodies that a strike may be prohibited during the peace obligation reflects the belief that the strike is disproportionate when there are other procedures for dispute resolution.[75] This is despite the fact that such a prohibition is difficult to reconcile with the notion of the strike as a human right. Similarly, the recognition by the same bodies that restrictions of various kinds (from bans to minimum service obligations) may be imposed on strikes in essential services is a recognition of the fact that the consequences of industrial action in some circumstances may be just too grave to contemplate.[76]

CONCLUSION

With the expansion of human rights law, labour lawyers can no longer lay a proprietary claim to the right to strike. Indeed, it is a matter about which labour law has failed to provide effective or enduring protection. Human rights law may provide a more secure and lasting alternative, and it is perhaps paradoxical that a strategy based on individual rights is better equipped to provide protection for the collective interest. Not only that,

---

[74] For a full account, see M Craven, *The International Covenant on Economic, Social and Cultural Rights* (2nd edn, Oxford, Oxford University Press, 1998), 257–59. On the corresponding provisions in Art 22(3) of the ICCPR, see D Harris and S Joseph (eds), *The International Covenant on Civil and Political Rights and United Kingdom Law* (Oxford, Oxford University Press, 1995) ch 14.

[75] Indeed, it is sobering to reflect that to the extent that there is a right to strike as a fundamental human right, it is at best a right to strike sometimes, and a right to strike infrequently. In many countries, most workers will be denied the right to exercise their human right most of the time, and such denials will generally be compatible with international human rights law, including ILO Convention 87.

[76] For a summary, see Gernigon, Odero and Guido, above n 36, at 450–54.

but also do so in a way that recognises the role and functions of trade unions beyond the workplace. The scope of the human rights perspective is wider than the classical labour law perspective to the extent that the right to strike cannot be confined to the notion of a 'trade' dispute rooted in collective bargaining. It is also the case that many of the classical restrictions on the right to strike are difficult to reconcile with the idea of a human right vested in individuals. This applies particularly to the peace obligation (though not a feature of labour law in Britain) where the right to strike may be banned as a result of an agreement, and an agreement to which the worker is not a party. It also applies to pre-strike ballots which have the effect of banning the worker from striking unless he or she has the approval of a majority of his or her colleagues who take part in the ballot. But for all that, it should not be overlooked that no human rights treaty guarantees an unlimited right to strike, and all recognise in one form or another the need to accommodate the rights of others who may be affected by the right to strike. This is true even of the ILO where the supervisory bodies have effectively introduced proportionality restraints on the right to strike, even though they are not articulated as such.

Space does not permit a detailed account of how these competing interests might be accommodated in a highly structured statutory system for the protection of the right to strike. But consistently with ILO Conventions, there are three overlapping considerations. The starting point would be formal recognition of the right to strike as a human right, with additional weight being extended to strikes designed to promote other human rights. But it ought not to be possible to restrain the exercise of the right to strike simply because it interferes with the performance of other human rights, reduces the value of other human rights, or makes them more difficult to enjoy.[77] The right to exercise one human right cannot be *removed or prohibited* simply because it causes *inconvenience* to the human rights of others or *burdens* the manner of their exercise: 'the inflicting of some damage is fundamental.'[78] Thereafter, it may be appropriate to consider the extent to which other available steps had been taken by individuals collectively to resolve the dispute. But even this ought not to weigh heavily where the action is in response to the unlawful or provocative conduct of the employer or where other avenues are likely to lead to a dead end and likely to be ineffective.[79] A third and final factor relates to the impact of the dispute. But this ought not to be persuasive, far less decisive, unless the impact was devastating, and there were no other steps available to

---

[77] Nor is it relevant that the exercise of the right may be 'irresponsible': see *Re L [2003] UKHL 9*, above, para 81 (Lord Walker of Gestingthorpe).

[78] See *N V Dutch Railways v Transport Unions FNV, FSV and CNV*, above n 18.

[79] Cf Employment Relations Act 1999, s 16 and Sch 5, inserting a new TULR(C)A 1992, s 238A. See esp s 238A(6).

minimise the damage caused by the strike. Even in the case of a strike by firefighters during a 'war' it is possible for steps to be taken to protect life and property by a combination of voluntary minimum cover arrangements and the use of the military.[80] An approach more clearly grounded in human rights would thus not prevent all laws against strikes, but it would require a much more active protection than is currently provided by contemporary British labour law.

---

[80] For further discussion, see G Morris, *Strikes in Essential Services* (London, Mansell, 1986) 201.

3

Trade Unions and Collective Bargaining: Law and the Future of Collectivism

WILLIAM BROWN AND SARAH OXENBRIDGE

INTRODUCTION

WHAT SORT OF laws might be appropriate for future forms of collective bargaining? It is, perhaps, more usual to discuss how the law shapes collective bargaining than how collective bargaining might shape the law. But collective bargaining in Britain has always been in a state of change, responding first and foremost to changing economic circumstances. One cannot expect any one regulatory structure to be appropriate to all power relationships. Legal intervention may be considered necessary to protect the interests of employees, of employers, or of the public at large. But which of these interests might be felt to be more in need of protection at any time will depend not only upon the political complexion of the government of the day, but also upon the prevailing economic pressures. Trade unions tend to call for protective legislation when they are under threat; employers tend to demand restraints on trade unions when there is a rising propensity to strike. Future legislative needs will be greatly influenced by market circumstances.

In what follows we first discuss the changing nature of collective bargaining over the past century or so, drawing attention both to the wider economic forces that have given it shape, and to the way in which the law has been used in response. Then we look at the experience of the most recent major legal intervention, the Employment Relations Act 1999, and at the extent to which it has achieved a change in behaviour. This leads to a discussion of current changes in the nature of collective bargaining. Finally, we draw out implications for future legislation.

THE TWO FACES OF COLLECTIVE BARGAINING

For Beatrice Webb, who originated the expression, collective bargaining took place when an employer 'meets with a collective will and settles, in a single agreement, the principles on which, for the time being, all workmen of a particular group, or class, or grade, will be engaged.'[1] The passage of a century suggests a broader definition might be appropriate. Of many analyses that have sought to redefine the notion from the viewpoints of different countries and times, perhaps the most fruitful for our purposes is that of Alan Flanders, who eschewed a narrowly economic conception of collective bargaining. For him it was 'a rule-making process and involves a power relationship between organisations' and he suggested that a more accurate description might be 'joint regulation.'[2] He quoted with approval Sumner Slichter's conception of the process as 'industrial jurisprudence' whereby:

> laboring men, through unions, formulate policies to which they give expression in the form of shop rules and practices which are embodied in agreements with employers or are accorded less formal recognition and assent by management; shop committees, grievance procedures, and other means are evolved for applying these rules and policies; and rights and duties are claimed and recognised.[3]

In a foreshadowing of New Labour rhetoric, Flanders also agreed with TH Marshall's suggestion that trade unions create 'a secondary system of industrial citizenship, parallel with and supplementary to the system of political citizenship.'[4]

Here we have a view of collective bargaining as a process in which trade unions are, in an unspecified way, involved in the management of the employment relationship. That is, they are involved in the creation and application of the rules and norms that define and reduce the uncertainty of that relationship. But there are both pragmatic and normative aspects in this view. For, on the one hand, labour is organised in trade unions partly in order to present a credible threat of collective sanctions against management. Collective bargaining embodies a power relationship, and the capacity of the trade union to weave and shape the 'web of rules' surrounding employment will depend to a large extent upon the collective strength it can mobilise. Strong unions in some industries have in the past been able to build dense rule structures that have substantially constrained management

[1] S and B Webb, *Industrial Democracy* (London, Longmans, 1897).
[2] A Flanders, *Management and Unions* (London, Faber & Faber, 1970), 220.
[3] S Slichter, *Union Policies and Industrial Management* (Washington DC, Brookings Institution, 1941) 1.
[4] TH Marshall, *Sociology at the Crossroads and Other Essays* (London, Heinemann, 1963) 98.

discretion. Weakened unions, by contrast, have been derecognised and their regulatory influence erased.

At the same time, however, there is an unavoidable normative aspect to the practice of collective bargaining.[5] Many employers and employer organisations have engaged in some form of collective bargaining not because they have been forced to do so by industrial action, but because they have felt it to be an appropriate form of industrial governance — a 'system of industrial citizenship' — which provides employees with due process and a representative 'voice,' whether or not their trade union has the muscle that would win this recognition against employer hostility. Employers in this position often speak of and value the legitimacy that they feel collective bargaining gives to their dealings with their employees.[6] There is a large econometric literature concerned with whether or not employers obtain tangible 'efficiency gains' from collective bargaining. As it happens, that research suggests that such gains have become more evident in recent years as unions have become weaker.[7] But that is beside the main point, which is that, whether or not greater profits may flow through collective bargaining than through autocratic management, employers may prefer collective bargaining because they feel it to be more respectful of their employees.

This normative aspect of collective bargaining is particularly evident in the realm of legislation. Individual employers may pragmatically see fit to recognise trade unions because the labour market is tight, or because the union is strong, and collective bargaining procedures are seen to be a practical way of managing the potentially damaging power relationship. To some extent governments also make a virtue of necessity, encouraging union recognition in times of rising union strength in order to avoid economic disruption.[8] But governments also have a preference for normative language and for justifying their legislation in terms of rights, rather than practical solutions to current problems. Whether at the level of ILO Conventions, or EU Directives, or of current UK recognition legislation, the support for collective bargaining is not presented as a handy management technique, but as a right and duty of employees and employers.

An echo of these two faces of collective bargaining is to be found in Flanders' observation that 'trade unions have always had two faces, sword of justice and vested interest.'[9] The 'vested interest' face was of a union

---

[5] H Clegg, 'Pluralism in Industrial Relations' (1975) 13 *British Journal of Industrial Relations* 309–16.
[6] W Brown, S Deakin, M Hudson, C Pratten and P Ryan, *The Individualisation of Employment Contracts in Britain* (London, DTI, 1998).
[7] W Brown, 'Industrial Relations and the Economy 1939–1999' in R Floud and D McCloskey (eds), *The Economic History of Britain, vol 3, 1939–99* (3rd edn, Cambridge, Cambridge University Press, 2004) pp 399–423.
[8] G Bain, The *Growth of White-Collar Trade Unionism* (Oxford: Oxford Universtiy Press, 1970).
[9] Flanders, above n 2.

concerned solely with defending and enhancing the material interests of its members, their pay, working arrangements and job security. In this role they deploy what collective coercive strength they can muster. They are engaged in what economists like to think of as a 'zero-sum game,' in which the union's gain equals the employer's loss, and *vice versa*. The 'sword of justice' was concerned with the union's role in upholding rights, protecting the weak more generally, and a sense of wider social purpose. In this role, collective strength is less important than political and advocacy skills. There is no necessary implication that it is part of a zero-sum game; both costs and benefits might be external to the immediate employment relationship. Writing in 1961, he argued that the trade union movement had won its place in public life in this latter role of having a social purpose. He went on: 'when it is no longer seen to be this, when it can no longer count on anything but its own power to withstand assault, it becomes extremely vulnerable.'[10] In other words, the public acceptability of trade unions depends fundamentally upon their demonstrating a sense of social purpose above and beyond the self-interest of their members.

THE EVER-CHANGING NATURE OF COLLECTIVE BARGAINING

Collective bargaining did not develop out of an economy in which workers enjoyed free wage contracts with their employers. An important early achievement of trade unions was to press successfully for legal structures that provided a basis of employment contracts around which collective bargaining could then take place. It was only during the nineteenth century that legislation developed to constrain the common law assumptions of British employment law. Until then, employers enjoyed, and magistrates enforced, extreme rights of control over employees that, among other things, denied opportunity for collective action.[11] But, by the end of that century, a system of mostly local agreements had developed between unions and employer associations for a number of industries. These agreements depended upon the success of trade unions in organising a credible and comprehensive strike threat across all employers in those product markets within which their members' employers sold their goods. Strike management was central to the formation of collective bargaining. Consequently, the most important legal protection that early trade unions needed was against being sued for strike damage. This had been achieved in 1875 and was confirmed in 1906.

---

[10] *Ibid* at 15.

[11] S Deakin, 'The Contract of Employment: a Study in Legal Evolution' (2001) 11 *Historical Studies in Industrial Relations* 1; R Steinfeld, *Coercion, Contract and Free Labour in the Nineteenth Century* (Cambridge, Cambridge University Press, 2001).

   Strikes were an inescapable part of collective bargaining in these early years. Some idea of this can be gained from Table 3.1, the second and third columns of which give the aggregate strike propensity of trade union members by decades from 1893. The first column gives the average percentage of employees in trade unions. Only a small minority of employees was in trade unions at the end of the nineteenth century, almost all of them relatively highly skilled and in the private sector. It is evident that the average propensity of these union members to strike, and the average number of days per year on which they were on strike, was far greater than for any subsequent decade. This was partly because even local strikes over industrial agreements involve many workers from many workplaces. But also the average duration of strikes was long; it continued to be measured in weeks rather than days until after the 1920s.[12] It was little wonder that the immunity from tortious liability provided by the law was so important for the

Table 3.1:   Trade Union Membership and Strike Propensity in Great Britain, 1893–2002

Years	Trade union density: membership as % of all employees (ave pa)	Number of strikes per 1,000,000 union members (ave pa)	Working days lost per 1,000 union members (ave pa)
1893–99	11	469	6,818
1900–09	13	216	1,601
1910–19	26	206	3,135
1920–29	31	104	5,791
1930–39	26	120	601
1940–49	40	204	244
1950–59	44	239	366
1960–60	44	264	383
1970–79	52	240	1,163
1980–89	49	110	700
1990–99	33	32	76
2000–03	29	22	97

Sources: G Bain and R Price, *Profiles of Union Growth* (Oxford, Blackwell, 1980); P Edwards (ed), *Industrial Relations: Theory and Practice* (2nd ed, Oxford, Blackwell, 2003); D Metcalf and S Milner, *New Perspectives on Industrial Disputes* (London, Routledge, 1993); Office of National Statistics, *Labour Market Trends*, various issues.

---

[12] D Metcalf and S Milner, *New Perspectives on Industrial Disputes* (London, Routledge, 1993) 249.

collective bargaining of the time. The cost to trade unions of striking on this scale was huge.

As the first half of the twentieth century progressed, product markets were extended geographically by improvements in transport and communications. In response, local industrial collective agreements had to give way increasingly to agreements that were nationwide. There was growing government support for collective bargaining on this basis. Collective bargaining spread across the public sector. By 1950 national agreements covered more than half the workforce, with half the remainder covered by Wages Councils. The status of trade unions was greatly enhanced by the constructive role that they were perceived to have played during wartime, and especially through the influence of Ernest Bevin during the 1940s. By 1950, although there were some individual employers who resisted trade union recognition, in general it was not a controversial issue. There was widespread view that an optimal system of collective bargaining had been achieved, all the better for having minimal legal intervention.[13]

Under this apparently stable system, industry-specific national agreements largely determined pay rates, working hours and other conditions across both private and public sectors. For most union members collective bargaining did not offer significant job control, although during the 1940s it offered some workplace consultation rights. More robust unofficial workplace bargaining occurred in some highly organised private sector industries such as shipyards, engineering and steel. But although this in-house bargaining imposed constraints on management's freedom of action, it was not seen to pose a major threat to the integrity of the national agreements. The big exception was coal-mining, where industrial agreements counted for little until the 1960s and the driving force behind pay was pit-level bargaining over piecework, which provoked the great majority of all British strikes through the 1940s and 1950s. Elsewhere, few observers during the early 1950s anticipated that the then minor stirrings of workplace bargaining might, within a decade or so, grow so much as to shake the structure of national agreements to its foundations.

This national system of collective bargaining fragmented over the subsequent quarter century. Initially it was tight labour markets, and later increasing international competition, which placed unsupportable strains on the shallow-rooted national industrial agreements. The locus of bargaining shifted towards the workplace where strong in-house trade union organisations reached more or less formal deals with individual local managements. Formal consultative arrangements which were introduced in the 1940s were soon eclipsed by workplace bargaining. In many private

---

[13] A Flanders and H Clegg (eds), *The System of Industrial Relations in Great Britain* (Oxford, Blackwell, 1954).

sector industries collective bargaining became a detailed activity conducted at the workplace that substantially constrained management with informal deals and strike-defended 'custom and practice'. By the late 1960s there was official encouragement to regain management control by means of 'productivity agreements.' Accompanying the growth of workplace bargaining was an increase in small strikes at individual establishments. It became a political and legislative objective of both Labour and Conservative governments to deal with the 'strike problem'. But until 1980 the only significant innovation that endured from a number of legislative false starts was an independent third-party intervention service, the Advisory, Conciliation and Arbitration Service (Acas).

Collective bargaining descended from the heights of national agreements throughout the private sector. In many industries, such as food processing and road transport, where it had never previously affected much more than pay rates and standard hours, local union activists now engaged in bargaining over the micro-management of work. In the 1970s even the hitherto largely docile public services became strike prone, and collective bargaining over matters such as work organisation emerged as a new feature of local management in much of health, education and government. Workplace bargaining became commonplace. Indeed, it was a sign of those times that serious commentators could argue that legal support should be given to enable collective bargaining to be extended to influence *all* management decisions.[14]

The next, very abrupt, change to collective bargaining came after 1980. Falling inflation, a sharp recession in manufacturing and (of great importance) national self-sufficiency in petroleum, substantially strengthened the government's position with regard to trade unions. These changed economic circumstances enabled it to legislate to increase the costs of both strikes and of union organisation. Government could also afford to ride out trade union resistance to a substantial programme of privatisation of state-owned industries, thereby smashing some of the most powerful union structures. The Conservative government broke with the official policy of decades by clearly signalling its hostility to collective bargaining. While private sector employers who took on trade unions in strike battles were officially encouraged, relatively few of them did. But the combination of government-backed trade union defeats and ever-more invasive competitive pressures brought about a substantial change in employer attitudes.

The consequences for collective bargaining were substantial and widespread. In 20 years the coverage of collective agreements contracted from over three-quarters to under one-third of the employed workforce. The

---

[14] W McCarthy and N Ellis, *Management by Agreement: An Alternative to the Industrial Relations Act* (London, Hutchison, 1973).

range of issues over which bargaining took place shrunk massively. By the end of the 1990s, in workplaces where 20 years earlier it would have been normal for managers to negotiate with union activists over questions of manning, overtime, recruitment, and working practices, it had become a rarity. For one-third of workplaces with union recognition there were no longer even annual pay negotiations.[15] For some strongly organised industries, such as national newspapers and car assembly, the upheaval of collective bargaining came in the 1980s; for some, such as the docks and banking, it came in the 1990s; and for some, such as firefighting and the postal system, it came more recently. But the net effect has been a profound change in collective bargaining. It has returned to covering a small minority of the workforce, and one that is relatively highly skilled and professional. Even where collective bargaining continues, its impact on the exercise of management discretion is greatly diminished.

Two general points can be drawn from this brief history. The first is that collective bargaining has never been static. The past century has seen it vary in terms of the level of bargaining (local, national, company or workplace), in terms of the intensity of negotiation and consultation, and in terms of the issues covered (pay, job control, strategic management etc). There is no reason to suppose that any phase into which collective bargaining is currently moving will be any more durable.

The second point to note is that, although the collective bargaining of the twentieth century was associated with heavy strike activity, in recent years this has diminished greatly. This diminution is especially marked for the private sector. There is no reason to suppose it will increase again. This is because the effectiveness of strikes is largely dictated by whether the sphere of trade union organisation encompasses the sphere of product market competition. Otherwise an effective strike jeopardises the strikers' jobs. Markets have been opened up and extended in almost all sectors: some to international competition, some with the ending of state monopolies. Unions are confronted with apparently insuperable difficulties of international organisation, and with widespread competition from and outsourcing to non-unionised firms. It has for most become irreversibly more difficult to mobilise, *in extremis*, the credible strength that might alter employer attitudes.

The law has played a part in this diminution with increased legal constraints on strikes, and it is hard to envisage political circumstances under which these constraints might be substantially reduced. This is partly because unions and their members have to some extent learned to live with them. Perhaps the most important legal innovation in altering strike activity has

---

[15] W Brown, S Deakin, D Nash and S Oxenbridge, 'The Employment Contract: From Collective Procedures to Individual Rights' (2000) 38 *British Journal of Industrial Relations* 611.

been the compulsory use of strike ballots. This has led to their widespread use by unions as an effective alternative to strikes: over 90 per cent of ballots go in favour of strikes but, in response to the great majority of those votes in favour, subsequent management concessions prevent the strike occurring.[16] It is, of course, foolish to deny that the occurrence of future labour shortages or a return of high inflation might raise strike propensities. But it is hard to envisage this happening on a sustainable basis. In historical terms, the future for the private sector is likely to be relatively strike free.

THE RETURN OF A MORE SYMPATHETIC GOVERNMENT

A change in employer attitudes towards collective bargaining was particularly evident during the 1990s. The trigger for individual employers was generally a commercial crisis that forced them to rethink their way of working if they were to survive. Its origins were various: sharper product market competition; challenging technical innovations; or privatisation or other change in ownership. One study of the 1990s looked at firms that responded to such crises with strategies that involved union exclusion, and then compared their experience with that of firms in comparable market niches which responded while retaining union recognition.[17] It established that the unionised firms achieved changes in productivity and working practices that were no less effective than those of the union excluders. The explanation for this lay in the fact that the firms retaining union recognition had done so on very different terms from in the past. They had, in effect, re-recognised their unions in a more consultative role, with a much diminished scope for negotiation. At enterprise level the unions for their part had accommodated to this changed role, shifting the emphasis of their activity towards the facilitation and legitimation of change by means of consultation. Firm by firm, market crises were altering the conduct of collective bargaining.

Trade unions experienced another, very different, stimulus to change their role in the 1990s. The steady and continuing growth of statutory individual rights since the 1970s has meant that, whether or not they have been able to win advances for their members through collective bargaining, they have had a growing battery of legal rights to uphold for them. It has been demonstrated from the 1998 Workplace Employment Relations Survey that a trade union presence is associated with not only better compliance with statutory

---

[16] W Brown, S Deakin and P Ryan, 'The Effects of British Industrial Relations Legislation, 1979–1997' (1997) 161 *National Institute Economic Review* 77.
[17] Brown *et al*, above n 6.

requirements, but also greater improvement on those requirements.[18] Legal innovation is providing ever-growing scope for unions to wield the 'sword of justice' and there is good evidence that they are taking advantage of it.

The arrival of a 'New Labour' government in 1997 brought a regime which, for the first time in 18 years, was sympathetic to trade unions and collective bargaining, albeit intending a more 'arm's length' relationship than in the past. The central legislation, the Employment Relations Act 1999, provided a procedure whereby unions could press employers for recognition by statutory means. It also provided a number of more minor rights, of which the right for a worker to be accompanied by someone of their choice in a serious disciplinary or grievance case was perhaps the most important for trade union organisation. Public speculation at the time revolved around whether this legislation would lead to a dramatic trade union revival, and a return to past collective bargaining practices with an upsurge in strike activity.

Neither of these things have happened. The contraction in trade union membership has bottomed out, with some signs of very modest growth. An important part has been played by ACAS, which has seen a quadrupling of its collective conciliation cases concerning recognition, and has seen a rise in the proportion of these resulting in full recognition from one-third to two-thirds. The most important effect upon employers has been to force them more generally to review their relationship with trade unions, in much the way that commercial crises had forced individual employers to review their position in the 1990s.[19]

Some have responded by acting pre-emptively to exclude unions, typically by establishing new consultative arrangements. Whereas collective bargaining was originally conceived of as a process whereby trade unions were involved in the management of the employment relationship, many employers who faced recognition approaches under the Employment Relations Act sought to reshape collective bargaining by actively 'managing' the union-employer relationship, and the recognition process itself. They did this by choosing the union or officials they would grant recognition to, and by actively limiting the scope of union involvement. These employers have taken a strategic approach to managing both their relationship with the union, and with the workforce via the union. The extent to which the union is able to exert independent power over employment relations matters in these organisations, is, however, another matter. Other employers have reconfirmed their recognition, but again on a basis that

---

[18] Brown *et al*, above n 15.
[19] S Oxenbridge, W Brown, S Deakin and C Pratten, 'Initial Responses to the Statutory Recognition Provisions of the Employment Relations Act 1999' (2003) 41 *British Journal of Industrial Relations* 315–34.

emphasises the consultative rather than negotiatory aspect of collective bargaining.

Indeed, a shift towards consultation, encouraged by the prospect of implementation of the Information and Consultation Directive 2002/14/EC, has been widespread. And accompanying it has been a growing interest in what has been widely termed workplace 'partnership' arrangements. The TUC itself took a lead in encouraging this in 1999 when it spelled out six principles of partnership, which included employer responsibilities to train employees, to provide them with job security in return for flexibility, and full consultation rights. Its setting up of its Partnership Institute two years later provided an instrument that has been successful in consolidating recognition and in shifting the emphasis of bargaining towards consultation in many traditionally well-organised firms where employer/union relations were in crisis. A further stimulus to more cooperative employer/union relations has been provided by a statutory procedure to introduce trade union 'learning representatives' as part of the Employment Act 2002.

Widespread talk of 'partnership' should not, however, suggest uniformity of managerial motive. Partnership agreements in contemporary Britain range from some that do indeed seek to nurture trade unions as genuinely representative and independent, albeit on a cooperative basis, through to some that are thinly veiled devices to limit and constrain union influence.[20] In much of employment where there are strong traditions of collective bargaining, employers and unions are developing cooperative relationships that meet the TUC's definition but avoid the increasingly politically-charged word 'partnership.' It is clear that any attempt to build cooperative employer/union relationships is likely to be short-lived unless it embodies a substantial element of mutuality. Unless the union can demonstrate to its membership that they gain from the relationship, that it is, as one union official described it, a 'two-way street,' there are likely to be serious internal union tensions and, worse still, membership apathy, cynicism and loss.[21] For employers, especially private sector employers, this requires a commitment to sustaining the union's role even when the collective strength that may once have enforced it is all but gone.

LEGISLATING FOR FUTURE COLLECTIVE BARGAINING

We have given an account of collective bargaining as a constantly mutating institution. Trade unions brought it into existence as a basis for the formation

---

[20] S Oxenbridge and W Brown, 'The Two Faces of Partnership? An Assessment of Partnership and Cooperative Trade Union Relationships' (2002) 24 *Employee Relations* 262.
[21] S Oxenbridge and W Brown, 'Does Formalisation Matter? Employer and Trade Union Motives for Formalising Partnership Arrangements in British Workplaces' mimeo, BUIRA Conference, Leeds, July 2003.

of an employment contract, and as a means of drawing on collective employee strength to mitigate the overwhelming intrinsic inequality of that contract. When markets were relatively localised — whether labour, product or capital markets — the exercise of collective strength was a sufficient basis for making collective bargaining effective, at least for those workers fortunate enough to be able to organise. British unions long made a virtue of this sufficiency, idealising 'voluntarism' and asking no more of the state than that it should protect the strike weapon. But, with the opening up of markets beyond the scope of either union organisation or of nation states, collective action no longer offers sufficient support to protect the interests of most private sector workers. There is ample evidence from across the world that, without either effective unions or state intervention, the basis of employment can degrade to something like the pre-contractual employer tyranny of 200 years ago. The need for legislative regulation of the employment relationship has never been greater.

A starting point for thinking about what legislation might be appropriate for collective bargaining in the future could be that industrial citizenship is a part of political citizenship. In a society characterised by, at least, aspirations of equality of opportunity, employees might reasonably expect a right to be involved, informed and consulted on matters related to employment. Past experience suggests that such rights are best upheld by independent worker collectivities, which are able to articulate worker interests even when lacking effective coercive power. For much of the twentieth century, British governments appeared, with varying degrees of pragmatism and principle, to support this view. But the collapse of the economic base of trade unionism at the end of that century was taken as an opportunity by the then British government to reject it. If New Labour has in part reinstated it, it is with union awareness that such reinstatement could be jeopardised again by a change in government. The challenge is to provide a legal framework within which trade unions can work in a way that is widely perceived to be socially and politically valuable. Such public approval was achieved in the 1940s. How might it be achieved again in the profoundly different market conditions of the twenty-first century?

A relatively new feature of the British labour market has been the rapidly increasing number of statutory individual employment rights. The employment tribunal system, with the involvement of ACAS, offers protections that some unions have ceased to be able to bargain for, and that many unorganised workers never had a hope of. As has been noted, these are generally more effectively upheld where there is a trade union presence and where they thus offer, to some extent, a union recruitment incentive. Of these new rights, the National Minimum Wage has the added strength of its own specialist enforcement agency, the Inland Revenue. Its experience is instructive. In its first three years of operation in this role, the Revenue carried out over 16,000 visits, issued over 450 enforcement notices, and had

£11 million arrears of pay restored. The very great majority of the many thousand workers who benefited from the Revenue's enforcement of the National Minimum Wage will not have been trade union members and, to be realistic, since they were mostly in small firms, stand little chance of ever becoming union members.

This raises the question of whether Britain should follow the example of most other industrialised countries in developing a comprehensive Labour Inspectorate, monitoring the enforcement of all individual rights. The recruitment incentive argument for unions has so far made the TUC unwilling to campaign for this. But perhaps the TUC argument that a Labour Inspectorate might blunt the role of unions as the 'sword of justice' should be reconsidered in view of the steady increase in statutory individual employment rights, and the very limited coverage that trade unions now have of the employed labour force. Unorganised workers are easily intimidated, often ignorant of their rights, and reluctant to stand up to their employers for those rights. A Labour Inspectorate would provide trade unions with a means to uphold labour standards in circumstances where they could not get members to take cases to employment tribunals.

There is a more fundamental reason why unions would benefit from a Labour Inspectorate. It would help to maintain a floor of rights in areas of employment where unions have difficulty winning members, but which have employers who undercut and thereby threaten those workers in the same areas who are members. A constant plea to the Low Pay Commission from hard-pressed small employers seeking to abide by the National Minimum Wage has been that it is easier for them to do so if effective enforcement mechanisms prevent their being undercut by employers who cheat. The enforcement of labour standards for the unorganised is an essential buttress for the labour standards of the organised. In short, British trade unions should see a Labour Inspectorate not as a potential rival, but as an essential complement.

There can be no doubt that government support for trade unions is important at both symbolic and practical levels. One can see it with the marked improvement in climate which trade union officials reported with the approach of the Employment Relations Act 1999.[22] It is evident in the European Union's upholding of the practice of mediating legislative innovation through high level 'social partnership' arrangements. Such arrangements in Britain have already contributed to the 1999 Act, the Employment Act 2002, the National Minimum Wage, the rejuvenation of ACAS, and the impending implementation of the Information and Consultation Directive 2002/14/EC. Government support is crucial to fulfilling so many manifestations of the social purpose of trade unionism.

---

[22] S Oxenbridge *et al*, above n 19.

The Information and Consultation Directive has potentially far-reaching implications for trade union involvement and recruitment. As has been noted, since the 1990s the form and scope of collective bargaining have changed markedly. Whereas in the past, bargaining processes revolved around setting terms and conditions, the sphere of union influence has now shifted to their involvement in what employers describe as 'consultation' over issues relating to reform of work organisation or change management more broadly. The Directive, with its focus on employers informing and consulting on the 'probable development' of workplace activities and changes in work organisation, will give greater scope for union involvement in these matters, in cases where unions dominate consultative structures. Its effectiveness would be increased with statutory protections against discrimination for elected employee representatives, whether or not they are in unions. If workers gain substantial rights to be consulted and, at least as important, if unions can make these valued in the eyes of both members and non-members, there is scope for unions both to recruit in workplaces where they already have some presence and also to win wider acceptability among the employers with whom they deal. Although some issues that once were at the forefront of bargaining, such as job control, may leave the agenda, others of considerable strategic significance, such as corporate governance and pension schemes, may join it. A legally-backed habit and expectation of consultation with elected representatives of workers has the potential to extend the cooperative style of trade unionism which is already emerging.

The greater challenge for trade unions lies where they have no presence. There are vast tracts of employment where employer hostility, worker insecurity and savage market conditions make recruitment all but impossible. This is not only a problem in itself; as already noted, the inferior employment conditions pose a constant competitive threat to those employers who do offer reasonable conditions and who do work with unions. To some extent well-enforced statutory individual rights assist in this; there are, for example, many anecdotal examples of jobs being brought back 'in-house' because the National Minimum Wage removed the benefits of outsourcing. There is also considerable scope for government action. A good example has been the recent agreement with the TUC on 'two-tier' terms and conditions, whereby outsourced public sector work should offer comparable conditions to those of the in-house workers. A major extension would be the re-introduction of the 1946 Fair Wages Resolution that applied to government contractors. When applied to all suppliers of goods to government, broadly defined, this could have a far-reaching impact through the many outsourcing companies.

An issue of ever-growing importance among the unorganised is that of immigrant labour, and especially of those many, and highly vulnerable, illegal immigrants. Trade unions in many parts of the world have traditionally defended new immigrants. They could be given statutory support with regard to, for example, recruitment access, to fulfil a valuable role in monitoring and representation as part of a broader government strategy of integrating migrants without friction into the legitimate workforce and thereby into the wider community. The independence of trade unions offers them scope for winning the confidence of immigrants that government officials are often denied.

The era is over when trade unions could rely upon their bargaining strength, backed by the 1906 'immunities,' to protect the vested interests of their members. Paradoxically, little would be gained from new legislation to reinforce the effectiveness of the strike weapon; the economics of private sector markets have moved irreversibly against it. The future role for legal support for collective bargaining lies instead in upholding unions' broader social purpose: as consultative channels; as upholders of statutory rights; as defenders of standards that can be extended to the unorganised; and as potential organisers of those unorganised. Legislation can assist trade unions to build on their traditional role as instruments of industrial citizenship and social inclusion.

4

Workers, Finance and Democracy

SIMON DEAKIN[*]

INTRODUCTION

WHILE LABOUR LAW and corporate governance could once have been thought of as discrete areas for analysis, it is clear that this is no longer the case. The relationship between them has become both complex and paradoxical. On the one hand, the rise to prominence of the shareholder primacy norm since the 1980s has undermined job security for many workers; on the other, workers have apparently acquired a more direct interest in the performance and conduct of large corporations in their capacity as the beneficiaries of the pension funds which collectively hold a large and growing proportion of UK equities. Unravelling and resolving this paradox is one of the key tasks facing labour lawyers as they attempt to renew and reconstruct their own field. With this goal in mind, the next section explores the negative implications of shareholder primacy for the stability and quality of employment, while the one after that examines how a parallel process of reducing the security of workers' savings has occurred as a consequence of change to the nature of pension provision. The focus then shifts to possible solutions. Three are outlined: strengthened representation rights for employees affected by corporate restructuring; direct share ownership by employees in the companies for which they work; and employee involvement in shareholder activism aimed at enhancing corporate accountability.

THE RISE OF SHAREHOLDER VALUE AND
ITS IMPLICATIONS FOR WORKERS

The meaning of the terms 'shareholder value' and 'shareholder primacy' is not immediately clear. Although they are currently in widespread use by

[*] I am grateful to Paul Davies and Bob Hepple for comments on an earlier draft. I alone am responsible for the views stated in the text and for any errors or omissions.

corporate law scholars (as well as economists, regulators and policy-makers concerned with corporate governance), they are not legal terms of art. In law, directors' fiduciary interests are owed to the *company*, not directly to the shareholders. In what way is this reference to the company more than just a rhetorical device? In practice, the company's interests will often be synonymous with those of its members, that is, the shareholders. But one of the many useful functions of the notion of a distinct corporate personality, separate from the shareholders, is to provide the directors, and through them the managers and other employees, with some degree of autonomy from day-to-day shareholder pressure. According to a point of view which has a long history in company law, the responsibility of management is not to bow to the demands of the shareholders at every turn, but to maximise shareholder wealth by organising the firm's physical and human assets in such a way as to generate a surplus. This implies that the corporation is not solely the property of the shareholders but is, rather, an exercise in 'team production' involving the contribution of many stakeholders.[1]

Thus, even the common law systems, which lack the distinctive civil law idea of the company's interest 'in itself,'[2] give boards discretion to set corporate strategy with regard to a series of *organisational* objectives, which are not reducible to the shareholders' interests in maximising *financial* returns. The shareholders are not entitled to engage directly in the management of the enterprise; this is the responsibility of the board. According to Delaware corporate law (Delaware is the principal jurisdiction of incorporation for larger American companies), 'The business and affairs of every corporation ... shall be managed by or under the direction of a board of directors.'[3] Many of the formative cases of English company law, dating from the early twentieth century, make the same point.[4]

A further relevant aspect of this issue is that company law says nothing of the level of returns to which shareholders are entitled, nor of the

---

[1] The team production model has been most extensively developed by Margaret Blair and Lynn Stout in work which demonstrates its importance as a long-standing principle of corporate law, and not just as normatively desirable way of organising the corporation. See M Blair and L Stout, 'A Team Production Theory of Corporate Law' (1999) 85 *Virginia Law Review* 247 and for a similar argument in the context of UK company law, S Deakin and G Slinger, 'Hostile Takeovers, Corporate Law and the Theory of the Firm' (1997) 24 *Journal of Law and Society* 124; J Parkinson, 'Models of the Company and the Employment Relationship' (2003) 41 *British Journal of Industrial Relations* 481.

[2] On this, see G Teubner, 'Company Interest.: The Public Interest of the Enterprise "In Itself"' in R Rogowski and T Wilthagen (eds) *Reflexive Labour Law* (Deventer, Kluwer, 1994).

[3] Delaware Code annotated title 8, s 141(a) (2001), discussed by D Millon, 'Why is Corporate Management Obsessed with quarterly Earnings and What Should be Done About It?' (2002) 70 *George Washington Law Review* 890, 902.

[4] In particular, *Automatic Self-Cleansing Filter Company Co v Cunninghame* [1906] 2 Ch 34; *Quin & Axtens v Salmon* [1909] AC 442; *Shaw & Sons (Salford) Ltd v Shaw* [1935] 2 KB 113. See generally the discussion in P Davies, *Gower's Principles of Modern Company Law* 6th edn, London, Sweet & Maxwell, 1997), 183–188.

timescale over which their expectations are to be met. This enabled the Company Law Review Steering Committee, in the review of UK company law which was concluded in 2002, to express its support for the idea of 'enlightened shareholder value': this implies '[a]n obligation on directors to achieve the success of the company for the benefit of the shareholders by taking proper account of all the relevant considerations for that purpose' including 'a proper balanced view of the short and long term, the need to sustain effective ongoing relationships with employees, customers, suppliers and others; and the need to maintain the company's reputation and to consider the impact of its operations on the community and the environment.'[5]

The idea that the company is an organisation or enterprise with a distinct set of interests beyond those of all the stakeholder groups combined is most clearly represented in the civil law systems. These recognise the 'enterprise' as a legal form which corresponds to the organisation. This is distinct from the concept of the 'company' which essentially describes a set of claims to income streams and property rights. The explicit recognition of the company's organisational dimension has implications for the way in which stakeholder interests are recognised, as the Viénot Report on French corporate governance recognised:

> In Anglo-Saxon countries the emphasis is for the most part placed on the objective of maximising share values, whilst on the European continent and France in particular the emphasis is placed more on the human assets and resources of the company ... Human resources can be defined as the overriding interest of the corporate body itself, in other words the company considered as an autonomous economic agent, pursuing its own aims as distinct from those of its shareholders, its employees, it creditors including the tax authorities, and of its suppliers and customers; rather, it corresponds to their general, common interest, which is that of ensuring the survival and prosperity of the company.[6]

The common law systems, strikingly, have no legal term which corresponds to the economic or sociological notion of the 'enterprise' as a organisation, and even the notion of 'enlightened shareholder value' does not go as far as recognising a distinctive interest of the company 'in itself,' as in the civil law. In the final analysis, the common law insists that the

---

[5] Company Law Review Steering Committee, *Modern Company Law for a Competitive Economy: Developing the Framework* (London, DTI, 2000), 12; see also Company Law Review Steering Committee, *Modern Company Law for a Competitive Economy: Final Report vol 1* (London, DTI, 2001), 41.
[6] M Viénot, 'Rapport sur le conseil d'administration des sociétés cotées' (1995) 8 *Revue de droit des affaires internationales* 935, cited in A Alcouffe and C Alcouffe, 'Control and Executive Compensation in Large French Companies' (1997) 24 *Journal of Law and Society* 85, at 91.

directors of a company are accountable to its shareholders. But the question of *accountability* is not the same as the issue of whose *interests* the directors are meant to be serving.

English company law clearly provides shareholders with significant rights to the exclusion of other stakeholders. In a company limited by share capital, the shareholders can be said to have the residual claim upon the surplus from production in the sense that all other stakeholders with legal claims on the enterprise (employees, trade creditors, banks) have fixed or determinate rights to a particular flow of income, as defined by the contracts which they have entered into with the company. Shareholders keep what is left after everyone else has been paid off, that is, after workers have received their wages, creditors the debts which are due to them, and the banks their loans with the agreed interest. It is true that shareholders have limited liability as a consequence of adopting this version of the corporate form, and that this, together with the doctrine of separate corporate personality, protects their personal assets from being attacked by the company's creditors should it become insolvent. But alone of all the stakeholders (it may be argued), they face both a downside, and an upside risk. If the company does not thrive, their investment is sunk, and cannot be retrieved; if it succeeds in its business, on the other hand, they gain in direct proportion to this success, either in the form of increased dividends (regular payments attached to the ownership of shares) or through the rise in share price which accompanies a growing business.

This is the crux of so-called 'agency theory.'[7] Agency theorists accept (in common with most company lawyers) that what shareholders own is not the company as such (in itself, almost a meaningless proposition) but their shares, and this, among other things, gives them the right, exclusively of all the stakeholder groups, to hold directors and managers accountable. In that sense, the claim that shareholders are the true principals for whom managers act as agents has some basis in a purely positive (as opposed to normative) analysis of company law. Shareholders can call directors to account by removing them from the board at the annual general meeting. (In English law this is a right guaranteed by legislation, whatever the articles of association say.)[8] Agency theory offers a functional explanation for this, telling us that company law grants shareholders these rights because they are in the best position of all the stakeholder groups, to exercise them. Because they have most at risk, they have the strongest incentives to

---

[7] See, in particular, E Fama and M Jensen, 'Separation of Ownership and Control' (1983) 26 *Journal of Law and Economics* 301.

[8] Companies Act 1985, s 303, re-enacting Companies Act 1948, s 184 (although, on the use of weighted voting rights in the context of a private company to frustrate s 303, see *Bushell v Faith* [1970] AC 1099).

engage in effective monitoring. In addition, internal governance costs are lower for shareholders than for other groups.[9] They have a common interest in maximising rates of return on their investments. This gives managers a clear target to focus on.

Employees, on the other hand, may prioritise many different objectives: job security, quality of employment, high wages. For this reason, it is suggested, we rarely observe firms in which managers are accountable to the workforce.[10] State-owned enterprises, likewise, suffer from the intermingling of commercial goals with wider political objectives. It is because these entities — worker-owned firms and state-run firms — are not particularly successful in resolving the separation of ownership and control, that they are being replaced, we are told, by enterprises in which external shareholders have priority.[11] In performing their monitoring role, shareholders enhance not just their own well-being, but that of all those with a stake in the enterprise. Thus they serve *both their own interests, and those of the other stakeholders*.

'Stakeholder approaches,' in various ways, challenge this view of shareholder primacy. A stakeholder, according to this point of view, is one who has an interest in the enterprise which is at risk it if fails. An employee who may find it difficult to relocate to another employment if the enterprise closes; a creditor whose claims will not be met in full if the company enters insolvency; suppliers with close ties to a particular producer; and a community which has come to depend upon a large local employer, are all in a position where they have a stake in the enterprise's sustainability. From this perspective, corporate governance is about more than the mechanisms by which shareholders hold management to account. The corporate enterprise cannot be sustained without the inputs of a series of constituencies: investors, lenders, suppliers, managers, workers, unions, communities; and the issue is how voluntary cooperation between these different stakeholder groups is to be achieved. Employees have a claim to be regarded as 'stakeholders' as one of the groups whose cooperation is, in this sense, required for the firm's success.

Today's debate between the 'shareholder' and 'stakeholder' views was largely prefigured in the 1930s in the well-known exchange between Adolf Berle and E Merrick Dodd.[12] In *The Modern Corporation and Private Property*, published in 1932,[13] Berle and his co-author the economist

---

[9] H Hansmann, *The Ownership of Enterprise* (Cambridge, MA, Bellknapp Press, 1996) ch 1.
[10] *Ibid*.
[11] H Hansmann and R Kraakman, 'The End of History for Corporate Law' (2001) 89 *Georgetown Law Journal* 439.
[12] See EM Dodd, 'For Whom are Corporate Managers Trustees?' (1932) 45 *Harvard Law Review* 1145; AA Berle, 'For Whom Corporate Managers *are* Trustees: a Note' (1932) 45 *Harvard Law Review* 1365.
[13] London, Macmillan, 1932.

Gardiner Means argued for increased shareholder rights as a counter to the growing lack of accountability of professional managers in large corporations. The fragmentation of share ownership had led to a 'separation of ownership and control' with adverse consequences for society as a whole. Dodd, by contrast, denied that managers should be accountable only to shareholders, and argued for public regulatory control of the corporation as the way forward. Dodd's argument essentially won the day, as Berle himself later recognised.[14] In the decades immediately following the end of the Second World War, through a combination of regulation and direct state ownership of large parts of the economy, the major corporations in most developed countries acquired the character of public and social enterprises.

What happened next is also well known. From small beginnings in the 1960s, the corporate governance debate was relaunched as a result of intellectual and political disenchantment with the policy of direct state ownership and regulation of the economy. The means to make managers accountable to society at large was now seen to lie in the mobilisation of market forces, and specifically those of the capital market. The mechanism by which this was achieved was the hostile takeover bid. By offering to buy shares in a company at a premium over the existing stock market price, so-called corporate raiders or predators could obtain control of the enterprise, remove the existing managerial team, and install one of their own. If the shareholders had no greater interest in the company than the financial investment represented by their shares, they could be induced to sell in return for the premium offered by the raider, in particular if they felt that the incumbent managerial team was not looking after their interests. For the bidder, the cost of mounting the bid and buying out the shareholders could be recouped, after the event, by disposing of the company's assets to third parties. If the company had not been well run before, these assets would, by definition, be worth more in the hands of others. Thus, in principle, the hostile takeover bid performed a number of tasks. It empowered the shareholders, who now had a means to call management to account if it was under-performing. Conversely, the hostile takeover disciplined managerial teams, who knew that their jobs and reputations were on the line if a bid was mounted. In addition, it provided a market-led mechanism for the movement of corporate assets from declining sectors of the economy to more innovative, growing ones.

The earliest hostile takeovers occurred in the late 1950s and early 1960s in the United Kingdom and USA. There had always been mergers and acquisitions of firms; what was relatively new was the idea of a bid for control directed to the shareholders, over the heads of the target board. In

---

[14] AA Berle, 'Modern Functions of the Corporate System' (1962) 62 *Columbia Law Review* 443. For discussion of the evolution of Berle's views, see P Ireland, 'Back to the Future: Adolf Berle, the Law Commission and Directors' Duties' (1999) 20 *Company Lawyer* 203.

the inter-war period, incumbent boards would 'just say no' to unwelcome approaches from outsiders, often without even informing shareholders that a bid was on the table. At this stage, accounting rules had not evolved to the point where companies were under an obligation to publish objectively verifiable financial information. This changed in the post-war period as a consequence of the legal and accounting reforms which were put into place in both Britain and the USA by way of response to the financial crises of the 1930s.[15] Greater transparency made it easier for unsolicited bids to be mounted and more difficult for incumbent boards to resist them. Institutional protection for minority shareholders followed, with the adoption in Britain in 1959 of the Bank of England's Notes on Reconstructions and Amalgamations and, in 1968, the City Code on Takeovers and Mergers (1968 was also the year in which the US Congress adopted the Williams Act, instituting a system of regulation for hostile tender offers for American listed companies).

One of the effects of the City Code (and parallel rules in the USA) was that the normal duty of the directors, to set strategy by reference to what they understood to be the best interests of the company over time, was displaced by a more specific obligation to give advice to the shareholders on the financial merits of the bid which had been placed in front of them. The target board was also required to maintain a position of strict neutrality once the bid was tabled. These were clear manifestations of the new philosophy that boards had a duty to prioritise shareholder interests.[16]

The dominance of the shareholder primacy norm in the context of takeovers has not gone completely unchallenged. Over two decades of empirical research on the impact of hostile takeovers, mainly focused on the United Kingdom and USA, has failed to show that they consistently lead to an improvement in corporate performance in the companies which are immediately affected. The winners from the bid process are in most cases the target shareholders, who may well receive a substantial premium, in return for ceding control, on top of the pre-bid share price.[17] For bidder

---

[15] See generally L Hannah, 'Takeover Bids in Britain Before 1950: An Exercise in Business "Pre-history"' (1974) 16 *Business History* 65; W Njoya, 'Ownership and Property Rights in the Company: A Law and Economics Analysis of Employee and Shareholder Interests,' PhD Thesis, University of Cambridge (2002), 144–45.

[16] On the takeover code and directors' duties see generally, Deakin and Slinger, above n1; on the importance of the hostile takeover in the emergence of shareholder primacy in the United Kingdom, see P Davies, 'Shareholder Value: Company Law and Securities Markets Law — A British View' in K Hopt and E Wymeersch (eds), *Capital Markets and Company Law* (Oxford: Oxford University Press 2002) 262–88.

[17] For illustrations from the UK takeover wave of the mid-1990s, indicating premiums mostly in the range 20–50 per cent, see S Deakin, R Hobbs, D Nash and G Slinger, 'Implicit Contracts, Takeovers and Corporate Governance: In the Shadow of the City Code' in D Campbell, H Collins and J Wightman (eds), *Implicit Dimensions of Contract* (Oxford, Hart, 2003), 312–14.

shareholders, while hostile bids do better than agreed mergers, on average there is only a small positive effect on share prices,[18] and the range of outcomes is extremely wide.[19] Thus, while target shareholders undoubtedly do well from hostile takeover bids, shareholders in bidder companies, on average, make only slight gains, if that, and the whole process is, from their point of view, fraught with risk.

It is also likely that hostile bids, on the whole, work against the interests of employees. One explanation for the high takeover premiums paid to target shareholders is that downsizing, following the merger, enables management to capture future 'rents' or income streams which would otherwise have accrued to employees in the form of continuing employment, the so-called 'breach of trust hypothesis.'[20] In so far as this practice directly benefits shareholders only at the employees' expense, it is a simple wealth transfer. Its impact on productive efficiency is at best neutral, but more likely negative: 'over time such policies are likely to discourage further investments by employees in firm-specific human capital.'[21]

The normative case for regulatory facilitation of takeover bids therefore depends on the extent to which they have value-enhancing, as opposed to merely redistributive, effects. This is a question for empirical research, but measuring the welfare effects of takeovers on all stakeholders, as opposed to the impact on shareholders' interests as expressed through stock price movements or corporate profitability, is extremely difficult. Martin Conyon and colleagues, in a 2002 paper,[22] found econometric evidence to the effect that firms subject to hostile takeovers in the United Kingdom between 1987 and 1996 experienced significant falls in both employment and output following the merger. After controlling for the change in output, this study found that labour was being used more productively post-merger, thereby returning greater value to shareholders. On this basis the authors claimed that 'the results are generally supportive of the view that merger activity, particularly related and hostile merger activity, promotes efficiency.'[23] However, they also recognised that downsizings following a takeover bid could be construed by workers as a breach of

---

[18] A Cosh and P Guest, *The Long Run Performance of Hostile Takeovers: UK Evidence*; Centre for Business Research Working Paper 215, (University of Cambridge, 2001).

[19] D Mueller and M Sirower, *The Causes of Mergers: Tests Based on the Gains to Acquiring Firms' Shareholders and the Size of Premia* Centre for Business Research Working Paper (University of Cambridge, 1998).

[20] A Shleifer and L Summers, 'Breach of Trust in Hostile Takeovers' in A Auerbach (ed) *Corporate Takeovers: Causes and Consequences* (Chicago, University of Chicago Press, 1988) 33–67.

[21] M Blair, *Wealth Creation and Wealth Sharing: A Colloquium on Corporate Governance and Investments in Human Capital* (Washington, DC, Brookings Institution, 1996) 12.

[22] M Conyon, S Girma, S Thompson and P Wright, 'The Impact of Mergers and a Acquisitions on Company Employment in the United Kingdom' (2002) 46 *European Economic Review* 31.

[23] *Ibid*, 40.

implicit contractual expectations of job security, an argument first made by Andrei Shleifer and Larry Summers in 1988:

> if the observed employment reductions constitute a reneging on the implicit terms of the labour contract, in the sense of Shleifer and Summers (1988), there may be associated costs generated through the subsequent reductions in firm-specific human capital investment by employees. These will be manifested in lower output levels but any such changes would be very hard to identify.[24]

In other words, employees in firms subject to the threat of hostile takeover may well, as a result, put in less effort and avoid investing in firm-specific skills and knowledge which will be wasted if they lose their jobs in a post-merger restructuring of the firm. The result will be a loss to the firm over the longer term. However, measuring this effect is problematic.

A different methodology, using interviews with bid participants and longitudinal case studies of high-profile mergers, also suggests that hostile takeovers marginalise employee interests. This study, carried out in the Cambridge Centre for Business Research, focused on some of the most prominent of the takeover bids of the mid-1990s wave in the United Kingdom.[25] These included the contests between Glaxo and Wellcome and Granada and Forte, respectively, and several of the major bids which led to the break-up and re-organisation of the electricity industry following privatisation. Directors, investment bankers, legal advisers and employee representatives were among those interviewed. There was general agreement that the City Code on Takeovers and Mergers was the most important regulatory determinant of the practice of takeover bids. Directors reported a strong tendency to focus on the concerns of target shareholders to the exclusion of other stakeholder groups during bids. A review of the case studies five years on from the initial interviews found, almost without exception, evidence of downsizing following mergers. Most striking is the mismatch between the expectations of those involved in the bids at the time they were mounted and shortly after they were completed, and the outcomes of mergers. When interviewed in the immediate aftermath of bids, the respondents were more or less unanimous in expecting shareholders in the bidder companies to be among the winners from the takeover process (in contrast to employees in the target who were expected to lose out). When the progress of the same companies was reviewed five years after the intial interviews, it was clear that, in the view of the financial community, most of them were seen to have failed to produce a return for shareholders over and above that of the market as a whole.

[24] *Ibid*, citing Shleifer and Summers, above n 20.
[25] Deakin *et al*, above n 17.

But even if it is the case that takeovers often destroy value as regards of the companies immediately involved in them, they may produce wider gains to the economy as a whole. This argument maintains that hostile bids, by prompting a continuous process of restructuring in companies subject to the discipline of the market for corporate control, help to recycle capital from traditional or declining sectors of the economy to newly developing ones. Assets disposed of either following or in anticipation of a hostile bid are thereby freed up to move to more highly valued uses elsewhere in the economy. More specifically, by underpinning the ability of shareholders to liquidise their assets, the market for corporate control reduces the cost of capital for new ventures, thereby supporting innovation and enterpreneurship. As Larry Summers put it in a speech to the London Stock Exchange in 2001:

> It was impatient, value-focused shareholders who did America a great favour by forcing capital out of its traditional companies, and thereby making it available to fund the venture capitalists and the Ciscos and Microsofts that are now in a position to propel our economy very rapidly forward.[26]

According to this argument, while certain groups of workers may suffer from the destabilising effects of asset disposals and downsizing, this is the price to be paid for maintaining the long-run competitiveness of the economy. It is in essence a revival of the Schumpeterian claim that capitalism renews itself through successive cycles of 'creative destruction'.[27] As such, it is difficult to verify in any meaningful way. While there is no doubt of the central importance of technological innovation in driving economic growth, it is far from clear that a hyperactive market for corporate control is the best way of bringing this about. Recent experience suggests otherwise: at the end of the 1990s, in the wake of the collapse of the dot.com boom, it appeared that the cost of capital may, if anything, have become too low, as investments were diverted from established sectors to start-up firms supported by little more than market speculation. As John Plender has put it, Anglo-American managers and shareholders were presiding over 'a takeover-based process of creative destruction that all too often turns out to be more destructive and less creative than the Washington prospectus proclaims'.[28]

Against the background of these competing claims it is perhaps not surprising that the Company Law Review Steering Committee should conclude that 'there is no clear case made out for inhibiting the takeover markets'.[29] The Review proposed to the UK Listing Authority that the Listing Rules be

---

[26] Cited in J Plender, *Going off the Rails* (London, Wiley, 2003) 7.
[27] JA Schumpeter, *Capitalism, Socialism and Democracy* (London, Allen and Unwin, 1943).
[28] Plender, above n 26.
[29] *Modern Company Law for a Competitive Economy: Final Report vol 1*, above n at 140.

strengthened so that a wider range of transactions would be referred to shareholders in the bidder company for their prior approval, and that parties to takeovers should issue stakeholder-related information at the time an offer is made. Thus it took note of the claim that 'synergies [from takeovers] were often exaggerated and ... employment and productive capacity were often destroyed by such deals, without economic benefit.'[30] But until such time as the Code is amended, or the Panel brought under closer regulatory or judicial control (something which the Panel has strongly resisted and for which it would appear there is currently no appetite among policy-makers and regulators), such a change is unlikely to have much impact on the way the market for corporate control operates in the United Kingdom.

CRISIS IN OCCUPATIONAL PENSION PROVISION

The rise of the shareholder value norm has put in doubt the ability of the corporation to provide long-term job stability for workers, without clearly offering, by way of compensation, an efficient basis for the 'recycling' of capital. What of the capacity of the corporation to act as guarantor of the long-term savings of the working population? It may be argued that since workers are the ultimate beneficiaries of the pension funds and unit trusts which between them own nearly 80 per cent of UK equities, they receive more than adequate compensation for increased job insecurity in the form of enhanced returns to shareholders. But this argument falls apart on closer inspection.

Pension provision in the United Kingdom has become increasingly insecure since the mid-1980s largely as a result of changes in the relationship between the social insurance schemes provided by the state, on the one hand, and private and occupational schemes on the other. For most of the twentieth century, the United Kingdom has had a hybrid system of pension provision. Social insurance provided for a basic state pension and a second pension (given a number of different names at various stages), payable on the basis of national insurance contributions and thereby accessible for those in regular lifetime employment and their dependants. Occupational schemes, provided by employers, received fiscal subsidies from the 1920s and, from the 1960s, could be 'contracted out' of the second state pension. These schemes favoured employees who had continuous service with a particular employer. Finally, for those whose employment record was insufficient to generate a meaningful pension either through the state scheme or through an occupational scheme, means-tested social security benefits of various kinds were provided directly by the state.

[30] *Ibid.*

The key period in the evolution of the system runs from the adoption of an ambitious version of the second state pension, the state earnings-related pensions scheme or SERPS, in the Social Security Act 1975, and its unravelling which began only a decade or so later in the Social Security Act 1986. SERPS aimed to provide a retirement pension equivalent to one-quarter of average earnings over the best 20 years of an individual's employment, within the range of the upper and lower earnings limits for national insurance contributions, payable on top of the basic state pension which at that point was indexed-linked to increases in earnings over time. In the early 1980s, the link between earnings and benefits for the basic state pension was broken, with subsequent upratings taking place by reference to price inflation only. Since prices rose more slowly than earnings during the 1980s, this led to a gradual but inexorable decline in the value of the basic pension which has continued to this day (the Labour government elected in 1997 controversially refused to restore the earnings link). The 1986 Act also substituted a new formula for SERPS under which the maximum a beneficiary could receive would be a pension equivalent to one-fifth of average earnings over an entire working lifetime (rather than the best 20 years).[31]

In addition, the 1986 Act also made significant changes to the conditions upon which occupational schemes could contract out of SERPS. Previously, schemes could only benefit from the contracted-out rebate on national insurance contributions if they took a particular form, that is, a defined benefit scheme under which the payment was calculated as a proportion of either the employee's final salary or their average salary calculated over a certain number of years. The 1986 Act permitted employers to offer, as an alternative to defined benefit schemes, defined contribution schemes under which the final payout was dependent solely on the financial performance of the fund into which the contributions were invested. In effect, this transferred the risk of the investment under-performing from the employer to the employee. The 1986 Act also made it possible for individual employees to take out personal retirement plans, opting out either of SERPS or an occupational scheme as the case might be. Subsequent legislation altered the minimum contracting out requirements for defined benefit schemes. Under the Social Security Act 1975, occupational schemes were required to provide a guaranteed minimum pension or GMP which was broadly the equivalent to the level of benefit which the employee would have received under SERPS. The Pensions Act 1995 replaced the GMP with a weaker

---

[31] On the changes made to the social insurance system at this time, including the decision to decouple the basic state pension from earnings and to weaken the pensions formula in SERPS, see S Deakin and F Wilkinson, 'Labour Law, Social Security and Economic Inequality' (1991) 15 *Cambridge Journal of Economics* 125.

'requisite benefits test' under which the link with SERPS was broken.[32] Additional changes to the contracting-out regime were made by the Child Support, Pensions and Social Security Act 2001, which also further restructured SERPS and renamed it the 'state second pension' (or 'S2P').[33]

The combined effect of these changes was to reduce the real value of social insurance benefits,[34] at the same time as removing the role which they had played in terms of providing a 'floor of rights' to occupational schemes. This began the process which has more recently led to many employers closing their defined benefit schemes to new entrants and replacing them with defined contribution schemes. In 2001, BT and ICI were among major employers which closed their defined benefit schemes to new members, and in the same year the rate of conversion to defined contribution schemes, which in 1993 was running at 1 per cent of all private sector schemes, had reached 4.5 per cent.[35] The trend towards increased regulation of defined benefit schemes, following on from the report of the Goode Committee in 1993 which was a response to the scandal of the Mirror Group pension funds, appears to have exacerbated the situation, by making defined benefit schemes costly to administer and organise by comparison to defined contribution schemes.[36] The difficulty is that no employer is obliged, as a matter of general law, to provide an occupational pension scheme for its employees or to make contributions to one. Employers did so in the past initially to attract and retain scarce labour,[37] and later because of the implicit competition provided by the state social insurance scheme. The contracting-out regime put in place first in the 1950s and 1960s and then strengthened in 1975 meant that occupational schemes had to come up to a high standard in terms of security of provision. In the 1990s and 2000s, in a weaker labour market and under

---

[32] For further details see S Deakin and G Morris, *Labour Law* (3rd edn, London, Butterworths, 2001), 364–65.

[33] The first phase of S2P differs from SERPS in focusing benefits on to lower earners, replacing the uniform accrual rate of 20 per cent with three separate rates according to earnings. In the second phase of S2P, which has not yet been brought into force, the earnings-related element would disappear altogether to be replaced by a flat-rate pension. See generally N Wikeley, *Wikeley, Ogus and Barendt's Law of Social Security* (London, Butterworths, 2002) 620–25. So-called 'stakeholder pensions,' introduced by the Welfare Reform and Pensions Act 1999, are intended to meet the demand for an earnings-related pension as the second phase of S2P comes into effect; under a stakeholder pension, the employer's obligation is not to contribute as such, but to grant employees access to a pensions provider. So far the take-up of stakeholder pensions has been limited.

[34] A major implication of this has been the increase in government spending on means-tested benefits for the elderly, at first in the form of the minimum income guarantee for pensioners, and more recently through pensions credits, under the State Pension Credit Act 2002.

[35] National Association for Pension Funds, *Twenty-seventh Annual Survey of Occupational Pension Schemes 2001* (London, NAPF, 2002).

[36] This argument has been advanced by the NAPF; see *ibid*.

[37] See generally L Hannah, *Inventing Retirement: The Development of Occupational Pensions in Britain* (Cambridge, Cambridge University Press, 1986).

circumstances where employers had much greater autonomy over the types of schemes they could offer while still retaining the benefit of the national insurance rebate, it was only a matter of time before they began to offer schemes under which the bulk of the risk passed to the employee.

Different types of pension scheme have distinct implications for the sharing and distribution of risk. Under the 'pay as you go' principle of social insurance, current contributions, paid by those in work, directly support the benefits received by current pensioners. With 'pre-funded' schemes, pension levels depend on the investment returns from contributions made in the past by the same individuals who are now drawing the relevant benefits. On the face of it, funded schemes thereby involve less of a call on the resources of the current generation of wage-earners. The shift from social insurance to funded pensions is therefore said to reduce the 'burden' of meeting the needs of pensioners at a time when the size of the working age population is falling relative to those who have retired. The true picture is more complicated. Past labour cannot be stored, so the 'fund' being drawn on in a private pension scheme is in essence nothing more or less than a set of contractual claims on the surplus generated from production at the time the pension is paid out. Social insurance, despite being organised by the state, has many contractual features, most notably the sense in which it represents a 'contract between generations.' While the 'ageing' of the population represents a potential threat to the ability of schemes to pay out, it is not necessarily the case that this problem is worse in systems which rely on transfers mediated through the social insurance system. Both types of claim are dependent, in practice, on the productivity of the workforce at the time the pension is being received. In all developed economies, improvements in technology and in the organisation of production over the course of the twentieth century have made it possible to provide for an ever-growing number of retirees. Thus, while changes in the age structure of the population may well require a change in the overall level of contributions, it is far from clear that they necessitate the running down of state-run, social insurance systems and their replacement with private provision.

It could be argued that public sector schemes are less secure than those provided through investment vehicles and provide a lower rate of return. However, public and private claims alike can be affected by economic shocks, such as inflationary episodes, as well as by unexpected changes to the terms of the underlying pensions contract. In the 1980s and 1990s, as we have seen, successive UK governments made changes to the social insurance system which amounted to an ex post realignment of the deal implicitly struck with contributors. But private sector pensions are also subject to ex post contractual adjustments: the decisions taken by the insurer Equitable Life in the course of the 1990s to offer guaranteed rates of return to one particular group of policy-holders led directly and inevitably to the expropriation of others in the early 2000s. Moreover, the claims made for higher rates of return from private-sector investment vehicles almost invariably depend upon extrapolations being made from particular periods of past stock market growth, and upon assumptions about future returns, which are often highly questionable.[38]

The distinguishing feature of social insurance schemes is not so much their use of 'pay as you go' in preference to 'pre-funding' as a basis for the financing of benefits, but their use of a particular set of criteria as the basis for setting the levels of benefits. Social insurance schemes tend to favour those with continuous employment and higher wages or salaries; conversely, they discriminate against those whose earnings records are interrupted or who do not have earnings which are consistently high enough to qualify for significant benefits. However, these inegalitarian features of social insurance can be (and in practice often have been) offset by the use of social insurance 'credits' in place of contributions for those spending time out of the workforce because of family responsibilities. The earnings limits for contributions can also be adjusted in such a way as to bring about redistribution between higher and lower earners. Defined benefit schemes have some of the collectivising features of social insurance, but introduce inequalities and market imperfections of their own. Because most defined benefit schemes are employer-specific, they introduce barriers to mobility between employers which are not present in social insurance schemes which cover entire sectors or countries. These barriers are only partially offset by the practice of transferring employee interests between schemes, which is highly complex to administer.

Thus it is far from obvious that the decline of social insurance has been brought about by efficiency considerations. A public choice perspective offers a more convincing explanation. The causes of the decline of social insurance in Britain during the 1980s and 1990s are complex but they certainly include powerful and concerted lobbying by the financial services industry, which had a direct stake in running down the state system in favour of private provision. In addition, there was opportunism by governments of both political parties, which continued to impose high levels of earnings-related national insurance contributions as a form of taxation at the same time as cutting the link between earnings and benefits.[39]

But whatever the reasons for the erosion of the social insurance system, its legacy is a pensions system in which expectations of a high and stable

---

[38] On the points made in this paragraph, see generally the excellent analysis of R Blackburn, *Banking on Death or Investing in Life: The History and Future of Pensions* (London, Verso, 2002).

[39] On the way in which legislation in the 1980s was used to alter the balance of funding of social security between, on the one hand, the National Insurance Fund and, on the other, general taxation, and the implications of this process for the erosion of the social insurance principle, see Deakin and Wilkinson, above n 31.

level of benefit provision are increasingly unlikely to be met. The unilateral changes made by employers to defined benefit schemes indicate that employees' interests lack a sound legal foundation. The precise nature of the employer's 'pension promise' has long been unclear: although in some cases courts have interpreted contractual documentation as giving rise to a legally protectible expectation that benefits will be paid if particular conditions are met, the terms of trust deeds are normally drafted by employers and confer discretion upon them to change the terms upon which they operate.[40] Recent decisions[41] have confirmed that there are few constraints upon the use by employers of pension fund surpluses built up during the boom years of the 1990s, and that employers may be able to avoid the obligation to meet statutory minimum funding requirements in the event of financial difficulty. Against this background, it is unlikely that decisions to close defined benefit schemes to new entrants, or even to dilute the terms of existing schemes for employees who have not yet reached retirement (and whose rights may not therefore have vested), will be successfully challenged in the courts. In practice it is extremely difficult to identify precisely what employees' property rights in pension funds amount to.

RESOLVING LABOUR'S 'PARADOXICAL INTERESTS' IN CORPORATE GOVERNANCE

Teresa Ghilarducci, James Hawley and Andrew Williams have pointed to the fundamentally 'paradoxical' nature of labour's interests in corporate governance.[42] As workers, employees make firm-specific investments in the companies for which they work, which cannot be easily transferred; on this basis they are likely to argue for a voice in the running of the enterprise. But as owners of the enterprise, in the sense of being the beneficiaries of pension funds, they have an interest in maintaining high investment returns which may not be compatible with worker voice at enterprise level. The dilemmas are particularly sharply posed for trade unions. As representatives of employees in the workplace, their role is to press for job stability and enhanced pay and conditions of employment; but when trade union officials act as pension fund trustees, they come under a duty to obtain the highest possible investment return for the scheme beneficiaries.[43]

---

[40] See generally R Nobles, *Pensions, Employment and the Law* (Oxford, Oxford University Press, 1993).

[41] In particular, the decision of the House of Lords in the National Grid litigation, *International Power plc v Healy* [2001] IRLR 394.

[42] T Ghilarducci, J Hawley and A Williams, 'Labour's Paradoxical Interests and the Evolution of Corporate Governance' (1997) 24 *Journal of Law and Society* 106.

[43] See generally *Cowan v Scargill* [1985] Ch 270.

The dilemma can be solved if those companies which offer their employees a form of participation and involvement in the enterprise, along with a commitment to job security, are also able to provide high and sustainable returns to shareholders. Under this scenario, unions can play a dual role of negotiating the conditions for effective cooperation with employers at enterprise level,[44] while using their influence as 'activist' investors to press for good practice in corporate governance. This scenario is perhaps a distant one but it is by no means incapable of being realised. It crucially depends, however, on a reconfiguration of the institutional forces which currently shape corporate governance.

In this chapter it has been argued that the modern corporation is, in essence, a complex exercise in engendering cooperation between the owners of the different inputs, including labour. Employees have claims to be treated as stakeholders because labour's contribution is essential to the productive success of the enterprise; if workers are poorly trained and motivated, the surplus from production which the corporation is capable of generating will be that much smaller than it would otherwise be. This is, of course, not the same thing as saying that shareholders in individual companies will *necessarily* be better off if employees' interests are taken into account. It is not difficult to imagine situations in which shareholders can make short-term gains from expropriating other stakeholders, including employees; as we have seen, the hostile takeover bid provides just such a case. However, the same example of the hostile takeover bid cautions against the long-term feasibility of this tactic for shareholders: again as we have seen, what they gain as investors in the target they frequently lose as investors in the merged company. In the final analysis, shareholders can have no interest in a system which reduces the scale of the surplus generated by corporate enterprise, in particular when so many of those shareholders are also workers with a direct interest in the way that the organisations they work for are run. But the question remains of how to give effective institutional expression to workers' interests.

If employees have a claim to be treated as stakeholders, is this not best expressed by encouraging them to become shareholders in the enterprise itself, thereby avoiding the problems which arise from relying on intermediaries, including pension fund trustees and fund managers, to act on their behalf? On closer inspection, it quickly becomes apparent that employee share ownership in itself is not the answer to the issues raised by the stakeholder debate. Most employee share ownership schemes provide for limited forms of financial participation; these can be a useful mechanism for rewarding employees, but they do not normally confer control of the kind which would provide a mechanism of countervailing power to set against

---

[44] See William Brown and Sarah Oxenbridge, Chapter 3 in this volume.

the influence of outside investors. Moreover, it is important here not to confuse the interests employees have in participating in decisions relating to the structure of the enterprise in which they work, with their interest in the use of the stock market to provide long-term security of savings. The fall of Enron in 2001 illustrated starkly the risks for employees of investing in their own company's shares: the company's defined contribution pension plan was locked into Enron stock at a time when its share price was plummeting in the autumn of 2001, and the company's subsequent bankruptcy left many employees with severely reduced pension claims.[45] In the United Kingdom, this type of 'self-investment' is much more limited, thanks in part to pensions legislation of the early 1990s which, in the aftermath of the depletion of the Mirror pension funds by Robert Maxwell, placed strict limits on the practice,[46] but Enron's experience should serve as a warning against the over-enthusiastic promotion of direct employee share ownership.

If direct share ownership is not the answer, there are other means by which the role of employee voice in the enterprise could be strengthened. There is considerable comparative evidence to the effect that employee information and consultation mechanisms offer an important institutional device for representing the interests of employees as stakeholders.[47] In this context, it is important to be clear that for employees to claim stakeholder status does not imply that their interests must *override* those of shareholders. Rather, the argument is that no single stakeholder group (shareholders included) should have the right to require management to put that group's interests above those of the enterprise *as a whole*. Again, the hostile takeover illustrates the point. The takeover mechanism enables the shareholders to liquidise their investment and remove it, by transferring their shares to the bidder in return for cash (at least if the bid is made in that form). The City Code on Takeovers and Mergers prevents the incumbent management from frustrating this power of the shareholders. Conversely, it offers employees no mechanism by which they may influence the decisions taken by management. The disenfranchisement of employees is total: they have no standing before the City Panel and no opportunity to make their voice heard in the bid process.

How very different the situation is when a corporate merger is brought about not by share purchase but by the transfer of the undertaking as a going concern from one employer to another. Now, by virtue of the rules contained in the Acquired Rights Directive 2001/23EC and the Transfer of

---

[45] See generally, W Bratton, 'Enron and the Dark Side of Shareholder Value' (2002) 76 *Tulane Law Review* 1275.
[46] Pension Schemes Act 1992, s 112; SI 1991/588.
[47] See in particular the overview by J Rogers and W Streeck, 'Workforce Representation Overseas: The Works Councils Story' in R Freeman (ed), *Working under Different Rules* (New York, Russell Sage Foundation, 1994).

Undertakings (Protection of Employment) Regulations 1981 (SI 1981/1794) ('TUPE'), employee representatives have the right to be informed and consulted about the effects of the impending transfer.[48] Because this right is triggered in relation to the transfer itself, it is the equivalent of requiring the incumbent board to enter into an information and consultation process once it receives a serious takeover bid.

Information and consultation rights do not provide employees with a veto over a restructuring; nor will the English courts nullify a commercial transaction entered into by an employer simply because it is in breach of employee information and consultation laws. But the effect of such a breach on the employer's part can nevertheless be substantial. The failure of the intended sale of the Rover Group by BMW to Alchemy Partners in 2000 shows that even the limited sanctions available under TUPE for an employer's failure to consult can shift the commercial balance of a deal. Many restructurings depend on knife-edge calculations of commercial advantage, as well as being highly sensitive to the timing of events; expectations can be upset by the introduction into the equation of employee claims which, as under TUPE, run with the assets, thereby binding the prospective bidder or purchaser. The effect, in Rover's case, was to help derail a plan for the company which would inevitably have led to mass redundancies, and to bring back into the picture a rival bid, put together by the Phoenix consortium of former Rover managers and local community interests, which was pledged to keeping Rover in existence as a large volume car producer.[49] Phoenix was ultimately successful in its offer to buy Rover, and three years later the company continues to support, directly or indirectly, several thousand jobs in the West Midlands of England.[50]

Although there are inevitably some difficulties in generalising from an isolated and possibly unique case,[51] Rover demonstrates strikingly that information and consultation laws can influence the outcome of a restructuring in a way which does not simply respect the involvement of particular non-shareholder constituencies, but also preserves the enterprise as a going concern. From a stakeholder perspective, then, a highly useful reform would be the extension of the duty to inform and consult to cases of merger and acquisition by share transfer. In particular, the obligation to consult

---

[48] See J Armour and S Deakin, 'Insolvency and Employment Protection: The Mixed Effects of the Acquired Rights Directive' (2003) 23 *International Review of Law and Economics* 443 on the nature of this requirement, and Deakin *et al* above n 17, on the reasons for and effects of its absence in the context of a takeover by share transfer.

[49] See generally Armour and Deakin, above n 48.

[50] As of autumn 2003.

[51] See the discussion in J Armour, S Deakin and S Konzelmann, 'Shareholder Primacy and the Trajectory of UK Corporate Governance' (2003) 41 *British Journal of Industrial Relations* 531.

should be triggered as soon as a hostile bid is received by the target board, as is currently the situation in French law.[52]

The third aspect of institutional reform to be considered here relates to the involvement of employees and their representatives in campaigns of shareholder activism. American unions have been successful in forging alliances with a wider shareholder activist movement which has placed corporate social responsibility on the governance agenda. This has been possible in part because of the important role, historically, which American unions have played in building up occupational pension provision: unions are co-owners with employers of so-called Taft-Hartley schemes, set up under the federal labour legislation of 1947, and they also have a prominent position on the boards of trustees of many public pension funds.[53]

In contrast, British unions are currently finding it more difficult to assert property-like claims in relation to occupational pensions schemes. The problem is the one identified earlier in our discussion: the law treats an occupational pension scheme as the property of the employer. An employer is under no prior obligation to set up a scheme, it can use pension fund surpluses to reduce contribution rates and can close the scheme to new members, leaving employees to rely on a defined contribution plan. Under these circumstances, 'the purpose of the fund is not to deliver superior returns to pension scheme members or savers. It is to provide a guarantee to back the pensions promise.' As a result, 'employees and pensioners, the so-called beneficiaries, have no substantive claim in this kind of [occupational] scheme on the fund's assets ... And they have little effective say in how the investments are managed.'[54]

Recent government initiatives to promote a socially responsible approach to investment policy, while useful, need to be seen in this light. The proposals laid out in the Myners Report[55] which aim to promote a longer-term approach to investment policy, and the requirement in pensions regulations for funds to disclose details of their approach to social, environmental and ethical investments, represent useful steps forward.[56] Until, however, the issue of pension fund ownership and participation is resolved, the extent of employee influence over the investment process will remain limited. An important reform would be to strengthen the involvement of employee representatives in their capacity as trustees of

[52] By virtue of Art L 432-1, para 9 of the Code du travail, introduced by the Law of 15 May 2001.
[53] Ghilarducci, Hawley and Williams, above n 42.
[54] Plender, above n 26 at 143.
[55] P Myners *Institutional Investment in the United Kingdom: A Review* (London, HM Treasury, 2001).
[56] See the Occupational Pension Schemes (Investment and Assignment, Forfeiture, Bankruptcy, etc.) Amendment Regulations (SI 1999/1849), reg 2(4), amending SI 1996/3127.

occupational pension funds. Although legislation requires the election of member-nominated trustees in both defined benefit and defined contribution schemes, it does not mandate parity of representation with employer-nominated trustees.[57] Nor is it clear, notwithstanding the new disclosure rules for pension funds, how far trustees have a discretion to take account of non-financial factors when making investment decisions; their duty continues to be to have regard to the best interests of the scheme beneficiaries.[58] The notion of employee interests in pension funds remains ill-defined and should be a major priority for legislative action in the future.

CONCLUSION

At the heart of corporate governance is the question of who exercises power and control in corporations, and the implications of the growing 'financialisation' of the economy for notions of democratic participation and accountability. As such, this set of issues is of direct and central concern to labour lawyers. The corporation has been a remarkably successful institution for most of the twentieth century, providing stable employment for workers and security for personal savings at the same time as facilitating the recycling of risk capital. What is striking from the point of view of the future of labour law is that, at the beginning of the twenty-first century, it is no longer clear that the corporation is succeeding in fulfilling these multiple functions. The logic of shareholder value, leading to restructuring and downsizing, has proved to be difficult to reconcile with the goal of job stability, at the same time as the erosion of social insurance has had the effect of undermining its private sector twin, the defined benefit pension scheme. All this has been justified on the grounds that 'creative destruction' will provide the conditions for future economic growth. But in the aftermath of the end of the dot.com bubble, the benefits of this process for the Anglo-American economies are, to say the least, contestable.

One conclusion to draw from this process is that we are witnessing the beginning of the end of neoliberalism; as Allan Kennedy has put it, 'the end of the era of shareholder value is drawing near.'[59] This is a useful conclusion, in so far as we can see that the inherent tensions of the neoliberal project are causing it to unravel. It is, of course, less clear what will come to replace it. In this chapter three institutional solutions to the problem of representing the interests of employees in corporate governance processes were considered. The first, direct share ownership in companies, was shown to provide no answer to the need to counterbalance the influence exercised

---

[57] Pensions Act 1995, s 16; Deakin and Morris, above n 32, at 367–68.
[58] *Cowan v Scargill* [1985] Ch 107.
[59] A Kennedy *The End of Shareholder Value* (Cambridge, MA, Perseus Publishing, 2000).

over management by external investors, and to give rise to considerable problems of exposure to the risk of stock market instability when employee shareholdings were used to support retirement pensions. By contrast, it was argued that the second mechanism, employee information and participation laws, could be used to penalise opportunistic attempts at corporate restructuring which expropriated employee interests. The third mechanism considered here was the involvement of employees and unions in campaigns of shareholder activism; this, it was suggested, could be a useful part of a wider strategy to promote the goals and values of corporate social responsibility, but a prerequisite to this is greater clarity in the nature of the employee interest in occupational pension funds, which requires, in turn, a fundamental policy and legislative review of state pensions policy. If the complexity of this task, and the difficulty of shifting established political positions and vested interests, can hardly be overestimated, the same is true of the urgent necessity for a new settlement in corporate governance.

5

Termination of Employment: Whose Property Rights?

STEVEN ANDERMAN*

INTRODUCTION

T HE LAWS OF termination of employment have been frequently analysed in the past by focusing on the 'property' rights of employees. An early contribution was made by Meyers in *Ownership of Jobs*, a comparison of dismissal law in four countries.[1] In 1984, Davies and Freedland suggested that:

> In its conception [the unfair dismissal] legislation made substantial steps in the direction of job property, a trend even more prominent in the reforms of the unfair dismissals legislation made by the Employment Protection Act 1975.[2]

In 1991, Collins wrote that the assertion of property rights in the job for employees was essentially a rhetorical device to express 'the idea that employees should enjoy greater job security than that accorded to them by the common law's doctrine of termination at will.' He added that the rhetoric of property rights had its uses because the inappropriate taking of the job by the employer would be regarded as void thereby leading to a natural right of reinstatement: there could be 'compensation for the forceful taking of the right' and as well as 'for the loss of economic value represented by the right.' Such a standard also implied a fair procedure for the taking of the property.[3]

* My thanks to my colleagues Janet Dine and Bob Watt for looking at the script in draft form, to Michael Rubenstein, with whom I have discussed the ideas for this contribution and to Hugh Collins upon whose shoulders I have stood in writing this chapter.
[1] F Meyers, *Ownership of Jobs: A Comparative Study* (Los Angeles, UCLA Press, 1964) 1.
[2] See P Davies and M Freedland, *Labour Law: Text and Materials* (2nd edn, London, Weidenfeld and Nicholson, 1984) 431. See at 428–32 for a more comprehensive analysis.
[3] See H Collins, *Justice in Dismissal: The Law of Termination of Employment* (Oxford, Clarendon Press, 1992) 88.

By comparison, much less effort has been made to look closely at the influence of judicial assumptions of the 'property' rights of employers in cases relating to employment law and in particular the way in which a view of employer 'property' rights underpins an acceptance of managerial pre-rogatives.[4] Yet if one looks closely at a number of judicial statements there is strong evidence of the endurance of a rather absolutist assumption of the employer's 'property' rights by the judiciary. A good recent example of this type of sole property rights assumption is offered by Lord Steyn's opinion in *Malik v BCCI* in which he used the following language to describe the implied term of mutual trust and confidence:

> the implied obligation as formulated is apt to cover the great diversity of situations in which a balance is struck between an employer's interest in *managing his business as he sees fit* and the employee's interest in not being unfairly and improperly *exploited*.[5] (emphasis added)

At first glance, this statement may be thought to be an endorsement of the 'balancing role' of the implied term.[6] If one concentrates on the factors being balanced, however, it is clear that Lord Steyn has adopted an implicit sole property rights perspective of the enterprise. In the first place, the man-agement of *the* business is the management of *his* business. Moreover this is coupled with *as he sees fit* which hints at a rather wide scope for manage-rial prerogative. Further, the relationship between employer and employee is viewed one of *exploitation* by the employer balanced by a responsibility not to do so unfairly and improperly. The quotation takes the view that ownership is solely vested in the employer and this ownership is viewed as giving exclusive rights to not only the physical property owned by the firm but the labour and product of the firm's employees, and by implication the 'job.' Perhaps it is unfair to isolate a single phrase from its context. However, the statement offers evidence of the implicit assumptions in judi-cial thinking and that is by no means an isolated occurrence in the context of the contract of employment.

The influence of sole property rights assumptions can help to explain a number of the historical decisions of employment law that otherwise have appeared puzzling, particularly those judicial decisions relating to the termination of employment. One example is the automatic termination

---

[4] See, eg B Hepple and S Fredman, *Labour Law and Industrial Relations in Great Britain* (Deventer, Kluwer, 1986) in which at 145 they stated 'In summary, then, the attempts to give "job property" or even "job security rights" to employees have proved no match for the prop-erty rights of employers'; see too J Atleson, *Values and Assumptions in American Labor Law* (Amherst, University of Massachusetts Press, 1983).

[5] [1997] IRLR 462, HL (*emphasis added*).

[6] See, eg D Brodie, 'Mutual Trust and the Values of the Employment Contract' (2001) *ILJ* 84, at 85.

rule in employment contracts.[7] There are also decisions interpreting the discrimination Acts, such as *Adekeye v Post Office (No 2)* which held that once the employer has chosen to terminate that relationship, even though the employee had a contractual right of appeal over the dismissal, he was to be classified as no longer employed by the employer for the purpose of bringing a claim of racial discrimination.[8] This decision has recently been reversed by the House of Lords.[9]

A further and particularly striking example of judicial protectiveness of employer property rights is the way many UK judges have been unwilling to allow specialist tribunals to make an independent determination of the fairness of the dismissal, applying a proportionality test under the Employment Rights Act 1996, section 98(4).[10] Instead most judges have insisted upon a wide 'range of reasonable responses' test curbing the scope of the tribunal's determination. This interpretation of the standard of fairness established by section 98(4) has kept the legal control of managerial power to dismiss in the United Kingdom to a level that fails to meet the ILO standard embedded in the UK legislation, and that falls below the standards established by other comparable European legislation.[11] The purpose of this contribution to a volume in honour of Bob Hepple is to attempt to draw greater attention to the role of assumptions about the sole property rights of employers in the judicial interpretation of UK unfair dismissals legislation.

This phenomenon of judicial deference to managerial discretion has often been explained in utilitarian or instrumental terms. One explanation has been that the judges doubt their capacity to second-guess managerial decisions. A second suggested explanation has been the judicial concern to avoid overstretching the capacity of the courts by too interventionist a standard of reasonableness, suggesting an instrumental trade-off between court resources and a desirable interpretation of the statute.[12] Perhaps the most common approach has been to explain the judges' reaction to the creation of statutory employee rights in terms of a need to balance managerial efficiency with employee rights, as if there were a trade-off between the two. Employment rights have been implicitly assumed to be a burden on business and if they are given too purposive an interpretation they will interfere with

---

[7] See, eg *Sanders v EA Neale Ltd* [1974] 3 All ER 327, at 333; see discussion in P Elias, 'Unravelling the Concept of Dismissal' (1978) *ILJ* 16. See too judicial comment in *Boyo v London Borough of Lambeth* [1995] IRLR 50.

[8] See, eg *Adekeye v Post Office* (No 2) [1997] IRLR 105.

[9] *Relaxion Group plc v Rhys Harper and other* [2003] IRLR 484.

[10] See, eg H Collins, *Justice in Dismissal: The Law of Termination of Employment* (Oxford, Clarendon Press, 1992); H Collins, 'The Meaning of Job Security' (1991) *ILJ* 227; H Collins and M Freedland, 'Finding the Right Direction for the Industrial Jury' (2000) *ILJ* 288.

[11] See B Hepple, 'Security of Employment' in R Blanpain and F Millard, *Comparative Labour Law and Industrial Relations* (Deventer, Kluwer, 1982) 367.

[12] See, eg Judge Ansell's remarks quoted by Lord Hoffman in *Johnson v Unisys Ltd* [2001] IRLR 279.

the efficient running of a business.[13] If, however, the impetus to interpretation were purely instrumental, why have the judiciary proved to be so unreceptive to arguments by academics and the findings of researchers that higher standards of treatment of employees in matters of discipline and dismissal can have efficiency enhancing effects?[14]

There is little doubt that the interpretation of statute law by the judiciary has been influenced in large measure by utilitarian factors. Yet to concentrate solely on an instrumental basis for the dominant judicial paradigm of deference to managerial discretion may be to miss out on the implicit deontological assumption by UK judges about the sole 'property' rights of the owners of firms as the foundation for a wide managerial prerogative.

A 'property right,' as recognised by legal systems, consists of a spectrum of rights against other people as well as correlative obligations by those other people to the property rightholder.[15] A 'property right' can also involve a spectrum of obligations to other people, beginning with a duty not to do harm with one's property and extending to other external legislative and common law obligations.[16] The concept of a 'sole property right' occupies the extreme end of the spectrum of ownership rights and encompasses *all* the core rights: to exclude others from one's property, (trespassory rights), to have exclusive use and control over one's property and a right freely to dispose of one's property.

In the context of employment, the exclusionary property rights that apply to protect property in inanimate things are inappropriate to reinforce control when that property is being exploited with the help of other people. At the crudest level, work may be an economic transaction of exchange whereby the employer trades his property in the form of money for the labour to be done. In a more sustained relationship of employment, however, there is an issue for the legal system to resolve. How should it define the extent of control by 'property' right owners over employees? The original source of the employer's power over labour may be economic in the sense that the work is done in return for a wage. However, the 'property' rights and power of the employer have been extended into control over labour in the continued employment relationship by terms implied in law.

---

[13] See, eg *RS Components Ltd v Irwin* [1973] IRLR 239; *Catamaran Cruisers Ltd v Williams* [1994] IRLR 386.

[14] See, eg S Deakin and G Morris, *Labour Law* (3rd edn, London, Butterworths, 2001); see too S Anderman, *Labour Law: Management Decisions and Workers' Rights* (4th edn, London, Butterworths, 2000).

[15] See, eg W Hohfeld, *Fundamental Legal Conceptions as Applied in Judicial Reasoning* (New Haven, Yale University Press, 1919) 71; L Becker, *Property Rights: Philosophic Foundations* (London, Routledge and Kegan Paul, 1977) 11–14, 21–22.

[16] See, eg J Harris, *Property and Justice* (Oxford, Clarendon Press, 1996) 130; AM Honoré, 'Ownership' in A Guest (ed), *Oxford Essays in Jurisprudence* (Oxford, Oxford University Press, 1961) ch 5; M Cohen, 'Property and Sovereignty' (1927) *Cornell L Rev* 8.

In employment contracts, even more than in commercial contracts, express terms and terms implied in fact would have been inadequate to ensure control.

In earlier times, the rules of status offered a mechanism for an extension of the master's 'property' rights into control over the labour of the servant. The master not only controlled the work on the job by the status obligations of obedience, loyalty and fidelity; he also had legal powers to prevent the servant leaving the job. In turn he had certain minimum obligations of care towards servants.

Once the rules of status were abandoned in 1875, the law of contract was looked to in order to provide a functional substitute for the extension of the 'property' rights of the employer into a managerial prerogative.[17] The mechanisms provided by the contract of employment to ensure control over work included the transformation of the rules of status into the contractual implied terms of obedience, loyalty and fidelity.[18] These allowed the employer to enjoy a legal right to control the servant's labour upon those assets and the product of that labour in return for the wage. Secondly, the law of contract also allowed the employer-owner to continue to enjoy an exclusive right to dispose of the job for reasons of 'his' choosing, subject to the giving of adequate notice. The rules of wrongful dismissal only applied to cases where inadequate contractual notice was given and the employer's wide freedom to dismiss underpinned the other contractual means of control and power.[19]

As we know, there were some important differences in the control mechanism introduced by the law of contract as compared to that provided by the rules of status. Quite apart from the basic difference that the setting of wages was freed from statutory maxima, there was the introduction of an employee's entitlement to leave with notice, the limits imposed by equity upon the legal compulsion of an employee to remain in service,[20] and the limits on the property rights of employers imposed by the doctrine of restraint of trade.[21]

---

[17] See, eg A Fox, *Beyond Contract: Work, Power and Trust Relations* (London, Faber, 1974), 181–86.

[18] See eg Deakin and Morris, above n 14 H Collins, K Ewing and A McColgan, *Labour Law: Text and Materials* (Oxford, Hart Publishing, 2001); Anderman, above n 14.

[19] See, eg Davies and Freedland, *Kahn Freund's Labour and the Law* (3rd ed London, Stevens, 1983) 18.

[20] *De Franscesco v Barnum* (1890) 45 Ch D 430 at 438.

[21] Here we have an early example of the common law forced by its own assumptions of freedom of contract to recognise the property rights of the employee in her own skill and knowledge and the freedom to offer that skill and knowledge to another employer upon the termination of employment or to engage in trade herself. The employer may enjoy the obligations of obedience, own the intellectual property of employees and protect its trade secrets but it could not use the mechanism of contract to extend its property rights over the employee's own right to her residual freedom to trade. See, eg *Herbert Morris v Saxelby* [1916] 1 AC 688,

Nevertheless, these limits on the employer's 'property' rights contained within the doctrines of the contract of employment did not prevent a high degree of control via the duty of obedience, the continued ownership of the employer in all products of the employee's labour, both physical and intellectual, and the freedom to terminate employment. The legal framework at common law could continue to reinforce an image of the employer as enjoying exclusive property rights in all aspects of 'his' business

The endurance of a rather absolute view of employer property rights is difficult to reconcile with the developments in UK labour law in the past few decades which clearly place limits upon the exercise of managerial prerogative. During an earlier period of master-servant law, a pure property rights view of businesses might have been a more understandable frame of reference for the judiciary. As the modern law of employment has developed, however, with legislation regulating unfair dismissal, redundancy and discrimination, etc, there should have been some modification of absolutist property rights thinking by judges. In the first place, the spectrum of exclusive rights enjoyed by the employer should have been adjusted to take into account the fact that the state now restricts by legislation the employer's exclusive right to dispose of his 'property' in the job. It will be argued later in this chapter that many European legal systems did make such an adjustment and had far less difficulty in winning acceptance by their judges.

The law of unfair dismissal in its design was meant substantially to restrict the exclusive property right of the employer to dispose of jobs via dismissals, particularly 'disciplinary' dismissals. The legislative motive was partly to create a test for dismissals that was fair to employees, particularly non-unionised employees, and partly to ensure that management behaved fairly so as to avoid precipitating industrial action in response to dismissal decisions. The legislation was an attempt to adjust the power relationship created by the property rights of the employer's capital assets and extended over employees in the employment contract. In particular, it was designed to make illegal the arbitrary dismissal decisions of employers, ie those decisions which ignored considerations of proportionality.

The statutory provision requires the balance between the employer's exclusive power to dismiss and the employee's right to fair treatment in dismissal decisions to be determined by an impartial tribunal making an independent assessment of the decision of the employer and applying a substantive test which incorporated a standard of equity. Nevertheless, the courts have been reluctant to accept the legislative requirement that the employment tribunals

---

at 709; *Faccenda Chicken Ltd v Fowler* [1986] IRLR 69. The doctrine of restraint of trade offered an early example of a regulatory mechanism to limit the scope of the express term, albeit in the crude form of rendering it void. See, eg *Mason v Provident Clothing and Supply Co* [1913] AC 724. There was, of course, the limited possibility of merely severing the offending clause under the 'blue pencil rule.'

should make an independent assessment of the equity of the employer's decisions. Instead, they have chosen to curb the degree of independence of employment tribunals.

Some judges have been prepared to acknowledge the way other employment legislation has modified the sole property rights of employers, but by and large this has been under the direction of the European judges and legislators. In the first place, it required the firm guidance of the ECJ to ensure that the discrimination laws received an interpretation that allowed them to reach into and sharply limit employer 'property' rights.[22] Secondly, also under the influence of European Union law, the concept of purposive interpretation has made its way into the interpretation of EU-based legislation like the Transfer of Undertakings (Protection of Employment) Regulations 1981 (S1 1981/1794) ('TUPE') Indeed, the impact of the Acquired Rights Directive 2001/23/EC and TUPE on the 'property' rights of UK firms initially produced shocks of a seismic scale. The development has been well described by Collins, Ewing and McColgan:[23]

> Governments, employers and insolvency practitioners simply could not believe that legislation could attempt both to prevent employers from carrying out dismissals in order to effect a sale and to prevent the purchaser from reorganising the business. They were astounded that, for the sake of protecting the contractual expectations of the workforce, legal controls might prevent employers from achieving the maximum value from the sale of the businesses and might block the use of outsourcing of parts of the business in order to take advantage of lower labour costs in the secondary labour market. Initially, the courts shared this disbelief, but before long they accorded respect to the decisions of the ECJ which laid bare the purposes of the Directive.

The experience of the judges' reaction to TUPE, as guided by the ECJ, however, appears to have remained largely compartmentalised. There is little evidence of 'spill over' of methods of purposive interpretation into other more 'home grown' statutory protections against termination of employment.[24] The one exception to this, perhaps, is the way that guidelines used by employment tribunals in the case of unfair redundancy dismissals have been influenced by the collective redundancy consultation provisions.

---

[22] The pregnancy cases offer a good example. On the whole, after a few spirited attempts at resistance the UK courts have accepted the need to give a robust interpretation to the discrimination laws, one that is consistent with ECJ reasoning. Yet, of course, the UK courts had little choice. They were bound by the European Communities Act 1972 to follow the judgments of the ECJ. Moreover, terminations of employment for prohibited discriminatory reasons were more in the nature of public interest dismissals.

[23] Above n 18, at 1068–69.

[24] See, eg discussion in S Anderman, 'The Interpretation of Protective Employment Statutes and the Contract of Employment' (2000) *ILJ* 223; see too S Honeyball, 'Employment Law and the Primacy of Contract' (1988) *ILJ* 97.

However, there is little evidence that the convention of purposive interpretation has been applied to the substantive test in section 98(4) of the 1996 Act.[25] Indeed, if anything the pattern of interpretation of employee rights has been noticably solicitous of employer 'property' rights.

To explore the way UK judges have retained a sole property rights perspective in the context of unfair dismissals, it will be helpful look more closely at four issues in turn: the common law of wrongful dismissal in a 'property' rights perspective; the law of unfair dismissal in a 'property' rights perspective; unfair dismissal law and 'property' rights in the EU; company law, labour law and 'property' rights in the EU.

COMMON LAW OF WRONGFUL DISMISSAL IN A 'PROPERTY' RIGHTS PERSPECTIVE

One major reason for retention of an unmodified employer 'property' rights perspective by the judiciary is the continued life of the implied terms of employment contracts at common law. Despite the rise of the term of mutual trust and confidence, these implied terms continue to perpetuate the image of the employer as the sole owner of the business as well as to rein-force the power inherent in that property right.

Any close study of the implied obligations of obedience, fidelity, loyalty, confidentiality and cooperation can easily point to elements of master-servant assumptions remaining in the substance of these implied contractual terms.[26] To take one example, why is it assumed in employment law that the intellectual property created by the employee in the course of employment is the sole property of the employer. There is no foundation for this in the law of patent or copyright. Indeed, the philosophy of the intellectual property laws would award the rights to a patent or copyright to its originator as an individual.[27] The employee's implied term of fidelity to the employer operates as a contractual mechanism to ensure that the employer's property right is extended to the intellectual product of the employee.[28]

---

[25] Other statutory provisions such as those of the Redundancy Payments Act 1965 may have been eventually rescued from their early common law interpretation. But these provisions do not strike at the heart of the property rights of the employer. Section 98(4) as it applied to disciplinary dismissals, if applied literally or purposively, did. See, eg Anderman, above n 24.

[26] See excellent discussion by Deakin and Morris, above n 14, at 326.

[27] See, eg L Bentley and B Sherman, *Intellectual Property Law* (Oxford, Oxford University Press, 2002), 4; W Cornish, *Intellectual Property* (4th edn, London, Butterworths, 1999). For the Lockean underpinnings, see J Locke, 'An Essay Concerning the True Original Extent and End of Civil Government' in E Barker (ed), *Introduction to Social Contract, Essays by Locke, Hume and Rousseau* (Oxford, Oxford University Press, 1947) 28.

[28] See, eg *British Syphon Co Ltd v Homewood* [1956] 2 All ER 897. The Patent Act 1977 modifies this property right to some extent but the Copyright Act makes no such provision. See, eg Wotherspoon, 'Employee Inventions Revisited' (1973) *ILJ* 11; J Philips, 'Employee Inventors and the New Patents Act' (1978) *ILJ* 30; *Reiss Engineering Co Ltd v Harris* [1985] IRLR 232.

In modern times, the contract of employment has been interpreted to be more protective of the interests of employees. The courts have accepted an elective theory of termination[29] and on occasion allowed interlocutory injunctions where the employer has breached the terms of the contract.[30] These cases acknowledge employee expectation interests in the contract and roll back the implicit property rights assumptions in the unilateral theory of termination. They have their limits in the sense that, in addition to all the other hurdles employees must overcome to obtain an injunction, they must also show that the employee is not one in whom the employer has lost trust and confidence. It is an open question whether this requirement is an integral feature of contract law or a residue of employer 'property' rights thinking.[31]

Moreover, the implied term of mutual trust and confidence has been developed as a general 'portmanteau' obligation requiring the employer not to engage in conduct likely to undermine the trust and confidence which the employment contract implicitly envisages.[32] The test ranges widely[33] including regulating the employer's discretion in applying express terms and exercising its powers to enforce the employee's obligations of obedience and cooperation. It reaches into the employer's powers to control employees during employment as well as placing limits on the employer's powers to terminate employment. It even appears to place obligations upon employers in respect of references given after employment terminates.[34] It has been described as creating a more balanced view of the employment relationship.[35]

Yet if we look more closely at the nature of that balancing exercise, we can see that the cases in which the employer's exercise of control has been found wanting have tended to be extreme cases involving arbitrary, unreasonable and capricious treatment. The landmark cases applying a balancing

---

[29] See, eg *Boyo v London Borough of Lambeth* [1995] IRLR 50 for the grudging quality of that acceptance. See now *Relaxion Group plc v Rhys Harper* [2003] IRLR 484.

[30] See, eg *Jones v Gwent County Council* [1992] IRLR 521. See too K Ewing, 'Remedies for Breach of the Contract of Employment' (1993) 52 *Cambridge Law Journal* 405.

[31] In cases like *Jones and Lee v Goulding* [1980] IRLR 67, where the judges applied straightforward contractual reasoning, the employer's breach of its own disciplinary procedure, an express term of the contact, was held to entitle him to interim relief. No mention of a need for the employer to have continued confidence in the employer; see too *Jones v Gwent County Council* [1992] IRLR 521.

[32] Lord Nicholls referred to it in these terms in *Malik v BCCI* [1997] IRLR 462, at 464. He also stated that 'Employers must take care not to damage their employees future employment prospects, by harsh and oppressive behaviour or by any other form of conduct which is unacceptable today as falling below the standards set by the implied trust and confidence term.'

[33] '[W]hether by statute or judicial decision, to care for the physical, financial and even psychological welfare of the employee': *Spring v Guardian Assurance plc* [1994] IRLR 460, HL at 474.

[34] *Ibid.*

[35] See D Brodie, 'Mutual Trust and the Values of the Employment Contract' (2001) *ILJ* 84.

test and favouring the employee may on occasion have suggested a good faith test.[36] However, in each of these cases, cautionary language has been used by the judges to restrict the scope of the penetration of the implied term into the property rights of the employer. *Aktar*,[37] *Johnstone*,[38] *Imperial Tobacco*,[39] *French v Barclay's Bank plc*[40] and *Scally*[41] are cases of harsh or unreasonable treatment of employees by employers. Moreover, we must be careful to factor in the limiting language used in the cases, in particular *White v Reflecting Roadstones*,[42] *Malik*,[43] and the post *Malik* cases of *Ali v BCCI*[44] and *Johnson v Unisys Ltd*.[45] In particular, Lord Hoffman in *Johnson* makes it clear that the courts are extremely reluctant to extend the implied term of mutual trust and confidence to the dismissals procedure of the employer and the manner of dismissal. His reason for not extending the implied term to certain heads of compensation is the existence of the unfair dismissals legislation.[46] However, his unwillingness to extend the implied term to the failure to provide an appeals procedure indicates a reluctance to accept the perfectly respectable contractual argument that the appeals procedure was an integral part of the employment relationship and could therefore continue to bind the employer after the employer has chosen *otherwise* to terminate the contract of employment.[47]

Although the implied term of mutual trust and confidence may have improved the employee's position by placing certain outer limits to the powers of the employer to exercise control without restraint, it does not seem to have dislodged the sole ownership image of the employer. The factors being balanced in the balancing test of the implied term, as we have seen from Lord Steyn's statement in *Malik*, weigh the employer's entitlement to control over its property as against the employee's entitlement not to be treated extremely unreasonably in the process. The employer's interest is defined by

---

[36] See, eg *Imperial Group Pension Trust Ltd v Imperial Tobacco Ltd* [1991] IRLR 66.
[37] *United Bank Ltd v Ahktar* [1989] IRLR 507.
[38] *Johnstone v Bloomsbury Health Authority* [1991] IRLR 118.
[39] *Imperial Group Pension Trust Ltd v Imperial Tobacco Ltd* [1991] IRLR 66.
[40] [1998] IRLR 646.
[41] *Scally v Southern Health and Social Services Board* [1991] IRLR 522.
[42] [1991] IRLR 331, 335.
[43] See, eg the language of Lord Steyn in *Malik*. The implied obligation of mutual trust and confidence, he stated 'applies only where there is no reasonable and proper cause for the employer's conduct, and then only if the conduct is calculated to destroy or seriously damage the relationship of trust and confidence. That circumscribes the potential reach and scope of the implied obligation'. See too comments by Lindsay J, 'The Implied Term of Trust and Confidence' (2001) 30 *ILJ* 1.
[44] *BCCI SA v Ali* [2001] IRLR 292.
[45] [2001] IRLR 279.
[46] See discussion by D Brodie 'Mutual Trust and the Values of the Employment Contract' (2001) *ILJ* 84.
[47] See *Relaxion Group plc v Rhys Harper* [2003] IRLR 484, HL.

its property rights; the employee's interest is defined by not being subjected to egregiously unreasonable treatment.

It might possibly be argued that the employer's property rights over the labour and product of the employee may have been retained at common law without necessarily being the reason for the restrictive interpretation given to the statutory provision. Yet it is impossible to ignore the fact that the interpretation of the implied term of mutual trust and confidence appears remarkably similar to that given to the range of reasonable employer responses test of section 98(4) of the 1996 Act. Both leave a wide berth to management discretion. Both require an almost indisputable display of poor judgement by management before finding a job termination unlawful. Both are extremely solicitous of the rights of the employer to dispose of its property as it wills. Both apply a *Wednesbury*[48] or *Bolam*[49] type unreasonableness test limiting control to the need to avoid 'arbitrary and capricious results.'[50] This convergence of standards applied by the courts to the two different legal tests indicates that the judges are willing to apply common law standards of limits on the power of employers to the statutory test of reasonableness. The value underpinning the common law standard is the implicit assumption of the property rights of the employer extending into the employment relationship to the point of terminating employment. It is difficult not to conclude that a similar assumption has underpinned the interpretation of the statutory standard.

LAW OF UNFAIR DISMISSAL IN A 'PROPERTY' RIGHTS PERSPECTIVE

Introduction

Historically, the legislation introducing unfair dismissal protection was meant to create a substantive and procedural test of fairness as well as the remedies of compensation for financial loss over and above pay in lieu of proper notice and reinstatement, all of which were lacking at common law. The statute was meant to replace the meagre protection then offered by the common law action of wrongful dismissal which was based on the freedom of the employer to exercise its power to terminate employment. This change in the nature of legislative policy expressed itself in the creation of individual rights for employees that emphasise the importance of placing limits on the employer's exercise of its power to dismiss in the interests of an

---

[48] *Associated Provincial Picture Houses Ltd v Wednesbury Corporation* [1948] 1 KB 223.
[49] *Bolam v Friern Barnett Hospital Management Committee* [1957] 2 All ER 118.
[50] Cf Brodie, above n 46, at 94.

improved measure of fair treatment for individual employees. This legislation went against the grain of the common law in that it placed tribunals and courts in the position of applying objective standards of fairness to managerial conduct in exercising the employer's extended 'property' rights.

The legislation also at first appeared to run against the grain of 'collective laissez-faire' in that it involved direct regulation of property rights and the managerial power they bring by the courts applying an independent legal standard.[51] Under collective laissez-faire, the trade unions had only unevenly challenged managerial power over the workforce at the workplace. It was this statute that Bob Hepple undoubtedly had in the forefront of his mind when he stated that 'matters which were entirely in the sphere of managerial prerogatives or collective bargaining are now directly regulated by positive rights and duties.'[52]

The starting point for the legislators was ILO Recommendation 119/1963 on Termination of Employment, adopted by the United Kingdom in 1964, and the recommendations of the Donovan Commission.[53] It is interesting to note that these two sources, despite proceeding from rather different assumptions, arrived at a similar conclusion. The ILO Recommendation was introduced quite clearly as a counterweight to the power of the employer at work. It explicitly incorporated the rationale of limiting abuses of a dominant power position by the employer and embraced a concept of introducing minimum standards of fairness reflecting the fact that labour had social value and was not reducible to a commodity.[54] The motives of the Donovan Commission Report were more complex. The Commission was concerned to fit the modification of the employer's powers over dismissals into a workplace bargaining context (para 409). However, it was also concerned to establish direct legislative protection based on an ILO standard to employees unprotected by collective bargaining (paras 525, 545).[55]

The eventual Employment Right Act 1996 adopted the form of the ILO Recommendation's two step-test: the first step was the isolation of the

[51] Collins, *Justice in Dismissal*, above n 10, at 26.

[52] B Hepple, 'Individual Employment Law' in G Bain (ed), *Industrial Relations in Britain* (Oxford, Blackwell, 1983) 394.

[53] The law was also influenced by the NJAC Report on Unfair Dismissals. It was also based on research by two part-time advisers, Geoffrey de Nys Clarke on remedies for unfair dismissal and by myself on dismissal procedures in both private and public sector industries. We both sat through certain preparatory stages consisting of the drafting of proposals by the civil servants and their exchange with the parliamentary draftsman during the course of succeeding drafts.

[54] See, eg Paul O Higgins, 'Labour is not a Commodity: an Irish Contribution in International Labour Law' (1997) 26 ILJ 225; see too B Napier, 'Dismissals: The New ILO Standards' (1983) 12 *ILJ* 17.

[55] This was the reason why so much effort went into the drafting of the statutory exemption for voluntary procedures. I found that more than half my work on the preparation of the legislation as a part-time adviser to the Department of Employment was directed towards this end.

employer's reason for dismissal; the second was to classify dismissals into three broad categories. The first category consisted of the 'invalid' reasons for termination of employment (Article 2(3)). These in the UK statute became the automatically unfair reasons initially covering rights to protection against dismissals for trade union membership and activity and later expanding into 14 categories of inadmissible reasons for dismissal.[56]

The second category consisted of the presumptively valid, 'economic dismissals,' ie those based on the operational requirements of the undertaking, establishment or service (Article 2(1)). These were meant to be subject to minimum standards of procedural fairness but had a less comprehensive substantive fairness test.

The third category consisted of the presumptively valid, 'disciplinary dismissals,' ie those connected with the capacity and conduct of the worker. These were intended to require considerably greater judicial oversight of the employer's decision to dismiss. The statutory test for presumptively valid reasons for dismissal was meant to be an objective test of the reasonableness of the employer's decision by an impartial tribunal.[57] ILO Recommendation 119/1963 proclaimed that dismissal without notice should not take place unless there has been serious misconduct and where the 'employer could not in good faith be expected to take any other course.' The Recommendation was therefore quite clear that a significant element of the test of the substantive fairness of the dismissal was an objective test of proportionality applied by the tribunal. It also suggested procedural standards of fair conduct by employers in cases of disciplinary dismissals.

The original legislative form, both in the Labour Government's Industrial Relations Bill in 1970 and the Industrial Relations Act 1971, strongly implied a test on the merits of the employer's dismissal as well as the fairness of the employer's procedure. The phrase 'equity and the substantial merits of the case' suggested that the test should be a question of fact in which the injustice to the employee should be a major factor in considering the reasonableness of the employer's decision to dismiss.[58] The legislation allocated the task of determining the fairness of the dismissal to industrial tribunals in the first instance, although this was subject to appeal to the forerunner of the EAT and to the higher courts.

As Collins has rightly pointed out, in order to understand how this task has been approached it is necessary to appreciate 'the predicament in which

---

[56] These were given special protection in the sense that fewer qualifications such as length of continuous service were imposed and in some cases interim relief was provided. Moreover, the substantive test of unfairness left little discretion to judges. If the employee can show that the employer had dismissed for an inadmissible reason, the dismissal will be automatically unfair.
[57] A later ILO Recommendation, No. 166 on Termination of Employment, expanded on this point. See Napier, above n 54.
[58] See, eg *Dobie v Burns International Security Services (UK) Ltd* [1984] IRLR 329.

courts and tribunals found themselves when called upon to apply the statute.' Moreover, as Collins has rightly stressed, the new statute went against the grain of the values and assumptions of the common law generally, such as autonomy, neutrality and formal equality, and particularly those values as they applied to termination of contracts.[59]

What needs to be added to the analysis of the core values of autonomy, neutrality and formal equality is a more explicit reference to the role of 'property' rights in the values and assumptions of the judges. The statute had introduced a legislative norm which challenged the basic values and assumptions of the judges about the 'property' rights paradigm at common law. The reason that neutrality and formal equality were viewed as appropriate was that they endorsed the 'property' rights assumptions of autonomy, and the reason that legislative measures as drafted were viewed as overly interventionist was that they appeared to reach too far into the 'property' rights of the employer to manage his own business and interfere with the employer's legitimate right to dispose of 'his' property. This perspective based on common law assumptions of the sole 'property' rights of employers resulted in a defensive response to any attempts to legislate a public policy requiring a more invasive review of employer's dismissal decisions.[60]

The evidence for this proposition can be found in a number of judicial interpretations of section 98(4). There is the evolution of a test of procedural fairness culminating in *Polkey* which allows employee's rights to procedural fair treatment to be subordinated to a test of the utility to management.[61] There is the evolution of the test of *British Home Stores* with its weak test of fact and reasonable investigation.[62] Furthermore, there is the weakness of the interpretation given to remedies both of reinstatement and compensation, particularly the compensation rules where procedural steps have been omitted by the employer.[63] For the purposes of this chapter, however, it will be more useful to look in detail at the judges' steadfast resistance to allowing

[59] Collins, *Justice in Dismissal*, above n 10, at 26. He also quite rightly pointed out that 'the fact that this abnegation in general leads to unbridled disciplinary power at the disposal of the employer did not weaken lawyers' faith in its appropriateness' (33).

[60] For an account of a similar defensive reaction of American judges to labour legislation threatening property rights, see J Atleson, *Values and Assumptions in American Labor Law*, above n 4.

[61] *Polkey v A E Dayton Services Ltd* [1987] IRLR 503.

[62] *British Home Stores Ltd v Burchill* [1978] IRLR 379. The EAT stated that in cases of dismissal for suspected misconduct, a tribunal need only find that the employer entertained a 'reasonable suspicion amounting to a belief in the guilt of the employee.' The EAT then went on to specify the following three-step test: first, 'there must be established by the employer the fact of that belief; that the employer did believe it.' Secondly, it must be shown 'that the employer had in his mind reasonable grounds upon which to sustain that belief.' The third requirement is that the employer must have 'carried out as much investigation into the matter as was reasonable in all the circumstances' before forming that belief.

[63] See excellent discussion in Collins, *Justic in Dismissal*, above n 10.

tribunals to impose a proportionality test on the merits of the employer's dismissal decisions despite its evident inclusion in the language of the statute.

This story is perhaps best told by starting with the interrelationship between economic and disciplinary dismissals.

Economic Dismissals in a 'Property' Rights Perspective

The weakest link in the substantive protections against unfair dismissals is to be found in the category of economic dismissals, ie those consisting of dismissals for redundancy or for reorganisation ('Some Other Substantial Reason' SOSR).[64] Some limits to the review of employer economic dismissal decisions were indicated in the ILO Recommendation 119/1963 but this does not fully explain the deference of the UK judiciary to employer economic decisions. A contributing factor may have been the enactment of the Redundancy Payments Act, with its legislative assumptions of non-interference with managerial discretion, in the period prior to the unfair dismissals legislation.[65] This tendency was reinforced by the inclusion of redundancy as a presumptively fair reason for dismissal, the general effect of which, as Collins has pointed out, was 'to grant the employer an immunity from the standards of unfair dismissal.'[66]

It seems likely that the substantive test for unfair dismissal for redundancy has been influenced in some measure by the implicit assumption of the redundancy payment provisions that the discretion of the employer in determining the numbers of employees to be made redundant is absolute.[67] This can be seen in the sweeping language used in the cases dealing with claims questioning the necessity for closures.[68] When the employer is facing economic difficulties, the judges seem instinctively to draw back from a close review of the employer's decision.

---

[64] See, eg S Anderman, *The Law of Unfair Dismissal* (3rd edn, London, Butterworths, 2001) ch 9; J Bowers and A Clarke, 'Unfair Dismissals and Managerial Prerogative: A Study of "Some Other Substantial Reason"' (1981) 10 *ILJ* 34; Deakin and Morris, above n 14, ch 5; Collins, Ewing and McColgan, above n 18, ch 5.

[65] A typical interpretation of the Act was that of Lord Denning in *Johnson v Nottinghamshire Combined Police Authority:* 'an employer is entitled to reorganise his business so as to improve its efficiency and in so doing to propose to his staff a change in the terms and condition of their employments: and to dispense with their services if they disagree': [1974] ICR 170.

[66] H Collins, 'The Meaning of Job Security' (1991) 20 *ILJ* 227, at 230.

[67] In *Orr v Vaughn* [1981] IRLR 63 the EAT, per Slynn J, underlined this point: 'at the end of the day, it is largely for the employer to decide, on the material which is available to the employer, what is to be done by way of reorganisation of the business; and it is for the employer to decide whether the requirement of the business for employees to carry out the particular work have ceased or diminished.'

[68] See *James W Cook & Co (Wivenhoe) v Tipper* [1990] IRLR 386, in which the court stated that 'it was not open to the court to investigate the commercial and economic reasons which

This can also be seen in the way a wide band of reasonableness test has been applied to cases of claims of unfair selection for redundancy under section 98(4). In this line of cases the courts have been troubled by the tribunals' role as reviewers of the employer's discretion. On the one hand, the courts realise that they cannot defer entirely to employer discretion.[69] On the other hand, if redundancy is really the reason for dismissal, the tribunals have been reluctant to apply too strict a test. The *via media* has been provided by a wide version of the 'range of reasonable employer responses' test for tribunal review of employer decisions. Yet even in the case of redundancy selection decisions there have been two judicial views about the width of the reasonableness test. On the one hand, there is a narrow version of the range, ie merely an observation that such a test must leave *some* room for a difference of view amongst reasonable employers.[70] On the other hand, some cases have articulated an extremely wide version of the range of reasonable employer responses test in the case of selection for redundancies. For example, in *Vickers v Smith Ltd*,[71] Cumming Bruce J stated:

> the test to be applied ... was not simply whether the tribunal thought that the employer's decision was wrong, but rather whether it was so wrong that no reasonable management could have arrived at the decision at which the management arrived.

This was reminiscent of the *Wednesbury* rule applied to public bodies for the purposes of judicial review or the *Bolam* rule applied to doctors for the purposes of determining the standard of care for medical negligence and appeared initially to apply only to redundancy selection dismissals. The interesting question is why this extremely deferential standard of substantive fairness for employers in economic dismissals has been transferred without modification to cases of disciplinary dismissals. There was an earlier case of disciplinary dismissals in which Philips J suggested a narrow version of the range test for tribunals in the case of disciplinary dismissals.[72] In *British Leyland UK Ltd v Swift*,[73] however, the wider version of the range test was

---

prompted the closure. [It] may be that the court should have this power, but it does not have [it] at present.' See too *Moon v Homeworthy Furniture Northern Ltd* [1976] IRLR 298, at 299 where the EAT said 'there could not and cannot be any investigation into the rights and wrongs of the declared redundancy.'

[69] This was prompted by the early test of automatically unfair selection and its continued prominence in that category of dismissal.

[70] See, eg *NC Watling & Co v Richardson* [1978] IRLR 255 in which the EAT held that the tribunal was entitled to find a selection for redundancy unfair when an employer ignored seniority considerations entirely. See too *Grundy (Teddington) Ltd v Willis* [1976] IRLR 118.

[71] [1977] IRLR 11.

[72] See *Trust House Forte Ltd v Aquilar* [1976] IRLR 251, EAT, at 254.

[73] [1981] IRLR 91, CA.

transplanted into the category of disciplinary dismissals test by Lord Denning.

Disciplinary Dismissals in a 'Property' Rights Perspective

The employer's decision to dismiss for disciplinary reasons is a foundation stone of managerial authority during the course of the employment relationship as well as a core right of the employer to dispose of its 'property.' The unfair dismissals legislation challenged this view by placing independent specialist tribunals into a position to determine standards of *reasonableness* for dismissal.

There were early indications that the tribunals were to be viewed as 'industrial juries' determining standards of reasonableness as a matter of fact[74] by applying an objective standard informed by their understanding of good industrial relations practice, accepting the good standards of industry operating at the relevant time and place,[75] subject only to misdirection and perversity. In the design of the legislation, this task was never meant simply to reflect existing managerial practice. The intention was to hold managers to a standard of *good* managerial practice. Tribunals were intended to apply a statutory standard which took into account 'equity and the substantial merits of the case.' This meant that they could question the reasonableness of the rules as well as the reasonableness of the employer's interpretation of the rules. They could also examine the severity of the dismissal. Most importantly, the determination of the equity standard was part of the fact-finding of the tribunals as part of the reasonableness test. This was stated initially by Sir John Donaldson in *Earl v Slater Wheeler* before the NIRC in 1972 and repeated by him in the Court of Appeal decision in *UCATT v Brain*[76] in 1981:

> where Parliament has directed a tribunal to have regard to equity a tribunal's duty is very plain. It has to look at the question in the round and without any regard for a lawyer's technicalities. It has to look at it in an employment and industrial relations context. It should therefore be very rare for any decision of an industrial tribunal to give rise to any issue of law, and where Parliament

---

[74] 'Whether someone has acted reasonably has always been a question of fact': see *UCATT v Brain* [1981] IRLR 224; see too *Piggot Bros Co Ltd v Jackson* [1991] IRLR 309.
[75] See, eg *Grundy (Teddington) Ltd v Willis* [1976] IRLR 118; see too *Williams v Compair Maxam Ltd* 1982] IRLR 83: 'the Industrial Tribunal is an industrial jury which brings to its task a knowledge of industrial relations both from the viewpoint of the employer and the employee. Matters of good industrial relations practice are not proved before an Industrial Tribunal as they would be proved before an ordinary court; the lay members are taken to know them. The lay members of the Industrial Tribunal bring to their task their expertise in the field where conventions and practices are of the greatest importance.'
[76] [1981] IRLR 224.

has given tribunals such a wide discretion, appellate courts should be very
slow to find that the tribunal had erred in law.

Yet the notion of a tribunal as a trier of the fact of reasonableness capable
of applying a test of proportionality based on its own industrial assessment
has not proved acceptable to the majority of courts. Some judges have
argued that the reason was purely pragmatic; a fear of 'palm tree justice,' ie
the variable treatment by tribunals of the question of fact and the development of inconsistent standards throughout the country.[77] That may have
been a contributory motive but a close look at the particular constraints
established by the courts to tribunal discretion under section 98(4) suggests
a second motive; a concern to defend the 'property' rights of the employer
as they manifest themselves in managerial prerogative.

The first decision of the House of Lords in an unfair dismissals case was
Devis & Sons Ltd v Atkins[78] in which it indicated considerable ambiva-
lence in defining the scope of the unfair dismissals protection against the
employer's exclusive right to dispose of its property as it wills. In the first
place, the Law Lords decided that the actual language of the statute directs
the tribunal to focus its attention upon the conduct of the employers, not
on whether the employee in fact suffered any injustice. This claimed to be a
literal reading of the statutory provision yet it proved to be rather selective.
It placed remarkably little weight upon the statute's requirement that the
reasonableness of the employer's decision was to be decided on the basis of
'equity and the substantial merits of the case.'[79]

The *Devis* decision set the stage for subsequent developments in the law
governing the standard of reasonableness. If the test of reasonableness was
to be concerned solely with the conduct of the employer and not the injustice to employees, it created the risk that the balancing test would be forever
skewed. The *Devis* rule appeared frequently in many decisions but its potential implications for the substantive test of fairness in disciplinary decisions
was made clear in 1981 when the Court of Appeal, in *British Leyland UK
Ltd v Swift*, introduced the concept of a wide band of reasonableness test.

---

[77] In *Williams v Compair Maxam Ltd* [1982] IRLR 83, Browne Wilkinson initially proposed,
in answer to this problem, providing greater guidelines to tribunals in the form of guidelines to
an expanded test of perversity.
[78] [1977] IRLR 314.
[79] In *Devis & Sons Ltd v Atkins* the Law Lords could accept that an employee was entitled to
fair warning that disobedience could or would result in dismissal under the predecessor of
s 98(4) and a failure to warn made the dismissal unfair. However, they were troubled by the
possibility that the evidence of the employee's possible fraudulent misconduct discovered by
the employer after the dismissal might lead to the employee being over-compensated. Yet they
chose to find an interpretation of the just and equitable test in s 123 to deny any compensation to the employee. In taking this view, the court drew directly upon the standards of
the common law of wrongful dismissal in interpreting the statutory provision governing
unfair dismissal. See Collins, *Justice in Dismissal,* above n 10, at 3. This meant that the court
in this instance also drew upon the property right assumptions of master-servant law.

The *Swift* case was one in which the industrial tribunal had applied a test of proportionality. Swift had served 18 years satisfactorily but was dismissed when the employer's tax disc was found on his own car. The tribunal found that the penalty was too severe for a minor offence. Lord Denning stated that the tribunal had applied the wrong test. The tribunal had said that they thought that 'a reasonable employer,' in their opinion would have considered a lesser penalty was appropriate. Lord Denning said that they had to say that 'no reasonable employer' would have reached that decision. He then reviewed the facts and charged the tribunal with not taking into account all relevant considerations.

Lord Denning's proposition clearly helps to reduce the authority of tribunals to apply a test of proportionality to unfair dismissals.[80] In addition, the Court of Appeal substituted its decision on the facts for that of the tribunal. The court allowed the appeal and held that the dismissal was fair. It did not remit to a tribunal and allow that tribunal to decide on the basis of a correct direction in law.[81]

Shortly afterwards, Browne Wilkinson J attempted to restore what he thought was a more balanced approach to the constraints the courts would place upon tribunals. In *Iceland Frozen Foods*,[82] he suggested guidelines to the interpretation of the mainstream issue of reasonableness in the case of conduct and capability dismissal decisions incorporating a more bounded version of the range of reasonable employer responses test.

Browne Wilkinson J thought the guidelines in *Iceland* would allow a better balance between injustice to employees and employer decisions as well as providing an objective approach to the assessment of the conduct of employers. It is true that his test endorsed the substitution constraint; it explicitly prevented tribunals from deciding what they subjectively thought that the employer should have done in the circumstances. This in itself could be taken merely as a reminder to tribunals that they must take an objective approach to the employer's dismissal decision without preventing them from deciding that a harsh decision was objectively unfair because of its harshness.

Browne Wilkinson in *Iceland* also thought that his formula would avoid the excess of the approach of the *Vickers v Smith* test which appeared to require a showing that the employer had behaved perversely in dismissing the employee. He stated:

Although the statement of principle in *Vickers v Smith* is entirely accurate in law, for the reasons given in *Watling v Richardson*, we think industrial tribunals will do well not to direct themselves by reference to it. The statement

---

[80] See Collins, *Justice in Dismissal,* above n 10, Collins and freedland, above n 10.
[81] Lord Denning seemed to be affronted by the fact that theft of property could be condoned by an industrial tribunal.
[82] [1982] IRLR 439.

in *Vickers v Smith* is capable of being misunderstood so as to require so high a degree of unreasonableness to be shown that nothing short of a perverse decision to dismiss can be held as fair.[83]

Brown Wilkinson J still hoped to leave to employment tribunals a measure of control over reasonableness as an issue of fact. He thought that he had ensured that there was an objective minimum test of the reasonable employer. His formula proposed that:

> the function of the industrial tribunal, as an industrial jury, is to determine whether in the particular circumstances of each case the decision to dismiss the employee fell within the band of reasonable responses which *a reasonable employer* might have adopted (*emphasis added*).

He retained the views he had expressed in *Compair Maxam* and thought they could be applied more generally to section 98(4) using the *Iceland Frozen Foods* guidelines.[84]

One feature of a test of reasonableness in section 98(4) is that it does presuppose *some* band of reasonableness. The issue is how wide the band is to be and who is to decide that question. Browne Wilkinson's formula, if read closely, would allow tribunals to impose constraints on the width of the band of the reasonableness test and even allow a proportionality test to determine its width. He seems, however, to have under-estimated the hostage to fortune created by the 'substitution' point as well as over-estimated his powers of persuasion *vis-à-vis* his colleagues in the Court of Appeal.

Browne Wilkinson's formulation in *Iceland Frozen Foods* has had as little success as the original statutory provision in creating a balanced treatment of employer decisions by tribunals. On the one hand, the tribunals have interpreted the band too widely using a loose standard and these decisions have not been appealed or have not always been overturned when they have been appealed.[85] Alternatively, when some tribunals have applied a robust standard of reasonableness to harsh and disproportionate employer decisions to dismiss they have been found to have made a subjective decision and have failed to remind themselves to decide not what they would have done but what they think that objectively a reasonable employer would have done.[86] Often, it seems that the tribunals have in fact applied what they consider to be an objective test but their real shortcoming in the eyes of the appeal judges is that they did not apply a wide enough range in their 'range of reasonableness' test.

---

[83] *Ibid.*
[84] In *Compair Maxam*, Browne Wilkinson had proposed guidelines in the more limited context of a widened test for *perversity*.
[85] See, eg *Haddon v Van Den Bergh Foods Ltd*, below n 87.
[86] See, eg *British Leyland v Swift; PO v Foley; HSBC Bank plc v Madden* [2000] IRLR 827.

Morison J drew attention to this point in Haddon[87] and even gave support to the language of *Iceland Frozen Foods,* pointing out that the problem of reciting 'the mantra' of the range test had produced the result that 'it has led tribunals into applying what amounts to a perversity test, which as is clear from *Iceland* itself, was not its purpose.' In fact, had he wished, he could probably have reversed the tribunal decision in *Haddon* on grounds of perversity but he was after bigger game. He therefore proposed that it would be better to go back to the language of the statute. In a sense, he gambled to achieve an interpretation of the statute that would do justice to its original purpose, but his gamble failed.

One difficulty with Morison J's approach, as the Court of Appeal in *Foley* correctly observed, is that the test in the statute is a reasonableness test and therefore presupposes *some* band of reasonable employer responses. Yet, the court in *Foley,* led by Mummery LJ, also revealed its lack of interest in dealing with the problem that Morison had illuminated, ie, the tendency of employment tribunals to apply too wide a range of reasonableness to employer dismissal decisions and therefore eschewing their role to apply minimum standards of reasonableness as stipulated in the *Iceland Frozen Foods* guidelines. Mummery LJ insisted that there was an objective test implicit in the range of reasonableness test and that test was higher than a perversity test but he gave little support for that latter proposition. He said nothing about the tendency of tribunals to be wary of applying a reasonable employer test to harsh employer decisions because of the fear of either deciding what they would do themselves or failing to respect the judicial view of the width of the range of reasonable employer responses. He was more forthcoming on the 'substitution point.' He acknowledged that if the tribunal applied the right test in respect of the band of reasonableness test, 'they are in effect substituting their judgment for that of the employer.'[88]

The need is to find a way, now that the *Iceland Frozen Food* formula, as interpreted by the courts, has palpably failed in its objective, to convince tribunals that harsh decisions by employers can be viewed as unreasonable under the range test.[89] The problem with the court's approach is that it makes the tribunals fearful of applying a limited range test and instead pushes them to a perversity test of the employer's decision. If they decide that because an employer's decision is harsh it is unfair they run the risk of being overturned on appeal for their failure to refrain from deciding for

---

[87] *Haddon v Van Den Bergh Foods Ltd* [1999] IRLR 672, EAT. See discussion in Collins and Freedland, above n 10.

[88] [2000] IRLR 827, para 53. He distinguished between tribunals substituting their decisions for that of the employer, which was acceptable, and tribunals substituting themselves for the employer, which was not.

[89] For one suggestion see Anderman, above n 14.

themselves what the employer should have done or that they have not applied an appropriate band of reasonableness test.[90] On occasion, the EAT does find that the band of reasonableness has been too widely interpreted and is upheld by the Court of Appeal.[91] But such cases are relatively rare.

The irony is that the language of section 98(4) is compatible with the guidelines in *Iceland Frozen Foods* if they are interpreted properly but the tribunals have not been allowed or have been inadequately directed to apply these guidelines.[92] By interpreting the language of section 98(4) in this way, the judiciary have precluded the possibility that the statutory provision could be used to restrict the exercise of employer 'property' rights according to the intentions of the legislators.

UNFAIR DISMISSAL LAW AND 'PROPERTY' RIGHTS IN OTHER EU COUNTRIES

Unfair Dismissal Legislation

The labour laws of a number of fellow European states have devised doctrines and remedies that are more invasive of the supposed 'property' rights of employers in respect of unfair dismissals and these are applied by the judges, on the whole, in a manner consistent with the purposes of the legislation. This can be seen in the standard of the substantive unfair dismissal test that invariably allows the courts, often the labour courts, to apply a test of proportionality to the employer's decision to dismiss.[93]

The European approach is also characterised by a greater willingness to insist upon a more effective remedy of reinstatement for unfair dismissals. A good example is offered by the Italian *Statuto di Lavoratori*, Article 18, which provides that if an employee claims that he or she has been unfairly dismissed, there is a right to interim relief until the tribunal pronounces upon the fairness or unfairness of the dismissal in accordance with the Individual Dismissals Law of 1996. Moreover, there is a minimum penalty for unfair dismissal of five month's pay which applies even if the employee is back at work in less than five months.

---

[90] In *Sainsbury's Supermarket Ltd v Hitt* [2003] IRLR 23, the Court of Appeal decided to extend the range of reasonableness-non-substitution constraint to the issue of a reasonable investigation. This, of course, would reduce the substantive test of disciplinary dismissals to a bare minimum. However, in *Panama v London Borough of Hackney* [2003] IRLR 278, a differently constituted Court of Appeal reiterated that the reasonable investigation requirement of the *Burchell* case had a minimum objective test. See, too, Elias J's views in *A v B* [2003] IRLR 405.
[91] See, eg *Panama v London Borough of Hackney* [2003] IRLR 278.
[92] See Anderman, above n 14.
[93] See, generally, B Hepple, 'European Rules on Dismissals Law?' (1997) *Comp Labour Law J* 204; see, too, R Blanpain and T Hanami (eds), *Employment Security: Law and Practice* (Deventer, Kluwer, 1994).

Reinstatement is the natural remedy for all firms of more than 15 employees and a failure to reinstate carries with it a penalty of compensation for every day of the continuing default. The existence of a reinstatement remedy for unfair dismissal where the firm is over 15 employees is significant. It indicates that for undertakings which are below a certain size, it is realistic to maintain a sole ownership perspective to some degree. For undertakings above a certain size, however, a sole ownership perspective is thought be inappropriate. Consequently, the exclusive right of the employer to terminate employment for the fault of the employee can be restricted in the interests of the humanity and dignity of the subordinate worker that the law must safeguard.[94] Wedderburn has drawn attention to the wider values built into the Statuto:

> the Statuto constituted, in individual terms, it has been said 'a primitive version of a Charter for the habeas corpus for the worker ... while in other provisions it introduced more specifically a nucleus of modification inside the normative structure of the individual employment relationship itself' (Arts 13, 18). The Amendment of the Civil Code concerning a worker's right to the 'job' for which he was hired, and to higher tasks (and pay) under certain conditions, went to the core of employment law. So too did the legislative control of disciplinary procedures (Art 7).[95]

It is difficult for an outsider to the Italian system to know whether to characterise Article 18 of the Statuto as creating a property right in the 'job' or simply as a forcefully imposed responsibility upon management not to dismiss an employee for misconduct or indiscipline without an independent assessment of the degree of fault by an impartial tribunal under the 1996 Individual Dismissals Law. At all events, it amounts to a significant restriction upon not only the managerial prerogative but also the sole property rights of the undertaking with more than 15 employees.

German and Scandinavian legislation place procedural obstacles in the way of dismissals involving employee representatives and the use of arbitration.[96] In these countries, not only is the standard set out in the legislation consistent with a robust fairness test; the pattern of judicial interpretation tends to be consistent with the values of the legislation.[97]

---

[94] Article 18, not entirely unexpectedly, has been a target for reform by the Berluscloni government, but a referendum in July 2003 resulted in continued support for the provision.
[95] Lord Wedderburn, 'The Italian Workers Statute: British Reflections on a High Point of Legal protection' (1990) 19 *ILJ* 154; also in Lord Wedderburn, *Employment Rights in Britain and Europe; Selected Papers in Labour Law* (London; Lawrence and Wishart, 1991), at p 239.
[96] See Hepple, above n 93, at 210–12.
[97] See, eg, M Weiss, 'Germany' in Blanpain and Hanami, above n 93, at 146; Adlercreutz, 'Sweden' in *International Encyclopaedia of Labour and Labour Relations* (Deventer, Kluwer, 1990) 266.

The duties of civil law judges can partly explain this phenomenon. They are required to apply legislation according to its purpose and seem to have embraced the concept of proportionality as an integral feature of the unfair dismissal test.[98] It would be difficult to imagine civilian judges adopting a standard as loose as a wide range of reasonableness test. The reason for this is partly in their training and partly the way Continental systems as a whole have moved away from a view of the employer as the sole owner of the 'property' rights in the firm.

The explanation for this approach to the property rights of employers lies partly with the development of Continental labour legislation. In post-war Continental Europe, labour legislation experienced none of the inhibitions of 'collective laissez-faire.' From an early stage, even the Scandinavians with their strong trade unions and extensive collective bargaining, took a pragmatic view that labour legislation could operate as a natural complement to collective bargaining.[99] At all events, the majority of EU Member States have been prepared to recognise that the powers of management are supposed to be directed to the promotion of the enterprise and their powers over the enterprise are understood to be modified by legislation.[100] 'Ownership' or 'property' in the sense of the right freely to exclude and to control people in employment have not been conceptualised as belonging solely to the employer. Moreover, the overlap between labour and company law on the Continent offered a further explanation.

Labour Law, Company Law and 'Property' Rights in the EU

In most of the Continental Member States of the EU, the 'property' rights of the employer *vis-a-vis* employees are curbed more comprehensively by the legal framework for company law. Legislation establishes information, consultation and participation rights of workers in the enterprise as well as individual statutory employment rights such as unfair dismissal protection.[101]

The Continental image of ownership has been modified by the fact that employee representatives have long been involved in the legal decision-making

---

[98] The French Code du travail L 122–43, for example, will find a dismissal decision unfair where it is shown to be clearly disproportionate to the employee's fault.

[99] See, eg R Nielsen, *Employers' Prerogatives: In a European and Nordic Perspective* (Copenhagen, Handelshogskolan Forlag, 1996).

[100] See, eg A Supiot, 'The Dogmatic Foundations of the Market' (2000) 29 *ILJ* 321.

[101] See, eg Annex to EC Commission's Proposal for a Council Directive Establishing a general Framework for Informing and Consulting Employees in the European Community (COM (1998) 612 final 98/0315 (SYN)); see too Davignon Report, *European Systems of Worker Involvement with regard to the European Company Statute*; P Davies, 'Workers on the Board of the European Company' (2003) 32 *ILJ* 75; O Edstrom, 'Involvement of Employees in Private Enterprises in Four Nordic Countries' (2002) *Scandinavian Studies in Law* 159.

of the enterprise. The socialist, social democratic, social catholic[102] and social market thinking in Continental European countries has responded to the separation of managerial power from share ownership by ensuring that company law reflects de jure the way managerial power is regulated and moderated by employee consultation and participation. In some models, collective bargaining is excluded from company law,[103] but in some models, collective bargaining is integrated into company law.[104] None of the Continental legal models cede much ultimate managerial decisional power to employee representatives, but they do recognise that employees have a 'stake' in the ownership of the enterprise. The 'enterprise' is viewed as the economic entity which brings together human, physical and intellectual assets as a going concern.[105]

This European concept of shared power in an enterprise is incompatible with a sole ownership paradigm. The shareholders are acknowledged as the owners of the shares of the enterprise but this is not equated with all ownership rights of the enterprise. Instead, the bundle of rights and responsibilities that is associated with ownership of the firm is viewed in less absolute terms. Owing to the legal integration of employee representatives in the organs of company decision-making and Works Councils in some form of consultation or co-decision process, it is difficult for judges or legislators to view the company as owned solely by the employer. This concept of significant limitations on the exclusive property rights of employers may help to explain the stronger substantive norms and remedial robustness of European standards of unfair dismissal.

As we know, this picture contrasts rather sharply with conditions in the United Kingdom. There have been some inroads made into sole ownership rights by 'home grown' UK labour laws. The National Minimum Wage, the recognition laws and the requirements for consultation over pension schemes with employee representatives offer examples. Moreover, EU social policy has required legally enforceable consultation over redundancies, health and safety and TUPE transfers as well as the information and consultation obligations in the European Works Council Directive 94/45/EC for enterprises which have a European dimension and in the European company. Furthermore, the Information and Consultation Directive 2002/14/EU will soon be implemented in the United Kingdom.

---

[102] See, eg P Misner, *Social Catholicism in Europe: From the Onset of Industrialisation to the First World War* (London, Darton, Longman and Todd, 1991).
[103] See the restrictions on employee boardroom representatives under the German co-determination system.
[104] See, eg the Swedish Law of Workers on the Board in which the worker board members are viewed as representatives of the trade unions.
[105] See, eg S Deakin, 'Enterprise-Risk: The Juridical Nature of the Firm Revisited' (2003) 32 *ILJ* 97, at 98.

The endurance of the sole property rights image of employers in UK labour law in the face of these developments may also be reinforced by the continued separation of UK company law from these labour law regulatory developments. As is well known, UK company law has retained an assumption that the 'company' is solely 'owned' by the shareholders. UK company law has not adjusted its concept of the 'company' to incorporate 'the idea of the enterprise as a productive entity.'[106] As Deakin rightly points out, UK company law offers no legal concept of the employer which adequately expresses the complex social and economic entity which is the enterprise.

Of course, labour law itself is directed at the regulation of the powers of management in the context of the productive enterprise. Indeed, the specific laws governing termination of employment have not only established individual rights and remedies against employer power; they have also created rights to information and consultation for employee representatives in management decisions on such issues as collective redundancies and TUPE transfers. In addition, they offer legal support for collective bargaining that indicates acceptance of joint rule-making in certain areas of management decision-making. These labour laws operate not only as de facto limits on employer power in the form of individual employment rights; they also on occasion enfranchise employee representatives in the institutional processes of managerial, ie company, decision-making.

However, this type of legal regulation has rarely if ever been incorporated explicitly in company law.[107] For example, there is little evidence of the array of director's duties being redefined to include, say, a duty of care to observe labour law norms. Labour law obligations have not yet disturbed the company law image of shareholder 'ownership' of the enterprise in any meaningful way. The new Works Councils legislation may ultimately change this picture but the endurance of the concept of the business as being solely owned by the employer has hitherto been reinforced by the evolution of a UK company law hermetically sealed off from labour law developments.

CONCLUSION

The unwillingness of UK judges to allow tribunals to apply a robust substantive test to unfair dismissals seems to be based not only upon a concern about its effects but also upon a reflexive defence of the employer's exclusive

---

[106] *Ibid.*

[107] Companies Act 1985, s 309, although requiring directors to have regard to the interests of the company's employees as well as the interests of its members, has done little to integrate company law and labour law, in part because the judges are all too aware that it is essentially a procedural requirement; employees cannot enforce it and it offers no guidance to directors on how to balance competing interests.

'property' rights in jobs. This judicial defence of property rights results in a reinforcement of the prerogative power of employers in a way that does little justice to the parliamentary intention to provide employees with a particular standard of protection against such powers.

The unfair dismissals legislation was introduced explicitly to prevent the misuse of power by employers when dismissing employees, by placing limits upon the power of management to make arbitrary and ill-considered disciplinary dismissals. Its purpose was to end a legal framework that allocated excessive power to managerial prerogative in employment deriving from the employer's property rights. Redressing the balance of power in this way was viewed partly as a means of recognising the entitlement of a citizen of a democratic society and partly as a useful method to reform management and collective procedures and thereby reduce disputes in industry. The insistence upon a wide range of reasonable employer responses test in section 98(4) has thwarted that parliamentary intention.

In the *Relaxion* case[108] Lord Nichols reminded judges of the need to interpret legislation carefully in its context and in the light of its purpose. Some judges have clearly understood the need to alter the current interpretation of section 98(4) to bring it more in line with the legislative purpose and for an acceptance of the judicial role in effectuating that purpose.[109] Others, however, seem unaware that the retention of a wide range of reasonableness test may fall outside the parameters of reasonable interpretation of legislative purpose and legislative context.

Mummery LJ made this eminently clear in *PO v Foley*[110] when he quoted the following statement in support of his insistence on *leaving unchanged* the existing wide range test in section 98(4):

> The courts are ever mindful that their constitutional role in this field is interpretive. They must abstain from any course which might have the appearance of judicial legislation. A statute is expressed in language approved and enacted by the legislature.

The inability of judges to see that the current interpretation of section 98(4) *is* a form of judicial legislation is evidence of their underlying assumptions about exclusive employer property rights in the contract of employment. They seem unable to adjust to the reality of labour legislation as an intended moderator of employer property rights.

The problem identified by Morrison in *Haddon* and the issues raised by the case of *PO v Foley* have yet to be addressed by the House of Lords.

---

[108] *Relaxion Group plc v Rhys Harper* [2003] IRLR 484, HL.
[109] See, eg efforts of Lindley J in *Midland Bank plc v Madden* [2000] IRLR 288, discussed by Collins and Freedland above n 10.
[110] [2000] IRLR 827, at para 12. Ironically, that statement was made by Lord Nicholls.

The Law Lords could adjust the pattern of judicial interpretation of section 98(4) by holding that the range of reasonableness test should be kept within narrow limits. Stressing the importance of the need to take into account 'equity and the substantial merits of the case' in tribunal decisions would be one way to achieve this aim. Their decision in *Polkey* indicated that they can interpret section 98(4) to raise the level of protection for employee procedural rights to fairness, even if it also showed that they tended to view employee rights through the lens of managerial efficiency. Unfortunately, their willingness to maintain relatively high procedural standards has tended not to carry over into their interpretation of substantive standards of fairness of dismissals.

If there is no sign of self-imposed judicial change, what will it take to produce a change in the UK pattern of judicial interpretation of section 98(4)? Despite all the arguments for deregulation, the case for adequate legislative protection of individuals against arbitrary dismissals by employers is as strong as ever. The arguments are based on the moral right of individuals to be fairly treated in cases of dismissals. Fair treatment of individual employees by management helps to remove a ground for resentment by the workforce collectively and contributes to a more efficient management.

One possibility, even if a remote one, is a legislative amendment of section 98(4) to spell out that it is a 'just cause' test in which tribunals apply a proportionality test to ensure that arbitrary dismissals cannot be found to be fair by employment tribunals.[111] Another possibility, less remote but still not likely to occur in the short term, is that the European influence can one day produce a change in the test of unfair dismissals.

Over the next decade, the introduction of employee representation in Works Councils may help to modify the rather absolutist view of employer property rights which is sometimes assumed by UK judges. Moreover, as Bob Hepple has suggested, it may be possible to add an obligation on the employer to inform and consult with employee representatives over *individual* dismissals under European law by adding it explicitly or by interpretation to the category of management decisions adversely affecting the interests of workers.[112] Finally, European social policy may one day produce a Directive on individual dismissals to improve the minimum standards of fairness in dismissals in the United Kingdom.

Until that time, the judicial interpretation of section 98(4) will stand as a notable example of property rights-based judicial resistance to legislative standards crying out for legislative reform or judicial modification.

[111] See B Hepple, 'The Fall and Rise of Unfair Dismissal' in W McCarthy (ed), *Legal Intervention in Industrial Relations: Gains and Losses* (Oxford, Blackwell, 1992) 95.
[112] B Hepple, above n 93.

6

Changing Perspectives Upon the Employment Relationship in British Labour Law

PAUL DAVIES AND MARK FREEDLAND

INTRODUCTION: THREE CHANGING PERSPECTIVES

THE COMMITMENT OF the contributors to this symposium is to engage in predictive speculation or forward-looking thinking about the future of labour law. In 1986 Bob Hepple published an article which did precisely that with regard to the core concept around which British labour law is organised, that of the individual employment relationship.[1] That core concept was then, is still, and perhaps ever shall be, constructed by British employment law in terms of the individual employment contract. In that ground-breaking article, Hepple argued that this equation was not a necessary one, and not a productive one. He advocated a shift of the frame of reference from that of the employment contract to that of the relationship itself. He regarded this as a way of creating a more inclusive core category for employment law. In this paper we suggest ways of revisiting that core conceptual territory in light of the many changes since 1986 in the functioning of the labour market, in the practice of management of production of goods and services, and in the outlook and objectives of governments and their perceptions as to how to realise those objectives through employment law and policy.

---

[1] BA Hepple, 'Restructuring Employment Rights' (1986) 15 *ILJ* 69. In that article, his special concern was with the form of legislation which protects workers, and he argued against the use of the contract of service, suggesting instead a broad concept of the 'employment relationship.' He has expressed the view to us, in very helpful comments upon an earlier draft of this chapter, that the legislature has preferred an ad hoc response to the problems which that article pointed out, and that a principled response to them would now be appropriate, including one which would deal with the requirement of mutuality which leaves many casual workers unprotected (as in the key case of *Carmichael v National Power Plc* [1998] ICR 1167).

Our revisiting of the legal analysis of the employment relationship pursues a somewhat different approach from that of Hepple's 1986 article. On the one hand, we are less committed than Hepple was in that article to the superseding or rejection of the contractual analysis. We are more agnostic as to whether or not the core legal construction of the employment relationship should be an essentially contractual one. But we are very clear that if that core construction is to continue to be in contractual form, as it has so far obdurately persisted in being, this has to be on the basis of an extensive reconceptualisation in various other respects. Here, we seek to go further than the various writings, including our own, which have concentrated particularly upon one very prominent aspect of the contractual analysis of the employment relationship, namely the scope of the contractual category in terms of the persons in work or business relations who are included in it or excluded from it.

In this chapter we seek to identify the aspect of personal scope as one of three dimensions of the employment contract or relationship, each of which deserves extensive re-examination. Those three aspects are (1) the definition and conceptualisation of the party providing services, that is to say the employee or worker, (2) the definition and conceptualisation of the party demanding services, that is to say the employer or employing entity, and (3) the analysis and understanding of the nature of the relations between them. Our suggestion is that each of these three aspects of the employment relationship or contract as understood by employment law would benefit from reconsideration in light of recent and current changes or developments in the working of the labour market, in the patterns of organisation of business structures, in the styles or methods of human resource management, and in the policy orientations of employment law.

Two further preliminary or introductory points remain to be made. First, we identify this process of 'rethinking' as a partly descriptive one but a more than slightly normative one. In its descriptive aspect it draws attention to some respects in which employment practice and employment law may be undergoing a series of changes or re-orientations in the three dimensions which we have identified. However, our concerns will also be the normative ones of pointing out various ways in which the legal response is an insufficient one which fails to take appropriate account of changes or developments in the commercial or organisational environment of employment relationships. Our normative stance is one which seeks to reconcile the worker's claims to autonomy, dignity and security with the needs of the employing enterprise for efficiency in the performance of its institutional tasks and maintaining its viability or profitability.

Secondly, we see this analysis and critique as being one which seeks not merely to identify but also to interlink arguments or themes arising in the three respective spheres of (1) the worker, (2) the employer, and (3) the relations between them. Our assertion is not merely that there are significant transformations going on in each of these three spheres, but that those transformations are interconnected and can be related to each other. Our order of proceeding will be first to consider changes in the practical and legal formulation of the employment relationship in each of those three spheres in turn, and finally to discuss the possibilities of synthesis between arguments arising in those respective areas.

THE WORKER

The prevailing account of the changing identity of the worker in current employment practice concentrates upon phenomena or tendencies which can be grouped together under the heading of casualisation.[2] The whole business of identifying the worker is, of course, a matter of recognising a person as being in a particular relationship which qualifies him or her as having the capacity of a worker; the term 'worker' depicts a relational capacity, as surely as does that of 'spouse' or 'cousin.' The prevailing account identifies an evolution by which the worker is more likely than was previously the case, let us say 20 years ago, to be in a work relationship which is a casual one in the sense especially that it is temporary, and perhaps also part-time, and that the mutual commitment between the worker and the employing enterprise is a correspondingly transient one.

That development falls within the larger category of 'vertical disintegration of production' which Hugh Collins so powerfully identified in the early 1990s as a challenge to the coherence of application of employment protection legislation.[3] At that stage, casualisation was the principal manifestation of a trend towards disintegration in which workers were externalised from the producing enterprise (which could easily result in their losing their legal identity as employees coming within the scope of employment protection legislation). Ten or more years later, this picture seems to have changed again; a more insidious form of disintegration seems to have become important, whereby the worker is more strongly individuated, in a more atomised pattern of relations *within* the producing enterprise, than was previously the case. The worker within the firm is often now subjected to a more elaborately personalised set of incentives and risks than in the previously typical pattern. We pursue this argument in greater detail later under the heading of the employment relationship; at this point it suffices to indicate an emergent phenomenon of *internal* disintegration of production which

---

[2] Compare S Fredman, 'Labour Law in Flux: The Changing Composition of the Workforce' (1997) 26 *ILJ* 337.
[3] H Collins, 'Independent Contractors and the Challenge of Vertical Disintegration to Employment Protection Laws' (1990) 10 *OJLS* 353.

occurs alongside the process of mainly *external* disintegration which was previously described.

The potential implications of that development or emergent phenomenon, for the legal conceptualisation of the worker, are very considerable. Our concern as labour lawyers with the phenomenon of external disintegration has been with the way in which it turns employees into ostensibly independent contractors. It may well be that we need to reflect upon a parallel transformation whereby workers are placed in a situation which is much more like the reality of independent contracting while continuing to be styled and categorised as dependent employees. The cumulative effect of both external and internal disintegration is to present an even deeper challenge than has hitherto been perceived to a system of employment law essentially premised upon a deep and fundamental distinction between the dependent employee and the independent contractor, and targeted almost exclusively upon the dependent employment relationship. It will be useful to say something about the legal response to external disintegration and to internal disintegration respectively.

So far as external disintegration is concerned, there has been a significant legal response, but it has been only a partial one. Some pieces of employment legislation have adopted broad and inclusive categories as to their personal scope. This is true of the various types of legislation against discrimination in employment, which deploy a very broad and inclusive notion of 'person employed'[4] and it is also true of some post-1997 legislation, notably the National Minimum Wage Act 1998,[5] the Working Time Regulations 1998 (SI 1998/1833),[6] and the Part-time Workers (Prevention of Less Favourable Treatment) Regulations 2000 (SI 2000/1551),[7] which invoke the only slightly less inclusive notion of the 'worker' as statutorily defined. However, this extension of the personal scope of new employment legislation has been very far from complete. Some of it has occurred only under the pressure of requirements to implement EC legislation, and even that pressure has latterly been resisted as far as possible, as witness the reversion to the narrower 'employee' category in the Fixed-term Employees (Prevention of Less Favourable Treatment) Regulations 2002 (SI 2002\2034).[8]

Moreover, many of the core items of individual employment protection legislation, such as the unfair dismissal legislation[9] and the Transfer of

---

[4] Sex Discrimination Act 1975, s 82(1); Race Relations Act 1976, s 78(1), Disability Discrimination Act 1995, s 68(1) (definition of 'employment').
[5] See s 54(3) (definition of 'worker').
[6] See eg 2(1) (definition of 'worker').
[7] See eg 1(1) (definition of 'worker').
[8] The confining of the scope of the Regulations to the category of 'employee' is effected by the Employment Act 2002, s 45, under the authority of which the Regulations are made.
[9] See Employment Rights Act 1996, s 94(1).

Undertakings (Protection of Employment) Regulations 1981 (SI 1981/1794) ('TUPE'),[10] remain confined to the narrower category of employees. If one takes the view that the category of 'worker' now forms the general outline category for employment legislation, then it is undoubtedly the case that there is a two-tier system within that general category, with 'employees' as the fully protected group and the 'other workers' as the marginally protected group. The government acquired powers under section 23 of the Employment Relations Act 1999 to close this gap by secondary legislation, but appears increasingly less inclined to use those powers.[11]

The picture is a similarly mixed one so far as collective labour legislation is concerned. The trade union recognition provisions introduced in 1999 extend to the wider category of 'workers'[12]; but the restriction to 'employees' of the core rights against detriment or dismissal on the grounds of trade union membership,[13] or against dismissal of those taking industrial action,[14] remains in place as an arguably egregious stratification of the law relating to freedom of association.

Charting the legal response or lack of response to the *internal* disintegration of the concept of the worker within the firm is more difficult, because internal disintegration is itself a more subtle development than that of external disintegration. Simon Deakin has effectively shown[15] that the whole notion of the 'employee' as an essentially homogeneous category is itself, far from being a perpetual and self-evident truth of employment practice or employment legislation, instead largely an illusion fostered by the architecture of the social security legislation of the post-1945 welfare state. But, even if artificially fostered, that tendency towards homogeneity or uniformity of the concept of the employee remained evident for the succeeding 40 years both in employment practice and employment law.

However, that trend was first halted and then reversed from the early 1980s onwards. An increasing de-collectivisation of the negotiation of terms and conditions of employment was part of an increasingly powerful centrifugal force exerted upon the stereotype of the 'standard' contract of employment. This became the vehicle for an increasingly diverse spectrum

---

[10] See eg 2(1) (definition of 'employee').

[11] See Department of Trade and Industry, *Review of the Employment Relations Act 1999* (URN 03/606 February 2003) 5.

[12] See Trade Union and Labour Relations (Consolidation) Act (TULR(C)A) 1992, Sch A1, paras 1, 165, referring to s 296(1) of the principal Act. (The extent of the exception for contracts between a worker and a person who is a 'professional client' of the worker is currently the subject of significant litigation and debate.)

[13] See TULRE(C)A 1992 (as subsequently amended), s 146.

[14] *Ibid* (as subsequently amended), ss 237–39.

[15] See S Deakin 'The Evolution of the Contract of Employment, 1900 to 1950: The Influence of the welfare state' in N Whiteside and R Salais (eds), *Governance, Industry and Labour Markets in Britain and France: The Modernising state in the Mid-Twentieth Century* (London, Routledge, 1998).

of employment arrangements within the employing enterprise, between extremes of, on the one hand, employment as a form of proprietorship of the employing enterprise or deep investment in it, and of, on the other hand, employment as a form of precarious daily or hourly provision of labour. It is unnecessary at this point to identify whether and how far all this amounted to a reversion to a pre-welfare-state formation of the labour market, suffice it to observe the extent to which the unificatory conception of the employee which underlay much of the practice of employment relations has thereby progressively been undermined.

What has been the legal response to this phenomenon? During the 1980s and early 1990s, employment legislation was of course positively contributing to this de-homogenising tendency. With hindsight one can begin to see how the legislation of the 1980s and early 1990s,[16] ensuring the portability and individuation of pension arrangements, plays an important part in this story. Latterly a degree of legislative reversal is apparent. The Part-time Workers and Fixed-term Employees Regulations[17] are significant in this respect, although rather qualified in their effect. One could regard the judicial formulation of the implied obligation of trust and confidence as an enterprise of reharmonisation of the core conception of the contract of employment. If so, its extrusion from the area of termination of employment describes the limitedness of that set of intentions. We proceed to turn our attention to the second focus of our argument, that of the issues concerning the formulation and conceptualisation of the employer.

THE EMPLOYER

Debate about defining the 'personal scope' of the employment relationship has focused to a very large extent on the 'supply side' of the contract. Should the party on that side of the contract be defined as the 'employee,' the 'worker,' something wider, in all or some cases? On the 'demand' side, at first sight the issue has seemed much less troublesome, though by no means free from debate. The 'employer' is simply the counterparty in whatever range of contracts is defined on the supply side as coming within the scope of labour law. However, on closer inspection it is possible to identify two broad areas where the definition of the employer has raised difficult problems for either judiciary or legislature, problems which in some ways are even more intractable than those raised by the search for an appropriate definition on the supply side.

---

[16] Especially significant in this respect is the Pension Schemes Act 1993, s 160: 'Terms of contracts of service or schemes restricting choice to be void.' See our concluding remarks below pp 157–58.
[17] See above, nn 7, 8.

The identification of these two problems takes as their point of departure the perception of Otto Kahn-Freund that 'the principal purpose of labour law is to regulate, to support and to restrain the power of management and the power of organised labour.'[18] As Kahn-Freund recognised, 'management' is an abstraction and the bearers of management powers as against workers may be many and various: 'a foreman on the assembly line, a production manager, a factory manager, or a board of directors or head of department'.[19] The purpose of the term 'employer', certainly in individual employment law and often more broadly in labour law, is to capture all the relevant bearers of management powers, so as to bring them within the fold of regulation. In the two situations to be discussed, it is doubtful whether the definition of 'employer' succeeds in achieving this objective.

The two problem areas can be defined in the following ways. The first is where it is possible to identify a coherent managerial unit, which one might expect to be recognised as the employer, but in fact the definition of the 'employer' captures only a part of that unit. This arises where the managerial unit is not recognised in law as a single entity but rather consists of a number of distinct legal entities which, however, are under common ownership and control. The prototypical example is the corporate group. The second, by contrast, is where managerial power has been diversified across two or more legal units which are clearly not under common ownership or control. Here, the separate legal entities may reflect the existence of separate foci of managerial power. However, if the law is restricted to recognising as the employer only that legal entity which has the relevant type of contractual relation with the worker, the concept of the 'employer' may fail to capture the reality of the managerial power located in the 'non-employer' entities. In other words, the question for labour law is how to conceptualise the multi-party nature of the employment relationship on the management side. Typical of this latter situation are agency-supplied workers, the multifarious forms which franchises or concessions may take and some forms of contracting out.

Although in both cases it can be said that the definition of employer is under-inclusive, the second situation is the more problematic. In the first situation, a coherent managerial unit consisting of two or more distinct legal entities, it may be that in many cases, if labour law applies its liability rules to any one of the entities, the unit as a whole will respond appropriately because of its managerial unity. However, it could be that those very liability rules are distorted in some cases by the existence of legally separate but managerially united units. Does a rule which treats two employers as

---

[18] P Davies and M Freedland (eds), *Kahn-Freund's Labour and the Law* (3rd edn, London, Stevens, 1983) 15.
[19] *Ibid.*

separate assume in policy terms managerial as well as legal separateness, and, if so, is the objective of the legal rule frustrated by the fact that there is managerial unity? Should, then, the rule cease treating the legal entities as distinct and instead bring them into congruence with the underlying managerial unity?

In the second situation, managerial diversification across a number of legal entities which are not under common control, by contrast, there is no reason to presume a response by the appropriate bearer of managerial power if the law itself does not accurately identify that person. In such a case, confining legal liability to the entity which has the appropriate contractual relationship with the worker seems inherently dangerous.

Employers Within Corporate Groups (Unified Management)

The first problem is the older problem[20] and stems mainly, if not entirely, from the fact that the typical employer of any size in the private sector is a company and that most corporate businesses above a very modest size are operated not through a single company but as a group of companies. In the public sector, employers also are typically corporate (though usually not Companies Act corporate bodies), but the pressures towards group structures which operate in the private sector have seemed less strong in the past in the public sector. This may be about to change, for example through the creation of NHS Trusts and, now, Foundation Hospitals, incorporated as 'community interest companies.'[21] However, it is not clear at this stage whether this development represents simply the creation of smaller units, in which management and legal structures are congruent, or the generation in the public sector of a mismatch between managerial and legal units.

In the private sector, by contrast, group structures are pervasive. This is not a characteristic simply of multi-national or large-scale national companies, though their group structures are indeed bewildering in their abundance and complexity. Even quite small businesses, run by individual entrepreneurs, outgrow the single company at quite an early stage. It is not entirely clear why this should be, nor is it crucially important to this chapter to identify the reasons, but it is probably a combination of historical accident (businesses started or acquired at different times) and the advantages of ring-fencing the liabilities of different business activities by putting them in separate companies.

---

[20] Recognised, for example, in Brian Bercusson's contribution to R Lewis (ed), *Labour Law in Britain* (Oxford, Blackwell, 1986). For recent discussion of the second problem which we have found helpful, see S Deakin, 'The Changing Concept of the Employer in Labour Law' (2001) 30 *ILJ* 72 and J Earnshaw, J Rubery and F Lee Cooke, *Who is the Employer?* (London, Institute of Employment Rights, 2002).

[21] DTI and HM Treasury, *Enterprise for Communities: Proposals for a Community Interest Company* URN 03/1460, March 2003.

For the purposes of this chapter, the important point is that, in principle, the common law identifies the contracting party on the employer side in this situation as a particular group company rather than the group as a whole, which does not constitute a legal entity, or rather than two or more group companies jointly. The crucial point to observe is that this in-principle rule applies even though the managerial structure of the group (or part of it) itself ignores the division of the group into separate legal entities. Where the legal structure of the group maps directly onto its managerial structure, the identification of a particular group company as the employer is probably not troubling. However, given that the legal construction of many groups is not driven by operational concerns, but by, for example, regulatory or tax goals or pure historical accident, it is in fact not uncommon for managerial arrangements to cut across the group's legal structure. Thus, a set of employees may be managed as a single unit, even though they are in fact employed by different companies within the group. Nevertheless, provided the legal formalities pertaining to the different companies making up the group are properly observed by group management, the fact that the business organisation of the group ignores the separate legal entities of the group companies will not enable the employee to go behind or beyond his or her employing company. Only if those formalities are not observed will the group structure be regarded as a 'sham' which the courts may ignore. This is the teaching of the highly important decision of the Court of Appeal in *Adams v Cape Industries*.[22] It means that ignoring the group structure will rarely be a policy available to the courts.

Cape was a tort case, and what it reflects is the unwillingness of the common law to override the principle of limited liability for shareholders, even where the shareholder is another company in a corporate group rather than a natural person holding shares in a free-standing company. However, limited liability is simply the default position: there is no public policy which restricts parties from contracting out of limited liability or the legislature from overruling it.[23] The direct significance of *Cape* for labour law is, thus, that it shows that it is unlikely that the common law of employment will adopt the 'single economic entity' theory. However, *Cape* probably also has an important, indirect, 'spillover' significance for statutory labour law, which may be described as a reluctance on the part of the courts to treat labour law statutes as breaching the principle of the separate legal entity within groups, in the absence of clear indications that Parliament intended to override that principle. In other words, the courts put the onus on the legislature to identify the situations where it is appropriate to treat group companies as a single unit. That the legislature is capable of recognising the group

[22] [1990] 1 All ER 929.
[23] As was recognised in *Cape* itself at 1019. Indeed, the Companies Act provides for the creation of a form of company without limited liability for its members: Companies Act 1985, s 1(2)(c).

when it wants to is clear, the most famous examples being in relation to financial disclosure (group accounts) and taxation. Labour law takes account of the group structure in some cases as well, principally through the definition of an 'associated employer.'[24] Whilst this definition does not treat the group as a single entity, it does recognise that, in some cases, the appropriate managerial decision may be located in a company other than the employing company, ie it recognises the linkages among companies within the same group.

Is the 'associated employer' enough to deal with the first problem identified above? Its deficiencies are clear enough. First, and most important, the legislature, national or Community, needs to remember to put it into the relevant piece of legislation. It is not included automatically and, as we have just seen, the courts seem unwilling to play an active role in repairing any legislative deficiencies. Sometimes the question of whether to include it seems not to have been addressed in the policy formation process; in others it may have been, but the question was not publicly debated. Where it is left out, sometimes, probably generally, this is to the benefit of employers (for example, *Dimbleby & Sons Ltd v NUJ*[25] in which an associated company was not treated as party to a trade dispute); sometimes to the benefit of workers (for example, *Allen:*[26] transfer regulations applying to a transfer between group subsidiaries subject to common ownership and control as much as to transfers across the group's boundaries).

Sometimes, the major impact of the failure to deal expressly with the group issue seems to be on the workability of the results produced by the law in question. Thus, it seems that applications under the recognition procedure, and so awards by the CAC, cannot embrace associated employers, even though the most sensible bargaining unit would be one which crossed the boundaries of the legal entities involved.[27] Similarly, in the current consultations on the transposition of the Information and Consultation Framework Directive[28] the government seems to take the view that the Directive requires only a 'single employer' approach and it does not propose to go further than that and to introduce compulsory information and consultation mechanisms embracing associated employers (though the

---

[24] TULR(C)A 1992, s 297. An analogous concept, sometimes found in domestic provisions derived from EU law, is that of a person 'controlling the employer': ibid s 188(7).

[25] [1984] ICR 386. The case is a clear example of judicial reluctance to pierce the corporate veil in the absence of clear legislative intention: see at 409G–410B.

[26] C-234/98 [2000] ICR 436.

[27] See CAC decisions *GPMU and Derry Print Ltd and John Brown Printers Ltd* (TUR1/113/2001) and *GMB and Northbourne Ltd* (TUR1/183/2002). Whilst stopping short of proposing that associated employers be included, the DTI has asked for views on such a proposal in its consultation document on the reform of the procedure: *Review of the Employment Relations Act 1999*, (URN 03/606, February 2003).

[28] Directive 2002/14/EC.

parties might agree such a structure).[29] If this approach is carried through, the transposition of the general Framework Directive will be less in tune with commercial realities than in the case of the transposition of the European Works Council (EWC)Directive.[30] In the case of the EWC Directive, the default rule (the parties can agree otherwise) is that the Directive operates at the level of the central management of 'groups of undertakings,' where there is a group structure.[31] In short, the EWC Directive sets the default position at the group level, whereas the Framework Directive, in the government's view, sets it at the level of the individual company.

In any case, the question that is left in the air is the question of substantive policy. Should rules about secondary action treat other group companies in the same way as fully independent companies; should transfers of employees within corporate groups be treated in the same way as transfers to outsiders; should bargaining units be capable of embracing more than one employer within a corporate group?

There are further problems about the associated employer concept. A third one is that the definition of an associated employer is a statutory concept and does not therefore apply to common law liabilities of employers.[32] A fourth and final one is that the definition of associated employer does not work well in the public sector.[33]

Is there any general solution to this set of problems or should one simply hang a big notice up in the DTI employment section, saying 'Don't forget to consider how these rules are to apply in corporate groups'? A radical alternative general principle would be to say that labour law claims can be asserted against and defences asserted by the parent company, as well as the employing company, or, even, against or by any corporate group member. However, if, as suggested above, the purpose of labour law is and should be to control the exercise of managerial power within an employment relationship, it would seem that the radical rule could be too broad. This is

---

[29] DTI, *High Performance Workplaces: Informing and Consulting Employees* (July 2003) paras 4.47–4.49. This proposal shows that the issue under discussion here does not evaporate just because Community law in this area uses the term 'undertaking' rather than the term 'employer.' 'Undertaking' is also an ambiguous term in this regard.

[30] Directive 94/45/EC.

[31] See the definitions of 'group of undertakings' and 'central management' in Art 2 of the Directive.

[32] See Collins (1990) 53 *MLR* 731, pointing to *McDermid v Nash Dredging* [1987] 1 AC 906, where the captain of a tug, whose negligence injured the claimant crew member, was employed by a different group company from that which employed the crew. The claimant's employer was not vicariously liable for the captain's negligence, but the problem was solved in that case by holding the claimant's employer in breach of a personal and non-delegable duty of care. In fact, the claimant employee then benefited from the group structure since a limitation of liability under the Merchant Shipping (Liability of Shipowners and Others) Act 1958, s 3 which would have operated if the crew and tug had been owned and operated by a single company, was avoided.

[33] *Allonby v Accrington and Rossendale College* [2001] ICR 1189: an example on its facts of the second problem identified above.

because, within corporate groups, a number of different and distinctly managed businesses may be carried on. It would be wrong to assume that corporate groups carry on only a single line of business. Very often this is not the case. If the current rule, focusing on the employing legal entity, is under-inclusive, a rule making the parent liable for all group companies' actions in the field of labour law would be over-inclusive. The radical rule tends towards the principle that distinctly managed businesses should be separately owned (ie not form part of the same corporate group). It is unclear what the rationale for this rule would be and the business ineffi-ciencies generated by it could be substantial.

An alternative approach would be to give the court in any particular case the power to permit claims to be made against or defences asserted by other companies in the same group where it is necessary to do so to give effect to the 'managerial unit' model of the employing entity (or for the court to treat the actions of other group companies as the actions of the employing com-pany). As a legal technique, however, it is unattractive, because of the uncertainty it would generate in operation. In other words, it is not clear that the benefits of such a principle, in terms of the better targeting of labour laws, would exceed its costs in terms of more protracted litigation. This might even be the case if the principle were confined to those legal provisions where the legislature had not expressly addressed the issue of group application, through deployment of the 'associated employer' con-cept or in some other way.

So, maybe ad hoc specification is (still) the way forward, although it will be important to ensure that legislative design is debated in an open and transparent way.

Employers and Dispersed Management

In this second problematic situation, management of the employees is again spread across two or more separate legal entities, but, whereas in the first example the separate legal entities were under unified management and ownership, in the second example they are not. However, it is crucial to see that the problem under discussion arises because the outsourcing entity retains some managerial powers in respect of the workers performing the outsourced functions. Where this is not the case, the problem we have identified does not arise: where the management of the workforce is entirely outsourced with the outsourcing of the product or service, that sit-uation need not detain us, as far as the definition of the employer is con-cerned. If a car manufacturer ceases to make its own gear-boxes and instead buys them from a separate and specialist manufacturer of gear-boxes, it would seem clear that management functions in relation to the workers who make the gear-boxes are located entirely with the specialist manufacturer. Where services are outsourced, some retention of managerial authority on the part of the outsourcing employer is more likely, though not inevitable. If a company outsources the maintenance of its share register, for example, there is no obvious reason why the company should wish to retain any managerial authority over the workers employed on that task. If the services are to be provided on the premises of the outsourcing company, by contrast, or are associated with the outsourcing company in the public mind, as in a franchise, some managerial control may well be located partly in the hands of a body which is not (or is no longer) the employer on a conventional analysis. A fortiori, the issue arises where the task side of the employment relationship is not outsourced at all, but only the recruitment, dismissal and payment functions, as with workers employed through an agency business.

There seem to be two policy questions in relation to outsourcing, as broadly defined in the previous paragraph. The first focuses on the possible loss of legal protection which the division of managerial functions between the outsourcing and outsourced entities generates for the worker, and seeks to remedy it. A paradigm, but by no means the only, example of an issue to address in this context might be the reluctance of the courts to find that agency workers have a contract of employment with the user or the agency or even either of them. The second, and broader, issue is whether outsourcing justifies specific regulation of the terms and conditions of the workers involved (beyond the obligation to meet general minimum standards) so as to redress the damage to the economic interests of the workers which often accompanies outsourcing.

The narrower question can be addressed either by making the outsourced entity liable for the acts of the outsourcing entity or by entitling the worker to take action against the outsourcing entity in relation to the exercise of the latter's managerial powers, even though that entity was not the employer of the worker in question. The latter seems to be the favoured technique in discrimination law, where the non-discrimination rule is applied to those who have work available to be done by workers supplied to them by another, even though the user of the workers' services is not itself their employer.[34] The outsourcing entity must not discriminate in relation to allowing the worker to do the work, the terms on which the work is done, in relation to benefits, facilities or services, or by imposing any other detriment. Although these provisions catch actions by the user entity in relation to agency work,[35] they go wider than that. Thus, in *Harrods Ltd v Remick*[36] they were applied so as to subject to the jurisdiction of the tribunal

---

[34] Sex Discrimination Act 1975, s 9; Race Relations Act 1976, s 7; Disability Discrimination Act 1995, s 12 (in all three cases referred to as discrimination against 'contract workers').
[35] *MHC Consulting Services Ltd v Tansell* [2000] ICR 789, CA.
[36] [1998] ICR 156, CA (Hepple QC for the unsuccessful employer!).

allegedly discriminatory acts by a store which reserved the power to vet the employees of licensees which operated concessions on its premises. The width of the interpretation is perhaps revealed by the subsequent decision in *O'Shea Construction v Bassi*,[37] where the provision was held wide enough to catch acts of a customer's employee where the respondent customer, under a contract with the applicant's employer, simply had the power to dictate where and in what quantities ready-mixed concrete, delivered by lorry, was to be discharged.

In principle, these provisions seem accurately to track the division of managerial functions between the outsourcing and outsourced entities. Thus, the outsourced entity is liable for the discriminatory acts it commits in its capacity as employer; the outsourcing entity for the acts it commits in the exercise of (retained) managerial powers, even though not itself the employer. If the outsourcing entity retains no employer powers, it cannot be liable. A narrower approach to this problem can be found in the provisions of the National Minimum Wage Act 1998[38] and the Working Time Regulations 1998.[39] The aim in these subject-specific pieces of legislation is not to spread liability across outsourcing and outsourced entities in accordance with their exercise of managerial powers. Rather the aim is to fix liability on the employer. However, to deal with the risk that an agency worker will be regarded as employed by neither agency nor user,[40] the legislation in such a case fixes liability on the entity which is responsible for paying the worker or does in fact discharge the payment function. These provisions thus apply only to outsourcing which takes the form of the use of agency workers and, even then, only where neither agency nor user is the employer.[41]

However, neither the wider nor the narrower set of provisions is typical of statutory labour provisions. Under the law of unfair dismissal, for example, no claim would seem to lie against the outsourcing entity (because there was no contract of employment with that person) and the success of the claim against the claimant's employer (the outsourced entity)[42] would seem

---

[37] [1998] ICR 1130 (though the case was so mishandled because of the incompetence of the claimant's representatives and the employment tribunal that it is probably not an unavoidable decision).

[38] See s 34.

[39] See reg 36.

[40] For the latest twist in this saga see *Franks v Reuters Ltd* [2003] IRLR 423, CA; *Stephenson v Delphi Diesel Systems Ltd* [2003] ICR 471; *Dacas v Brook Street Bureau (UK) Ltd* [2004] IRLR 358 CA.

[41] As the side-note to the relevant provisions indicates: 'agency workers who are not otherwise "workers"'.

[42] Assuming, of course, that the tribunal did not find that the division of managerial functions between the outsourcing and outsourced entities had not deprived the worker of a contract of employment with both entities.

to depend upon the tribunal's application of the general fairness test to the actions of the outsourced entity, not those of the outsourcing entity.[43] There is a good case for extending the principle of the discrimination statutes to labour law statutes in general, perhaps under the powers contained in section 23 of the Employment Relations Act 1999.[44]

In the paragraphs above, we have discussed the issue of how to respond to the impact of outsourcing on the legal protections of the workers providing the outsourced service. The broader question arises out of the impact of the outsourcing upon the economic interests of the workers involved, usually because of a worsening of their terms and conditions in comparison with those afforded when the service was provided in-house. The equivalent question in this respect to that asked in the previous paragraphs is whether the workers of the outsourced entity should be entitled to the same terms and conditions as those of the outsourcing entity doing, or previously doing, the same or similar work, where the outsourcing entity retains control over the terms and conditions of employment provided by the outsourced entity.

Despite the failure of the claimants in *Lawrence v Regent Office Care Ltd*,[45] the answer is that arguably in the situation hypothesised the claimants could successfully prosecute an equal pay claim. In *Lawrence* the dinner ladies now employed by the respondents failed in their claim for equal pay with equivalent workers employed by their previous employer, North Yorkshire Country Council. The claim failed because the ECJ was not willing to give direct effect to Article 141 of the EC Treaty where two separate organisations were responsible for setting the terms and conditions in question: 'the differences ... cannot be attributed to a single source, there is no body which is responsible for the inequality and which could restore the equal treatment.'[46] However, in the hypothesised case this is not the situation: there the outsourcing entity does retain control over the outsourced entity's formulation of its terms and conditions of employment. Since the ECJ accepted that there was no requirement in Article 141 EC that the dinner ladies and their comparators work for the same employer,[47] there is nothing in *Lawrence* which stands in the way of a successful equal pay claim in the situation envisaged.

However, this is likely to be of little help to the employees of outsourced entities. Outsourcing entities may expect to reap economic rewards from worsened terms and conditions offered by the outsourced entity, but it is

---

[43] *Dobie v Burns International Security Services (UK) Ltd* [1984] IRLR 329.

[44] But see above n 11 and associated text for indications of governmental reluctance.

[45] C-320/00, [2002] IRLR 822 ECJ, now followed in relation to contractual comparison in C-256/01, *Allonby* [2004] IRLR 224 ECJ.

[46] *Lawrence*, above n 45, judgment at para 18.

[47] *Ibid* at para 17.

highly unlikely that this result will be achieved by means of stipulations in the commercial contract between the two entities as to what terms and conditions should be offered by the outsourced entity. That contract will normally simply stipulate a price for a prescribed service and leave it to the outsourced entity to work out how it is profitably to deliver the service for that price. The economic pressure on the outsourced entity to worsen terms and conditions may derive from the commercial contract, but the outsourced entity will remain legally free to set its own terms and conditions of employment. In this, more typical, situation *Lawrence* would indeed seem to block access to a successful equal pay claim.

A more powerful principle, although one confined to only one form of outsourcing, is to be found in the proposed Temporary Work Directive.[48] It proposes mandatory equality with the user's employees for agency workers, unless the worker is engaged under a contract of indefinite duration with the agency, under which he or she is paid even during periods when not assigned to a user. The principle here seems to be that equality of pay with the user's employees is justified because the agency worker is being integrated into the user's workforce on the task side, even though the user has not sought to stipulate the terms and conditions upon which the agency should employ the worker. In this light it is not surprising that the debate revolves around the time threshold below which the coercive comparison should not operate, because there has been no integration.

In short, one might say that the principle underlying the proposal is that a high degree of managerial control on the part of the user over the worker supports a claim to equality of terms, even though that control does not specifically relate to the reward side of the work contract. However, it is unclear how far this principle can be generalised so as to cover a wider range of outsourcing arrangements. Agency work is at the far end of the outsourcing spectrum, because the outsourced entity provides no service itself to the user other than the recruitment and payment of the worker. Where the outsourced entity itself provides the service for which the workers are required (even if it is only under a cleaning contract), it is clear that the notion of a high degree of integration of the workers into the client's workforce may be difficult to sustain. And the idea would seem to have no purchase at all in the case of, for example, a franchise.

To provide economic equality in a wider range of outsourcing situations requires the identification of a principle which is broader than that of managerial control and thus outside the scope of this section of this chapter. Accordingly, the possibilities will be only briefly sketched. The Transfers Directive[49] recognises that where there is a shift of an activity carried out

---

[48] COM(2002) 149 final.
[49] Originally Directive 77/187/EEC, amended by Directive 98/50/EC and consolidated in Directive 2001/23/EC.

by an identifiable group of workers from one entity to another, the workers should be both entitled to transfer with the activity and retain their existing terms and conditions of employment. However, the theory upon which the Transfers Directive operates does not turn on the retention of managerial control by the transferor. That Directive preserves the transferred employees, terms and conditions, whether or not the transferor maintains managerial control. Thus, it applies in the share register example above[49a] as much as in the outsourcing of the running of the works canteen where the outsourcing company lays down rules for the dress and conduct of the supplier's staff. The theory of the Directive seems rather one of the attachment of the employees to the business transferred.

The British guidance for local authority contracting out[50] now carries that principle a stage further by applying a 'not less favourable' requirement to workers hired directly into the transferred workforce. However, the comparator here is the transferred workforce and their current terms of employment, not their previous terms of employment with the transferor or those of any workers retained by the transferor. Again, no question of managerial control retained by the transferor arises.

Finally, a solution which would not depend wholly upon legal rules would be the re-emergence of sectoral bargaining, but that is a topic way beyond the scope of this chapter. One might conclude, therefore, that the managerial concept of the employer has greater potential to deal with the legal disadvantages of the outsourced worker than with his or her economic disadvantages. We turn, therefore, to consider the third aspect of our subject, that of the relationship between the worker and the employer.

THE EMPLOYMENT RELATIONSHIP

If, since the 1980s, there have been significant changes in the ways that the worker, and to some extent the employer, are formulated and conceptualised in employment practice, there have been no less important, and in many ways associated, changes in the way that the employment relationship itself is approached. Again there is a set of questions, first, about the nature of those changes and secondly about the role of employment law in relation to them. The changes are strongly associated with the reconceptualisation of the social and economic practice or conduct of the employment relationship, formerly analysed as 'industrial relations' or 'employment relations,' into the very different framework of 'human resource management.'

That change in the name of the social science of the employment relationship has significant connotations in and of itself; it implies, first, in its

---

[49a] See above, p 141.
[50] Office of the Deputy Prime Minister Circular 03/2003.

shift from 'relations' to 'management,' an emphasis on the conduct of the relationship by the employing enterprise rather than on the relationship as a mutual interaction, and secondly, in its change from the terminology of 'industry' or 'employment' to that of 'human resources,' a special concern with the skills and capacities of workers as economic goods, a species of capital. These might be regarded as rhetorical rather than practical shifts; but they describe a set of changes of approach which it is useful to think of in terms of a combination of individuation and flexibilisation of the employment relationship. We proceed to elaborate upon each of those two notions in turn.

We touched upon the question of individuation earlier in connection with the changing notion of the worker.[51] It was observed that individuation consists in the first instance of decollectivisation of the employment relationship, in the sense of a resiliing from collective bargaining, and from collective representation more generally in the sense of the processing of workplace issues and grievances through trade union representatives or officials. It is, of course, debatable how strong and prevalent a trend that has been, and whether it has been arrested or reversed by the introduction of the statutory trade union recognition mechanism. However, our present concern is not so much to resolve that question, but rather to consider a distinct and deeper sense in which the employment relationship is tending to be individuated.[52]

This deeper sense of individuation can be understood by considering the prevailing methodology of human resource management. That methodology provides a practice of management which can, as it were, fill the vacuum which might otherwise be left behind by de-collectivisation. When decollectivisation occurs, we perhaps tend to assume that the practice of collective bargaining and collective representation is replaced by a situation in which the employing enterprise either imposes unilaterally upon the workforce as a whole the terms and conditions previously settled in collective bargaining, or contracts with workers one by one, being in a position to deal on more favourable terms with workers who are contracting severally than with workers who are contracting jointly.

The actual practice of the individuated employment relationship may be rather different, and in a sense lying between or outside those two assumed stereotypes. A consideration of the literature of human resource management[53] suggests instead that the practice of the individuated

---

[51] See above, p 133–34.

[52] Probably the most important contribution to the understanding of this phenomenon, both at a theoretical and practical level, is the research paper for the DTI by W Brown, S Deakin, M Hudson, C Pratten and P Ryan, *The Individualisation of Employment Contracts in Britain* (London, DTI, 1988).

[53] Specially useful in this respect is the collection of essays, R Schuler and S Jackson (eds), *Strategic Human Resource Management* (Oxford, Blackwell Business, 1999).

employment relationship consists not so much of individual contracting or of unilateral imposition of codes of terms and conditions, though both of those things may occur, but rather of continuous management of the worker and the work process on a more individuated basis than was typical in the heyday of collectivised industrial relations. This is essentially achieved by systems of behaviour management and payment (the latter often regarded as 'reward management')[54] which permit, indeed are premised upon, detailed continuous or frequently recurrent appraisal and evaluation of the individual worker's performance and approach to his or her work.

Of course, much of this may be no more than a formalisation, even the representation as a science, of what was occurring anyway in the normal course of the typical employment relationship. However, the new style appears in a more distinctive guise when the element of individuation is combined with that of flexibilisation. We are accustomed to understanding the notion of flexibility in employment in terms of the abolition of specific rigidities in working arrangements or practices, which restrict the worker's availability to particular locations, or tasks or timetables. We suggest that the evolving practice of human resource management is designed to combine individuation with flexibilisation to achieve a more profound kind of behavioural adaptability on the part of the worker, according to which the human resources of the enterprise are maintained as malleable ones in a more far-reaching sense.[55]

We suggest that the legal response to this evolution has been a patchy one, perhaps at times superficial. The struggle against individuation as a violation of the right of freedom of association, culminating in the decision of the European Court of Human Rights in *Wilson and Palmer v United Kingdom*[56] has been extremely important, but perhaps does not get to the very heart of the matter. In order to explain this point we have to examine in some little detail both the practice of imposition of 'personal' employment contracts which was the subject of the *Wilson and Palmer* saga, and the exact nature of the legal response to it.

The practice which was at stake was that of offering workers incentives, in the form of pay increases, to move to 'personal' contracts; those incentives were withheld from those who refused to accept that change. The exact nature of the change in situation which is involved in the move to 'personal' con-

---

[54] An equally useful general overview of this topic is provided by G White and J Druker (eds), *Reward Management: A Critical Text*, (London, Routledge, 2000).

[55] A revealing account of the underlying aims, according to the perceptions of that author at least, is given by S Tyson, 'Human Resource Strategy: A Process for Managing the Contribution of HRM to Organisational Performance' in Schuler and Jackson, above n 53, ch 6.

[56] [2002] IRLR 128. See, for an admirable analysis of this decision and its ramifications, KD Ewing, 'The Implications of *Wilson and Palmer*' (2003) 32 *ILJ* 1.

tracts is quite hard to specify and has perhaps been insufficiently examined. In the *Wilson and Palmer* saga, it was identified[57] in terms of the loss to the worker of the benefit of collective bargaining and of recourse to 'the essential services of the trade union' in the conduct of relations with the employer. In this identification, it was emphasised that the 'personal' employment contract did not seek to bind the worker not to belong to a trade union; to attempt so to bind the worker would clearly have been illegal.

Identified in that way, the imposition, or introduction by incentive, of this kind of transformation did not seem specially offensive to the notions of the rights of workers or proper governance of the employment relationship which the British courts and legislature entertained at that time (and perhaps still entertain, though in a more muted way since the decision of the European Court of Human Rights in *Wilson and Palmer v United Kingdom*). Employing enterprises were at that time legally free to resile from recognition of trade unions and from arrangements for collective bargaining. To judicial eyes, it might therefore appear that on the one hand, the workers therefore had no underlying legal claim to collective bargaining, and on the other hand were not being deprived of their legally protected claim to belong to a trade union. In a certain sense one feels that the Employment Appeal Tribunal[58] and the House of Lords,[59] in deciding the *Wilson and Palmer* cases, could not, in those circumstances, see what all the fuss was really about.

This considerable judicial myopia towards the collective dimension of the employment relationship is in no small part due to the depth with which the courts have internalised the construction of the employment relationship as an essentially individual contract, and moreover one which is capable of being fully articulated or spelt out at that individual level at and from the moment of its formation. When Otto Kahn-Freund so brilliantly in the 1950s provided British lawyers with a convincing way of transposing collective bargaining theory into that individual contractual form,[60] there was always the risk that this might turn out to be a Faustian pact in which the underlying claim to collective joint regulation might be traded away in

---

[57] We suggest that this approach permeates the argument and treatment of these cases at least in the British courts through which they progressed. For a critical analysis of this approach, see KD Ewing, above n 56, especially at 7–13.

[58] [1992] ICR 681, [1993] ICR 101.

[59] [1995] ICR 406; but contrast the Court of Appeal, [1994] ICR 97.

[60] See O Kahn-Freund, '*Legal Framework*' in A Flanders and H Clegg (eds), *The System of Industrial Relations in Great Britain: Its History, Law and Institutions* (Oxford, Blackwell, 1959) ch II at 57–60, especially at 59 where the notion of the collective agreement as 'crystallised custom' is proposed.

return for recognition of the legal effectiveness of the normative provisions of particular collective agreements.

It was this risk which essentially materialised in *Wilson and Palmer*. Because, in the eyes of the courts, the workers were employed under individual contracts in the first place, it was hard to view the transformation of those contracts into 'personal' ones as specially momentous. Moreover, and no less important, because this theoretical approach identified those contracts as capable of being fully articulated or spelt out at the individual level at and from the moment of their formation, it was hard to see why and in what respect the continuing recourse to 'the essential services of the trade union' was particularly significant to those contracts or to the relationships which they embodied.

Herein lies the double invisibility of the collective dimension of the employment relation to those brought up religiously wearing the spectacles of the British law of the contract of employment. For in truth, the terms of the employment relation are typically not capable of being fully articulated or spelt out at the individual level at and from the moment of its formation; they are specified and transformed in the course of the relationship. That process of specification and transformation can usefully be thought of as one of continuous administration or management. It is of crucial significance whether and how far that process is subject to collective and joint regulation, which normally depends upon whether and how far trade unions have an effective role or voice in that process. It is that which is really at stake when the rather nebulous concept is evoked of 'recourse to the essential services of the trade union.' Yet it is that which is effectively masked from view by this special and subtle opacity of the British law of the contract of employment.

Another way in which to express this particular phenomenon might be to say that the British law of the contract of employment has a narrowly bounded conceptual horizon, beyond which lies a broad unconfined space for continuous managerial adjustment and adaptation of the real conduct of the employment relationship. Kahn-Freund and the theorists of industrial relations of the 1950s and 1960s could afford to be reasonably optimistic about the prospects for a reasonable degree of effective joint regulation within that area, and so could confidently maintain it as a kind of secret garden beyond the gaze of labour law theory.

The juridification of employment relations in the 1970s would erode this space, but, even more significantly, their rapidly increasing de-collectivisation in the 1980s and early 1990s would reveal just how lightly defended it was by the forces of joint regulation. It was this particular piece of territory, therefore, which was ripe for occupation by the protagonists of individuation and flexibilisation of employment relations from that time onwards. Operating under the banner of human resource management, and at a safe distance from attack from an always basically unaggressive and now much weakened legal apparatus of joint regulation, those protagonists could recapture this space as a territory for the free working of managerial prerogative in a way that would not have been predicted, and has, even now, perhaps not been fully understood. This process does more than merely marginalise trade unions, momentous though that alone would be. It also tends to individuate and demutualise the employment relationship at an even deeper level.

It is of no small importance that, for much of the 1990s at least, that evolution could proceed not merely in safety from the courts, but with the positive acquiescence, even at times the active approval, of the legislature and the government. Certainly this was manifest in the way that, in 1993, the 'Ullswater Amendment'[61] was allowed to become a crucial limitation on the capacity of the British legislation concerning the right to trade union membership to halt the advance of individuation and flexibilisation of the employment relationship. The 'Ullswater Amendment' precisely covered, legitimated and protected that advance by providing that an action on the part of the employer which might otherwise have been construed as intended to encroach upon trade union membership or activity was not to be so construed where it had the purpose of 'furthering a change in the relationship with all or any class of his employees'.[62]

If one allows for the undoubted fact that the main kind of 'change in the relationship with employees' which managements were seeking consisted precisely of their individuation and flexibilisation, then it becomes apparent that, if ever a legislative proposal succeeded in beguiling Parliament into enacting that the greater should be deemed *not* to include the lesser, this was the one which most nearly did so. The question thus raised by the Ullswater Amendment, of whether and how far the imposition of this kind of change in the nature of relations between the employing enterprise and its workforce (that is to say, their individuation and flexibilisation at a deep level) has a distinct legitimacy in and of itself, is not yet resolved,[63] and seems to be an element in the current deliberations[64] about the appropriate

[61] This refers to an additional clause proposed by Lord Ullswater, at that time the Conservative government spokesman on employment law matters in the House of Lords, during the passage through Parliament of the Bill that was to be enacted as the Trade Union Reform and Employment Relations Act 1993.

[62] The provison was later re-enacted as, and is currently contained in, Employment Rights Act 1996, s 148(3).

[63] Further complication was caused by the re-iteration of a similar notion in another amendment to a Bill passing through Parliament, this time proposed by Lord Miller and enacted as Employment Relations Act 1999, s 17(4), which limited the power conferred by s 17 to deal with the *Wilson and Palmer* problem by ministerial regulations, as the New Labour government was at that time hoping or intending to do.

[64] As evidenced by the proposals canvassed in DTI, *Review of the Employment Relations Act 1999* (URN 03/606, February 2003) paras 3.12–3.13 'Freedom to enter individualised contracts.' Compare the subsequent Employment Relations Bill 2003–4.

legislative response to *Wilson v United Kingdom*. However, rather than pursing that particular discussion in further detail, we put forward the general theme about individuation and flexibilisation as forming the basis of an argument which seeks to link together the three hitherto distinct elements in this chapter, and forms the conclusion to it.

CONCLUSION: THE THREE PERSPECTIVES BROUGHT TOGETHER

**The Employment Relation Under New Management:
HRM as a New Paradigm?**

Our concluding suggestion is that the evolution which we have described in the management of the employment relationship may come to assume a transcendent significance, so that it feeds back into our discussion of the reconceptualisation of the worker and of the employer. The proponents of human resource management have an increasingly proactive vision of what they are about. They increasingly describe their pursuit as *strategic* human resource management[65]. This is more than mere grandiloquence. It identifies the practice of human resource management as having the purpose of managing the adaptation of the workforce not merely to the day-to-day variations in demand and task specification, but to the most fundamental changes in the nature and structure of the work process and the employing enterprise. It extends to managing situations in which the worker is called upon to adapt to complete reconfigurations of his or her role vis-à-vis the employing enterprise, and of the employing enterprise itself.

That last observation suggests the sense in which the individuation and flexibilisation of employment relations, which is at the heart of much of current thinking about 'human resource management,' may come to embrace a certain kind of redesigning or reconceptualising, both in general terms and in particular situations, of the other two elements in the firmament of employment which we have explored, those of the 'employee' or 'worker,' and the 'employer' or employing enterprise. Eventually, and in its most strategic forms, human resource management does not merely accustom the workforce to the individuality and flexibility of the relations of its members to the employing enterprise; it actually tends to reconceive the employing enterprise as an essentially mutant and almost virtual institution, and to reconceive the 'employee' as a working agent capable of operating in such a loosely jointed structure.

An earlier practice of 'industrial relations' was, broadly speaking, directed at constructing and maintaining (whether on a unitary or pluralistic basis) a

---

[65] Compare CA and ML Lengnick-Hall, 'Strategic Human Resources Management: A Review of the Literature and a Proposed Typology' in Schuler and Jackson, above n 53, ch 2.

coherent and solidaristic sense of institutional identity of and within the employing enterprise, and formed its conceptions accordingly both of the employer, of the worker, and of the relations between them. There is a real sense in which there may now be, in the current practice of 'human resource management,' something of a reverse trend in all those three perspectives. At some risk of coining phrases which may turn out to be more bright than weighty, we could venture to speak of a combination of the semi-detached worker with the amorphous employer in the demutualised employment relationship; and we could begin to regard that as a possible new paradigm of human resource management.

The Legal Response

This argument opens up very large questions about the adequacy and appropriateness of the legal response, which we have touched upon earlier but should now look at in a more general sense. This could easily turn into an evaluation of New Labour employment law, and may yet do so in another context; but such presumption is to be avoided on this occasion. The course and duration of that scenario is far too unclear, and in any event this is too small and specific a canvas on which to paint such a picture. Equally to be avoided is the assumption that there is such a thing as a single or even a unified 'legal response' to the evolutions in the theory and practice of the management of the employment relationship which we have sought to identify and to describe. That assumes a unity of purpose and action between and within the legislative, executive and judicial arms of government which is far from realistic.

Most firmly to be avoided of all, however, is the sense that the evolution of employment law in recent years is to be understood, even remotely, in terms of a simple dialectic between 'problem' and 'response.' That would connote a largely counterfactual sense of the evolution of the practice of the employment relationship as creating a perceived set of negativities or difficulties, for which the legal system was offering a positive set of ameliorations or remedies. There is one part, but almost one part only, of the mid-1990s, late 1990s and early twenty-first century evolution of British domestic employment law which could be seen in those simple terms. The higher courts, in shaping the law of the contract of employment, do seem to have been concerned to offset the more extreme asperities of modern approaches to the management of the employment relationship. Their promulgation of the implied obligation of trust and confidence[66] is

---

[66] See the series of articles by Douglas Brodie on this topic, especially 'The Heart of the Matter: Mutual Trust and Confidence' (1996) 25 *ILJ* 121.

an eloquent testimony to their good and worthy intentions in that regard, even if that enterprise has been largely derailed by the House of Lords, when it drew back in some disarray in *Johnson v Unisys Ltd*,[67] in the face of their perception that the implied obligation was producing an emergent very expensive and overblown common law of unfair dismissal in parallel with the securely capped and confined statute law of unfair dismissal which had been in existence since the early 1970s.

For the executive and legislative branches of government — the latter so tightly yoked to the former after 1997 as to have no effective independence for most of the ensuing time — the approach to the post-Fordist evolution of employment relations was a more complex and compromised one, in which the new style of human resource management has often been perceived more as part of the solution than as part of the problem with regard to the labour market and the practice of employment relations. So much is this the case that we think we can begin to see New Labour employment law as having and seeking a kind of auxiliary role with regard to the post-Fordist system of human resource management, rather in the way — and there is a more than slight irony in this — that Kahn-Freund depicted post-Second World War governments as accepting or even carving out an auxiliary role for labour law[68] in relation to the then prevailing voluntary collectivism of British industrial relations.

In one respect, indeed, post-1997 New Labour governments seem to have devised quite an exact parallel with the auxiliary role of employment law as the hand-maiden to collective *laissez-faire*. Despite their initial concerns about its pusillanimity, even the left-wing critics of the trade union recognition legislation of the Employment Relations Act 1999 might admit that it has had a more than expected success in encouraging a resurgent pattern of voluntary trade union recognition, and has halted if not reversed the previously relentless-seeming trend of de-unionisation of the late 1980s and early 1990s.

However, a possible perception of post-1997 New Labour governments as being committed to a vigorous rekindling of strong and universal collective bargaining starts somewhat to fade when one considers the conspicuously narrow subject matter[69] of the mandatory recognition which is offered by the new statutory system; and one starts to realise than in many of its manifestations, New Labour employment law has come to praise the new individuated and flexibilised style of human resource management rather than to bury it. Thus, for example, although there is a new willingness

---

[67] [2001] ICR 480.
[68] Compare his chapter in M Ginsberg (ed), *Law and Opinion in England in the Twentieth Century* (London, Stevens, 1959) especially 222 *et seq*.
[69] Defined, in effect, as 'pay, hours and holidays' by [(inserted by the Employment Relations Act 1999)] TULR(C)A 1992, Sch A1, para 3(2).

to acquiesce in and implement EU law measures designed to promote and increase arrangements for collective workforce consultation,[70] those measures are allowed to depend upon such a notoriously flimsy institutional base in British employment practice that their application in the British context can be seen more as supporting than as undermining an increasingly individuated rather than collectivised system of human resource management. A similar comment might be made with regard to the provisions concerning representation in disciplinary or grievance proceedings;[71] these provisions were, in the event,[72] informed by a concern to ensure that the worker had the right to be accompanied by a 'companion' and spokesperson in what would remain essentially individual proceedings, rather than that the proceedings would themselves be partly collectivised by the intrusion of a representative in an essentially collective role.

In a broader sense, the same set of intentions to buttress an individuated and flexibilised style of human resource management rather than to replace it with a juridified or, still more, a collectivised one, can be seen to permeate much of the policy of post-1997 New Labour employment legislation. Such a set of intentions is perfectly consistent with the formulation of the minimum wage legislation,[73] which is constructed in such a way as to make no attempt to revive the statutory substitute for sectoral collective bargaining in weakly organised occupations which the earlier Wages Councils system had attempted, however imperfectly, to provide. The same aims are equally consistent with the British implementation[74] of the Working Time Directive, especially given the breadth of scope which is allowed for individual as well as collective opting-out.

In a rather different sense, similar goals manifest themselves in the formulation of the by now decidedly elaborate package of 'family-friendly' employment measures introduced since 1997.[75] It is no accident that a measure, which is in fact a decidedly cautious version[76] of the requirements

---

[70] As exemplified by the transnational Information and Consultation of Employees Regulations 1999 (SI 1999/3323), and, most recently, by the draft Information and Consultation of Employees Regulations by which it is proposed to implement the National Information and Consultation Directive 2002/14/EC. But there is some restrictiveness of approach; cf above n 11 and associated text.

[71] Employment Relations Act 1999, s 10.

[72] The proposals in the White Paper, *Fairness at Work*, paras 4.29–4.30 had seemed to hint at the contrasting possibility.

[73] National Minimum Wage Act 1998 and associated Regulations.

[74] Working Time Regulations 1998 (SI 1998/1833).

[75] Contained especially but not solely in the provisons of the Employment Act 2002 concerning statutory leave and pay in connection with parenthood (Part 1 of the Act), and concerning 'Flexible Working' (s 47, inserting new Part 8A into the Employment Rights Act 1996).

[76] Part-time Workers (Prevention of Less Favourable Treatement) Regulations 2000 (SI 2000/1551).

of the Part-time Work Directive[77] to ensure opportunities for part-time work, should be presented as a major initiative for the promotion of 'flexible working,' or that it should display as much solicitude for the needs for managerial 'flexibility' as for those of the workforce. The former concern with the need for managerial flexibility also seems to explain a growing negativity towards EU measures or proposals to combat less favourable treatment of workers in various types of 'non-standard' work pattern; a mounting caution displayed in the implementation of the Directives on Part-time Work[78] and Fixed-term Work[79] has hardened into outright resistance to proposals for corresponding measures with regard to temporary agency workers.[80]

Finally we might refer to one of the most recent post-1997 New Labour initiatives in the employment law field which is by no means the least indicative of the government's preferred approach to the practice of employment relations, namely the provisions of Part 3 of the Employment Act 2002 concerning statutory dispute resolution procedures, the implementation of which is at the time of writing the subject of a consultative document.[81] As Bob Hepple and Gillian Morris have shown in their illuminating exploration of these provisions,[82] they represent primarily a strategy of choking-off the enforcement of individual employment rights by means of employment tribunal litigation, because of the costliness of that litigation both to employing enterprises and to the public purse, mainly by the diversion of such claims into internal disciplinary, dismissal and grievance procedures.

It might appear on the face of this legislation as if workers were being drawn down the path of internal dispute resolution by the carrot of statutory enhancement of the employer's internal procedures. However, that apparent enhancement consists in reality of the imposition of studiedly exiguous minimum procedural requirements for discipline or dismissal,[83] coupled with the *downgrading* of procedural considerations in unfair dismissal claims,[84] while the much more forceful thrust of this set of measures is to beat workers down the internal procedural path with the stick of a strong set of requirements to invoke internal grievance procedure as a total

---

[77] Directive 97/81/EC.
[78] *Ibid.*
[79] Directive 99/70/EC.
[80] See above, n 48 and associated text.
[81] *A Consultation on Proposals for the Introduction of Statutory Dispute Resolution Procedures* (DTI, July 2003).
[82] 'The Employment Act 2002 and the Crisis of Individual Employment Rights' (2002) 31 *ILJ* 245.
[83] Employment Act 2002, Sch 2, Part 1.
[84] *Ibid*, s 34, inserting new Employment Rights Act 1996, s 98A(2).

or partial pre-condition to the enforcement of individual employment rights in tribunal proceedings.[85]

It is notable how markedly that latter set of requirements might operate as quite a coercive auxiliary reinforcement of an individuated and flexi-bilised style of human resource management. It means that workers may face the prospect, when they seek tribunal enforcement of individual employment rights, that they may be met with the rejoinder that they should, as individuals, have anticipated the issue in question and opened a discussion with their managers at some earlier point in such a way as to permit an essentially ad hoc and ad personam managerial response before the issue became problematical.[86] It is important in this regard that, as we observed earlier, the provisions about accompaniment of the worker in such discussions have carefully protected the possibility of an essentially de-collectivised framework for such proceedings.[87] However, this particular set of provisions or proposals seems to be one which is particularly good at provoking polemic among employment lawyers, and rather than becoming too deeply engaged in that polemic, we turn to some more general concluding reflections.

Approaching a New Paradigm: Re-conceptualisation, Crisis or Equilibrium in Employment Law?

We suggest that the arguments which we have advanced in the course of this chapter do provide broad support for the hypothesis of the emergence of a kind of new paradigm for the structuring and conduct of employment relations according to the approaches or discipline of human resource management. This seems to involve or to be associated with a degree of reconceptualisation of employment relations, from three distinct perspectives, or in three distinct dimensions, those of the worker, the employer, and the nature of the relations between them. This practical reconceptualisation, itself not uninfluenced by changes in the policy and approach of employment law, demands and evokes further changes in the policies and approaches of employment law.

Opinions of course differ widely as to the appropriateness or adequacy of those latter responses. Those immediately responsible for the current

---

[85] Employment Act 2002, ss 31, 32.

[86] Thus Gerry Sutcliffe, Parliamentary Under-Secretary of State for Employment Relations, Competition and Consumers, in the Ministerial Foreword to the consultative document: 'Discussing problems in the workplace will not solve all of them; but in many cases dialogue can be expected to result in quick and flexible solutions, which preserve the employment relationship.' The whole tenor of this document is such as to suggest that the dialogue which is envisaged is with the individual worker as a potential, but to be discouraged, party to tribunal litigation to enforce his or her individual employment rights.

[87] See above, nn 70–71 and associated text.

fashioning of employment law, whether as judges, or parliamentary or administrative legislators, tend to see themselves as arriving at a balanced equilibrium between competing forces or claims or tendencies. The theorists of employment law are much more apt to interpret such changes as manifesting a state of crisis in employment relations or in employment law. Bill Wedderburn and Jon Clark were speaking eloquently of a crisis of fundamental concepts in labour law in the early 1980s;[88] Bob Hepple and Gill Morris now speak, no less convincingly, of a crisis in individual employment rights.[89]

We do not seek in this chapter to reach any grand conclusions, with regard to a possibly emergent new paradigm for employment relations and the legal responses to it, as between analysis in terms of crisis and analysis in terms of equilibrium. However, we suggest that, in evaluating the kind of reconceptualisation which seems to be taking place in employment practice and employment law, it may be useful to draw a distinction between, on the one hand, equilibrium or crisis in a theoretical sense and, on the other hand, equilibrium or crisis in a political or social sense. In the long term, such a distinction is not sustainable; a crisis in one sense in due course becomes a crisis in the other sense.

In the short term, however, it is more possible for there to be equilibrium, actual or perceived, in one sense, while there is crisis, actual or perceived, in the other sense. For example, the theorists of employment law have long maintained, in our view very cogently, that there is a theoretical or conceptual crisis in the way that the contract of employment is defined, and even more particularly in the way that it is distinguished from the contract for services. Yet we would have to admit that, at least until very recently, that particular crisis has not assumed any great political or social dimensions.

Equally real, in our suggestion, is the possibility that there may be a crisis of social and political dimensions in the sphere of employment practice or employment law, but whose theoretical implications are not perceived in the short term. This is, in a sense, what Hepple and Morris are pointing out with regard to the impending measures requiring internal dispute resolution. We suggest that there may be other such instances, whose implications for employment law are even more unexpected and less quickly perceived. For example, there is widely perceived to be a current political, social and economic crisis with regard to occupational pension provision; but it has not been seen as strongly interconnected with the main theoretical issues of employment law.[90] In fact our hypothesis is

[88] KW Wedderburn and J Clark, 'Modern Law: Problems, Functions and Policies', in Wedderburn, Lewis and Clark (eds), *Labour Law and Industrial Relations: Building on Kahn-Freund* (Oxford, Clarendon Press, 1983) ch 6.
[89] 'The Employment Act 2002 and the Crisis of Individual Employment Rights' (2002) 31 *ILJ* 245.
[90] Cf above n 16 and associated text.

that this may turn out to be an unfamiliar location in which fundamental questions of the kind which we have been pursuing in this chapter are posed in urgent form, as much against the 'old' perspectives upon the employment relationship and its legal regulation as against the 'new' ones which we have been canvassing. That is an inquiry which we hope to pursue in further and separate work. In the meantime we offer the foregoing reflections in affectionate supplementation to Bob Hepple's ground-breaking labours in this particular conceptual and practical field.

7

The Future of the Public/Private Labour Law Divide

GILLIAN S MORRIS

INTRODUCTION

I N THE INTRODUCTION to their ground-breaking study of public employee trade unionism in 1971, Bob Hepple and Paul O'Higgins wrote that 'there is no clear demarcation in British law between public and private employees, just as the sharp distinction which exists in some European continental systems of law between "public law" and "private law" has no counterpart in Britain.'[1] Nevertheless they demonstrated that, despite the absence of a formal divide, collective bargaining and dispute settlement operated differently in public services, reflecting the special position of the state as employer. Seventeen years later Sandra Fredman and I examined these and other aspects of labour law in the public services, and again concluded that the state had distinctive characteristics that rendered it unique among employers.[2] Since that time the legal and institutional framework governing employment in public services has become considerably more complex due, in part, to policies that attempt to replicate the disciplines of a private sector competitive market. Provisions to ensure that nationally-determined terms and conditions of employment were applied throughout an individual service have been replaced by a more fragmented structure, with individual employer or managerial units having much greater discretion at a local level to determine terms and conditions of employment.[3] Moreover, 'public' services are no longer necessarily delivered

---

[1] BA Hepple and P O'Higgins, *Public Employee Trade Unionism in the United Kingdom: The Legal Framework* (Ann Arbor, Institute of Labor and Industrial Relations, University of Michigan / Wayne State University, 1971).
[2] S Fredman and GS Morris, *The State as Employer: Labour Law in the Public Services* (London, Mansell, 1989); see also GS Morris and S Fredman, 'Is there a Public/Private Labour Law Divide?' (1993) 14 *Comparative Labor Law Journal* 115.
[3] See GS Morris, 'Fragmenting the State: Implications for Accountability for Employment Practices in Public Services' [1999] *Public Law* 64.

by public bodies; they may instead be delivered by private organisations, either alone or in tandem with public sector providers, usually under contract to the state or pursuant to a statutory regulatory regime. This development has given the role of the state as contractor, as well as employer, enhanced importance for labour lawyers.[4] From the converse perspective, the public/private divide also needs to be assessed in the light of developments both in common law and statute that expose employment practices in both sectors to greater external scrutiny and control, most notably through the implication of principles associated with public law in relation to the exercise of contractual powers or discretion.[5]

What are the implications of this restructured landscape for a public/private labour law divide? Do contemporary patterns of public service delivery make such a distinction otiose? I have argued elsewhere that, despite the apparent convergence of the public and private sectors in terms of their employment practices, the case for special treatment of employment in the public service remains.[6] This case is justified by reference to two distinct sets of principles which it is important to keep separate. The first is the principle of democratic accountability and the nature of state power. This entails constraints on the actions of state employers which could not realistically be applied to employers in the private sector, but does not (contrary to earlier 'state sovereignty' arguments for limiting rights such as freedom of association and the right to strike)[7] of itself justify restricting the employment rights of workers. The second category — the 'functional' approach — examines the role in society which public services perform, and acknowledges that the function of a particular service, and that which individual workers perform within it, may justify regulation of a kind which has no counterpart in the general law. By contrast to the first, functional justifications are equally applicable to the public and the private sectors and to workers as well as their employers.

The normative approach outlined above is reflected in arguments in this chapter. However, the main task of the chapter is not to examine the substantive provisions applicable to individual services which this approach may entail — restrictions on conflicts of interest or requirements to 'whistle-blow,' for example. Rather, it is to assess at a broader level whether, in the light of current policies and trends, the labour law of the future is likely to

---

[4] See B Hepple, 'Tort Law in the Contract State' in P Birks (ed), *Frontiers of Liability, vol 2* (Oxford, Oxford University Press, 1994).
[5] See M Freedland, *The Personal Employment Contract* (Oxford, Oxford University Press, 2003) especially 154–70, 186–95, 223–33, 332–47.
[6] GS Morris, 'Employment in Public Services: The Case for Special Treatment' (2000) 20 *Oxford Journal of Legal Studies* 167.
[7] See KW Wedderburn, 'Industrial Action, the State and the Public Interest' in B Aaron and KW Wedderburn (eds), *Industrial Conflict: A Comparative Legal Survey* (London, Longman, 1972) 367–77.

be based upon an essentially uniform regime, albeit with distinctive statutory provision made for particular groups in specific areas (industrial action or participation in political activities, for example), or whether some form of public/private divide is likely to continue to exist. The chapter begins by assessing the extent to which public and private employment are moving towards a common legal framework, the barriers to full convergence that currently exist, and whether there are principled arguments for those barriers to remain. It then examines the respects in which the conduct of the state as contractor is creating a rather different form of divide in the sense that the state is imposing obligations on the private sector employers it uses to perform public services that go beyond those that contracts in the purely private sector are likely to require. The conclusion finds that, despite some infusion into general labour law of concepts associated with public law, obstacles to a uniform labour law regime are likely to remain. However, it will be necessary to talk not of a 'public/private' divide, as such, but rather a series of divides whose location varies according to the context, not always on a coherent or easily justifiable basis.

PUBLIC AND PRIVATE: TOWARDS A COMMON LEGAL FRAMEWORK?

The United Kingdom is unusual in never having subjected public employees as a whole to a separate legal regime, although some categories of worker, such as the police, have long been subject to distinctive statutory rules and procedures designed to cater for the perceived requirements of the individual service. The employment protection legislation introduced from the 1960s onwards continued the traditional position of not distinguishing between the public and the private sectors, and (with some exceptions) such legislation generally now accords homogenous protection to all groups other than the police and the armed forces,[8] although even these groups are not excluded from all rights. This reflects the position in post-war international treaties on workers' rights, which do not accord public employees differential treatment from other groups merely because of their status as such,[9] although some EU Social Policy Directives exclude from their ambit, expressly or by implication, areas of public employment or activities, a point returned to in the concluding section.

To focus purely on the scope of statutory employment rights overlooks important differences between the public and the private sectors in other

---

[8] For an overview of the current position see S Deakin and GS Morris, *Labour Law* (3rd edn, Butterworths, London 2001) 182–88.
[9] See, eg, ILO Conventions. 87, 98 and 151; European Convention on Human Rights 1950 and the European Social Charter 1961.

respects, however. These differences can be divided into three main areas. The first concerns the anomalous common law status of two important public sector groups, civil servants and the police, which, despite being increasingly difficult to defend, seems likely to remain unchanged by legislation. The second lies in the availability of judicial review of the decisions of public bodies which, although confined to limited circumstances in the context of employment, has no counterpart in the private sector. The third is a by-product of the public/private divide contained in the Human Rights Act 1998. I explore each of these differences in turn and conclude that, whilst the first should be abolished and the third may ultimately be of limited practical importance, the second constitutes a principled reason for the barrier to full convergence between the public and the private sectors to remain.

Police and Civil Servants: Barriers to a Common Legal Framework?

At common law, police constables are regarded as independent officers capable of exercising legal powers derived from the nature of their office. On this ground it was held that they were not employees of the relevant police authority for the purposes of vicarious liability in tort.[10] Statute now deems chief officers of police to be liable in respect of any unlawful conduct by constables in their force in the performance of their functions,[11] and in the context of negligence claims the House of Lords has treated the relationship between officer and Chief Constable as analogous to a contract of employment for the purposes of determining the nature of the duties the Chief Constable owes.[12] However, this flexible approach does not apply to statutory interpretation, and the absence of an employment relationship has produced a welter of litigation regarding the application of anti-discrimination legislation to the police, most recently in relation to the liability of Chief Constables for discriminatory acts perpetrated by one member of the force against another.[13]

The concept of the independent police officer has long appeared to sit uneasily with the high level of control that in reality accompanies membership of a hierarchical disciplined force. It has been argued strongly that the traditional position is anachronistic, and that it would be more appropriate

---

[10] *Fisher v Oldham Corporation* [1930] 2 KB 364.
[11] Police Act 1996, s 88(1).
[12] *White v Chief Constable of South Yorkshire Police* [1999] IRLR 110; *Waters v Commissioner of Police of the Metropolis* [2000] IRLR 720.
[13] *Liversidge v Chief Constable of Bedfordshire* [2002] IRLR 651 (but see now Race Relations Act 1976, s 76A); *Chief Constable of Cumbria v McGlennon* [2002] ICR 1156; *Chief Constable of Kent County Constabulary v Baskerville* [2003] EWCA Civ 1354 (but see now Sex Discrimination Act 1975 (Amendment) Regulations 2003 (SI 2003 1657).

to treat police officers as employees of the police authority, a position that would epitomise and reinforce their relationship with the local community which they serve.[14] Such a measure would also create, in the context of statutory employment protection rights, a presumption of homogenous treatment with other groups rather than the presumption of exclusion from such rights that currently applies in the absence of provision to the contrary.[15] The presumption of inclusion could, of course, be overridden, but it would remove the need for time-consuming and expensive litigation over the unintended consequences of legislative drafting and require consideration of the justification for exclusion in each specific case. The capacity for a Chief Officer of Police to authorise civilians employed by police authorities to exercise specified police powers is a further argument in favour of re-examining the status of police constables.[16] However, in 2002, when this power was being debated, the government gave no indication that this would lead to a change in the traditional position, and it seems likely, therefore, that the police will continue to remain outside the general framework of labour law for the foreseeable future.

In contrast to the police, civil servants already benefit in practice from the majority of statutory employment rights.[17] However, anachronistically, they still work in 'Crown service,' reflecting their original status as members of the royal household, a position that has anomalous consequences in the modern state. The Crown's power to employ derives from the royal prerogative, which is exercised through Orders in Council, in contrast to the statutory authority upon which other public employers depend. In practice the power to determine matters relating to employment in the civil service is delegated to the Minister of the Civil Service.[18] Orders in Council can be promulgated and amended without recourse to Parliament, so enabling fundamental changes to the governance and conduct of the civil service to be made outside the democratic process.[19] The fact that civil servants are

---

[14] L Lustgarten, *The Governance of Police* (London, Sweet and Maxwell, 1986) 31. Possession of the powers of a constable has not been regarded as incompatible with employee status in relation to members of the British Transport Police: *Spence v British Railways Board* [2000] ICR 232.

[15] *Commissioner of Police of the Metropolis v Lowrey-Nesbit* [1999] ICR 401. Special provision is currently made for the police, for example, in the context of health and safety, whistle-blowing, and working time.

[16] Police Reform Act 2002, s 38. See GS Morris, 'Extending the Police Family: Issues and Anomalies' [2002] *Public Law* 670.

[17] The main exceptions are the right to a minimum notice period and the right to a statutory redundancy payment. Separate provision for redundancy is made in the Civil Service Compensation Scheme.

[18] Civil Service Order in Council 1995, as amended. The Civil Service (Management Functions) Act 1992 authorises the Minister for the Civil Service to delegate any of his functions to any other servant of the Crown: s 1(2).

[19] A recent controversial example being the provision in 1997 for the Prime Minister to allow up to three special advisers in his office to exceed the function of providing advice to ministers to which special advisers are generally confined.

regarded as working for the Crown has resulted in arcane debates as to their common law employment rights. Although the courts eventually (a mere 15 years ago) concluded that it was constitutionally possible for civil servants to have contracts of employment,[20] the traditional doctrine of dismissal at will has survived, albeit that it is not generally relied upon in practice. This doctrine is invoked in the model contract for senior staff to deny them any entitlement to notice of termination, although it states that normally notice will be given and compensation paid if it is not. It is difficult to justify maintaining a legal basis for employment which leads to contortions of this kind.[21]

In recent years there has been pressure from a variety of quarters for the constitutional status of civil servants to be enshrined in a Civil Service Act.[22] The Labour government has committed itself in principle to this, but has refused to give an undertaking as to the timing of such a measure and progress has been 'disappointingly slow.'[23] In its submission to a recent Wicks Committee Inquiry,[24] it indicated that any steps in this direction would, in any event, be confined to placing the Civil Service Code and Code of Conduct for Special Advisers on a statutory footing. This falls far short of the more comprehensive legislation required to locate civil service employment within the framework of a modern democratic state. At a basic minimum, legislation should address the legal status of civil servants, the identity of their employer and the source of the power to employ; recruitment and pre-employment vetting; the disciplinary procedure; wider aspects of conduct than those covered in the current Code, including political activities and restrictions on activities post-employment; the role of Agency Chief Executives; and accountability for civil service employment matters.[25] Given that the government lacks the political will for such reform, it seems likely that civil service employment, like that of the police, will continue to be based on outmoded historical principles for some years to come.

[20] *R v Civil Service Appeal Board, ex parte Bruce* [1988] ICR 649, affirmed by the Court of Appeal in *R v Lord Chancellor's Department, ex parte Nangle* [1991] IRLR 343.
[21] See M Freedland, 'Contracting the Employment of Civil Servants: A Transparent Exercise?' [1995] *Public Law* 224 for the argument that dismissal at will could be excluded by contract.
[22] Report of the House of Lords Select Committee on the Public Service, HL Paper 55, Session 1997–98, paras 403–14; Sixth Report of the Committee on Standards in Public Life (January 2000), Recommendation 17; Ninth Report of the Committee on Standards in Public Life, (April 2003), Recommendation 34.
[23] Ninth Report, above n 22, at para 10.17; see generally *ibid* ch 10.
[24] Ninth Report, above, n 22. *The Government's Response to the Ninth Report of the Committee on Standards in Public Life* (Cm 5964, 2003), does not reiterate this, but states that any legislation would need to be 'short and succinct' (at 10) and emphasises that any legislation on the civil service 'has to compete for its place alongside many other priorities' (at 5).
[25] For a wider discussion, see N Lewis, 'A Civil Service Act for the United Kingdom' [1998] *Public Law* 463.

Judicial Review

An important distinction between private sector employers and their public sector counterparts is that decisions of the latter, unlike the former, are potentially subject to judicial review. In practice, as is well known, since *R v East Berkshire Health Authority ex parte Walsh*[26] it has been accepted that the fact that an employer is a public body does not of itself constitute the requisite 'public' element for judicial review to lie; rather, where the dispute concerns the exercise of 'private' contractual rights, the remedy should be confined to private law. In order for the presumption that the employment relationship lies principally in the private realm to be overridden, exceptional circumstances must be present. These include where a specific aspect of the employment relationship is underpinned by prerogative or statute, or otherwise restricted by the state (such as a statutory discipline code of the type governing the police);[27] where the challenged act is of 'general application';[28] and, more broadly where, in the exercise of its discretion, the court considers that there are special factors that accord the decision the necessary quality of 'publicness.'[29] Moreover, even then an application may be rejected if the court considers there to be an alternative remedy available, such as those available under contract or general unfair dismissal law, even if this remedy is not equivalent in its effect to those which public law may offer.

The arguments against this restrictive approach to judicial review, which fails to accord sufficient recognition to the fact that decisions in the field of employment, no less than in other fields, involve an exercise of public power for which the bearers should be judicially accountable, have been discussed in detail elsewhere and are not repeated here.[30] Far from being accepted, however, the courts have erected a further obstacle to judicial review in the context of employment with the adoption of a test that asks not only whether the function being performed by the public body was public or private in its nature but further whether 'the defendant was performing a public duty owed to the claimant in the particular circumstances under consideration.'[31] On this basis the Court of Appeal concluded that the decision to send a detective inspector of police seconded to the National Crime Squad back to his local force because of perceived deficiencies in his skills

---

[26] [1985] QB 152.
[27] *McLaren v Home Office* [1990] IRLR 338, 342.
[28] *Ibid*; see also *R v Hillingdon Health Authority, ex parte Goodwin* [1984] ICR 800; *R v Liverpool City Council, ex parte Ferguson and Ferguson* [1985] IRLR 501.
[29] *R v CPS, ex parte Hogg* (1994) 6 Admin LR 778.
[30] S Fredman and G Morris, 'Public or Private? State Employees and Judicial Review' (1991) 107 *Law Quarterly Review* 298.
[31] *R (on the Application of Tucker) v Director General of the National Crime Squad* [2003] EWCA Civ 57, [2003] IRLR 439, Scott Baker LJ at para 24.

and conduct was a 'decision tailor-made' to him and of an 'operational nature,' and for these reasons did not involve the performance of a public duty.[32] The line between the operation of formal disciplinary proceedings, which the court acknowledged remained amenable to review, and 'operational and management decisions, where the police are entitled to run their own affairs without the intervention of the courts'[33] may not be as clear cut in practice as the judgment in this case suggests, given that 'management' decisions may have crucial implications for individuals' reputations and career prospects within a monopoly public employer.[34] Moreover, it fails to provide a remedy for the individual who is subject to a detrimental decision that may be *Wednesbury* unreasonable[35] but 'tailor-made' to her, such as (to take the paradigm example) the colour of her hair. The outcome of closing the review jurisdiction to 'management' decisions may be, ironically, that workers with a contract of employment may have a cause of action based on a breach of principles associated with public law (in particular rationality and compliance with legitimate expectations) in the exercise of a contractual power or discretion[36] in circumstances where those who have no contract, such as the police, are denied a remedy. However, despite the assiduity with which access to judicial review is guarded, its potential availability in even limited circumstances will continue to represent a form of public/private employment law divide, albeit of a fragmented and incoherent nature.

Human Rights Act 1998

The public/private divide created by the Human Rights Act 1998 is of a rather different nature to that applied by the courts to judicial review. An individual 'victim' may bring proceedings against a 'public authority' he or she alleges has acted, or proposes to act, incompatibly with a Convention right.[37] The Act states that a 'public authority' includes 'any person certain of whose functions are functions of a public nature' but then provides that

---

[32] *Ibid* at para 25.

[33] *Ibid* at para 35.

[34] Cf *R (on the Application of Morgan) v Chief Constable of South Wales* [2001] EWHC Admin 262, para 19, where Scott Baker LJ opined that the courts should only in the most exceptional circumstances, if ever, interfere with a decision to remove the applicant from a pool awaiting promotion due to an operational incident that resulted in admonishment.

[35] In the sense of being 'so unreasonable that no reasonable authority could ever come to it': *Associated Provincial Picture Houses Ltd v Wednesbury Corporation* [1948] 1 KB 223, Lord Greene MR at 229–30.

[36] This cause of action may be derived from breach of the implied term of trust and confidence, which increasingly draws upon these principles, or from free-standing principles: see Freedland, above n 5.

[37] Human Rights Act 1998, ss 6, 7.

a person is not a public authority by virtue only of this provision 'if the nature of the act is private.'[38] This means that there are effectively two categories of public authority for the purposes of the Act. First, there are 'core' public authorities, whose acts will be susceptible to challenge even if they occur in the context of the employment relationship which, as discussed above, is generally regarded as private for the purposes of judicial review. In deciding whether a body is a 'core' public authority the House of Lords has emphasised the need to examine whether its functions are in the broad sense 'governmental' so that its actions would both engage the responsibility of the state before the European Court of Human Rights and it would fall outside the definition of a 'victim' for the purposes of Article 34 of the Convention, which allows applications only by 'any person, non-governmental organisation or group of individuals.'[39] Secondly, there are 'hybrid' bodies with 'mixed' functions, where it will be necessary to decide whether the act in question falls within the public or the private realm. Bodies of this nature may themselves be 'victims' when performing private acts.[40]

To date the courts have adopted a restrictive approach to the question of whether a body is a public authority on the basis of the 'functional' test. According to the Court of Appeal, this test is not designed without more 'to make a body, which does not have responsibilities to the public, a public body merely because it performs acts on behalf of a public body which would constitute public functions were such acts to be performed by the public body itself'[41]; there must be features or a combination of features which impose a public character or stamp on the act. The existence of statutory authority for what is done can help, as can the extent of control over the function exercised by another body which is a public authority, but supervision by a public regulatory body of itself would not necessarily suffice.[42] This reasoning has been criticised as contrary to constitutional principle in making the application of rights contingent on the method

---

[38] *Ibid* s 6(3)(b), (5).

[39] *Parochial Church Council of the Parish of Aston Cantlow and Wilmcote with Billesley, Warwickshire v Wallbank* [2003] UKHL 37, Lord Nicholls at paras 7–8; Lord Hope at paras 51–52; Lord Hobhouse at para 87; Lord Rodger at paras 159–62. The Human Rights Act 1998 uses the Art 34 definition of a 'victim' for the purposes of the Act: s 7(7). Lord Nicholls regarded as the 'most obvious examples' of 'core' public authorities government departments, local authorities, the police and the armed forces: para 7.

[40] *Ibid*, Lord Nicholls at para 11.

[41] *Poplar Housing and Regeneration Community Association Ltd v Donoghue* [2001] EWCA Civ 595, [2001] 4 All ER 604, para 59.

[42] *Ibid* at para 65. See also *R (on the application of Heather and others) v Leonard Cheshire Foundation* [2002] EWCA Civ 266, [2002] 2 All ER 936. No reference was made to *Donoghue* or *Leonard Cheshire* in *Aston Cantlow*, above n 39. In *Hampshire County Council v Graham Beer t/a Hammer Trout Farm* [2003] EWCA Civ 1056 the Court of Appeal, whilst considering this omission 'perhaps somewhat surprising' did not regard the earlier decisions as thereby overruled.

of service delivery and as illogical in deeming a function to be public if conducted on an in-house basis but private if contracted out.[43] Its implications for employment law depend partly on the answer to the question whether, in the case of a body which is deemed to be a public authority according to the functional test, acts relating to employment are regarded as public or private in their nature; unless the courts are persuaded by the argument that bodies performing public functions should be liable for breaches of Convention rights in relation to the treatment of their workers engaged in the performance of those functions,[44] rights will be enforceable directly only where the employer is a 'core' public authority. This issue has yet to be determined, but the decision of the House of Lords that enforcement of a civil debt does not constitute a public act[45] suggests that the argument that most employment-related acts are private may prevail. Nevertheless the public/private divide will remain significant, at least unless and until the common law absorbs Convention rights to the extent that such rights can be invoked directly by all workers, regardless of the legal status of their employer.

THE STATE AS CONTRACTOR: A SPECIAL CASE?

Historically, the state has been a major purchaser of goods and services from the private sector. The significance of this procurement role for labour lawyers was enhanced by the policies of market testing and contracting-out adopted by the 1979–97 Conservative governments, which involved staff employed by private sector bodies delivering public services in place of those employed directly by the state. The priority accorded to the operation of market forces in determining the terms and conditions of employment of such staff led to the reversal of long-standing policies, including the termination of the 1946 House of Commons Fair Wages Resolution, which, embodying a practice dating back to 1891, had required government

---

[43] P Craig, 'Contracting Out, the Human Rights Act and the Scope of Judicial Review' (2002) 118 *Law Quarterly Review* 551. The argument that a public authority could be required to contract with a private sector provider to protect an individual's Convention rights is explored in the following section.

[44] See GS Morris, 'The Human Rights Act and the Public/Private Divide in Employment Law' (1998) 27 *Industrial Law Journal* 293; 'Public Employment and the Human Rights Act' [2001] *Public Law* 442; P Elias and J Coppel, 'Freedom of Expression and Freedom of Religion: Some Thoughts on the *Glen Hoddle* Case' in J Beatson and Y Cripps (eds), *Freedom of Expression and Freedom of Information* (Oxford, Oxford University Press, 2000) 51, 58. Cf B Hepple, *Human Rights and the Contract of Employment* (London, Employment Lawyers Association, 2001).

[45] *Aston Cantlow*, above n 39, Lord Nicholls at paras 16–17, Lord Hope at para 64, Lord Hobhouse at para 89.

departments to include a term in contracts with private sector employers that contractors should pay their workers the generally accepted rate for the job.[46] Local authorities and other public bodies were prohibited by statute from taking account in the procurement process of the wages paid by contractors, and a wide range of other workforce matters labelled 'non-commercial,' to ensure that this neo-liberal approach was generally applied.[47] Only the Transfer of Undertakings (Protection of Employment) Regulations 1981 (SI 1981/1794) ('TUPE'), where applicable, served as a partial impediment to the race to the bottom by safeguarding existing terms and conditions of employment when services were contracted out,[48] although their application was frequently contested.

The Labour government modified the policies of its Conservative predecessor towards the delivery of public services in a number of respects. Private sector involvement was not abandoned; indeed, the variety of 'public/private partnerships' has increased, and the private finance initiative (PFI), initiated by the Conservatives, has been embraced with enthusiasm; commitments have been made to around 520 projects, with a capital value approaching 23 billion pounds,[49] despite some well publicised failures and strong opposition within trade unions and some quarters of the Labour Party to the concept. However, the 'prior options' test previously applied, which favoured provision by the private sector whenever possible,[50] has been replaced by the criterion of 'best value,'[51] with no ideological preference for any particular form of provision.[52] Moreover, the government has emphasised that 'partnerships with the private and voluntary sectors should be selected where these will drive up service performance standards, not in order to drive down staff terms and conditions.'[53] 'Best value' is not to be equated with the cheapest; rather it means 'the optimum combination of whole life costs and benefits to meet the customer's requirements,' which may include social factors such as good workforce management in addition to other factors relating to sustainability and quality.[54]

The abandonment of the explicit preference for private sector provision of public services has been accompanied by a series of measures designed to

---

[46] The effectiveness of the Resolutions in practice has been doubted, however: see B Bercusson, *Fair Wages Resolutions* (London, Mansell, 1978).

[47] Local Government Act 1988, s 17.

[48] SI 1981/1794, reg 5. See generally Deakin and Morris, above n 8, at 216–33.

[49] *Financial Times*, 22 November 2002.

[50] Efficiency Unit, *The Government's Guide to Market Testing* (1993).

[51] *Government's Response to the Report from the House of Lords Select Committee on the Public Service* (Cm 4000, 1998) paras 12 and 13.

[52] See, eg, circular on *Best Value and Performance Improvement* (ODPM Circular 03/2003) para 24.

[53] *Ibid* at para 37.

[54] *Ibid* at para 62.

accord greater protection to staff interests where services are transferred. These are unlikely to be adopted in a purely private sector context. In addition, modest moves have been made in the direction of the adoption of contract compliance strategies by public bodies, requiring as a condition of the contract that specific public policy objectives are furthered. These developments are each examined in turn. Finally, the capacity of the state to impose obligations beyond the realm of the contractual by means of legislation is examined briefly, a unique and enduring attribute which is not shared by any private sector body.

Contracting Out and Staff Interests: Beyond the General Law

Four principal measures have been adopted to ameliorate the detrimental impact on staff interests when services are contracted out to the private sector. Two, at least, are the product of overt political negotiations designed to reduce union opposition to private sector involvement in the provision of public services (although they have not been wholly successful in this regard). Nevertheless, this does not reduce their significance as exemplars of state practice that is highly unlikely to be replicated in agreements between private sector bodies.

First, a Cabinet Office Statement of Practice on Staff Transfers in the Public Sector, issued in January 2000, affirmed that public sector organisations should conduct contracting-out exercises with the private sector, including second and subsequent round contracts (and functions returning to the public sector), on the basis that staff will transfer and TUPE will apply unless there are exceptional reasons not to do this. In circumstances where TUPE does not apply to a transfer within the public sector,[55] TUPE principles should nevertheless be followed, where possible on the basis of specific statutory provision.[56] Highly significantly, the Statement requires the new employer to offer transferring staff membership of a pension scheme which is actuarially certified as 'broadly comparable' to the public service scheme the staff transferred are leaving, subject to appropriate compensation if exceptional circumstances preclude this. This also applies where staff originally employed in the public sector transfer from one contractor to another. Given that occupational pension arrangements are

---

[55] An administrative reorganisation of public administrative authorities, or the transfer of administrative functions between public administrative authorities, is outside the scope of the Directive: Directive 2001/23/EC, Art 1(c).

[56] In addition, Employment Relations Act 1999, s 38, permits the Secretary of State to apply TUPE principles in circumstances not covered by the Acquired Rights Directive: see the Transfer of Undertakings (Protection of Employment) (Rent Officer Service) Regulations 1999, (SI 1999/2511).

currently outside TUPE,[57] this requirement (enshrined in statute for local government)[58] confers a substantial benefit.

Secondly, since April 2003 local authorities have had a statutory duty to consult recognised trade unions and organisations representing relevant staff, and staff themselves, in conducting best value reviews,[59] and it is recommended that contractors should have policies that ensure consultation with the workforce on key issues following a transfer.[60] In addition, the terms and conditions of employment applicable to a contractor's workforce, the composition of and opportunities afforded to its members, and the conduct of contractors or workers in industrial disputes have ceased to be prohibited 'non-commercial' matters to the extent that they are relevant to the achievement of best value or the purposes of a TUPE transfer.[61] Indeed, local authorities are now required to take account of workforce issues in the procurement process to the extent compatible with EU law obligations, discussed below.[62]

Thirdly, a Code of Practice on Workforce Matters in Local Authority Service Contracts, announced in March 2003, is designed to end the 'two-tier' workforce by requiring contractors who employ staff transferred from local authority employment to offer new recruits terms and conditions (other than pensions) 'which are, overall, no less favourable than those of transferred employees.'[63] Such terms should be the subject of consultation and preferably agreement by contractors with recognised union or other employee representatives. The Code is to be part of the commercial contract, enforceable by the local authority in the event that attempts to resolve a complaint of non-compliance against the contractor by other methods are unsuccessful. Employers and unions have agreed to independent and binding arbitration as a means of settling disputes in this area if attempts at

---

[57] At the time of writing the government proposes that, on a TUPE transfer, where an employee is covered by a pension scheme to which the transferor employer is required to contribute, the transferee will be required to make payments, capped at 6 per cent limit, into a stakeholder pension or equivalent alternative: *Simplicity, Security and Choice: Working and Saving for Retirement* (Cm 5825, 2003). Clearly this falls short of what the Cabinet Office Statement of Practice requires.

[58] Local Government Act 2003, s 102; see also s 101, which is designed to give statutory effect to other principles in the Cabinet Office Statement.

[59] Local Government (Best Value) Performance Plans and Reviews Order 1999 (SI 1999/3251), as amended by SI 2003/662.

[60] Above n 52, at para 29. In the light of the emphasis on consultation, it is anomalous that the prohibition on a requirement to negotiate or consult with union officials remains in the Trade Union and Labour Relations (Consolidation) Act 1992, ss 186 and 187.

[61] Local Government Best Value (Exclusion of Non-Commercial Considerations) Order 2001, (SI 2001/909).

[62] See above, n 52 Annex C for guidance issued by the Secretary of State to which local authorities must have regard on taking into account workforce issues in local government tendering.

[63] Above n 52, paras 36–39 and Annex D. The Code requires new joiners to be offered one of three specified pension arrangements.

conciliation fail. Local authorities will be required to certify compliance with their obligations under the Code in their 'Performance Plan,' which will be subject to scrutiny by the auditor. The adoption of a 'package' rather than a term-for-term comparison accords contractors flexibility that may not exist for TUPE-transferred staff in the light of *Daddy's Dance Hall*,[64] and leaves scope for argument as to when the stipulated formula has been met.[65] There may also be difficulties in determining when jobs are comparable. Nevertheless, the adoption of this formula is seen as a substantial concession to unions, which are pressing for its extension to other areas of the public sector.

Finally, in the NHS, a 'retention of employment' model has been agreed, which will result in staff engaged in specified ancillary activities (catering, cleaning, laundry, portering and security) in PFI hospitals remaining in Trust employment on secondment to the private sector operator to which they would otherwise have transferred, possibly for several years. This outcome is achieved by staff formally objecting to employment by the contractor,[66] at which point the Trust will offer new contracts to the staff concerned. New staff in the categories concerned will also be employed by the Trust, but those promoted to other jobs will become employees of the contractor.

All these four measures mark a significant departure from previous practice. The third and fourth, in particular, are likely to have long-term consequences because of the longevity of the arrangements of which they constitute an integral part. It is highly unlikely that a contract between two private organisations would include provisions of this nature, and to that extent these developments will accord the state as contractor a distinctive status for the foreseeable future. At a time when occupational pension schemes are under threat, the safeguards accorded to workers transferring from public sector bodies also constitute a substantial difference from their private sector counterparts.

Contract Compliance

The Code of Practice on Workforce Matters in Local Authority Service Contracts, described above, contains one example of contract compliance, a strategy that was all but outlawed or abandoned under the Conservative government. This strategy harnesses the enormous purchasing power of state bodies to further social policy objectives, and at one time was widely used by public bodies.[67] Limited steps have been taken to revive it. The

---

[64] 324/86, [1988] IRLR 315, paras 14–17; see Deakin and Morris, above n 8, at 227–29.
[65] Cf the approach under the Equal Pay Act 1970: *Hayward v Cammell Laird Shipbuilders Ltd* [1988] IRLR 257.
[66] Under TUPE, reg 5(4A). See generally R Davies, 'Contracting Out and the Retention of Employment Model in the National Health Service (2004) 33 *Industrial Law Journal* 95.
[67] See Fredman and Morris, above n 2, ch 12.

Race Relations (Amendment) Act 2000 obliges a wide range of public authorities to promote race equality,[68] which, in certain contexts, can extend to a requirement for contractors to promote equality of opportunity within their workforce.[69] This duty is to be extended to gender and disabilities 'when parliamentary time allows,'[70] and the Commission for Racial Equality has suggested that public authorities should also consider other equality issues, including those concerning disability, religion or belief, sexual orientation and age, in the contract specification.[71]

Public authorities are uniquely constrained by public procurement regulations that govern contracts exceeding specified thresholds,[72] resulting from EC Directives designed to prevent barriers to the operation of the internal market.[73] At one time these were regarded as obstacles to the pursuit of contract compliance strategies. However, in 2001 the European Commission indicated that contracts may require compliance with obligations such as the promotion of sex equality or racial diversity, or compliance with the substance of ILO core Conventions, provided that such requirements do not discriminate against non-national tenderers and are mentioned in the contract notice.[74] Moreover, member states may define as 'grave professional misconduct' justifying exclusion from a procurement procedure altogether non-compliance with provisions of social legislation, which could include, if mandatory in national law, the introduction of an equal opportunities policy.[75] This suggests that EU law may not constitute as formidable a barrier to contract compliance strategies as was sometimes thought, although the extent to which the UK government will permit or pursue such strategies more widely than at present is a matter of speculation.[76]

---

[68] Race Relations Act 1976, s 71. Bodies subject to the duty are listed in Sch 1A.

[69] Commission for Racial Equality, *Race Equality and Public Procurement*, Consultation Draft, (2003) 25. The CRE confines this to contracts highly relevant to the duty to promote race equality, which are likely to be front-line services.

[70] Above n 52, at para 25. See the draft Disability Discrimination Bill, December 2003.

[71] Above note 69, at 29. See also the Equality Bill 2003, introduced by Lord Lester, cls 25–27 and Sch 2, Part 2.

[72] Public Works Contracts Regulations 1991 (SI 1991/2680); Public Service Contracts Regulations 1993 (SI 1993/3228); Public Supply Contracts Regulations 1995 (SI 1995/201). The authorities affected are identically defined in reg 3 of each set of regulations.

[73] Even where contracts are not subject to the Directives, public purchasers must adhere to general obligations in the EC Treaty such as non-discrimination on grounds of nationality.

[74] Interpretative Communication of the Commission on the Community Law Applicable to Public Procurement and the Possibilities for Integrating Social Considerations into Public Procurement (COM (2001) 566 final) para 1.6. See also Common Position adopted by the Council on 20 March 2003 with a View to the Adoption of a Directive of the European Parliament and of the Council on the Co-ordination of Procedures for the Award of Public Works Contracts, Public Supply Contracts and Public Service Contracts, Preamble, recital 31.

[75] Interpretative Communication, above, n 74, at para 1.3.1.

[76] See the general discussion in B Hepple, M Coussey and T Choudhury, *Equality: A New Framework* (Oxford, Hart Publishing, 2000) 79–85.

One area where contract compliance may be required by law is human rights. It has been suggested obiter that under the Human Rights Act 1998 it would arguably be possible for the individual recipient of a service (in the case in question a resident of a care home to whom the local authority owed a duty to provide accommodation) to require a 'public authority' to enter into a contract with the private sector provider which fully protected that individual's Convention rights, even though the provider was not itself thereby regarded as performing a public function. The individual may then be able to rely upon the contract as a person for whose benefit the contract was made.[77] There seems no reason in principle why such an argument, if accepted, could not equally apply to the treatment of the contractor's workers. There are substantial conceptual and practical objections to this approach in either case, however.[78] Why should there be an obligation to secure the application of Convention rights against a party not itself bound by the Human Rights Act? What if workers did not know of their rights, or lacked the capacity to enforce them when the contract was being made? If incorporated, would workers then be regarded as beneficiaries of the term for enforcement purposes?[79] The 'contract compliance' obligation is a less attractive course in this context than an approach that categorises as 'public' a function that would be regarded as such if performed in-house by the public authority itself, although this leaves the difficulty that acts in the employment sphere by bodies with 'mixed functions' may be seen as 'private.'

The State as Legislator

A fundamental distinction between the state and private sector bodies as contractors is the ability of the state to impose obligations on contractors' workers enforceable by remedies beyond the realm of the contractual. The legislation governing the police and prison services respectively exemplifies this process. The Police Reform Act 2002 enables the Secretary of State to bring detention and escort officers employed by contractors within the remit of the Independent Police Complaints Commission.[80] It is a criminal offence, not merely a breach of contract, for private sector prison staff to disclose information acquired in the course of employment about individual prisoners.[81] Clearly, the imposition of sanctions of this nature is not a facility open to private sector bodies.

---

[77] R *(on the application of Heather and others) v Leonard Cheshire Foundation*, above n 42, Lord Woolf CJ at para 34.
[78] See Craig, above n 43, at 559–61.
[79] See the Contracts (Rights of Third Parties) Act 1999.
[80] Police Reform Act 2002, s 39(9), (10).
[81] Criminal Justice Act 1991, s 91; Criminal Justice and Public Order Act 1994, s 14.

CONCLUSION

This chapter has sought to assess whether the labour law of the future will be based on an essentially uniform regime or whether the divisions between the public and the private realms are likely to constitute an obstacle to this. The evidence suggests that these divisions are likely to remain, but not on a clear-cut basis; rather there are a series of 'public/private' law divides, the location of which varies according to the context: for the purposes of judicial review the divide is located differently from that applicable to the Human Rights Act, for example. This variable geometry is also reflected in EU law;[82] whereas the Directives on equal treatment cover both the public and the private sectors, the Collective Redundancies Directive excludes 'workers employed by public administrative bodies or by establishments governed by public law (or, in Member States where this concept is unknown, by equivalent bodies).'[83] By contrast, the Acquired Rights Directive applies to 'public and private undertakings engaged in economic activities whether or not they are operating for gain,'[84] although only those who are protected as employees under national employment law are covered.[85] This wider formulation also applies to the Information and Consultation Directive,[86] although the issues on which it requires employers to inform and consult are more extensive than those specified in the Collective Redundancies Directive, whose more restricted application seems hard to justify.

An assessment of the position of the state as contractor in English law produces public/private divides of a rather different nature, relating to the obligations imposed on private sector employers that contract with the state. Here, too, the picture is fragmented; the safeguards against the 'two-tier' workforce currently apply only to those transferred from local authority employment, the 'retention of employment model' is confined largely to the NHS.

The introduction to this chapter referred briefly to two distinctive sets of arguments in favour of differential treatment of employment in public services. The first justification derives from the principle of democratic accountability and the nature of state power, and thus relates to the employer's legal status. The second, the 'functional' approach, is based on the nature of the role that those who operate public services perform,

---

[82] For differential treatment of specific categories of public service worker in Treaties covering freedom of association see GS Morris, 'Freedom of Association and the Interests of the State' in KD Ewing, CA Gearty and BA Hepple (eds), *Human Rights and Labour Law: Essays for Paul O'Higgins* (London, Mansell, 1994).
[83] Directive 98/59/EC, Art 1(2)(a).
[84] Directive 2001/23/EC, Art 1(1)(c). This requires the activity to derive from the exercise of public authority: C-298/94 *Henke* [1996] IRLR 701; C-173/96 and C-247/96 *Sanchez Hidalgo* [1999] IRLR 136. See also above n 55.
[85] Directive 2001/23/EC, Art 2(d).
[86] Directive 2002/14/EC, Art 2(a).

whether in the public or the private sector. The first of these argues against a uniform labour law regime in that it requires mechanisms to be in place to ensure that the state does not exceed its legal powers as an employer, as well as adequate mechanisms of political accountability. Judicial review is designed to provide a remedy against excess or abuse of legal powers, but the restricted access to it permitted by the courts in the context of employ-ment means that it operates as a very incomplete constraint. The principle in *Walsh*[87] that confines workers employed by public bodies to remedies in private law where the complaint relates to the exercise of contractual pow-ers has long been open to the criticism that the pattern of contractual and non-contractual relations in the public services is the product of historical accident rather than coherent principle.[88] More fundamentally, the *Walsh* principle ignores the fact that judicial review is concerned with the exercise of public power, scrutiny of which should not be obstructed by a co-existent remedy concerned only with private rights. Reconsidering *Walsh* also needs to be combined with a reversal of the exclusion of decisions from the purview of the courts on the ground that they are 'operational' or 'manage-rial.' It is ironic that, as the courts have demonstrated an increased willing-ness to subject the exercise of contractual powers and discretion in private law to principles associated with public law,[89] the areas of decision-making in which judicial review may lie are, if anything, becoming more restricted. In that respect, a group such as the police that lacks access to a contractual remedy may be disadvantaged other than in the important area of dismissal, where the courts have held back from applying public law principles to con-tractual powers in deference to a statutory regime which itself is set to reduce standards of procedural fairness.[90]

To view the existence of a contract as synonymous with an exclusively private law relationship also overlooks the growing tendency for contrac-tual terms themselves to be the product of an exercise in public power. The Fire Service Act 2003, enacted following the ending of a long-running dis-pute over pay and modernisation in the fire service, empowers the Secretary of State unilaterally to fix or modify the conditions of service, including pay, of fire brigade members.[91] This power is intended to be used in the event that the government's modernisation agenda is not delivered by the firefighters and their local fire authority employers or renewed industrial

---

[87] Above n 26.
[88] See generally Fredman and Morris, above n 2, chs 3 and 8.
[89] See above n 36.
[90] *Johnson v Unisys Ltd* [2001] UKHL 13, [2001] IRLR 279; Employment Rights Act 1996, s 98A, inserted by Employment Act 2002, s 34(2). See further B Hepple and GS Morris, 'The Employment Act 2002 and the Crisis of Individual Employment Rights' (2002) 31 *Industrial Law Journal* 245.
[91] Subject to a duty to consult the negotiating body on the proposals.

action is threatened.[92] It is intended to be a temporary measure[93] pending more radical statutory reforms of the fire service, including revised collective bargaining machinery.[94] However, its significance should not be underestimated. There are other services for which the government, although not the direct employer, formally determines terms and conditions of service, but this happens following either negotiations by employers and representative organisations or a report by an independent body such as a review body or arbitrator, whose recommendations the government will be under political pressure to implement.[95] It remains to be seen whether the fire service legislation constitutes a model for imposing government reforms in other public services. The susceptibility of employer and employee to this far-reaching form of external regulation has no counterpart in the private sector of a capitalist economy.

Finally, in any consideration of the public/private labour law divide, it is important not to lose sight of the framework of political accountability within which public services operate. As informed participants, public service workers can play a significant role as guardians of public service standards of efficiency, safety and propriety, not only by 'blowing the whistle' on unlawful practices,[96] but by themselves challenging practices that endanger public safety[97] or infringe the principle of equal access, for example. Discussion to date has tended to focus on the obligations owed by public service workers: selflessness, integrity, objectivity, accountability, openness, honesty and leadership.[98] However, practical adherence to these principles, and fulfilment of a wider constitutional role, may necessitate safeguards for public service workers against detrimental treatment that

---

[92] Lord Rooker, Minister of State, Office of the Deputy Prime Minister, HL Debs vol 651, GC 45, 7 July 2003. The legislation itself does not limit the circumstances in which the power may be invoked. It could thus be used in violation of Art 6 of the European Social Charter and Art 8 of ILO Convention 151: see Joint Committee on Human Rights, Eighth and Twelfth Reports (2002–03).

[93] No orders may be made under the legislation more than two years after its commencement, except to revoke provisions in a previous order.

[94] White Paper, *Our Fire and Rescue Service* (Cm 5808, 2003); Fire and Rescue Services Bill 2004, Part 4.

[95] See S Corby, *Public Sector Disputes and Third Party Intervention* (London, ACAS, 2003). In 1987 the Conservative government abolished collective bargaining machinery for schoolteachers and introduced unilateral determination of terms and conditions, following only limited consultative procedures, by the Secretary of State. This was replaced by a statutory Review Body in 1991: see S Fredman and G Morris, 'School Teachers Pay and Conditions Act 1991' (1992) 21 *Industrial Law Journal* 44.

[96] See L Vickers, *Freedom of Speech and Employment* (Oxford, Oxford University Press, 2002).

[97] *Johnstone v Bloomsbury Health Authority* [1991] IRLR 118. I am indebted to Mark Freedland for this suggestion.

[98] The seven principles of public life identified by the Nolan Committee, *Standards in Public Life: First Report of the Committee on Standards in Public Life, vol 1* (Cm 2850-I, 1995) 14. See also House of Commons Public Administration Select Committee, *The Public Service Ethos*, Seventh Report of Session 2001–02, HC 263-I.

exceed those in the general law.[99] These and other issues relating to public service workers would benefit from consideration by a Public Services Commission. There are strong justifications for the continuation of a public/private labour law divide, but it should rest on coherent principles that are rooted in the framework of a twenty-first century democracy rather than arcane doctrines that are frequently arbitrary and unpredictable in their application. In this area, the future should break with the past; it is time to start again.

[99] See Morris, above n 6, at 180 for some examples.

8

Episodes on the Path Towards the European Social Model: The EU Charter of Fundamental Rights and the Convention on the Future of Europe

BRIAN BERCUSSON

INTRODUCTION

BOB HEPPLE'S PRESCIENT recognition of the impact of European legal developments on national labour law is well-known.[1] It is fitting, therefore, that the European Union's (EU) Charter of Fundamental Rights should be recognised in this volume as one source of the renewal of labour law. For the EU Charter of Fundamental Rights proclaimed at the summit at Nice on 7 December 2000 includes provisions which are at the heart of labour law in Europe.[2] It has the potential to renew labour law in the Member States and at EU level.

On the one hand, the Charter breaks new ground by including in a single list of fundamental rights not only traditional civil and political rights, but also a long list of social and economic rights. On the other hand, although the EU Charter was approved by the European Council at Nice, it was limited to a political declaration. A 'Convention on the Future of Europe' was

---

[1] As acknowledged on the first page of my book on *European Labour Law* (London, Butterworths, 1996) n 4.
[2] Freedom of association (Art 12), right of collective bargaining and collective action (Art 28), workers' right to information and consultation within the undertaking (Art 27), freedom to choose an occupation and right to engage in work (Art 15), prohibition of child labour and protection of young people at work (Art 32), fair and just working conditions (Art 31), protection of personal data (Art 8), non-discrimination (Art 21), equality between men and women (Art 23), protection in the event of unjustified dismissal (Art 30).

to consider whether and, if so, how the Charter should be integrated into the Treaties.[3]

The 'Convention on the Future of Europe' was established by the Heads of Government of the EU Member States to prepare the answers to a series of difficult questions facing the European Union. The answers take the form of a new draft Treaty which is proposed as the future Constitution of the European Union. The Convention included representatives of the European Parliament, the national Parliaments of the Member States, the governments of Member States and the European Commission. It was chaired by Valerie Giscard d'Estaing, together with a Praesidium. The Convention began work in early 2002 and produced its report in mid-2003.[4]

The working methods of the Convention included the establishment at the beginning of its deliberations of ten Working Groups to report to the plenary Convention on a number of specific topics. Working Group II was concerned with the EU Charter of Fundamental Rights. The Final Report of Working Group II was presented to the Plenary of the Convention on 29 October 2002. It recommended that the EU Charter be integrated into the Treaty. The Convention accepted this recommendation and has incorporated the whole of the EU Charter as Part II of the proposed Constitutional Treaty.

If incorporated into the Treaties, the Charter will have an impact not only on the EU's institutions, but perhaps even more, on the Member States, also bound by the Charter through the doctrine of supremacy of EU law. The consequences for national labour laws of such incorporation could be significant. The EU Charter includes at least three Articles on fundamental trade union rights: Article 12: Freedom of assembly and of association, Article 27: Workers' right to information and consultation within the undertaking and Article 29: Right to collective bargaining and action. Their inclusion in the Charter may well confer on them a constitutional status within national legal orders.

The European Court of Justice may be willing to recognise as protected by the EU Charter those fundamental trade union rights which all, or most, or even a critical number of Member States insist should be protected. The Court may interpret the Articles of the EU Charter on fundamental trade union rights consistently with other international labour standards and will be sensitive to where national laws have protected trade union rights.

---

[3] This chapter is derived principally from a number of memoranda prepared during 2002–03 for various Members of the Convention on the Future of Europe and for the European Trade Union Confederation, which was accorded Official Observer status at the Convention.
[4] Exhaustive information on the Convention may be obtained from the European Union's website: (http://europa.eu.int).

The EU Charter broke new ground in recognising social and labour rights on a par with classic civil and political human rights. Despite this, conspicuous by its absence from the agenda of the Convention on the Future of Europe was any apparent consideration of the future social dimension of the European Union. The Praesidium of the Convention appears to have regarded social issues as peripheral to the concerns of the Future of Europe, and to have assumed that such issues would be dealt with in the margins of the reports of the other Working Groups.

However, a number of organisations at national and European level, including the European Trade Union Confederation, considered that commitments to full employment, improved labour standards and trade union rights were central to their vision of the future of Europe. Together with members of the Convention, they worked towards building pressure to establish a specific Working Group on Social Europe. Their efforts finally succeeded when the Convention decided on 22 November 2002 to establish such a Working Group. This late decision meant work had to proceed very rapidly. The first constitutive meeting of the Working Group was held on 10 December 2002, the second meeting on 10 January 2003. Working Group XI produced draft reports and presented its Final Report to the Plenary of the Convention on 6 February 2003, to be considered by the Plenary during its final deliberations in the following months.

The Final Reports of Working Group II on the EU Charter and of Working Group XI on Social Europe provide important insights into the conflicting perspectives on the role of fundamental rights in the EU and Member State legal orders, and in particular, their potential for the renewal of labour law.

FINAL REPORT OF WORKING GROUP II ON THE EU CHARTER[5]

The EU Charter, by including fundamental social and labour standards, sets up a specific political dynamic. Failure to make the promised fundamental rights effective will create bitter disillusionment, especially among those who are promised specific social and labour rights, and will undermine their loyalty to the European integration project. The values of the Charter are a declared part of the construction of Social Europe. Its objectives are to be secured through the exercise of the competences allocated under the Union's Constitution.

The proposal in the Final Report of Working Group II that the EU Charter be integrated into the Constitutional Treaty of the European Union

---

[5] Final Report of Working Group II (CONV 354/02, 22 October 2002).

was endorsed in the Draft of Articles 1 to 16 of the Constitutional Treaty produced by the Convention's Praesidium on 6 February 2003.[6] Draft Article 5(1) provided:

> The Charter of Fundamental Rights shall be an integral part of the Constitution. The Charter is set out [in the second part of/in a Protocol annexed to] this Constitution.

A footnote added: 'The full text of the Charter, *with all the drafting adjustments given in Working Group II's final report* (CONV 354/02) will be set out either in a second part of the Constitution or in a Protocol annexed thereto, as the Convention decides.' Annex II of the Praesidium's draft, the 'Explanatory Note,' repeated that the Charter was to be incorporated 'with all the drafting adjustments mentioned in the Working Group's final report.'[7]

This endorsement was reinforced by the Final Report of Working Group XI on Social Europe.[8] A footnote in the Final Report of Working Group XI stated:[9]

> Regarding the ways and means to integrate the Charter itself in the Constitutional treaty, the Group referred to and confirmed the conclusions of the Final Report of Working Group II.

This unfortunate endorsement in a footnote raises the question of how closely Working Group XI considered the Final Report of Working Group II, in particular, the contentious 'adjustments' proposed by Working Group II.[10] Some of the conclusions reached by Working Group II, such as the extent to which Member States are bound by the Charter, were ambiguous, and

---

[6] CONV 528/03.

[7] The final draft Constitution produced by the Convention re-affirms this position.

[8] The Praesidium produced its draft of Arts 1–16 on 6 February 2003, the same day that the Final Report of Working Group XI was presented by its Chair to the Plenary of the Convention. The Praesidium's draft texts were introduced by acknowledging that they 'reflect the reports of the Working Groups on Legal Personality, the Charter, Economic Governance, Complementary Competencies, the Principle of Subsidiarity and External Action, as well as the guidelines that emerged on the basis of their recommendations during the plenary debate.' Manifestly, the draft failed to take account either of the Final Report of Working Group XI, or of any debate on the Report in the Plenary. This failure compounded the Praesidium's inability to recognise the importance of Social Europe by failing to establish a Working Group early in its proceedings.

[9] See below n 27, at 8, para 11.

[10] In the discussion in the Plenary, a number of Members of the Convention from the European Parliament criticised the Working Group's proposed 'adjustments' to the horizontal clauses. Sylvia-Yvonne Kaufmann referred to the dangers of the proposed 'adjustments' introducing new elements by the back door. Elena Paccioti warned that 'adjustments' to the horizontal clauses evinced an attempt to water down the Charter. However, the Member of the Convention representing the German Parliament, Jürgen Meyer, argued that the new clauses were mere clarifications which did not change the substance of the Charter.

render ambivalent the apparent endorsement by Working Group XI. It is vital, therefore, that these proposed 'adjustments' be critically scrutinised.

The 'adjustments' to the EU Charter proposed by Working Group II on the Charter were described as follows in its Final Report:[11]

> It is important to note that these adjustments proposed by the Group do not reflect modifications of substance. On the contrary, they would serve to confirm, and render absolutely clear and legally watertight, certain key elements of the overall consensus on the Charter on which the previous Convention had already agreed ... all drafting adjustments proposed herein fully respect the basic premise of the Group's work, i.e. to leave intact the substance agreed by consensus within the previous Convention.

On the contrary, I suggest that the proposed 'adjustments' may be characterised as, first, an attack on fundamental rights in general; and secondly, an attack on social rights in particular. Further, despite its statement to the contrary, Working Group II re-opened questions resolved by the earlier Convention, relying in one case on 'understandings' reported by a few members of that Convention who happened to be in this Working Group, or the 'important guidance provided by the "Praesidium's Explanations"',[12] though the Praesidium itself explicitly denied that it represented the Convention's authority and the Working Group conceded 'they have no legal value'.[13] The Working Group had no authority to re-open these questions, let alone propose 'adjustments' which change the consensus reached in the earlier Convention.[14] Two 'adjustments' in particular warrant close scrutiny.

Attack on Fundamental Rights in General

Working Group II proposed the following additions (in italics) to Article 51(2) of the EU Charter:

> This Charter does not *extend the scope of application of Union law beyond the powers of the Union or* establish any new power or task for [the Community or] the Union or modify powers and tasks defined *by the other [chapters/parts]* of [this Treaty/the Constitutional Treaty].

[11] Above n 5, at s A.II.1.
[12] *Ibid* at s A.II.6.
[13] *Ibid* at s A.III.3.
[14] Professor Grainne de Búrca has written one of 'Ten Reflections on the Constitutional Treaty for Europe' prepared by the European University Institute, a contribution submitted to the Convention by Giuliano Amato (CONV 703/03, 28 April 2003). Professor de Búrca analyses Working Group II's proposed 'adjustments' and recommends that, with one minor exception, they should be rejected. Amato says he does 'not endorse every single word of this study.'

If there is a potential conflict between the scope of Treaty competences and some Charter rights, the solution should be to reinforce the status of fundamental rights, not abandon them or allow their violation in order to protect the Treaty.

At least, it should be left to the European Court of Justice (ECJ) to resolve this conflict. The ECJ has played a cautious but essential role in protecting fundamental rights. It has done this, contrary to the line proposed in the 'adjustments,' in the interests of protecting the Treaty from national constitutional courts which would reject it precisely because the Treaty appeared to contradict fundamental rights in national constitutions. By recognising fundamental rights as not conflicting with the Treaty, thus giving way to the objections of these national constitutional courts, the ECJ has preserved the Treaty. Working Group II's proposed 'adjustments,' by seeking to stifle this development, threaten a confrontation with national constitutional courts which the ECJ, and the earlier Convention, wisely sought to avoid.

In making a proposal in its Final Report to 'adjust' Article 51(2):[15]

> the Group considers it useful to confirm expressly, in Article 51(2), in light of established case law, that the protection of fundamental rights by Union law cannot have the effect of extending the scope of the Treaty provisions beyond the competences of the Union.

A footnote referred to the judgment of the ECJ in C-249/96 *Grant v South-West Trains*.[16] This claim of support by the ECJ of the Working Group's view is suspect.

First, the decision in *Grant* has been widely criticised as retreating from the principle of the prohibition of discrimination on grounds of sex established in the earlier ECJ decision in *P v S and Cornwall County Council*.[17]

Secondly, the ECJ's refusal in *Grant* to prohibit discrimination on the grounds of sexual orientation as outside EU competence was reversed by the insertion by the Treaty of Amsterdam of Article 13 of the EC Treaty. This was pointed out by the Court itself in its judgment,[18] implying that the fundamental right at issue in *Grant* could have been protected in the event of Article 13 conferring EU competence. Arguably similar to Article 13 EC in the case of discrimination, the EU Charter confers competence as regards a wide range of human rights, including labour rights.

---

[15] Above n 5, at s II.2.
[16] [1998] ECR I-621, at para 45.
[17] C-13/94 [1996] ECR I-2143.
[18] At para 48.

Finally, Working Group II specifically cited paragraph 45 of the judgment in *Grant*:

> However, although respect for fundamental rights which form an integral part of those general principles is a condition of the legality of Community acts, those rights cannot in themselves have the effect of extending the scope of the Treaty provisions beyond the competences of the Community (see, *inter alia*, on the scope of Article 235 of the EC Treaty as regards respect for human rights, Opinion 2/94 [1996] ECR I-1759, paragraphs 34 and 35).[19]

The ECJ was responding to the argument that the scope of the Community's respect for fundamental rights was to be interpreted in light of national law and international conventions. The reference in brackets is to one of those: Opinion 2/94 concerned the European Convention on Human Rights. However, the position is arguably very different with respect to an EU Charter of Fundamental Rights which is itself incorporated into the Constitutional Treaty. This is not an *external* human rights standard laid down in national or international law by which to measure EU competences as regards fundamental rights. It is the *internal* EU standard establishing the competence of the EU in the areas covered by the EU Charter.

Attack on Social Rights in Particular

This attack is expressed in an 'adjustment' in the form of an additional paragraph added to Article 52 (Article 52(5)):

> The provisions of this Charter which contain principles may be implemented by legislative and executive acts taken by the institutions and bodies of the Union, and by acts of Member States when they are implementing Union law, in the exercise of their respective powers. They shall be judicially cognisable only in the interpretation of such acts and in the ruling on their legality.

Again, this is a new limitation. Most importantly, it aims to prevent 'principles' being interpreted in future as containing elements of positive rights for individuals. This proposal was vainly resisted by members of Working

---

[19] The argument as to limitation of competences as the basis of the decision in *Grant* is also undermined by the later decision in C-125/99P *D v Council* [2001] ECR I-4319, where the issue was clearly within EU competence as it involved the EU's treatment of its own employees. The claim for a household allowance for the same-sex partner was rejected, but there was no hint in the judgment that the EU lacked competence to deal with it, only that the EU legislature had not adopted legislation to allow same-sex partners that allowance as 'married' persons (para 38). See P Craig and G de Búrca, *EU Law: Text, Cases and Materials* (3rd edn, Oxford, Oxford University Press, 2003) 388.

Group II, who complained that it resurrected the distinction between rights and principles which had been rejected by the drafting Convention.[20]

This is an outrageous attempt to reverse what was a central compromise in the earlier Convention which drafted the Charter: that social and economic rights should not be separated from traditional 'rights' by characterising them as 'principles' which are not justiciable positive rights.[21] That Convention decided that all rights should have the same status.[22] This was a compromise in exchange for the Convention's not seeking to assert that the Charter should have legal constitutional status. That final legal status would be determined by the Member States, but the Convention which drafted the Charter rejected the view, advocated by a number of its members, that there should be differences in the legal status of different parts of the Charter.

The language of the Charter uses the word 'rights.' By asserting that 'principles' are weaker, Working Group II is trying to open the door to transforming some 'rights' into mere 'principles.' The Working Group even admits that it is aiming at social rights when it says: 'This is consistent both with case law of the Court of Justice and with the approach of the Member States' constitutional systems to "principles" *particularly in the field of social law.*'[23] To single out social rights for weaker protection is not acceptable.

However, it is submitted that the 'adjustment' may not have the effect claimed for it, and it does not apply to most of the provisions in Chapter IV 'Solidarity' of the Charter. Articles 27 to 38 are formulated mostly as rights, not principles. But it sets a bad precedent.[24]

---

[20] In criticising the Working Group's amendments during the Convention Plenary's debate on the Final Report of Working Group II, Olivier Duhamel, a Member of the Convention from the European Parliament, stated they were 'unnecessary and retrograde' and singled out the alleged distinction between 'rights and principles,' as did Anne Van Lancker, who specifically identified the distinction between rights and principles as attempting to limit the Charter. The French government representative, Pierre Moscovici, warned that the distinction between rights and principles could limit the interpretation of those principles.

[21] The distinction between hard (justiciable) rights and soft (programmatic) rights arose in discussions over whether social and economic rights, as contrasted with civil and political rights, were appropriate for inclusion in the EU Charter. On one side were those who wanted to exclude social rights entirely, or minimise their content, or marginalise them into a separate 'programmatic' section, or make them purely declaratory, or subject them to special 'horizontal' conditions to prevent the EU acquiring any further social competences. On the other side were those who wanted to include social rights, maximise their content, grant them the same status as civil and political rights, make them justiciable or otherwise enforceable, and not limit them by reference to existing EU competences. The latter prevailed.

[22] As affirmed in a dissent in Working Group II by Mme Elena Paciotti, a Member of the Convention from the European Parliament.

[23] Final Report of Working Group II, above n 5, at 8, s A.II.6.

[24] Some members of the Convention, including MM Giuliano Amato and Peter Hain, are putting forward the argument that some parts of the Charter (again 'principles,' as contrasted with 'rights') are not 'justiciable.'

Its impact could be seen in the Draft of Articles 1 to 16 of the Constitutional Treaty produced by the Convention's Praesidium on 6 February 2003.[25] On the one hand, in an apparently casual aside in Annex II's 'Explanatory Note' commenting on their draft Article 2 ('The Union's values'), which did not even mention the EU Charter, the Praesidium said of the Charter of Fundamental Rights: 'which, unlike this Article, does not, however, apply to autonomous action by the Member States'. This dismissal of the Charter's application to 'autonomous' action by the Member States raises serious questions about the Praesidium's commitment to the fundamental rights protected by the EU legal order.

On the other hand, this statement appeared to be contradicted by the provisions in the Praesidium's draft Article 9(1) and (4):[26]

(1)   The Constitution [Article 5(1): 'The Charter of Fundamental Rights shall be an integral part of the Constitution'] *and* law adopted by the Union institutions in exercising competences conferred on it by the Constitution, shall have primacy over the law of the Member States...

(4)   Member States shall take all appropriate measures, general or particular, to ensure fulfilment of the obligations flowing from the Constitution *or* resulting from actions taken by the Union Institutions.

Both draft Articles 9(1) and 9(4) appeared to envisage Member States being bound by the EU Charter, as part of the Constitution, *apart* from laws adopted and actions taken by Union institutions exercising Union competences. There seems to be a lack of clarity in the Praesidium regarding the application of the EU Charter to the Member States.

FINAL REPORT OF WORKING GROUP XI ON SOCIAL EUROPE

The mandate of the Convention's Working Group XI on Social Europe included a number of questions. The first three listed in the mandate concerned the European Union's social values, objectives and competences. Three others were concerned with processes of social policy-making: the open method of coordination, legislation and the role of the social partners. Finally, the question was raised of the relationship between coordination of economic and social policies. Analysis of the Final Report of Working Group XI on Social Europe reveals a number of indicators of the path towards a European social model.[27]

---

[25] CONV 528/03.

[26] Now in Art I–10 ('Union law') of the proposed Constitutional Treaty presented to the Thessaloniki European Council, (CONV 797/1/03, Rev 1, vol I, Brussels, 12 June 2003).

[27] Final Report of Working Group XI (CONV 516/1/03, Rev 1, Brussels, 4 February 2003).

Basic Values

Working Group XI explicitly noted the consensus on integration of the EU Charter into the Treaty and 'that the Charter should not be reopened.'[28] But it also 'noted that the Charter and Article 2 [of the draft Constitutional Treaty of 28 October 2002][29] have *different* scopes.' This raises the question of the legal effect of the Charter if it is acknowledged that its values *differ* (in scope) from those in Article 2 of the future Constitutional Treaty.[30]

Nonetheless, the Draft of Articles 1 to 16 of the Constitutional Treaty produced by the Convention's Praesidium on 6 February 2003[31] did not include the EU Charter among 'The Union's values' in its draft Article 2.[32] There is thereby opened a dangerous distinction between the Constitution's 'Fundamental rights' in draft Article 5[33] and draft Article 2's 'respect for human rights,' on which '[t]he Union is founded.'[34] The relegation of the Charter to a 'separate second part of the Constitution or as a Protocol' was justified by the Praesidium in its 'Explanatory Note' in Annex II:

> that technique will ... avoid making the first part of the Constitution more lengthy. At the same time, the reference to the Charter *in the first few articles of the Constitution* will underline its constitutional status.

---

[28] *Ibid* at para 8.

[29] CONV 369/02, 28 October 2002, Art 2: 'This article sets out the values of the Union: human dignity, fundamental rights, democracy, the rule of law, tolerance, respect for obligations and for international law.' Article 6 was destined for the EU Charter, depending on the proceedings of Working Group II.

[30] Now Art I-2 ('The Union's values') of the proposed Constitutional Treaty presented to the Thessaloniki European Council, above n 26: 'The Union is founded on the values of human dignity, liberty, democracy, equality, the rule of law and respect for human rights. These values are common to the Member States in a society of pluralism, tolerance, justice, solidarity and non-discrimination.' In the Final Report, para 11, Working Group XI cited Art 136 EC, which refers to the Social Charters of 1961 and 1989. The paragraph continues: 'the Group recommends that a specific reference be made to [the EU Charter] in the Constitutional Treaty provision alongside the current Article 136 TEC.' This is still not the case in the proposed Constitutional Treaty presented at Thessaloniki (Art III-98), nor in the subsequent revised Part III (CONV 836/03, vol II, 27 June 2003).

[31] CONV 528/03.

[32] Nor is the Charter mentioned among the Union's values in Art I-2 of the proposed Constitutional Treaty presented at Thessaloniki, above n 26.

[33] Now Art I-7 ('Fundamental rights') of the proposed Constitutional Treaty presented at Thessaloniki, above n 26.

[34] Language retained in Art I-2 ('the Union's values') of the proposed Constitutional Treaty presented at Thessaloniki, above n 26. Perhaps more alarming still is the apparent precedence of the guarantee accorded in Art I-4: 'Fundamental freedoms and non-discrimination' (on grounds of nationality only) to '[f]ree movement of persons, goods, services and capital and freedom of establishment.'

It is a questionable judgement to sacrifice the EU Charter to achieve stylistic brevity, particularly when its language is notably of superior literary quality to the Praesidium's draft Articles. The casual reference to its inclusion 'in the first few articles' implies that the Praesidium did not particularly care in which of these it is placed.

Application to Member States

Some Member States, including the United Kingdom, are attempting to deny that Member States have any obligation to comply with the EU Charter.[35] It is important to make clear that Member States are under a general obligation to comply with the EU Charter and respect its values, not only those of Article 2 of the draft Constitutional Treaty. To support this, Working Group XI on Social Europe recommended that Article 2 include also other social values.[36] Member States should comply with social values in general, and those in the EU Charter in particular.

The EU Charter was proclaimed by EU organs, and its Preamble ends by saying: 'The Union therefore recognises the rights ... .' But this is not the same as being addressed exclusively to the EU. On the contrary, there is the explicit reference in Article 51(1) of the Charter, which states:

> The provisions of this Charter are addressed to the institutions and bodies of the Union with due regard for the principle of subsidiarity and to the Member States only when they are implementing Union law.

The word 'implementing' could be interpreted as confining the Charter's impact to specific implementing measures of national law. The European Court takes a wider view, that EU law applies to all national laws falling within the scope of EU competence, whether or not there are specific implementing measures.

---

[35] For the continuing resistance of some Member States to the inclusion of the EU Charter in the Constitutional Treaty, see the letter dated 12 May 2003 from Peter Hain, a member of the Convention representing the UK government, replying to a letter from the President, Giscard d'Estaing concerning the Charter: 'Your letter suggests that it is now settled that the Charter should form Part II of the Constitution. As you know, our Government has always held the view that we could make no commitment to the incorporation of the Charter until we had sight of the whole package outlined in the recommendations of the Working Group ... The challenge is to find ways to give our citizens legal certainty and clarity in relation to the Charter's ambiguous or conflicting texts': CONV 736/03 13 May 2003. On the same lines, others are trying to argue that some parts of the Charter ('principles', as contrasted with 'rights') are not 'justiciable' (see the proposals of Working Group II on the EU Charter, attack on social rights in particular (new Art 52(5)), above n 23 and associated text).
[36] Final Report of Working Group XI, above n 27, at para 9.

In its Final Report, the Convention's Working Group II on the EU Charter confirmed that:[37]

> it is in line with the principle of subsidiarity that the scope of application of the Charter is limited, in accordance with its Article 51(1), to the institutions and bodies of the Union, and to Member States *only* when they are implementing Union law.

To this is attached a footnote which states:

> It should be noted that, upon possible incorporation of the Charter into the Treaty, the current wording of Article 46(d) TEU would *have to be brought in line with* existing case law and Article 51 of the Charter on the (limited) application of fundamental rights to acts of Member States.

Article 46(d) of the Treaty on European Union asserts that the powers of the European Court as regards provisions of the EC Treaty (and other Treaties) shall apply, as regards Article 6(2) TEU (fundamental rights) *only* 'with regard to action of the institutions'. Whatever the debate over exactly how limited it is, it appears that the Charter is intended to apply to the Member States.

With respect to some Charter rights, there is a question as to whether they fall within EU competences. But this argument allows for at least two interpretations. First, if the Charter is only addressed to the EU organs, and the EU has no competence, then these Charter rights are completely meaningless. Can this have been intended? Alternatively, these rights (and the others) in the Charter are within EU competence and also affect Member States.

Indeed, some Charter rights seem to be specifically targeted on Member States. For example, Chapter VI, ('Justice'): Article 47 refers to remedies and fair trial as regards 'rights and freedoms guaranteed by the law of the Union.' But this must include claims based on Union law before national courts. In Article 48, the presumption of innocence and right of defence does not limit itself to rights and freedoms of the EU. Article 49 excludes liability where there is no criminal offence under national law. Article 50 prohibits 'double jeopardy.' If a Member State repealed this last rule, arguably this could be challenged as a violation of the Charter.[38]

Of particular interest are the explicit guarantees of freedom of association and the right to take collective action in Articles 12 and 28 of the Charter.[39]

---

[37] Above 5, at 5 II.2, page 5.

[38] This is particularly pertinent to current draft legislation on double jeopardy in the United Kingdom.

[39] Article 12 of the EU Charter provides for 'freedom of association at all levels, in particular in ... trade union ... matters ... , which implies the right of everyone to form and to join trade

Article 137(5) of the EC Treaty[40] appears explicitly to exclude the right of association and the right to strike.[41] A potential conflict with Article 137(5) therefore emerges if the EU Charter is incorporated into the Constitutional Treaty.

One argument is that Article 51(1) of the EU Charter precludes any contradiction between the Charter and Article 137(5). It is argued that by virtue of Article 137(5), freedom of association and the right to strike fall *exclusively within Member State competence*. By virtue of Article 51(1) of the Charter, Member States are affected 'only when they are implementing Union law.' As there can be no Union law on these matters, there is no contradiction between the EU Charter and Article 137(5).[42]

However, this argument is based on the questionable assumption that there is no EU competence over the matters listed in Article 137(5). Article 137(5) begins: 'The provisions *of this Article* shall not apply to pay, the right of association, the right to strike or the right to impose lock-outs.' There is nothing which excludes Community competence as regards these matters being exercised under *any other Article* of the Treaty.[43] It can be argued that the Community *could* take action to achieve the rights of association and collective action in the EU Charter if these rights were not being sufficiently achieved by the Member States.[44]

Incorporation of the Charter into the Treaty is unavoidably linked to the question of EU competences.[45] The Treaty needs to reflect the values of the

---

unions for the protection of his or her interests.' Article 28 of the Charter provides for 'the right ... in cases of conflicts of interest, to take collective action to defend their interests, including strike action.'

[40] Before Nice, Art 137(6).

[41] 'The provisions *of this Article* shall not apply to pay, the right of association, the right to strike or the right to impose lock-outs.'

[42] In other words, *if* Art 137(5) provides that such action falls outside Community competence, the EU Charter does not affect the position as Art 51(2) states: 'This Charter does not establish any new power or task for the Community or the Union, or modify powers or tasks defined by the Treaties.'

[43] Indeed, the Final Report of Working Group XI, above n 27, states: 'Although Article 137(5) TEC rules out the adoption of uniform minimum requirements on pay, it does not rule out the possibility of adopting measures under other provisions of the Treaty, even if these measures have an impact on pay. The result is that a number of Community instruments contain provisions on pay': para 28. Examples are the EC Directives on equal pay and equal treatment, which were adopted on the legal basis of Art 308 (ex 235) of the EC Treaty.

[44] According to the principle of subsidiarity defined in Art 5 EC: 'In areas which do not fall within its exclusive competence, the Community shall take action ... only if and insofar as the objectives of the proposed action cannot be sufficiently achieved by the Member States and can therefore ... be better achieved by the Community.'

[45] Admittedly, the argument just presented that the Union has the competence to act to protect fundamental trade union rights is technically legalistic. Otherwise, however, the proclamation of fundamental values in a Constitutional Treaty confronts Art 137(5) which appears to deny the Union competence to implement those values. This contradiction undermines both these values and the Union. It would be more consistent with the Convention's endorsement of the EU Charter to delete Art 137(5).

Charter. If fundamental rights are subordinated to EU competences, they are only protected to the limit of EU competences. Instead, the Treaty should be amended to accommodate the Charter, not the Charter to fit the Treaty.

The Final Report of the Convention's Working Group II went further in a statement which implied that the Charter *does* bind Member States:[46]

> The fact that certain Charter rights concern areas in which the Union has lit-tle or no competence to act is not in contradiction to it, given that, although the Union's *competences* are limited, it must *respect* all fundamental rights wherever it acts and therefore avoid indirect interference also with such fun-damental rights on which it would have the competence to legislate.

When Member States act *within* the sphere of EU competence, they must comply with, or at least respect, the fundamental rights in the Charter. The implication that even where there may be *no* EU competence, the EU must *still* respect fundamental rights also arguably affects Member States. Even when Member States act outside EU competence, they too must respect fun-damental rights.[47]

INTERPRETING THE EU CHARTER

The Convention on the Future of Europe made another 'adjustment' to the EU Charter, one which was not proposed by its Working Group II on the EU Charter in the Annex to its Final Report. In that Report, Working Group II had restricted itself to stating:[48]

> Upon possible incorporation of the Charter, attention should then be drawn in an appropriate manner to the Explanations which, though they state that they have no legal value, are intended to clarify the provisions of the Charter. In particular, it would be important to publicise them more widely.

The Praesidium of the Convention drafting the Constitutional Treaty has gone far beyond this remit in its proposed 'adjustment' to the Preamble to the EU Charter. Far from being aimed at drawing attention to and publicising the 'Explanations,' the 'adjustment' appears intended to attribute a legal value to the 'Explanations' disclaimed by their authors, and repeated by Working Group II's acknowledgement that 'they have no legal value.'

---

[46] Above n 5, at 5, s II.2.
[47] See also below n 51.
[48] Final Report of Working Group II, above n 5, at 10, s III, para 3.

The inspiration and source of this 'adjustment' is questionable. It is suggested that it was yet another concession to those Member States seeking to dilute the potential content of fundamental rights guaranteed by the EU legal order. It is notable, for example, that the Praesidium of the Convention drafting the Constitutional Treaty did not include in the Preamble the Working Group's emphasis on a 'rule of interpretation' whereby 'rather than following a rigid approach of a 'lowest common denominator', the Charter rights concerned should be interpreted in a way offering a high standard of protection which is adequate for the law of the Union.'[49]

The additional 'adjustment' made by the Convention was to the Preamble to the EU Charter, now Part II of the proposed Constitutional Treaty. This was the only substantive alteration made to the Charter's Preamble. It reads ('adjustment' in italics)[50]:

> The Charter reaffirms, with due regard for the powers and tasks of the Union and the principle of subsidiarity, the rights as they result, in particular, from the constitutional traditions and international obligations common to the Member States, the European Convention for the Protection of Human Rights and Fundamental Freedoms, the Social Charters adopted by the Union and by the Council of Europe and the case law of the Court of Justice of the European Union and of the European Court of Human Rights. *In this context, the Charter will be interpreted by the Courts of the Union and the Member States*[51] *with due regard for the explanations prepared at the instigation of the Praesidium of the Convention which drafted the Charter.*

This contrasts with the Charter's own careful disclaimer, reproduced twice in footnotes to the text of the Charter on the EU's website. That text includes the Articles of the Charter alongside the 'Explanations' of the Praesidium which drafted the Charter; the footnotes state:

> These explanations have been prepared at the instigation of the Praesidium. They have no legal value and are simply intended to clarify the provisions of the Charter.

Only the first sentence of that disclaimer is reproduced in the Convention's 'adjustment' to the Preamble. The second sentence, which is not reproduced, states precisely the opposite to the positive assertion of the 'adjustment' to

---

[49] *Ibid* at 7, s II, para 5.
[50] Draft Constitution, vol II, draft revised text of Parts Two, Three and Four, (CONV 802/03, 12 June 2003).
[51] It is worth noting here that the reference to courts of the Member States is further evidence of the expectation that the Charter will be accorded legal status in disputes before national courts as well as the ECJ.

the Preamble that '… the Charter *will* be interpreted by the Courts of the Union and the Member States with due regard for the explanations.' This purports to attribute to the 'Explanations' the status of mandatory interpretative rules which the Praesidium of the Charter Convention was careful not to claim. Their caution was fully justified, among other reasons, because of the changing composition of the Praesidium[52] and differing extent of its members' involvement during its activities.

Perhaps the Praesidium of the current Convention, responsible for this 'adjustment', was hoping to set a precedent, anticipating that a similar reference to its own 'explanations' to the Constitutional Treaty might be similarly immortalised! In this it was anticipated by Working Group II, which said of its own proposed 'adjustments': 'To the extent that the Convention takes on board the drafting adjustments proposed by this Group, the corresponding explanations given in this report should be fully integrated with the original explanations'. But Working Group II at least retained some modesty by following this immediately with the affirmation that those original 'Explanations' 'have no legal value'.[53]

More important, however, there is a clear contradiction insofar as the Praesidium's 'Explanations' often fail to refer to 'international obligations common to the Member States' which the Preamble states are 'in particular' the inspiration and source of the EU Charter's provisions. In the case of those provisions referring to individual employment and collective labour rights, the absence in the Praesidium's 'Explanations' of references to the core ILO Conventions which bind all Member States is particularly noticeable, and regrettable.

For example, the Praesidium's 'Explanations' to Article 12 ('Freedom of assembly and of association') state that 'Paragraph 1 of this Article corresponds to Article 11 of the ECHR' and further asserts that 'The meaning of the provisions of paragraph 1 is the same as that of the ECHR, but their scope is wider since they apply at all levels, including European level.' This wider scope, which applies to all levels from the workplace up to the EU level, could have immense implications for the exercise of freedom of association going beyond the ECHR provisions.

The Praesidium's 'Explanations' go on to add 'This right is also based on Article 11 of the Community Charter of the Fundamental Social Rights of Workers'. The precise scope of Article 11 of the Community Charter ('Freedom of association and collective bargaining') has also been the subject of scrutiny and could extend beyond the confines of the provision in the ECHR.[54]

---

[52] See the Preface to the Charter on the EU's website.
[53] Final Report of Working Group II, above n 5, at 10, s III, para 3.
[54] B Bercusson, *European Labour Law* (1996) 585–89.

Again, the Praesidium's 'Explanations' to Article 28 ('Right of collective bargaining and action') state:

> This Article is based on Article 6 of the European Social Charter and on the Community Charter of the Fundamental Social Rights of Workers (points 12 to 14). The right of collective action was recognised by the European Court of Human Rights as one of the elements of trade union rights laid down by Article 11 of the ECHR ... Collective action, including strike action, comes under national laws and practices, including the question of whether it may be carried out in parallel in several Member States.

First, there is an obvious contradiction between requiring respect for the ECHR and the assertion that collective action 'comes under national laws and practices.' The contradiction is evident when the European Court of Human Rights finds a Member State's law to be in violation of the ECHR, as was recently the case with the United Kingdom in respect of Article 11.[55]

Secondly, collective action 'carried out in parallel in several Member States' engages precisely the transnational dimension of collective action in the European single market. Confining it to national laws and practices contradicts a fundamental right of European collective action. It is inevitably addressed at EU level,[56] not least by the ECJ.[57]

However, apart from these references to European international instruments, there are other international obligations binding EU Member States. These are not mentioned by the Praesidium's 'Explanations,' though the Preamble emphatically states that the Charter re-affirms these obligations. This indicates the incompleteness of the Praesidium's 'Explanations,' which no doubt explains the admirable caution expressed by that Praesidium with respect to the use to be made of its 'Explanations.' It would seem that, under pressure from some Member States anxious to restrict the ambit of the EU Charter's rights, the proposed 'adjustment' is attempting to elevate the 'Explanations' to a status never intended by its authors, the Convention which drafted the Charter, or even the Convention's own Working Group II, which did not include any such recommendation its own list of 'adjustments.'

---

[55] *Wilson and the National Union of Journalists; Palmer, Wyeth and the National Union of Rail, Maritime and Transport Workers; Doolan and others v United Kingdom* [2002] IRLR 128, decided 2 July 2002. For a detailed discussion of the potential impact on British labour law of what has been called 'probably the most important labour law decision for at least a generation,' see K Ewing, 'The Implications of *Wilson and Palmer*' [2003] 32 *Industrial Law Journal* 1.

[56] See Council Regulation 2679/98, 7 December 1998, on the functioning of the internal market in relation to the free movement of goods among the Member States [1998] OJ L337/8 (the 'Monti' Regulation').

[57] See C-112/00 *Eugen Schmidburger, Internationale Transporte Planzuge v Republic of Austria*, 12 June 2003.

The Preamble's reference to international obligations must have important consequences for the interpretation of the EU Charter. For example, trade union collective action has often been restricted, allegedly to protect public and/or essential services. The ILO's Freedom of Association Committee has established international standards on collective action in public/essential services. Relying on Article 28 of the EU Charter (right to collective action), trade unions could promote challenges to more restrictive national laws.

As the Constitutional Treaty's 'adjustment' to the Preamble begins, after the re-affirmation 'in particular [of] international obligations common to the Member States', with the phrase '[i]n this context,' the 'Explanations' should be read, and the EU Charter interpreted, with full weight attached to this context of the international obligations of the EU and its Member States.

VALUES AND COMPETENCES

Social Europe, as manifest in the values of the EU Charter, potentially stretches, if not goes beyond, a narrow view of the present competences of the EU. The paradox is clear: fundamental/universal rights are confronted with limited EC/EU competences. The central problem is the clash between limited EU competences and the EU Charter's fundamental human rights. If fundamental human rights are subject to competences, it undermines the concept of fundamental human rights. Values elevated by the EU to the status of fundamental human rights are only protected to the limit of EU competences. The EU would have to ignore fundamental human rights where they come up against the limitations of its competences.

Incorporation of the Charter into the Constitutional Treaty is unavoidably linked to the question of EU competences. The Treaty needs to reflect the social values of the Charter and to accommodate the values of Social Europe. However, a potential tension exists between EU competences to achieve Social Europe and the alleged democratic deficit of the EU. Some, if not most, Member States may be reluctant to grant to the EU institutions the new powers and tasks of implementing Social Europe.

The record of the United Kingdom in holding back progress towards Social Europe is second to none, and has been amply manifested in the Convention on the Future of Europe. The earnest appeal of the UK government's representative, Peter Hain, to the Convention for fairness at work and social justice[58] might carry more conviction were the Blair government's

---

[58] Peter Hain, 'The Way to Get Europe to Work,' *Financial Times*, 29 January 2003.

record in obstructing and then failing adequately to implement EC labour legislation were not so abysmal.[59] His claim of wanting 'to strengthen social dialogue and improve partnership between employer and employee representatives' is breathtaking when, carrying on where the previous Conservative government left off, the Blair government played a central role in obstructing the Information and Consultation Directive.[60] This record belies the claimed support for a 'new social agenda' and the disingenuous 'yes to employment rights' of the UK government's representative.[61]

In the Convention, the UK government evidently hoped, once again, to delay, obstruct and claw back any ambitions the EU has to progress towards a European social model of improved working conditions and dialogue between management and labour, which are declared to be its objectives in Article 136 of the EC Treaty. The United Kingdom, having lost the battle to exclude from the list of fundamental human rights those of workers to information and consultation, to collective bargaining and collective action, including strike action,[62] there was little surprise at the Blair government's next shameless attempt to downgrade these rights as mere 'principles' unworthy of judicial protection.[63] Not everybody in the Convention on the Future of Europe was seduced by Mr Hain's siren

---

[59] Attempting to exclude children born before the date of implementation of the Directive on parental leave, seeking to impose an entitlement threshold of 13 weeks on paid annual leave, the only Member State allowing opt-outs from the maximum 48-hour working week, to name but a few examples.

[60] Directive 2002/14/EC, 11 March 2002, establishing a general framework for informing and consulting employees in the European Community [2002] OJ L80/29. See B Bercusson, 'The European Social Model Comes to Britain' (2002) 31 *Industrial Law Journal* (September) 209. In an article in the *New Statesman*, Mr Hain even had the gall subsequently to claim the Directive was supported by the government, presumably on the basis that the United Kingdom finally accepted the result after leading a three-year rearguard battle to delay, if not kill it, and exploiting every opportunity to weaken it.

[61] Once again belied by the UK government's successful mobilisation of a minority of Member States sufficient to block the draft Directive granting rights to equal treatment of agency workers (May 2003). See again, the letter dated 12 May 2003 from Peter Hain challenging the legal status of the EU Charter (CONV 736/03, 13 May 2003), above n 35. In that letter, he appears to indicate support from other members of the Convention by referring to an earlier contribution (CONV 659/03, 14 April 2003). This is misleading because that contribution merely raised the question of the method of incorporating the Charter into the Treaty, not the principle of incorporation. The United Kingdom's fall-back position is doubtless already being prepared: a specific provision limiting the application of the Charter to the EU institutions.

[62] Now in Art 27 and 28 of the EU Charter of Fundamental Rights.

[63] Similarly, the cynicism of Mr Hain's appeal in his article in the *Financial Times* for 'diversity and flexibility,' 'with 10 countries joining the EU next year' is not lost on the workers of those countries, for whom it means lower wages, poorer working conditions, weakened trade unions and disregard for health and safety standards. Characterising efforts to establish basic minimum labour standards across Europe as a 'crude policy of harmonisation,' or 'intrusive, detailed rules' rings hollow against the United Kingdom's domestic record in legislating watered down employment rights. Hopefully, Mr Hain's invoking the firefighters' right to

song of a Social Europe with lofty values and objectives, but, crucially, without basic and enforceable labour standards.[64]

THE EU CHARTER AND THE RENEWAL OF LABOUR LAW AT EU AND NATIONAL LEVELS

At EU level, the resistance of some Member States to the EU taking on the task of implementing a European social model means that other institutions and processes may come to the fore. One proposal is to reinforce horizontal subsidiarity, the exercise of the new powers and competences of the Union through the action of the social partners.

The exercise of EU competences in social and labour policy requires legitimate institutional structures of social governance. The EU Charter can play a major role in building the legitimacy of these governance structures. The Charter's fundamental rights ascribe legitimacy to collective bargaining and collective action, and information and consultation on a wide range of issues at the level of the enterprise. Affirming rights to engage in work, vocational training, equal opportunities and other social and labour standards provides support for arrangements in the European Employment Strategy. The Charter can be used to legitimise the actors, processes and outcomes of Social Europe. It could provide support for the necessary legitimacy of the governance structures of an EU system of industrial relations.

At national level, the fundamental social and labour rights guaranteed by the Charter were the source of most of the disputes among and objections from some Member States in the Convention which drafted the Charter. What this process revealed is the urgent need for renewal of national labour laws. A requirement to respect the fundamental rights of labour guaranteed by the EU Charter in a new Constitutional Treaty offers the opportunity.

The inclusion of fundamental rights concerning employment and industrial relations in an EU Charter incorporated into the EU Treaty may well confer on them a constitutional status within national legal orders. The ECJ

---

strike in Britain was a mere failure to anticipate the government's subsequent proposal to impose a legislative settlement, and not further cynicism.

[64] The UK government's objective of full employment in a high-skill economy is admirable, and shared by other Member States. Its espousal is undermined by the government's continuing opposition to European labour standards, which other Member States do not see as incompatible with this economic and employment policy objective. Getting Europe to work is only half the story and rendered less plausible when accompanied by active opposition to basic employment rights. Far from suffering 'enormous damage,' working people in Britain have benefited greatly from European employment rights.

may interpret the Charter consistently with the labour laws in most Member States, which may exceed the protection of some Member State laws, or consistently with international labour standards, where again national labour laws may fall short. The EU Charter promises a renewal of labour law, both at transnational and national levels.

9

The 'Making' of EU Labour Law and the 'Future' of Labour Lawyers

SILVANA SCIARRA

INTRODUCTION

IN HIS 'INTRODUCTION' to *The Making of Labour Law in Europe*, Bob Hepple describes the methodology adopted in that work as a combination of historical and comparative approaches. This method, he argues, reflects the nature of labour law as a 'process,' rather than as a 'relatively static and neutral set of rules and institutions which regulate employment.'[1] Such a process — he suggests in a later contribution on the 'future' of labour law — is the result of 'conflict between different social groups and competing ideologies.'[2] The outcome is a constantly changing equilibrium in law-making, whereby the future has to be constructed by looking at ways to innovate, without losing sight of the past.

Bob Hepple's vision of the future includes a realistic appraisal of the grounds on which a new social consensus can be built. The 'tasks of modernisation' are vividly illustrated by his work. To revise the 'auxiliary' function of labour law, he suggests, it is necessary to adapt it to decentralised industrial relations; to expand its 'regulatory' function, non-standard contracts must be included in the area of legal guarantees. The fight against social exclusion, which is clearly exemplified in a number of European-level policies and programmes, opens up the space for a new 'integrative' function, aimed at introducing positive measures, rescuing the unemployed from marginality, and improving the conditions of the under-employed.[3] It is

---

[1] B Hepple (ed), *The Making of Labour Law in Europe: A Comparative Study of Nine Countries up to 1945* (London and New York, Mansell Publishing Ltd, 1986) 1. The book is, significantly, dedicated to Otto Kahn-Freund.
[2] B Hepple, 'The Future of Labour Law' (1995) 24 *Industrial Law Journal* 305.
[3] *Ibid* at 320. See also the inspiring writing of M D'Antona, 'Labour Law at the Century's End: An Identity Crisis?' in J Conaghan, RM Fischl and K Klare (eds), *Labour Law in an Era of Globalization* (Oxford, Oxford University Press, 2002) 31 and in particular 45 *et seq*.

above all this last 'integrative' task which opens up an important field of expansion for labour law.

In this chapter I argue that two key words — the 'making' and the 'future' — borrowed from Bob Hepple's enduring contribution to the European and comparative debate, are crucial in understanding the role of EU law in the shaping of labour law, both at a national and at a supranational level.

The hypothesis which I want to explore is that EU law, in particular through the 'open method of coordination' (OMC), is contributing to changes in the national law-making process by empowering branches of the administration which in the past were either invisible or completely inactive. These branches of the administration may sometimes operate in isolation from national governments and never come close to the legislative arena. They depend on assistance from external experts, or simply rely upon the contribution of high level bureaucrats.[4]

Regardless of the cultural background of particular national administrations, the OMC is insinuating into all national legal systems new techniques and new procedures of compliance with EU soft law. These procedures are generating a vast number of documents, some of which are only relevant to the internal workings of the administration, in the exchanges between different areas or departments of governmental apparatus.[5] Yet other documents become visible outside the domestic law and/or policy-making apparatus in the process of representing the Member States' official and formal responses to the issues raised by the EU institutions as part of OMC.

The national action plans (NAPs), the final outcomes of such procedures, have a '*sui generis*' legal nature,[6] which is difficult to evaluate by reference to both national and supranational systems of norms. They can be interpreted as mere promises by the Member States to reach certain targets set

---

[4] C de la Porte, 'Is the Open Method of Coordination Appropriate for Organising Activities at European Level in Sensitive Policy Areas?' (2002) 8 *European Law Journal*, 38.

[5] Examples are drawn from the Italian case in M Ferrera and E Gualmini, *La strategia europea sull'occupazione e la governance domestica del mercato del lavoro: verso nuovi assetti organizzativi e decisionali*, a paper which is part of the project launched by the Commission on the evaluation of national responses to the European Employment Strategy. See C Dell'Aringa (ed), *Impact Evaluation of the European Employment Strategy* (Rome, ISFOL Papers, 2002). The Swedish and the Danish cases are illustrated by K Jacobbson and H Schmid, 'Real Integration or Just Formal Adaptation?: On the Implementation of the National Action Plans for Employment' in C de La Porte and P Pochet (eds), *Building Social Europe Through the Open Method of Co-ordination* (Brussels, PIE, 2002). A discussion on the way different departments are involved in the drafting of NAPs in the United Kingdom — albeit with specific reference to employment measures and part-time in particular — is in C Kilpatrick and M Freedland, 'How is EU Governance Transformative? Part-time Work in the UK' in S Sciarra, P Davies and M Freedland (eds), *Employment Policy and the Regulation of Part-time Work in the EU: A Comparative Analysis* (Cambridge, Cambridge University Press, 2004).

[6] As suggested in the chapter by D Ashiagbor, 'The European Employment Strategy and the Regulation of Part-time Work' in Sciarra *et al*, above n 5.

by the central EU bodies, in relation both to employment policies and social inclusion. The aspirations contained in the NAPs may also be viewed as the basis for legal initiatives to be taken by national Parliaments. Furthermore, NAPs can lead to the adoption of other measures, of an extra-legislative character, whose aim is to fulfil a specific objective set at supranational level.

In order to improve the methodology inaugurated at Lisbon and to consolidate the success of the same, the European Commission issued a series of national studies on the impact of employment strategies and of the OMC. The results of the comparative research promoted by the Commission are visible in the extensive documentation to which this process gave rise.[7] In the attempt to standardise national responses and provide a coherent frame of reference, the Commission had to acknowledge that national interpretations of employment strategies remain very different.[8] The NAPs inevitably end up reflecting internal struggles among different policy options and set priorities which are only partially influenced by supranational guidelines.

The wide range of diversity in the different NAPs makes the measurement of outcomes difficult, if not impossible. One should not forget, however, that these new governance techniques are not primarily concerned with harmonisation; rather, they accept the need for recognition of national differences. The OMC is therefore achieving innovative results in the 'making' of labour law not by attempting to impose uniform rules, but rather by laying down certain broad indications to the Member States, calling upon them to follow general directions in the formulation of policy and to fill in the gaps left by existing modes of intervention. The final choices remain within the Member States' domain, as do the mechanisms of implementation.[9]

It is also significant that within the current 'making' of European labour law, academic expertise plays a remarkably prominent role. It is particularly noteworthy that this expertise does not emerge directly from traditional labour law scholarship, but rather from an interdisciplinary approach to labour market reforms. Employment policies have, since their first appearance in the Amsterdam Treaty, attracted the attention of experts

---

[7] Communication from the Commission, *Taking Stock of Five Years of the European Employment Strategy* (COM (2002) 416 final, 17 July 2002); Communication, *The Future of the European Employment Strategy: A Strategy for Full Employment and Better Jobs for All* (COM (2003) 6 final, 14 July 2003).

[8] Communication from the Commission, *Taking Stock of Five Years of the European Employment Strategy*, above n 7, at 22.

[9] Ashiagbor, above n 6, conducts an analysis of recent NAPs and observes an improvement in the account given to policy implementation, in comparison to the early NAPs. The lack of traditional sanctions seems to be counterbalanced by 'policy learning.' See on this point S Regent, 'The Open Method of Coordination: A New Supranational Form of Governance?' (2003) 9 *European Law Journal* 210.

in different fields.[10] In designing policies on social inclusion, employment measures are frequently required to operate in conjunction with family and housing policies. Measuring results thus becomes yet another facet of an interdisciplinary exercise which may be extremely enriching, but also end up in a dilution of the regulatory responsibilities of government. This approach runs the risk that in two separate, and yet interconnected, processes — employment and social inclusion — overlapping areas of inter-vention will arise. The attempt to build up a theory of legal evolution in the field of European labour law must take these elements of the current trajec-tory of OMC into account, and consider, in particular, their implications for the shifting boundaries of the discipline of labour law.

ACADEMIC EXPERTISE

Following the White Paper on governance,[11] the Commission highlighted a number of issues related to the transparency of decision-making processes. Guidelines for recourse to external expertise were announced in a Communication, in order to provide for its 'accountability, plurality and integrity.'[12] From Lisbon onwards the style of national presidencies of the Council has become highly proactive, at the same time as taking increased account of the academic background to policy-making; this can be seen in the meetings of the Council as well as in the work of research groups called upon to intervene on specific policy issues.

To take one example: the decision taken at Lisbon to extend OMC to the field of social inclusion must be seen from the point of view of a long-lasting commitment to this goal on the part of the Belgian Minister for Social Affairs and Pensions, Frank Vandenbroucke. In his speech delivered

---

[10] de La Porte and Pochet, above n 5. See also S Sciarra, 'The Employment Title in the Amsterdam Treaty: A Multi-language Legal Discourse' in D O'Keeffe and P Twoney (eds), *The Legal Issues of the Amsterdam Treaty* (Oxford / Portland Oregon, Hart Publishing, 1999) 158; E Szyszczak, 'The Evolving European Employment Strategy' in J Shaw (ed), *Social Law and Policy in an Evolving European Union* (Oxford / Portland Oregon, Hart Publishing, 2000) 197; C Barnard and S Deakin, 'Corporate Governance, European Governance and Social Rights' in B Hepple (ed), *Social and Labour Rights in a Global Context* (Cambridge, CUP, 2002) 122; JS Mosher and DM Trubek, 'Alternative Approaches to Governance in the EU: EU Social Policy and the European Employment Strategy' (2003) 41 *Journal of Common Market Studies* 63.

[11] European Commission, *A White Paper on European Governance*, (COM (2001) 428 final, Brussels, 25 July 2000, [2001] OJ C287, 1.

[12] Communication from the Commission, *Towards a Reinforced Culture of Consultation and Dialogue: General Principles and Minimum Standards for Consultation of Interested Parties by Commission*, (COM (2002) 704 final, Brussels, 11 December.2002), p. 16; Communication from the Commission, *On the Collection and Use of Expertise by the Commission: Principles and Guidelines 'Improving Knowledge Base for Better Policies'*, (COM (2002) 713 final, Brussels, 11 December 2002).

at a conference organised by the Portuguese Presidency,[13] he proposed to transform the then existing High Level Group on Social Protection into a Committee, with a more clearly defined institutional basis. The Nice Council followed up on this proposal and introduced a new Article 144 into the EC Treaty, thus formalising the promotion of cooperation between the Commission and the Member States on social protection policies.[14] In the same speech, delivered by one who is both an academic expert and a politician, the idea of setting objectives in terms of outcomes, rather than measuring welfare state expenditures, was advanced, and was linked to the proposal to establish a set of social indicators. The Conclusions of the Lisbon European Council incorporated this proposal, with the intention of arranging objective instruments of analysis and offering to Member States the opportunity to measure the progress made in these terms, the matter to be reviewed further at the Spring European Council to be held in 2001.

The Belgian Presidency then took the matter further by launching research on social indicators in such a way as to highlight the role of academic expertise, opening up the field of inquiry to a wide audience.[15] One of the immediate results of this process was to provide useful indications of the way forward for the specialised sub-group which was set up, in February 2001, within the Social Protection Committee. This sub-group, composed of qualified representatives of national ministries, has since been particularly active in the elaboration of the relevant indicators.[16]

It was through these different preparatory phases, driven on both by academics and by the institutions of the EU, that a new experimental field was prepared for the application of the OMC. It appeared potentially highly effective, even though it had no formal basis in the EC Treaty and was not subject to Council Guidelines, as was the case for employment policy.[17] The attractiveness of this process lay in the fact that the Member States retained their freedom to choose what for them were the most effective formulae and mechanisms, in view of the final aims to be achieved. In addition, the Member States continued to be active in the formulation of social indicators and in building consensus around them. But perhaps the most significant aspect of this process is the comparability of data which it

---

[13] F Vandenbroucke, Speech given at the conference on 'Europe, Globalisation and the Future of Social Policy', available at www.vandenbroucke.com/T-000506.htm

[14] A full account of these events is given by M Ferrera, M Matsaganis and S Sacchi, 'Open Coordination Against Poverty: The New EU "Social Inclusion Process"' (2002) 12 *Journal of European Social Policy* 231.

[15] The Belgian government commissioned the study by T Atkinson, B Cantillon, E Marlier, and B Nolan, *Social Indicators: The EU and Social Inclusion*, (Oxford, Oxford University Press 2002). The results of the research were discussed at the conference on 'Indicators for Social Inclusion: Making Common EU Objectives Work,' held in Antwerp, 14–15 September 2001.

[16] This is underlined by F Vandenbroucke in the 'Foreword' to Atkinson *et al*, above n 15 at viii.

[17] The first NAPs on social inclusion were prepared by Member States in mid-2001 and taken into account into the first Joint Report on Social Inclusion, below n 18.

requires: Member States retain autonomy in domestic decision-making, while at the same time the evaluation of their performances is grounded on objective comparisons.

It is also striking that whereas, in employment policy, the process of coordination occurs on the basis of loose compliance mechanisms, in social inclusion policy targets have been set in such a way that, within a given time, specific results can be measured. The Social Protection Committee, described in Article 144 of the EC Treaty as a body with advisory status, has progressively acquired a significant role in preparing 'Common Outlines for the drafting of National Action Plans on social inclusion' (the 'NAPs incl').

The Commission assisted Member States closely in the preparatory phase of the social inclusion OMC with the intention of making them fully aware of the technicalities involved in the process as well as the expected outcomes. The *Joint Report on Social Inclusion* of 2002 illustrates the Commission's commitment to closely observe the 'NAPs incl' and, at the same time, to offer an analytical evaluation of them.[18] The exchange of 'good practices' is, once more, put forward as the best way to stimulate ideas and to challenge national policy-makers.

At the same time, it has been argued that the employment policy OMC and the equivalent process for social inclusion processes suffer from similar weaknesses. These shortcomings mainly have to do with a recurring lack of rigour and precision in the estimation of costs, and in the description of implementing measures. At times, it is argued that the relevant guidelines lack imagination and tend to concentrate on existing measures, rather than trying to propose new ones.[19]

This criticism may indicate that the sophistication of academic expertise displayed in European Council meetings is not always matched by initiatives taken by national administrations, especially when the latter are left without experts to consult. The system of open coordination reveals in such cases an unstable equilibrium between ends and means, and may appear over-ambitious. It frequently happens that the recommendations of high level Committees of experts, appointed by governments or by individual ministries, result in limited, or even non-existent, legislative implementation.[20] However, even in these cases, the drafting of the NAPs in itself may be conducive to analysis of the status quo which assists in the evaluation of

---

[18] European Commission, *Joint Report on Social Inclusion* (Luxembourg, Office for Official Publications of the European Communities, 2002).

[19] M Ferrera *et al*, above n 14, at 235.

[20] Several examples taken from the Italian case are analysed by M Ferrera and E Gualmini, *Salvati dall'Europa?* (Bologna, Il Mulino, 1999). See also the forthcoming and updated English translation of this work: *Rescued by Europe? Social and Labour Market Reforms in Italy from Maastricht to Berlusconi* (Amsterdam, Amsterdam University Press, 2004).

possible reforms. Thus, in the area of social inclusion the OMC has, in some cases, brought about the 'Europeanisation' of national policies and favoured the creation of specialised committees, working groups and agencies to advance this process.[21] The simple meeting of deadlines set at a supranational level and production of reports and documentation may contribute to the creation of new and specialised branches of the administration and thereby to the slow but meaningful 'Europeanisation' of national policies.[22]

In particular, an integrated analysis of employment and social inclusion processes seems to suggest that in the European 'making' of labour law there is the possibility of rediscovering one of the original functions of the discipline, that is to say, the linking up of its individual and collective components with those of social security legislation. The notion of 'protection,' so central in the European policies on social inclusion, thereby becomes part of a newly defined function of labour law. Rather than simply addressing the protection of workers who are occupied in remunerative employment, labour law addresses the need for new forms of protection for those who have never been included in the labour market, or are present within it, but in a very marginal position.

In this context, it is interesting to observe how processes based on OMC are capable of re-inventing the rules of the game, in particular by amplifying the existing powers of the actors involved in them. For example, in the course of implementing the OMC, the Social Protection Committee is acquiring what seems to be a double role: on the one hand it creates consensus on data to be gathered and on techniques to measure them; on the other hand it signals to national administrations on how to transfer all this information into proactive policies.

The normative[23] impact of the social inclusion process — and consequently its potential success — is based on the accuracy of the investigations preceding the coordination of national policies and on the visibility of targets. The latter, in particular, have a high political value and can be put at the centre of the concrete recommendations given to governments. It is, therefore, not surprising that the Greek Presidency, in common with its predecessors, should have put a strong emphasis on social inclusion. The tradition, established in previous Council meetings, of combining political

---

[21] Information on Italy is in T Alti, 'Le politiche antipovertà: una questione europea' in S Fabbrini (ed), *L'europeizzazione dell'Italia* (Roma-Bari, Laterza, 2003), 212. See also S Giubboni, 'L'incerta europeizzazione. Diritto della sicurezza sociale e lotta all'esclusione in Italia' (2003) 18 *Giornale di Diritto del lavoro e di Relazioni Industriali* 563. The Italian NAP is reproduced at p 129 in the Joint Report, above n 18.

[22] Joint Report, above n 18, at 129, specifically referring to the Italian National Social Plan adopted in 2001, which then became the basis for the preparation of the NAP.

[23] The 'normative connotation' of social indicators is explained by Atkinson *et al*, above n 15, at 19.

direction with academic expertise has been followed by this Presidency.[24] Such continuity in setting the research agenda adds to the coherence of the arguments on which the OMC process is based, and heightens the visibility of the institutions of OMC to national governments.

In a paper presented by some of the scholars responsible for previous research on social indicators, a correlation is demonstrated between academic proposals and current practice, particularly in the formulation of indicators by the Social Protection Committee.[25] This work clearly shows how the research team in question monitored the enforcement of the measures which had been proposed, and in some cases even offered a re-interpretation of the suggested measures. The political commitment of the Council is thereby grounded on an evolutionary learning process, guided from outsides the political decision-making arena by academic expertise.

It could be argued that references by academics to the impact of their own work[26] on the functioning of such a complex machinery represent nothing more than an exercise in self-justification. However, they could be seen as giving rise to a deliberative process, as part of which data, whose objective status is generally agreed, provides a basis for action by both national and supranational actors. Academic research has created a stable and well-constructed frame for comparative policy evaluation.

The net effect of all this is that institutions and collegial bodies, such as the Social Protection Committee, receive inputs from outside the narrow institutional circuit of European-level decision-making. The signals sent out to national governments are mediated by academic research and strengthened by the rituals of Council meetings. Much of the initiative for stimulating this interaction of academic research and practical policy-making rests with the decisions taken by the successive national Presidencies. At the same time, mutual learning between the Member States appears to be a more focused exercise in the case of social inclusion than in the context of employment policy. The experience of social inclusion shows that distributive goals can be set and answers given to such questions as 'when is it fair to require equal treatment and when is it fair to require different treatment.'[27]

If we return to the key words borrowed from Bob Hepple's contributions, we notice that in the 'making' of European labour law, there is an extraordinary opportunity to observe how spontaneous orders re-invent legal principles. Open coordination in employment policies contributes

---

[24] The international conference on 'Modernization of the European Social Model and EU Policies and Instruments' was held at Ioannina, 21–22 May 2003. The proceedings are now published in T Sakallaropoulos and J Berghman (eds), *Connecting Welfare Diversity within the European Social Model* (Antwerp, Intersentia, 2004).

[25] T Atkinson, E Marlier and B Nolan, 'Indicators and Targets for Social Inclusion in the European Union,' Paper presented at the international conference, above n 24.

[26] Namely in the conference paper quoted above 25, in which references are made to previous work of the same research team.

[27] H Collins, 'Discrimination, Equality and Social Inclusion' (2003) 66 *Modern Law Review* 40.

through a soft law procedure to fulfilling the objective of a 'high level of employment' set out in Article 2 of the Treaty on European Union. It does so by combining 'work and welfare' in ways which involve a 'variety of institutional arrangements and policy legacies among the participating units.'[28] At the same time, social inclusion policies, again using a soft law procedure, have expanded the traditional functions of labour law at national level and contribute to building the 'future' of European labour law. In this way, a new 'integrative' function of labour law, rightly identified by Bob Hepple as one of its central tasks of modernisation,[29] has been imposed on national political agendas. The adoption of European-wide targets in this field, as in the employment field, has a significant symbolic value as well as facilitating political decisions at national level.

It has been suggested that in order to bring about effective policy outcomes, the two processes — social inclusion and employment policy — ought to operate more closely together.[30] The concept of 'work' is the obvious link between the two, since it represents the best way to include the excluded within the labour market. Work must be flexible and secure; it must not depart from principles of social justice, while accepting that inclusion may bring about specific measures, addressed differently to different groups. OMC is the appropriate vehicle for this policy agenda since it creates the right environment for the understanding of new ways in which to pursue policy-making and institutional construction; it forces national administrations out of the inertia which is so often the result of a lack of information and uncertainty about the use that can be made of available resources. Mutual learning between the two OMC processes might be seen as the next phase in the evolution of soft law regimes. The 'representation' of expertise[31] could, in this case, go beyond exercising an influence on policy-makers, and aim at a more enduring institutional outcome.

CONCLUDING REMARKS: A COHERENT LABOUR LAW

In the scenarios created by OMC, labour lawyers are not immediately visible, and it is sometimes difficult for those who observe policy-making in these

---

[28] A comparison between the the USA and the EU is offered by J Zeitlin and D Trubek (eds), *Governing Work and Welfare in a New Economy* (Oxford, Oxford University Press, 2003). See in particular the chapter by J Zeitlin, 'Introduction: Governing Work and Welfare in a New Economy: European and American Experiments', at 1 and at 17 for the quotation in the text.

[29] See above nn 1 and 2.

[30] Ferrera *et al*, above n 14, at 237. Criticism of some aspects of the EES is expressed to the commision in the Report of the Employment Taskforce chaired by W Kok, 'Jobs, Jobs, Jobs: Creating More Employment in Europe' (November 2003) section 3.5, in particular arguing for more effective policies towards the integration of minorities and migrants and non-EU nationals.

[31] C Radaelli, 'The "Representation" of Expertise in the European Union' in S Saurugger (ed), *La représentation dans l'Union Européenne* (Paris, L'Harmattan, 2003).

fields to imagine what their role should be in building social consensus in the way that they have often done in their national legal environments. This is mainly due to the way in which OMC interacts with national-level governments. It was suggested above that responses to the 'soft' requests coming from EU institutions are elaborated at various levels of state bureaucracies, often without the support of national experts. The occasional nature of coalitions created inside government offices, combining together actors with different cultural backgrounds, makes it, nevertheless, possible to get closer to European targets and to appreciate their relevance for the development of domestic institutions and policy-making. Again, even though the inspiration behind the employment and social inclusion OMCs is not predominantly legal, the combination of various regulatory techniques within OMC creates, both at national and supranational level, a space for productive interaction among different disciplines.

European labour law has, over the course of its history, benefited in several ways from contact with other disciplines, and this has been a vital means of extending its modernising function, as Bob Hepple predicted. The forging of links between the individual and collective aspects of employment relations on the one hand, and between labour law and social security legislation on the other, is crucial to this process, as is the broadening of the notion of 'protection' to include those who occupy a marginal position in the labour market.

A glance at the 2003 employment guidelines[32] helps to explain how this beneficial 'contamination' can work, while at the same time allowing labour law to retain its internal coherence. Under the heading 'active and preventing measures for the unemployed and the inactive' we read that Member States should 'ensure that at an early stage of their unemployment spell, all jobseekers benefit from an early identification of their needs and from services such as advice and guidance, job search assistance and personalised action plans.' Further on we learn that 'by 2010, 25% of the long-term unemployed will participate in an active measure in the form of training, retraining, work practice, or other employability measure, with the aim of achieving the average of the three most advanced Member States.'[33]

The individualised assistance described in the guidelines does not adopt a language of rights, but rather inclines towards the identification of 'needs,' giving rise to mere expectations in individuals — the jobseekers — identifiable as members of a specific group. The target for Member States is then set in quantitative terms, according to a criterion which gives prominence to best practices and pushes towards emulation of all other actors involved in the game.

---

[32] Council Decision of on Guidelines for the Employment Policies of the Member States (2003/578/EC, 22 July 2003), 2003 OJ L197 13.
[33] *Ibid*, at 19.

This is but one example chosen to illustrate the struggle between governance by guidelines and labour law's internal coherence. OMC safeguards Member States' sovereignty in highly sensitive fields, such as the setting of priorities within employment policies and the choice of the means to be adopted. Compliance with the guidelines takes place outside the core of labour law's fundamental principles. Thus, most recent legal measures dealing with the reform of labour markets and with measures to fight unemployment, of the kind which are frequently highlighted in the employment and social inclusion guidelines, have their most immediate effects upon employment and placement services, in both the public and private sector.

These developments are part of the evolution of labour law at national level and highlight the inextricable link between soft law policies and hard law responses. They also illustrate the tension between the 'making' and the 'future': new regulatory techniques may seem, at times, sceptical toward the distinctive, fundamental values which have so far characterised the strengthening of national labour law. The future of European labour lawyers can be projected into this still uncertain space: between policy-making and law-making, they can articulate a new discourse on the role of fundamental rights within OMC. Rather than simply trying to mark the boundaries of the discipline, they should be active in defending its internal coherence.

10

The Future of Equality Law: Equality and Beyond

CATHERINE BARNARD*

INTRODUCTION

I T SEEMS IMPOSSIBLE to add anything new to a consideration of the future of equality law when Bob Hepple, among others, has devoted his academic career to reflect on this subject.[1] Because I agree with much of the contribution he has made — about the inadequacies (both technically and substantively) of the present laws and about the urgent need for the law to be supplemented by practical flanking measures — I do not wish to go over this ground since I am sure to do so with less elegance and far less insight. Instead, I want to consider how we might (re)conceptualise the principles on which 'equality law' is based, drawing on the recent experience of European Community law, especially in the field of free movement of citizens.

Hugh Collins makes an eloquent case that the principle of social inclusion provides a more satisfactory intellectual framework to underpin (British) anti-discrimination legislation than existing approaches based on substantive equality.[2] I shall argue that, at European Union level at least, it is the principle of citizenship which provides the legal justification for giving equal rights to those seen to be disadvantaged and that, at the heart of citizenship, lies the concept not so much of social inclusion but solidarity.

The Oxford English Dictionary defines 'solidarity' as a 'mutual dependence, community of interests, feelings, and action'. In his Opinion

---

* I am grateful to Simon Deakin, Sandy Fredman, Bob Hepple and Tammy Hervey for their comments.
[1] See, eg, B Hepple, M Coussey and T Choudhury, *Equality: A New Framework: Report of the Independent Review of the Enforcement of UK Anti-Discrimination Legislation* (Oxford, Hart, 2000) and more generally, the Bibliography below; S Fredman, *Women and the Law* (Oxford, Oxford University Press, 1997); S Fredman, *Discrimination Law* (Oxford, Oxford University Press, 2002); S Fredman (ed), *Discrimination and Human Rights: The Case of Racism* (Oxford, Oxford University Press, 2001).
[2] H Collins, 'Discrimination, Equality and Social Inclusion' (2003) 66 *MLR* 16.

in *Sodemare*[3] Advocate General Fennelly develops this idea further. He says: 'Social solidarity envisages the inherently uncommercial act of involuntary subsidisation of one social group by another.'[4]

From these definitions we can see that these two concepts — solidarity and social inclusion — overlap significantly. However, I would suggest that 'solidarity' is more positive than social inclusion. While both have inclusiveness at their core, solidarity does not suggest that those suffering from discrimination are necessarily disadvantaged, marginalised victims. Often, in the free movement context, they are not: they are successful, skilled, highly motivated individuals who wish to take advantage of the opportunities offered by the single market but who are faced with detailed regulation imposed by the host state (concerning qualifications, licences and registration) which obstructs them from being fully integrated into the (host state) community. The same can often be said about those litigants bringing claims for equal treatment on the grounds of sex — indeed this is one of the criticisms of the existing law — because it is generally invoked by those already empowered (such as men bringing claims for equal occupational pension age).

Solidarity is partly to do with equality but it goes beyond that. Underpinning the idea of solidarity is the notion that the ties which exist between the individuals of a relevant group justify decision-makers taking steps, both negative and positive, to ensure that all individuals are integrated into the community, thereby enabling them to have the chance to participate and contribute fully. The negative steps include removing obstacles to integration and participation; positive steps include active programmes to encourage participation of those otherwise excluded. If this reading is correct then the use of solidarity as a guiding principle can help liberate decision-makers and decision-takers from the straight-jacket of formal equal treatment.

In the context of the EU, I shall argue that the principle of solidarity provides a useful framework to explain the European Court of Justice's emerging jurisprudence on equality between migrant citizens and nationals. It is a concept that the ECJ itself uses in its own case law,[5] enabling it legitimately to tailor the equality on offer: limited equality in the case of temporary migrants where there is only limited solidarity between nationals of the host state and migrants; full equality where the migrant is permanently established in the Member State where there is (or should be) greater solidarity between the migrant and the national. In this respect solidarity helps to facilitate the migrant's integration into the host state while also justifying the equal treatment. If this is the case then the integration argument helps explain

[3] C-70/95 *Sodemare SA, Anni Azzurri Holding SpA and Anni Azzurri Rezzato Srl v Regione Lombardia* [1997] ECR I-3395.
[4] At para 29.
[5] C-159/91 and C-160/91 *Poucet and Pistre v AGF and Cancava* [1993] ECR I-637; C-67/96 *Albany International BV v Stichting Bedrijfspensioenfonds Textielindustrie* [1999]

the relatively recent evolution in the ECJ's jurisprudence which justifies going beyond a model based on discrimination towards one based on removing the impediments of access to the market.

These interesting developments in the *transnational* context might inform our thinking about equality in the *national* context where principles of citizenship and solidarity are much more firmly rooted. I begin by examining the EU developments in respect of free movement of citizens before considering the implications they may have for domestic labour law.

CITIZENSHIP AND SOLIDARITY: THE EU CONTEXT

While a desire to create a 'Europe for Citizens'[6] or a 'People's Europe'[7] dates back to the early 1970s it was not until the Spanish pressed the issue at Maastricht[8] that the idea of Union citizenship took concrete form. A new Part Two, entitled 'Citizenship of the Union,' was added to the EC Treaty at Maastricht with a view to fostering a sense of identity with, and loyalty to, the EU. Article 17(1)EC establishes the concept of citizenship of the Union. This is conferred on every person holding the nationality of one of the Member States. Article 17(2) provides that citizens of the Union are to enjoy the rights conferred by the EC Treaty. These rights include the principle of non-discrimination on the grounds of nationality found in Article 12. Article 18 EC provides that every citizen of the Union has the right to move and reside freely within the territory of the Member States 'subject to the limitations and conditions laid down in this Treaty and by the measures adopted to give it effect.' The ECJ's case law on Article 18 provides an interesting illustration of how it has used the strong language of citizenship to justify a decision based on solidarity to ensure the attainment of equality between migrants and nationals. *Grzelczyk*[9] shows this very clearly.

Grzelczyk, a French national, began a four-year course of university studies in physical education at a Belgian university. During the first three years, he covered the costs of his studies by taking on various jobs and

---

ECR I-5751, para 87. See further C Barnard, 'Citizenship and "Incremental Inclusion" in M Dougan and E Spaventa (eds), *Social Welfare and EU Law* (Oxford, Hart, forthcoming).

[6] See the Tindemans Report on the European Union which contained a chapter entitled 'Towards a Europe for Citizens' (Bull EC (8) 1975 II no 12, 1) which was drawn up at the request of the Paris summit in 1974.
[7] See the two Adonnino Reports of 1985 to the European Council on a People's Europe (Bull EC Suppl 7/85).
[8] For a full discussion of the background see S O'Leary, *The Evolving Concept of Community Citizenship* (The Hague, Kluwer, 1996) ch 1. See also the Spanish memorandum on citizenship, 'The Road to European Citizenship' (Co.SN 3940/90, 24 September 1990).
[9] C-184/99 *Rudy Grzelczyk v Centre public d'aide sociale d'Ottignies-Louvain-la-Neuve* [2001] ECR I-6193.

loans. At the beginning of his fourth and final year, he applied to the Belgian authorities for payment of the minimex, a non-contributory social benefit designed to assist individuals in need. Under Belgian law as it then stood, Community nationals could receive the benefit but only if they were workers. Because the authorities thought Grzelczyk was a migrant student and not a worker he was denied the benefit; Belgian students in the same circumstances did, however, receive the benefit.[10] Grzelczyk was therefore suffering from discrimination on the grounds of nationality.

The ECJ said that, as a citizen of the Union lawfully resident in Belgium, Grzelczyk could rely on the Article 12 prohibition of discrimination on the grounds of nationality[11] in respect of those situations which fell within the material scope of the EC Treaty,[12] which included the right to move and reside freely in another Member State.[13] It then said that:

> Union citizenship is destined to be the fundamental status of nationals of the Member States enabling those who find themselves in the same situation to enjoy the same treatment in law irrespective of their nationality, subject to such exceptions as are expressly provided for.[14]

One such exception can be found in Article 1 of Directive 93/96/EC which provides that the migrant student must have sufficient resources. However, the ECJ used the citizenship provisions to limit the scope of the derogation. It said that where a migrant student did have recourse to social assistance a Member State could either withdraw his residence permit or not renew it,[15] but it added that such acts could not become the *automatic* consequence of a migrant student having recourse to the host state's social assistance system[16] since the Preamble to the Directive provided that migrant students could not become an 'unreasonable' burden on the public finances of the host state.[17]

The implications of this ruling were spelt out in *Baumbast*,[18] this time in respect of Directive 90/364/EC on persons of independent means. Baumbast, a German national, had been working in the United Kingdom, first as an employee and then as a self-employed person. He brought his family with him and they continued to reside there even after his work had ceased, funding themselves out of their own savings. They also had comprehensive medical insurance but this was for treatment in Germany and did not cover them for

---

[10] *Ibid* at para 29.
[11] *Ibid* at para 30.
[12] *Ibid* at para 32.
[13] *Ibid* at para 33, citing C-274/96 *Bickel and Franz* [1998] ECR I-7637.
[14] *Gizelczyk*, above n 9, at para 31.
[15] *Ibid* at para 42.
[16] *Ibid* at para 43.
[17] *Ibid* at para 44.
[18] C-413/99 [2002] ECR I-7091, para 91.

the United Kingdom. For this reason, the Secretary of State refused to renew Mr Baumbast's residence permit and the residence documents of his Columbian wife and children. The ECJ insisted on reading the limitations in Directive 90/364/EC subject to the principle of proportionality[19] and found that, given neither he nor his family had become a financial burden on the state, it would amount to a disproportionate interference with the exercise of the right of residence conferred on him by Article 18(1)EC if he were denied residence on the ground that his sickness insurance did not cover the emergency treatment given in the United Kingdom.[20]

The careful articulation of the proportionality principle in *Baumbast* helps to explain *Grzelczyk*: Grzelczyk could not be refused a minimex under Article 1 of Directive 93/96/EC because he had been lawfully residing in Belgium for three years during which time he had had sufficient resources (and medical insurance). Now that he was suffering 'temporary difficulties' it would be disproportionate to deny Grzelczyk the minimex to cover this. However, *Grzelczyk* goes further than *Baumbast* by requiring the Belgian authorities to grant Grzelczyk the benefit (minimex) which he would undoubtedly take advantage of, rather than merely granting him the possibility of the benefit (access to the host state's health service) which Baumabst and his family may never need to take up. Therefore, in *Grzelczyk* the ECJ recognised that there was 'a certain degree of financial solidarity' between nationals of a host Member State and nationals of other Member States,[21] and the same reasoning must apply to *Baumbast*. From these cases it would seem that in 'emergency' situations (pressing financial or medical need) the Court recognises that there is sufficient solidarity between nationals and migrants to justify the host state providing assistance to the migrant on equal terms with nationals, especially in respect of benefits which are non-contributory.

How then does this limited version of solidarity explain *Martínez Sala*?[22] Martínez Sala was a Spanish national who had been living in Germany since 1968 when she was 12. She had various jobs and various residence permits in that time. When she gave birth to a child in 1993, she did not have a residence permit, but she did have a certificate saying that an extension of the permit had been applied for. The German authorities refused to pay her a child raising allowance on the grounds that she was neither a German national nor did she have a residence permit. The ECJ said that, as a citizen of the Union lawfully residing in the territory of another Member State, she was entitled under Article 17(2)EC to benefit from the principle of equal treatment laid down in Article 12 EC in respect of 'all situations falling within the scope *ratione materiae* of

---

[19] *Ibid.*
[20] *Ibid* at para 93.
[21] *Ibid* at para 44.
[22] C-85/96 *Martínez Sala* [1998] ECR I-2691.

Community law'[23] which included payment of a child raising allowance.[24] Because she was suffering from direct discrimination on the grounds of nationality, this contravened Article 12.[25]

Why then was Martínez Sala granted full equal treatment in respect of a social benefit when she did not satisfy any of the criteria laid down in Directive 90/364/EC on persons of independent means? I think that part of the explanation lies in the fact that the ECJ did not consider her to be a temporary migrant but a migrant who was fully integrated into the host state's community, having lived there for 25 years. Given that she had spent most of her life in Germany (and had at times contributed to the German exchequer when she had worked), she was effectively more integrated into German society than Spanish society and so she was entitled to be treated in exactly the same way as a German national.

On the face of it, *Martínez Sala*, *Grzelczyk* and *Baumbast* tend to support the Court's confident assertion in *Grzelczyk*[26] that Union citizenship is 'the fundamental status of nationals of the Member States' with the result that, in the name of solidarity, migrant citizens who are not economically active now have the right to claim all benefits available in the host state on the same terms as nationals, unless the benefits are expressly excluded by Community law.[27] If this analysis is correct, then the creation of citizenship of the Union leads to what Iliopoulou and Toner describe as the 'perfect assimilation' approach, where the treatment of Community migrants is placed on a completely equal footing with nationals of the host Member State unless Community law specifically provides otherwise.[28] This is what Advocate General Léger had in mind in *Boukhalfa*[29] where he said:

> If all the conclusions inherent in that concept [Union citizenship] are drawn, every citizen of the Union must, whatever his nationality, enjoy exactly the same rights and be subject to the same obligations. Taken to its ultimate conclusion, the concept should lead to citizens of the Union being treated absolutely equally, irrespective of their nationality. Such equal treatment should be manifested in the same way as among nationals of one and the same State.

[23] *Ibid* at para 67.
[24] *Ibid*.
[25] *Ibid* at para 64.
[26] *Grzelczyk*, above n 9, at para 31, echoing AG La Pergola in *Martínez Sala* above n 22, at para 18.
[27] An example of an express exclusion is maintenance grants for students in Art 3 of Directive 93/96/EC.
[28] A Iliopoulou and H Toner (2002) 39 *CMLRev* 609, at 616.
[29] C-214/94 *Ingrid Boukhalfa v Bundesrepublik Deutschland* [1996] ECR I-2253, para 63 and S Friess and J Shaw, 'Citizenship of the Union: First Steps in the European Court of Justice' (1998) 4 *EPL* 533.

But, when looked at carefully, the cases do not support the full assimilationist approach and actually suggest an incremental approach to residence and equality: the longer migrants reside in the Member State, the greater the number of benefits they receive on equal terms with nationals. Therefore, Grzelcyzk, a medium-term resident, received the minimex for a temporary period. By contrast, Martínez Sala, a long-term resident (she had lived in Germany for 25 years) received child benefit on the same terms as nationals. It therefore seems that these cases turn on two principles: integration and solidarity.[30] Martínez Sala was fully integrated into the host state's community and so the ECJ required her to be treated like nationals. She therefore benefited from the principle of *national* solidarity which underpins national welfare systems (national taxpayers pay their taxes which help to provide benefits for their fellow nationals who are in need). By contrast, Grzelczyk was not considered fully integrated into the Belgian community (he was expected to return to France on the completion of his course). He therefore could not enjoy full, unlimited equal treatment with Belgian nationals in respect of the minimex. However, the ECJ noted that, as a result of the creation of Union citizenship, there was now sufficient *transnational* solidarity (national taxpayers pay their taxes to help provide benefits for their fellow nationals in need *and* for migrant EU citizens who are in temporary need) to justify requiring the host state to pay the minimex to Grzelczyk in respect of *temporary* difficulties.[31]

Thus, this case law suggests a spectrum: at one end is Martínez Sala who is fully integrated into the host state and so enjoys full equal treatment (the payment of the benefit on exactly the same terms as nationals); and in the middle lies Grzelczyk who is only partially integrated and so enjoys only limited equal treatment (he receives the benefit on the same terms as nationals but only until he becomes an unreasonable burden on public funds when his right of residence can be terminated). At the other end of the spectrum should be those migrant citizens who have just arrived in the host state. While Article 18(1)EC gives them the right to move and reside freely in the host state,[32] the logic outlined above suggests that because they are not yet integrated into the host state's community they should not enjoy equal treatment in respect of social welfare benefits (eg the minimex) although they might receive some social advantages on a non-discriminatory basis (eg emergency medical help, as *Baumbast* suggests).[33] This was the view taken by Advocate General Ruiz-Jarabo Colomer in *Collins*.[34] Collins, who was Irish, arrived in the United

---

[30] In the case of the economically active this is assumed.

[31] *Grzelczyk*, above n 9, at para 44.

[32] See also AG Geelhoed in C-413/01 *Franca Ninni-Orasche v Bundesminister für Wissenschaft, Verkehr und Kunst* [2003] ECR I-000.

[33] Although on the facts of *Baumbast* his length of residence suggested that his case might be closer to the full integration end of the spectrum.

[34] C-138/02 *Brian Francis Collins v Secretary of State for Work and Pensions* [2004] ECR I-000.

Kingdom and promptly applied for a jobseeker's allowance which was refused on the grounds that he was not habitually resident in the United Kingdom. The Advocate General distinguished *Grzelczyk*[35] and concluded that Community law did not require the benefit to be provided to a citizen of the Union who entered the territory of a Member State with the purpose of seeking employment while lacking any connection with the state or link with the domestic employment market.[36]

The incremental approach to the principle of equal treatment suggested by the case law was also recognised by Advocate General La Pergola in *Stöber*. He said that the ultimate purpose of the citizenship provisions was to bring about *increasing* equality between citizens of the Union, irrespective of their nationality.[37] The idea is further fleshed out in the Directive on Citizens' Rights,[38] which replaces the various Directives on workers, the self-employed and service providers and the three Residence Directives, with a single Directive giving rights to all Union citizens who move to or reside in another Member state and to their family members as defined.[39] The Directive envisages three categories of migrants. The first group are those wishing to enter the host state for up to three months. They are not subject to any conditions (eg as to resources, medical insurance) other than holding a valid identity card or passport. They enjoy the right to reside in the host State for themselves and their families and the right to equal treatment but they have no entitlement to social assistance during the first three months of their stay.

The second group are those residing in the host state for more than three months. They have a 'right to residence' if they are engaged in gainful activity as workers or are self-employed; or have sufficient resources for themselves and comprehensive sickness insurance cover; or they are students with comprehensive sickness insurance cover and sufficient resources.[40] They have the right to engage in gainful activity and the right to equal treatment. The third group concerns those legally residing in the host state for a continuous period of more than five years.[41] These citizens (and their family members who are not nationals but who have resided with the Union citizen for five years) will have the right of permanent residence. None of the conditions applicable to the second group apply to those seeking permanent residence. As with the second group, the third group also enjoy the right to work and

---

[35] *Ibid* at para 66.
[36] *Ibid* at para 76.
[37] C-4 and C-5/95 *Stöber and Pereira* [1997] ECR I-511, para 50.
[38] Parliament and Council Directive 2004/38/EC (OJ [2004] L158/77).
[39] *Ibid* Art 3(1).
[40] *Ibid* Art 7.
[41] Art 7.

to equal treatment. In addition, they can enjoy student maintenance in the form of grants or loans.[42]

There are three striking features of the citizenship case law outlined above. First, because the solidarity principle is used to justify giving — even limited — equality rights to migrants it tailors equality according to the circumstances and so makes it more flexible. This avoids the political problems of ensuring full equal treatment to all migrants from the first day of their arrival in the host state.

Secondly, the equality rights conferred by the case law in the name of solidarity have the effect of imposing corollary duties on national authorities to make payments (*Grzelczyk*) and to provide benefits (*Baumbast*) to migrants where they are already given to nationals. In the future it could be envisaged that the solidarity principle might justify other policies necessary to help the migrant feel integrated into the host state, including some of the positive duties of monitoring that Bob Hepple has advocated and which now find their way into OMC (open method of coordination) processes.

Thirdly, this case law shows how the principle of solidarity shades into notions of integration and social inclusion. In its pre-citizenship case law, the ECJ justified extending equality in respect of social advantages under Article 7(2) of Regulation 1612/68 to family members on the grounds that it was necessary to secure their integration into the community of the host state. This was first seen in *Even*[43] where the Court said that social advantages included those:

> which, whether or not linked to a contract of employment, are generally granted to national workers primarily because of their objective status as workers or by virtue of the mere fact of their residence on the national territory and the extension of which to workers who are nationals of other Member States *therefore seems suitable to facilitate their mobility within the Community* (emphasis added).

With its reference to residence, the decision in *Even* paved the way for Article 7(2)EC to be applied not just to workers qua workers but also to their families qua lawful residents.[44] The ECJ justified this on the grounds that, first, Article 7(2) was essential to encourage free movement not just of workers but also of their families, without whom the worker would be discouraged from moving;[45] and secondly, it

---

[42] Art 24(2).

[43] Case 207/78 *Ministère public v Even* [1979] ECR 2019.

[44] S Peers, "Social Advantages" and Discrimination in Employment: Case Law Confirmed and Clarified' (1997) 22 *EL Rev* 157, at 164; E Ellis, 'Social Advantages: A New Lease of Life' (2003) 40 *CML Rev* 639.

[45] See, eg Case 94/84 *ONEM v Deak* [1985] ECR 1873 where a Hungarian national, the son of an Italian working in Belgium, applied for unemployment benefits. Since unemployment

encouraged the integration of migrant workers into the working environment of the host country.[46]

So far we have seen how the principle of solidarity has been used to justify extending equality to both temporary and permanent migrants. However, as we have seen, solidarity goes beyond that and justifies taking steps — to remove impediments to the individual's participation in and integration into the community. The ECJ's case law on persons (workers, establishment and services) shows this clearly. The jurisprudence has moved beyond prohibiting direct and indirect discrimination[47] to removing any (substantial)[48] obstacle[49] which prevents or restricts access to the market. This change of approach was highlighted in *Säger*[50] where the ECJ said that Article 49 EC on the freedom to provide services required:

> *not only* the elimination of all discrimination against a person providing services on the ground of his nationality *but also* the abolition of any restriction, even if it applies without distinction to national providers of services and to those of other Member States, when *it is liable to prohibit or otherwise impede* the activities of a provider of services established in another Member State where he lawfully provides similar services.

The Court continued that any such restriction could only be justified by imperative reasons relating to the public interest.[51]

The facts of *Kraus*[52] demonstrate the importance of this change in approach. Kraus, a German student, complained that he was not allowed to use his British LLM title in Germany without prior authorisation from the German authorities. If he had obtained an academic diploma from a German university, no such authorisation would have been required. *Kraus* concerned discrimination not on the grounds of nationality (after all Kraus was German) but rather on the grounds that he had received the training in another Member State which disadvantaged him when he returned to his

---

benefit was found to constitute a social advantage within the meaning of Art 7(2), the son was entitled to receive it, irrespective of the fact that he was not a Community national.

[46] See also Joined Cases 389 and 390/87 *Echternach and Moritz v Minister van Onderwijs en Wetenschappen* [1989] ECR 723; C-308/93 *Bestuur van de Sociale Verzekeringsbank v Cabanis-Issarte* [1996] ECR I-2097.

[47] C-384/93 *Alpine Investments BV v Minister van Financiën* [1995] ECR I-1141 and Case C-275/92 *Customs and Excise v Schindler* [1994] ECR I-1039.

[48] C-190/98 *Graf v Filzmozer Maschinenbau GmbH* [2000] ECR I-493.

[49] C-415/93 [1995] ECR I-4921, para 104. See also C-18/95 *Terhoeve* [1999] ECR I-345, para 39; C-275/92 *Schindler* [1994] ECR 1039, para 45. See also C-221/89 *ex parte Factortame Ltd and others* [1991] ECR I-3905, para 32; C-114/97 *Commission v Spain* [1998] ECR I-6717, para 44.

[50] C-76/90, [1991] ECR I-4221, para 12, emphasis added.

[51] *Ibid* at para 15.

[52] C-19/92 [1993] ECR I-1663.

country of origin (German)[53] — in other words, he suffered discrimination based on the fact that he had exercised his rights of free movement.[54] Focusing on the obstacles to free movement created by the German rule, the ECJ said that Articles 39 EC and 43 EC precluded any national measure governing the conditions under which an academic title obtained in another Member State could be used, where that measure, even though applicable without discrimination on grounds of nationality, was *'liable to hamper or to render less attractive* the exercise by Community nationals, including those of the Member State which enacted the measure, of fundamental freedoms guaranteed by the Treaty'.[55] The Court then said that the national court had to consider whether the rules could be justified on the grounds of 'the need to protect a public which will not necessarily be alerted to abuse of academic titles'[56] and the steps taken were proportionate.[57]

Kraus was not an isolated decision. Its formulation has been repeated in more or less similar terms in a number of subsequent cases.[58] The court is also moving in this direction in the context of the case law on citizenship.[59] The significance of these cases is that, as Advocate General Jacobs argued in *Leclerc-Siplec* in the context of goods, a discrimination test is inappropriate since the central concern of the EC Treaty provisions on the free movement of goods, was to prevent unjustified obstacles to trade between Member States. He said that 'If an obstacle to trade exists it cannot cease to exist simply because an identical obstacle affects domestic trade'.[60] This argument is familiar to discrimination lawyers. The consequence of this approach is that many more obstacles are in principle prohibited and the burden shifts to the decision-maker not only to justify the restriction but also to demonstrate that the steps taken were no more restrictive than necessary (ie proportionate).

An approach based on removing obstacles is an example of the sort of negative step that can be taken in the name of solidarity to help facilitate integration. An example of a more positive step can be found in the

---

[53] See also C-370/90 *Surinder Singh* [1992] ECR I-4261, para 23.
[54] See also C-224/98 *D'Hoop v Office national de l'emploi* [2002] ECR I-6191, para 34, where the ECJ said that by linking the grant of tideover allowances to the condition of having obtained the required diploma in Belgium, Belgian law thus *'places at a disadvantage certain of its nationals simply because they have exercised their freedom to move* in order to pursue education in another Member State'.
[55] *Kraus*, above n 52, at para 32, emphasis added.
[56] *Ibid* at para 35.
[57] *Ibid* at para 42.
[58] See, eg C-369 and C-376/96 *Arblade v Leloup* [1999] ECR I-8453, para 33, C-3/95 *Sandker* [1996] ECR I-6511, para 25, C-55/94 *Gebhard* [1995] ECR I-4165, para 37 and V Hatzopoulos (2000) 37 *CMLRev* 43, at 70.
[59] C-224/98 *D'Hoop v Office national de l'emploi* [2002] ECR I-6191; see also AG Jacobs' Opinions in C-148/02 *Garcia Avello* [2003] ECR I-000 and C-224/02 *Heikki Antero Pusa v Osuuspankkien Keskinäinen Vakuutusyhtiö*, AG's Opinion, 20 November 2003.
[60] Case C-412/93 *Leclerc-Siplec v TF1 Publicité SA* [1995] ECR I-179 para 40.

EC Treaty: the rights for migrants to vote in local elections in the host state and European elections (Article 19 EC). *Grzelczyk* and *Baumbast* suggest that solidarity implies a positive obligation on the state to provide, in limited circumstances, health and social benefits at least on equal terms to nationals. The question we now turn to is the extent to which the developments in the field of free movement of persons might inform any future developments in the field of (domestic) equality law.

APPLYING SOLIDARITY PRINCIPLES TO EQUALITY LAW

In the previous section, I argued that the ECJ is using the solidarity principle to justify extending (at least limited) equality rights to migrant citizens in order to help to integrate them into the host state community or at least recognising their level of integration. The negative dimension of this approach is removing restrictions or obstacles to the migrant's integration (the *Säger/Kraus* approach); the positive aspect is that the solidarity principle can be used to impose obligations on the state to help integrate the individual. All of this has been developed in the context of the rather shaky foundations of EU citizenship. How might these principles be transplanted into the more fertile soil of national citizenship where the solidarity principle is much more firmly rooted? Could it be argued that discrimination law at national level is really about integrating individuals into the workplace while maintaining a balance between work and private life, that the removal of discrimination is really about ensuring solidarity between workers?

If we look first at the 'negative' dimension of this approach, then national law might provide that not only is discrimination prohibited but so is any measure, policy or practice which constituted an obstacle to or impeded the individual's participation in the economic life of a community. Such measures would be unlawful unless the obstacle could be justified and the steps taken were proportionate. This approach is resonant of that adopted by the Supreme Court in Canada in two seminal decisions on the meaning of the equality clause found in section 15(1) of the Canadian Charter, *Andrews v British Columbia*[61] and *Turpin v the Queen*.[62] In *Andrews*, McIntyre J rejected the Aristotelian 'similarly situated test' as 'seriously deficient' (since if applied literally it could be used to justify the Nuremberg laws of Adolf Hitler) and the separate but equal doctrine of *Plessey v Ferguson*. Instead, the court favoured an approach

---

[61] [1989] 1 SCR 143. See M Gold (1989) 34 *McGill LJ* 1063.
[62] [1989] 1 SCR 1296. Subsequent developments have been less positive: see, eg, D Lepofsky, 'The Canadian Judicial Approach to Equality Rights: Freedom Ride or Roller Coaster?' (1992) 55 *Law and Contemporary Problems* 167; D Beatty, 'The Canadian Charter of Rights: Lessons and Laments' (1997) 60 *MLR* 481, at 490; T Ison, 'A Constitutional Bill of Rights: The Canadian Experience' (1997) 60 *MLR* 499, at 500.

to discrimination based on disadvantage rather than difference.[63] McIntyre J said:

> [D]iscrimination may be described as a distinction, whether intentional or not but based on grounds relating to the personal characteristics of the individual or group, which has the effect of imposing burdens, obligations or disadvantages on such individual or group not imposed upon others, or which withholds or limits access to opportunities, benefits, and advantages available to other members of society.

This view was endorsed in *Turpin* where Wilson J added 'A finding of discrimination will, I think, in most but not all cases, necessarily entail a search for disadvantage that exists apart from and independent of the particular legal distinction being challenged.'

The advantages of applying the *Säger/Kraus* approach are threefold. First, it individualises the right. This means that the claim does not depend on proving (often by complex statistical analysis) group-based stereotypes (eg women have primary child-care responsibilities). Instead, it allows all individuals (both men with primary child-care responsibilities and women) to argue that an obstacle (eg evening or night working) stands in their way of being able fully to participate in the workplace. Secondly, since the existence of any such rule would need to be justified, employers would be obliged to think about their practices in order to be able to justify them. Thirdly, the application of the proportionality principle might allow for some degree of mediation between the parties by requiring the employer to consider whether there are less restrictive ways of achieving the same objective (eg working a limited number of evenings/nights only on fixed days of the week?). In this way the proportionality principle could be used to achieve some form of 'reasonable accommodation.'

There are obvious disadvantages to such an approach, too. First there are problems as to definition (what constitutes an obstacle?). Secondly, it would increase the burdens on employers. Thirdly, it would disrupt the well-established framework that direct discrimination can be saved only by reference to the express list of genuine occupational qualifications, while indirect discrimination could be objectively justified (although this model has been diluted somewhat by the Genuine Occupational Requirements in the Employment Directives). Fourthly, the individualised nature of the claim would leave many feeling exposed.

However, perhaps the most striking feature of any such claim would be that, unlike discrimination law, it does not expressly identify any suspect

---

[63] See also N Lacey, 'From Individual to Group?' in B Hepple and E Szyszczak, *Discrimination: The Limits of the Law* (London, Mansell, 1992) 104 and C Mackinnon, 'Reflections on Sex Equality under Law' (1991) 100 *Yale Law Journal* 1281, at 1325.

grounds. In one sense this is liberating. Claims would no longer have to be shoe-horned into existing, established prohibited grounds (eg discrimination against gays and transsexuals as sex discrimination, and sex or race-plus discrimination as sex and race discrimination) and it would also pave the way for those presently without grounds to make a claim (eg those wishing to engage in other community-related activities, not connected with child or elderly care, such as being a school governor who are prevented from participating by an employer's practice or policy). On the other hand, it loses the clear public statement found in existing legislation that discrimination on certain specified grounds (eg sex, race, religion) is unlawful. However, under EC law the *Säger/Kraus* approach *supplements* the existing discrimination model and the ECJ resorts to the discrimination approach in clear cases of discrimination. It would also be possible to envisage a permutation of the approach found in the USA to the Fourteenth Amendment, where restrictions which are based on, for example, race could be justified only according to a strict scrutiny review, while other restrictions might be subject only to intermediate (or less) review.

So far we have concentrated on the implications for national law of a negative approach to solidarity. In respect of the *positive* aspect of an approach based on solidarity, this could liberate governments/employers from the strait-jacket of formal equality: where individual workers are not fully integrated or need special support, action could be taken on the grounds of solidarity. For Hepple this is crucial since he sees that some positive different treatment is an essential part of the process of integration.[64] When considering the case of the Roma, he argues that negative rights not to interfere are insufficient. He argues that the Roma need positive rights, such as the right to adequate housing, education and health-care. In respect of employers, such positive acts might involve monitoring programmes, other positive action measures such as child-care provision or special training for the disadvantaged individual. This issue is of great practical importance given the current importance of the diversity agenda to human resources managers.[65] When viewed through the lens of solidarity, such programmes could be put in place without fear of challenge under formal discrimination law by groups who have not benefited from that particular programme.

However, the ECJ's case law does pose one serious threat for existing equality law: it suggests that there are varying degrees of equality (full equality for long-term residents, limited equality for new arrivals). However, this aspect of the case law must be judged in the immigration context. It has long been the case that migrants acquire a greater number of rights the longer they remain in the host state. Equality law (sex, race,

---

[64] B Hepple, 'Race and Law in Fortress Europe,' (2004) 67 *MLR* 1.
[65] See L Barmes with S Ashtiani, 'The Diversity Approach to Achieving Equality: Potential and Pitfalls' (2003) 32 *ILJ* 274.

ethnic origin etc), when looked at in the domestic context, applies to all residents and is premised on the idea that the beneficiaries are all established in the state. In this regard, the staggered equality envisaged by the ECJ's case law is not strictly transposeable to the domestic arena. However, the Court's notion could be used for beneficial purposes, assisting in the integration process. It could be argued that in a transition phase, certain groups need particular assistance to help integrate them into the workplace and so, as we saw above, in the name of solidarity it could be argued that differential treatment is permitted.

CONCLUSIONS

In this chapter I have argued that the future of equality law may well lie beyond equality. I have argued that it needs to be buttressed by another principle — solidarity — to achieve the broader social objectives intended by equality, namely integration and participation. I have argued that while the principle of non-discrimination was (and still us) a useful tool for eliminating the more egregious examples of inequality (ideally subject to the many modifications suggested by Hepple, Coussey, Fredman and others) we should look elsewhere for other guiding principles which might help eliminate the remaining disadvantages suffered by workers. Here, the ECJ, confident in its role of reinforcing negative integration, has shown an interesting way forward with its *Säger/Kraus* case law. More interesting still is the positive use of the solidarity principle in *Baumbast* and other cases by the Court. Couched in the careful rhetoric of equality, the ECJ has taken an important step towards imposing obligations on the states in respect of migrant citizens.

Yet, a wider use of this approach to secure positive rights for individuals may well have been frustrated by the legislator, through the enactment of the equality Directives, especially the Article 13 Directives. The language used in the Preambles to the two Article 13 Directives appears to locate them firmly within the context of our discussion on solidarity. For example, paragraph 8 of the Preamble to the Race Directive refers to the Employment Guidelines 2000 which stress the need to foster conditions for a socially inclusive labour market formulating a coherent set of policies aimed at combating discrimination against groups such as ethnic minorities.[66] Paragraph 9 goes on to say that discrimination based on racial or ethnic origin may undermine the achievement of the objectives of the EC Treaty

---

[66] Council Directive 2000/78 establishing a general framework for equal treatment in employment and occuption (OJ 2000 L303/16) Preamble, para (8) to the Horizontal Directive adds that the reference to groups includes persons with a disability and refers to the need to support older workers.

including 'social cohesion and solidarity.'[67] Paragraph 9 of the Horizontal Directive adds that employment and occupation are key elements in guaranteeing equal opportunities for all and contribute strongly to the full participation of citizens in economic, cultural and social life and to realising their potential.

Yet despite this rhetoric, the substance of the Directives is based firmly on the 'third generation' non-discrimination model, strongly influenced by the United Kingdom's Race Relations Act 1976.[68] The drafting took no account of 'fourth generation' rights which place positive duties on decision-makers; nor did it look to the rather innovative *Säger/Kraus* line of case law to inform its approach, despite the fact that the Commission's explanatory memorandum made express reference to the ECJ's case law on persons to inform the Directive's definition of indirect discrimination. Confined as they are to a fairly narrow conception of equality, the existence of the Directives may well curtail the ECJ's willingness to make more imaginative uses of the solidarity principle outside the confines of the free movement of persons[69] and, in so doing, constrain national courts from demonstrating any similar creativity.

---

[67] Similar language is used in respect of the Horizontal Directive in para 11.
[68] B Hepple, above n 64.
[69] Recent case law demonstrates that the ECJ has become sensitive to accusations that it has overstepped the limits of its judicial competence: See Case C-249/96 *Grant v South West Trains* [1998] ECR I-621; Case C-376/98 *Federal Republic of Germany v European Parliament and Council of the European Union* [2000] ECR I-8419; Case C-50/00P *Unión de Pequeñas Agricultures v Council of the European Union* [2002] ECR I-6677.

11

The Future of Workers' Participation in the EU

MANFRED WEISS

INTRODUCTION

T HE FUNCTION OF labour law, as well as the institutional arrangements which it creates, very much depend on the historical, political, cultural and economic context of specific countries and specific regions. Therefore, it would not make much sense to speculate on the functions and institutions of labour law on a global scale, even if globalisation is advancing. This insight implies that the discussion on the future of workers' participation has to be embedded into a specific environment. The focus in this chapter is exclusively on the EU.

Two different approaches could be chosen: either to provide an analysis of the system of each Member State or to analyse the European Community's strategy as a basis for an assessment of future development in this area. In making such a choice it needs to be appreciated that, up to now, the differences between the industrial relations systems of the EU Member States are nowhere greater than in the area of workers' participation.[1] Some countries, for example Germany, Austria, the Netherlands and Luxembourg, have systems with a dual structure where workers' participation institutionally is separated from the trade unions, even if in actual practice the links between the two are significant. In other countries, workers' participation is based on two pillars: both the trade unions and a body elected by all employees. This is the case in France, Greece, Portugal and Spain. In the Scandinavian countries, workers' participation is exclusively in the hands of the trade unions. In countries like Ireland and the United Kingdom, workers' participation for a long time was more or less a taboo subject for the trade unions. The fear of being compromised in opposing

---

[1] For an instructive overview see European Commission (ed), *Industrial Relations in Europe* (Luxembourg, Office of the Official Publications of the European Communities, 2000) 30.

measures through their industrial strength prevented them becoming integrated into the mechanism of decision-making in companies. Only recently, mainly due to the EU input, is this attitude gradually beginning to change. Italy has developed an interesting mixture of its own. Even if it may be possible, as just indicated, to discover organisational similarities between the systems of different countries, the remaining differences should not be overlooked. It should be added that in some countries, workers' participation is based exclusively on legislation (as, for example, in Germany), in others exclusively on collective agreements (as, for example, in Scandinavia) and again in others on a mixture of both (as, for example, in Belgium). The subject matter of workers' participation is as different as the degree of participation, which ranges from mere information to co-determination. And only some countries have provisions for workers' participation in company boards, which several systems again differ significantly from each other. In short, there is a wide spectrum of patterns of workers' participation and some countries where such participation is virtually unknown.

Even if an effort were to be made to analyse in detail all the existing systems, thereby showing the institutional similarities and differences, this would not be very helpful. It would not tell us anything about their functions. The functional perspective could be revealed only by putting the system of workers' participation into the overall context of the respective country, thereby analysing not only the other parts of the overall system (such as collective bargaining, the system of conflict resolution, the minimum level of protection guaranteed by employment law etc) but also the shape of the actors, the prevailing attitudes, the cultural, political and economic environment etc. This evidently is an impossible task. Therefore, the second option indicated above is chosen in this chapter, and its purpose is much more modest. The discussion focuses on the input by the European Community in the area of workers' participation in order to assess whether and in what way this will have an effect on the overall structure of workers' participation in the EU as well as on the systems in the different Member States.

THE EUROPEAN COMMUNITY'S APPROACH

The European Community from the very beginning has been confronted with the diversity of the Member States' systems indicated above. The intervention of Community legislation in the area of employee involvement started in the 1970s with Directives referring to specific issues. The second phase was devoted to employee involvement in transnational companies.

And finally a framework for employee involvement at the shop-floor level in the Member States was developed.

The sequence of these legislative interventions is by no means based on a coherent concept. The 1970s Directive on employee involvement in relation to collective redundancies was the result of a reaction to a high-profile case in which it was shown that uneven structures among Member States in this area might be abused by transnationally operating companies. The Directive of the same period on transfer of undertakings was driven by an attempt to increase job security in such situations. And the Framework Directive on health and safety was built on the widespread consensus of a need for employee involvement in this area.[2] The real break-through for employee involvement as a mainstream strategy in the European Community was the Directive on European Works Councils 94/45/EC, which after long and controversial debates was passed in 1994. Without this success, the Directive on employee involvement in the European Company of 2001 and the Directive on a framework for consultation and information of 2002, setting minimum standards for shop-floor participation within the Member States, would have been unthinkable. Therefore, in order to understand the dynamics of the European Community's achievements in this field it is necessary to follow the chronological sequence of the Community's legislative acts.

The brief description of the different Directives is not designed to deliver a profound analysis but merely to provide a basis for an assessment of the role of workers' participation in the EU in the future. In the latter perspective, of course, the implications of EU-enlargement have to be included.

'SPECIALISED' PARTICIPATION

In 1975 the Directive on the approximation of the laws of the Member States relating to collective redundancies[3] was passed and two years later the Directive on safeguarding of employees' rights in the event of transfers of undertakings, businesses and parts of businesses[4] followed. Both Directives establish an information and consultation procedure in the context, respectively, of collective redundancies and transfers of undertakings. The actors on the employees' side are the workers' representatives according

---

[2] For a detailed discussion of these first Directives see M Weiss, 'Workers' Participation in the European Union' in P Davies, A Lyon-Caen, S Sciarra and S Simitis (eds), *European Community Labour Law: Principles and Perspectives* (Oxford, Clarendon Press, 1996) 213 at 218.

[3] [1975] OJ L48.

[4] [1977] OJ L61.

to 'the laws or practices' of the respective Member State. However, there was and is no guarantee that a body acting as workers' representative will be available everywhere. To take just the most interesting example, in the United Kingdom, according to the Employment Protection Act 1975, 'workers' representative' in this context meant an independent trade union recognised by the employer. Until 1979, recognition of trade unions was obligatory under certain conditions. As a result of the changes made by the Thatcher government it was left to the employer's discretion whether a trade union was recognised and, if so, which one. The employer was entitled not only to refuse recognition but also to withdraw it without giving any reasons. Owing to the decline in practice in trade union power in Britain, derecognition increased significantly.[5] This situation was considered by the European Court of Justice (ECJ)[6] not to be in line with the spirit of the Directives. Therefore, the United Kingdom had no choice but to amend its legislation[7] to make sure that, at least in principle, workers' representatives are available. In addition, by the Employment Relations Act 1999, a new statutory recognition procedure has been introduced.[8]

Both Directives related only to cases where the decision on collective redundancies or on transfer of undertakings was made within the particular company concerned. However, they did not cover cases where employees of a subsidiary are affected by decisions taken by the holding company of a group which may be located within the same country or abroad. Consequently, the Directive on collective redundancies was amended in 1992[9] and 1998[10] and the Directive on transfer of undertakings in 1998[11] and 2001.[12] According to the amended versions, the Directives now apply irrespective of whether the decision on collective redundancies or on transfer of undertakings is made by the employer or by the parent undertaking controlling the employing company. The amended version of the Directive on collective redundancies further specifies and enlarges the minimum requirements for the content of information and consultation. The amendment to the Directive on transfers of undertakings tried to integrate the enormous amount of case law of the European Court of Justice and in particular offered a definition for transfer of undertakings, although this definition still leaves open many questions.

---

[5] For this development see G Morris and T Archer, *Trade Unions, Employers and the Law* (Oxford, Blackwell, 1991) 139.
[6] C-382/92 and C-383/92, *Commission v United Kingdom* [1994] ICR 664.
[7] See S Deakin and G Morris, *Labour Law* (3rd edn, London, Butterworths, 2001) 792–96.
[8] For a detailed analysis of this procedure see *ibid* at 766–81.
[9] [1992] OJ L245/3.
[10] [1998] OJ L225/16.
[11] [1998] OJ L201/88.
[12] [2001] OJ L82/16.

EMPLOYEE INVOLVEMENT IN
TRANSNATIONAL CORPORATIONS

The Directive on European Works Councils

Evidently national institutional arrangements on employee involvement can operate only within the national framework. If the decisions are taken by the headquarters outside the country concerned, information and consultation rights become useless. It is therefore no surprise that the main initiative to establish a framework for information and consultation on a European scale came from the labour movements in countries where such arrangements already existed and where the degree of frustration had steadily increased because, on the one hand, the transnational perspective was becoming more and more important but, on the other hand, it was not subject to the traditional instruments available within the national framework.

The first attempt to overcome this deficiency was the so-called 'Vredeling proposal' of 1980,[13] amended in 1983.[14] The proposal did not affect the pre-existing structure of employees' representation. As in the Directives on specific issues, the actors in the case of information and consultation were 'the employees' representatives provided for by the laws or practices of the Member States'. The chain of information had to go down from the parent company to the subsidiary where information and consultation were supposed to take place. The content and procedure of information and consultation were prescribed in detail. Largely due to this prescription the proposal was considered much too inflexible and therefore had no prospect of becoming a Directive. The attempt was given up in the mid-1980s.

The Directive on European Works Councils was the result of fresh efforts to revitalise social policy. The notion of the social dimension became a key issue in the discussions on the realisation of the internal market. In addition, the institutional strengthening of the social dialogue at EC level by the Single European Act's amendment of the EC Treaty led to an increased involvement of the social partners throughout the Community. This explains why the initiative to adopt a Community Charter of the Fundamental Social Rights of Workers[15] enjoyed widespread public attention and became the subject of very heated and controversial debates. When in December 1989 the Charter was adopted by 11 Member States in Strasbourg the content was reduced to a minimum on which practically everybody could agree. Hence, the topics contained in the Charter were also agreed upon by at least the majority of business organisations and their

---

[13] [1980] OJ C297/3.
[14] [1983] OJ C217/3.
[15] Com (1989) 248 final.

spokespersons. It is important in this context to mention that section 17 of the Charter reads as follows:

> Information, consultation and participation for workers must be developed along appropriate lines, taking account of the practices in force in the various Member States. This shall apply especially in companies or groups of companies having establishments or companies in two or more Member States of the European Community.

In section 18, the main situations requiring such information, consultation and participation were specified. And in the Commission's Social Action Programme to implement the Charter the introduction of a Community instrument on employee information, consultation and participation procedures in transnational undertakings was proposed. In short, both the legitimacy of such an instrument and the pressure to introduce it had increased tremendously compared with the period when Vredeling was being debated.

Furthermore, the Commission had succeeded in involving the social partners to an astonishing degree in the initial preparation of the draft of the new proposal. Nevertheless, the proposal, first presented in 1991[16] and then modified several times, in the end was not accepted unanimously by the Council. Therefore, there was no alternative but to follow the path opened by the Social Protocol of Maastricht. On 22 September 1994, the Council adopted the EWC Directive 94/45/EC[17] which was extended to the United Kingdom only after the integration of the Maastricht Protocol into the Amsterdam Treaty in 1997.

The Directive on the establishment of a European Works Council seeks to achieve the same goal as the Vredeling proposal, but uses a very different strategy: the change of paradigm from substantial regulation to a merely procedural solution. It covers only transnational undertakings and groups of undertakings with at least 1,000 employees within the EU and with at least 150 employees of the undertaking or of different undertakings of the group in each of at least two different Member States.

The focus of the Directive is on the establishment of a body representing the interests of all employees of the undertaking or group of undertakings within the Community: the European Works Council (EWC). In order to establish such an EWC a relatively complicated procedure is provided for. First, the employees' representatives in each undertaking or each group of undertakings must form a so-called special negotiating body composed of representatives of each Member State in which the Community-scale undertaking or group of undertakings employs at least 100 employees. Then the EWC has to be set up by written agreement between the central management

---

[16] [1991] OJ C39/10.
[17] [1994] OJ L254/64.

of the Community-scale undertaking or of the controlling undertaking of the group on the one hand and the special negotiating body on the other. Where a Community-scale undertaking or group of undertakings has its central management or its controlling undertaking outside the EU, the EWC must be set up by written agreement between its representative agent within the EU or, in the absence of such an agent, the management of the undertaking or of the group of undertakings with the largest number of employees on the one hand and the special negotiating body on the other.

This agreement (according to Article 6) must determine specific matters: the nature and composition of the EWC; its functions and powers; the procedure for informing and consulting the EWC; the place, frequency and duration of its meetings; and, lastly, the financial and material resources to be allocated to the EWC. Whether such an agreement is concluded, and in what manner, depends entirely on the parties on both sides. If the special negotiating body decides by a two-thirds majority not to request such an agreement, that is the end of the matter. Only if the central management refuses to commence negotiations within six months of receiving such a request or if after three years the two partners are unable to reach an agreement do the subsidiary requirements of the Annex to the EWC Directive apply.

These subsidiary requirements are the only form of pressure available to the special negotiating body. They expressly limit the EWC's competence to information and consultation on matters which affect either the transnationally operating undertaking or group of undertakings as a whole, or at least two subsidiaries of the undertaking or two undertakings of the group situated in different Member States. The organisational structure of the EWC is prescribed to a certain extent. In addition to the EWC, a specific committee consisting of at most three members is provided for. The EWC must be informed and consulted once a year on general aspects of the undertaking's or the group's policy. If measures with significant disadvantages for employees are at stake, additional information and consultation of the committee is required before these measures are executed. Those members of the EWC representing the constituency affected by measures in question are entitled to participate in the meeting. It is important to stress that the right of the EWC or the committee to meet alone before the meeting with the central management is guaranteed and that support by experts is provided if necessary. All costs are to be borne by the central management. However, the Member States are entitled to lay down budgetary rules regarding the operation of the EWC, and may in particular limit funding to cover one expert only.

The EWC Directive contains an article (Article 13) which was intended to confirm already existing voluntary agreements and to stimulate the conclusion of new ones up to the deadline for national implementation. Under this Article 13, the Directive did not apply to undertakings or groups of undertakings which at this date already had an agreement on a system of transnational information and consultation covering 'the entire workforce'. The content of such a agreement was left entirely to the parties. This possibility was understood as an expression of the principle of subsidiarity.

In the meantime, although the Directive is implemented into national law throughout the EU, fewer EWCs have been established than might have been expected.[18] Indeed, at first glance the quantitative side does not look very encouraging. More than 1,800 undertakings and groups of undertakings are covered by the Directive. This corresponds to about 10 per cent of the workforce in the EU. Out of these 1,822 undertakings, only a little more than one-third (which corresponds to a little more than 650 undertakings) have established one or more EWCs. This means that almost two-thirds of the companies covered by the Directive still are missing. The picture becomes even more modest if the existing EWCs are divided into those based on voluntary agreements according to Article 13 of the EWC Directive and those based on agreements according to the Directive: only one-third is linked to the latter, all the others are voluntary agreements. This means that the offer to conclude voluntary agreements was accepted extensively, whereas the EWC Directive as such has had only a rather modest effect. However, such a perspective would be misleading for several reasons. First, it was clear from the very beginning that Article 13 would be the main stimulus to initiate EWCs: this was intended by the Directive. Therefore, it is no surprise that this channel in reality turned out to be more successful than the mechanism embedded in the Directive itself. Secondly, voluntary agreements did not need to cope with the difficulty of putting together a special negotiating body as a partner for negotiations. This special negotiating body has such a complex structure that the efforts in establishing it should not be under-estimated. Finally, the undertakings in which voluntary agreements were concluded may have been exactly those where the climate for such a step was better than elsewhere. In other words, if they had not had the opportunity of voluntary agreements, many of them would have implemented the normal pattern of the Directive. In short, the division between voluntary and non-voluntary agreements does not tell us much about the EWC Directive's efficacy.

The question, however, still remains as to why two-thirds of the undertakings covered by the Directive do not yet have an EWC. Whether this is due to the central management or whether this is due to the lack of interest among the employees in establishing such an institutional structure is an open question. However, it should be clear that it would have been a

---

[18] As to the following, see S Demetriades, 'European Works Councils Directive: A Success Story ?' in M Biagi (ed), *Quality of Work and Employee Involvement in Europe* (The Hague, Kluwer, 2002) 49.

totally unrealistic expectation to obtain full coverage in such a short time. The EWC Directive has succeeded in raising the number of workers' representative bodies at a transnational level from almost zero in 1994 to one-third of all companies covered by the Directive, in spite of all difficulties connected with the establishment of such a body, not least the language barrier. This is, of course, not comprehensive coverage. But it is by far enough to experiment with the potential implied by the Directive. If looked upon from this angle, the present situation turns out to be an interesting laboratory for developing best practices. The ongoing intensive research on existing agreements is allowing a very useful exchange of information. In short, if the EWC is understood as a learning process in how to develop decent structures for employees' representation at a transnational scale, it is proving an excellent case study. The models of EWC are by no means homogenous but very different, an ideal setting for learning from each other. And of course quite a few deficiencies of the EWC Directive in the meantime have been observed in the course of this learning process. They have given rise to the still ongoing debate on how to amend the Directive. The requests for amendments refer to clarifications concerning the timing and comprehensiveness of information and consultation, to the improvement of training possibilities for members of European Works Councils, to the right to meet in the absence of the central management in order to improve possibilities for autonomous acting, and to the improvement of the trade unions' role in establishing not only the EWC but also the special negotiating body, to mention just the main topics. Whether it is a good idea also to request the lowering of the minimum size of the undertaking or the group of undertakings may well be doubted in view of the fact that among those companies which are covered by the Directive and which nevertheless are failing to establish EWCs, the smaller ones are in the majority. It has to be accepted that up to now and most probably for some time in the future the EWC is and will remain a pattern mainly for big companies. However, of primary interest is not the content of this debate on amending the Directive. The mere fact that the need for amendments has become the subject of controversial debate shows that the learning process is working.

Of course, there is an uneven distribution of EWCs by country. The fact that the United Kingdom is ranking second behind Germany demonstrates that it would be too simple to assume that EWCs are mainly established in countries with a tradition of workers' participation. Relatively speaking, the EWCs have the broadest coverage in the metal and chemical sectors, traditional areas for workers' participation schemes. However, again, simplistic conclusions would fail: the service sector has the biggest number of EWCs and as far as coverage is concerned, does fairly well. This distribution by country and by sector shows again the spreading of this new pattern into new areas for workers' participation.

One of the most important aspects in this context is the fact that groups of undertakings which have subsidiaries from the new Member States for EU enlargement voluntarily agree to include representatives of companies from those countries in the EWCs. This has already helped to overcome to a certain extent the hostile approach to workers' participation (due to the abuse by former regimes) in those countries. This shows that the EWC structure is an appropriate instrument to spread the idea of employee involvement even beyond the borders of the present EU. It thereby should definitely help to facilitate the integration of the candidate countries.

It is much too early to attempt an assessment of the qualitative aspects of the functioning of EWCs. The mere analysis of the agreements — as it has been conducted to a remarkable extent, mainly by the European Foundation in Dublin — does not tell us very much. At least the fact that several joint agreements have already been negotiated[19] shows that the EWCs cannot simply be denounced as puppet institutions. And in particular, it shows that the EWCs' influence will not remain at the mere level of information and consultation. The EWC Directive has put in place a dynamism of its own which may well develop to stronger forms of employees' influence in management's decision-making in the future.

It is evident that the composition and the meetings of EWCs lead to an intercultural exchange of ideas among workers' representatives which goes beyond any prevalent experience. In order to know more, qualitative in-depth studies are necessary. To this end there is great hope of the pioneer case studies on the functioning of the European Works Councils which are presently being prepared by the Dublin Foundation. These studies, covering four sectors, will focus on the internal operations of the European Works Councils as well as on their relationship with management on the one side and with the workforce on the other. The results of these studies will not only refer to positive effects, but will certainly also reveal deficiencies. In this respect, they are an important step on the way to improving the structure of EWCS and to making progress in the search for best practices.

From a merely legal point of view, there are still many open questions to be resolved. The normative effect of an agreement according to Article 6 of the EWC Directive is unclear, as is the legal status of an agreement between the EWC and the central management. To take another example, where the Directive in Articles 6(1) and 9 refers to a 'spirit of cooperation', it is clear from a German perspective that this means exclusion of a strike or lock-out as a means of resolving conflict. It may well be doubted whether this understanding is shared by other Member States. Therefore, in these and other cases the ECJ will have no choice but to decide on the interpretation of these and many other questions. This is not only a problem for the EWC

---

[19] For an assessment of these agreements, see Demetriades, above n 18, at 52–55.

Directive. The more recent Directives pose similar questions, and they, too, contain the 'spirit of cooperation' as a basic concept.

Employee Involvement in the European Company (Societas Europaea)

The Commission, impressed by the success of the Directive on European Works Councils, considered whether the method applied there could be repeated in the case of employees' involvement in the European company.[20] It established in 1996 a group of experts on 'European Systems of Workers Involvement' chaired by the former Deputy President of the EC Commission, Etienne Davignon. The Davignon group presented its Report in 1997; it was no surprise that its recommendations were based on the logic and principles of the Directive on European Works Councils. It merely defined actors for negotiation and left in principle everything to negotiations. As in the Directive on European Works Councils, in the case of failure of such negotiations a safety net, so called subsidiary requirements, was proposed, guaranteeing the employees' representatives at least one-fifth (in any case two) of the seats in the supervisory board or the corresponding body. In order to prevent companies already covered by schemes, of workers' participation escaping such schemes, the Davignon group suggested limiting the option for a European company to three situations: (1) creation of a joint holding company for companies of different countries within the EU; (2) merger of companies in different EU Member States; and finally (3) creation of a joint subsidiary by companies situated in different EU Member States. Transformation of an existing company into a European company was excluded on the grounds that such a conversion was seen as endangering the existing participation structure and thereby promoting the possibility of escape from participation schemes.

In spite of the very positive reaction which the Davignon Report received throughout the EU, it soon became clear that it still was very difficult to transfer the ideas of this Report into legislation. The crucial points of controversy were (1) the level of employees' board representation to be guaranteed by the subsidiary requirements and (2) the situations in which a European company was to be available. In the latter case, a consensus was reached relatively easily by adding transformation of a company as a fourth

---

[20] Council Directive 2001/86/EC of 8 October 2001 supplementing the Statute for a European company with regard to the involvement of employees (OJ 2001 L294/22) For a more detailed discussion of the genesis, content and impact of the Directive supplementing the Statute of the European Company see M Weiss, 'Workers' Involvement in the European Company' in Biagi, above n 18, at 63.

possibility. Safeguards were established to prevent the danger of escaping from existing participation schemes. The more difficult problem was linked to the safety net in the default model. The minimum level of representation continued to remain controversial. Member States with a higher level of employees' representation in company boards were reluctant to accept such a low proportion of employees' representation as suggested by the Davignon group. In spite of the fact that the European company was not supposed to be available for the foundation of a company, the danger that companies might try to escape the scope of application of the national system by way of mergers still seen to be too high. Therefore, in its first phase the attempt to turn the Davignon Report into law failed, mainly through German and Austrian opposition. The Report's proposals were also attacked from the other side, however; Member States which did not have a system of employees' representation in company boards considered the level suggested by the Davignon group to be too high. Under the United Kingdom's presidency in the first semester of 1998, a compromise was developed in order to overcome this resistance of both sides. The 'magic formula' invented by the United Kingdom was the 'before and after perspective': if, in a certain percentage of companies engaging in a merger, a given level of employees' representation existed before the merger, this same level had to be guaranteed afterwards. If, before the merger, none of the merging companies had any employees' board representation, the safety net should not establish any requirement for such a system afterwards. The zero solution was the trade-off for the maintenance guarantee. This pattern has not only survived but the maintenance guarantee was even weakened as a result of Spanish pressure when finally, after quite a few attempts at the summit in Nice in December 2000, a consensus was reached on the draft Directive which then was finally passed on 8 October 2001[21] together with the Statute on the European Company.

Unfortunately, the Directive supplementing the Statute for a European Company with regard to the involvement of employees was based on a wrong EC Treaty base or 'competence norm,' Article 308 of the EC Treaty. The correct basis would have been Article 137(3) of the Amsterdam Treaty; the specific competence norm excludes recourse to the Annex competence as provided in Article 308. Reliance on Article 137(3) would have made a significant difference in the legislative procedure. First, the social partners would have been entitled to be consulted and to regulate the matter by way of agreement. In the event that no agreement was reached, the co-decision procedure (Article 251EC) would have to have been applied which would have given the European Parliament a much stronger position than the one

---

[21] [2001] OJ L294/22.

implied by recourse to Article 308. Evidently, the involvement of the social partners as well as the co-decision procedure were considered to be too risky in a situation where the enactment of the Directive only looked to be a question of time. There was evidently a fear that the social partners and the Parliament might question the consensus reached so far and re-open the discussion. However, such a tactical use of the provisions of the EC Treaty is not very helpful for maintaining the legitimacy of the Community's legislative process. In the meantime, however, it has turned out that this deficiency will not be challenged in the European Court of Justice.

The European Company Directive has to be read together with the Statute on the European Company which contains the rules on company law. The main goal of establishing a European company as an option is to save transaction costs, and to increase efficiency and transparency. It should no longer be necessary to create complicated structures of holding companies in order to overcome the problems arising from national company law. Ideally, this goal could only be achieved if the Statute regulated all the details of company law at stake. Then the company law structure of the European company would be identical, no matter where its seat was. However, the Statute does not meet these expectations. It only contains rules for about one-third of the problems to be resolved. For the solution of the remaining issues it refers to the national law on joint stock companies (Statute, Article 9). Even if, in some important aspects, national company law has been harmonised, there are still significant differences. Therefore, the recourse to national law means that the company law structure of the European company will be very different, depending in which country it is situated. It is therefore, very doubtful whether this still very scattered pattern will really lead to the intended saving of transaction costs.

There are four types of foundation of a European company (Statute, Article 2): (1) a merger between several companies, if at least two of those are covered by the law of two different Member States; (2) the establishment of a holding company by several companies if at least two are covered by the law of different Member States; (3) the creation of a joint subsidiary by several companies if the respective companies have their headquarters and their seat within the Community and if at least two of these companies are covered by the law of different Member States, or if a company has for at least two years had a subsidiary in a different Member State covered by the law of that state; (4) transformation of an existing company into a European company, if this company has for at least two years had a daughter company or a subsidiary in a different Member State. In this latter case of transformation, the provision of Article 37(8) of the Statute is of utmost importance; according to this Article, the Member States are entitled to permit the transformation only if the body in which the workers are represented agrees with either qualified majority or unanimously. In addition, according to Article 37(3), it is not possible to transfer the company's seat to another Member State in the course of transformation. Thereby, the fears already indicated that transformation into a European company could lead to an escape from the national system of workers' participation are significantly reduced.

The Statute provides for two organisational alternatives: a two-tier system and a one-tier system. In addition to the shareholders' assembly, the two-tier system has a managing board and a supervisory board whereas the one-tier system has only an administrative board (Article 38). In the two-tier system, the members of the managing board are appointed and recalled by the supervisory board whose members are elected by the shareholders' assembly (St Article 40(2)), whereas in the one-tier system all members of the administrative board are elected by the shareholders' assembly (Article 43(3)).

A European company can be registered only if the requirements of the Europen Company Directive are met. Thereby, it is guaranteed that the provisions on workers' involvement cannot be ignored (Articles 12, 16). A precondition for the creation of a European company is a minimum capital stock of 120,000 euro (Article 4(2)). This implies that a European company by no means needs to be a large entity.

The structure of the European Company Directive is very much the same as in the Directive on European Works Councils; it provides for a special negotiating body (Article 3), lists the topics for negotiation (Article 4) and leaves everything to negotiations. In case the negotiations fail, there is a safety net, the so-called standard rules (Article 7 in combination with the Annex). Again in line with the scheme of the Directive on European Works Councils are the provisions on confidentiality (Article 8) and on protection of employees' representatives (Article 9).

The European Company Directive contains two different topics which have to be distinguished carefully. The first refers to information and consultation. Here, the structure is very similar to the one developed in the Directive on European Works Councils, even if it has to be recognised that some improvements which are in line with the foreseeable amendments of the Directive on European Works Councils are already contained in the European Company Directive (eg the definitions of information and consultation). According to Article 13(1), the application of the Directive on European Works Councils is excluded in the European company. It may well be asked whether it makes sense to develop two different structures of information and consultation. It would have been much easier simply to extend the scope of application of the Directive on European Works Councils to the European company. However, there is a big difference: whereas the scope of application of the Directive on European Works Councils only covers large undertakings with a certain minimum size of employees, the structure of information and consultation is meant for each European company no matter how small it is and no matter how many workers are employed therein.

Again, no minimum number of employees is required for the crucial and most interesting topic of the European Company Directive: employees' participation, which is defined as:

> the influence of the body representative of the employees and/or the employees' representatives in the affairs of a company by way of (1) the right to elect or appoint some of the members of the company's supervisory or administrative organ, or (2) the right to recommend and/or oppose the appointment of some or all of the members of the company's supervisory or administrative organ (Article 2(k)).

Normally, it is left to negotiations how such a scheme should look. Only in case of transformation the agreement must 'provide for at least the same level of all elements of employee involvement as the ones existing within the company to be transformed into' a European company (Article 4(4)). If in other cases a reduction of the participation level would be the result of the negotiations, qualified majority requirements apply which make sure that by way of agreement the existing highest level cannot be easily or carelessly reduced (see Article 3).

According to Article 12(3) of the Statute, a European company can be registered irrespective of employees' participation if none of the participating companies has been 'governed by participation rules prior to the registration of the European Company.' In this case, neither an agreement is needed nor do the standard rules apply. This is the already indicated trade-off for the maintenance structure: the zero solution.

Whether the standard rules on participation are to be applied is regulated by Article 7(2) of the European Company Directive. The most controversial point in this context has been the case of merger. Two situations are to be distinguished. The first is where at least one of the companies before the merger is covered by a scheme of participation and this scheme covers at least 25 per cent of the total number of employees engaging in the merger. The second is where this coverage is less than 25 per cent, and the special negotiating body decides that the standard rules on participation are to be applied. This pattern was strongly opposed by Spain which was worried that its effect would be the forcible import, through corporate mergers, of board-level employee representation. Therefore, a compromise had to be reached which now is to be found in Article 7(3), according to which the Member States may provide that the reference provisions in Part 3 of the Annex shall not apply in case of merger. If this option is chosen it means that irrespective of the percentage of companies already covered by a participation scheme, there is no maintenance guarantee: everything is open to agreement. Such an agreement, however, remains necessary: it is a precondition for registration of the European company (Article 12(3) of the Statute).

In the case of setting up a holding company, again there are two possible situations where the standard rules on participation apply. The first is where, before registration of the European company, one or more forms of participation applied in one or more of the participating companies covering at least 50 per cent of the total number of employees in all the participating companies. The second is where fewer than 50 per cent of the employees are so covered but the special negotiating body decides the standard rules should apply.

According to the standard rules laid down in the Annex to the European Company Directive, in the case, of transformation all aspects of employee participation have to remain as they were before. In other cases, the highest level in force in the participating companies is the decisive criterion for the level of participation in the European company.

It is up to the representative body established for purposes of information and consultation to decide on the allocation of seats within the administrative or supervisory body among the members representing the employees from the various Member States, or the way in which the European company's employees may recommend or oppose the appointment of the members of these bodies according to the proportion of the European company's employees in each Member State. Each Member State has the right to determine the allocation of the seats it is given within the administrative or supervisory body. In any case, the employees' representatives are full members with the same rights and obligations as the members representing the shareholders, including the right to vote.

FRAMEWORK FOR A MINIMUM OF
INFORMATION AND CONSULTATION

In the context of the action programme on social policy for the years 1995 to 1997, and again inspired by the success of the Directive on European Works Councils, the Commission in November 1995 presented a Communication containing a very ambitious goal: to establish throughout the EU a minimum framework for informing and consulting employees. The first and second phase of consultation of the social partners took place in June and November 1997. The European Trade Union Confederation as well as the Confédération des Enterprises Européans Publiques were ready to try to negotiate an agreement, whereas the Union des Industrics de la Communauté Européenne was firmly opposed to the idea. Due to the failure of negotiations implied by the resistance of UNICE, the Commission presented a first draft for a Directive in November 1998. For a long time it was not at all clear whether this initiative based on Article 137(2) of the Amsterdam Treaty and thereby only requiring qualified majority might have any chance of succeeding. In particular, the United Kingdom strongly opposed the idea of such a Directive. Nevertheless, after an extended debate, the Council and the European Parliament involved the conciliation committee in December 2001. Directive 2002/14/EC was finally passed[22] in March 2002.

UNICE's opposition to this project was based mainly on the argument of subsidiarity.[23] The Commission, as well as all other actors involved in the legislative process, rejected this argument. In the recitals in the Preamble of the Directive, reference is made to the need for workers to be involved in the affairs of the undertaking employing them and in decisions which affect them (recital 6). It also refers to the need properly to balance the internal market, 'maintaining the essential values on which our societies are based' (recital 11). The conclusion then is that:

> the objectives of the proposed action ... cannot be adequately achieved by the Member States, in that the object is to establish a framework for employee information and consultation appropriate for the new European context (recital 17).

It is exactly this context which has to be understood in discussing the topic of subsidiarity. The mere fact that in the Charter of Fundamental Rights of the EU the workers' right to information and consultation within the undertaking is considered to be a fundamental right (Article 27) shows that there is a consensus among the Member States that this right is identical with a basic value within the Community to be promoted and respected by the Community authorities. If subsidiarity could be used as a tool to undermine the Community-wide respect for such values, this notion would be perverted. If, evidently, some Member States are not willing to establish at least a minimum framework to be in conformity with such a value, it must be possible for the Community to take initiatives. If the workers' right to information and consultation is considered to be an essential part of industrial relations in the Community, the legislator on the level of the Community must have a possibility to overcome Member State's abstention in this area. The ECJ's judgments of 1994 in reference to the Directives on collective redundancy and on transfer of undertakings were indeed based on this philosophy.

The Information and Consultation Directive covers public or private undertakings of at least 50 employees in any Member State or establishments of at least 20 employees in any Member State. In the original version of the proposal, reference was only made to undertakings. The change is due to the fact that in some Member States, the entity which serves as the

---

[22] [2002] OJ L80/29.
[23] For this debate see A Neal, 'Information and Consultation for Employees: Still seeking the Philosopher's Stone?' in Biagi, above n 18, at 83.

reference point for information and consultation predominantly is the establishment (as for example in Germany). According to Article 1, the purpose of the Directive is 'to establish a general framework setting out minimum requirements for the right to information and consultation of employees in undertakings or establishments within the Community'.

From the mere wording it is not very clear whether the employees or only the employees' representatives according to national law and practice are entitled to information and consultation. The contextual analysis, however, reveals that the latter must be the case. This mainly can be deducted from the provision on confidentiality (Article 6).

The Information and Consultation Directive defines the structure of information and consultation in a much more comprehensive way than this is done so far in other Directives. The definitions contain important procedural requirements. The timing, content and manner of provision of information must be appropriate to enable, in particular, employees' representatives to conduct an adequate study and, where necessary, prepare for consultation (Article 4(3)). Consultation has to meet several requirements (see Article 4(4)): (1) it has to be ensured that the timing, the method and the content are appropriate; (2) information and consultation have to take place at the relevant level of management and representation, depending on the subject under discussion; (3) the employees' representatives are entitled to formulate an opinion on the basis of the relevant information supplied by the employer; (4) the employees' representatives are entitled to meet with the employer and to obtain a response, and the reasons for that response, to any opinion they may formulate; and finally (5) in case of decisions within the scope of the employer's management powers, consultation must be conducted with a view to reaching agreement. Unfortunately, the Directive does not state what is to happen if an agreement is reached but the employer does not implement it.

Information has to cover the recent and probable development of the undertaking's or the establishment's activities and economic situation in its broadest sense (Article 4(2)(a)). Information and consultation has to take place on the situation, structure and probable development of employment within the undertaking or establishment and on any anticipatory measures envisaged, in particular where there is a threat of unemployment (Article 4(2)(b)). Finally, information and consultation has to take place on decisions likely to lead to substantial changes in work organisation or in contractual relations, including those covered by the Community provisions (Article 4(2)(c)). According to the original draft, in this latter case the Member States were supposed to ensure that in case of grave violation of the employer's duty to inform and to consult, the decisions remained null and void as long as the employer did not meet the requirements (Article 8(3)). However, this provision did not survive the conciliation committee; it has been abolished.

According to Article 5 of the Information and Consultation Directive, Member States may permit the social partners on all levels, including undertakings and establishments, to conclude agreements on information and consultation that differ from those defined in Article 4. However, the agreements have to respect the principles expressed in Article 1. This, of course, is rather vague to serve as a clear-cut demarcation line. In any case, this permission of derogation goes far beyond the possibilities provided by Article 13 of the EWC Directive, which referred only to the transitional period until the transposition of that Directive into national law.

The Information and Consultation Directive allows particular provisions for 'undertakings or establishments which pursue directly and essentially political, professional, religious, charitable, educational, scientific or artistic aims, as well as aims involving information and the expression of opinions' on condition that provisions of that nature are already in existence in the national legislation at the date on which the Directive comes into force (Article 3(2)). It may well be doubted whether, in the case of information and consultation, such an exception is necessary at all. In addition it is very unclear to what extent the patterns of information and consultation for those undertakings and establishments can be different. Again the principles and goals as expressed by the Information and Consultation Directive have to be met. However, one conclusion certainly can be drawn from this: it would not be compatible with the Directive to provide no information and consultation whatsoever for those undertakings and establishments, as for example is still the case in Germany for the churches and their charitable institutions.

The implementation of Article 7 will be very interesting. It is the first attempt to harmonise the level of protection and the guarantees for workers' representatives to enable them to perform their activities. The Member States have to make sure that employees' representatives when carrying out their functions, 'enjoy adequate protection and guarantees to enable them to perform properly the duties which have been assigned to them.' The meaning of 'adequate' and 'proper' in this context, of course, is very debatable. There will be much room for argument as to their interpretation which may give rise to many references to the ECJ.

On the whole, the Information and Consultation Directive remains very flexible and leaves the structural framework and the modalities to a great extent to the Member States. Nevertheless, in practice the opposition of some countries could be overcome only by granting transitional provisions. These are to apply if, on 23 March 2005 'the date of the entry into force of the Directive', in the respective Member State there is:

> no general, permanent and statutory system of information and consultation of employees, nor a general, permanent and statutory system of employee representation at the workplace allowing employees to be represented for that purpose.

In the transitional period (which was shortened significantly by the conciliation committee) the minimum size is lifted in a first phase of two years to undertakings employing at least 150 employees or establishments employing at least 100 employees. In the second phase of another year this is lowered to 100 and 50. Only afterwards, from 23 March 2008 on wards, will the Directive apply generally. In short, member states which do not currently have an institutionalised system of employees' information and consultation are not exposed to 'shocktherapy' but are given the opportunity of a smooth transition.

Once the Information and Consultation Directive is in force, it remains unclear what will happen if employees in an undertaking or an establishment covered by the Directive do not elect or appoint employee representatives. Are the Member States obliged to make sure that, even in such a case, a body representing the employees' interests is established? Or is it left to the employees' discretion whether they want to make use of this possibility or not? In the course of the proceedings in the conciliation committee, the European Parliament, the Council and the Commission published a joint declaration which refers as regards this question to the ECJ's judgments of 8 June 1994 in the context of collective redundancies and of transfer of undertakings. This reference, however, does not clarify the problem, as the relevant judgments are rather ambiguous. It may well be that in actual practice it turns out to be necessary for the European legislator to define more specifically the minimum conditions for the establishment and structure of workers' representative bodies. It, however, may well be doubted whether such an attempt would find the necessary majority in the Council.

Since the Information and Consultation Directive only provides for a minimum framework, it of course does not affect more favourable arrangements in Member States. In addition, the Directive cannot be used to justify the reduction or destruction of existing patterns.

IMPLICATIONS FOR THE FUTURE OF WORKERS' PARTICIPATION IN THE EU

There is no longer any doubt that the promotion of workers' participation in company's decision-making has become an essential part of the Community's mainstreaming strategy in its social policy agenda. It has definitely crossed the 'point of no return'. This policy is in line with Article 27 of the Charter of Fundamental Rights of the EU. The change of paradigm from a naïve attempt to harmonise by prescribing institutional arrangements, to a more procedural input, has made this achievement possible. Also in the future there will be institutional variety throughout the Community, a competition in search of best practices. Workers' participation in essence is nothing but a concept to be observed in building-up institutions.

The Community's contribution has an important implication: countries with a tradition of exclusively adversarial structures have no longer a choice but to restructure their systems towards a concept of partnership and cooperation. The Community's input by way of the Directives discussed above is in particular an important signal for the new Member States for EU enlargement of how to shape their systems of industrial relations. For them the question is no longer whether they establish a system of workers' participation, but only how they do it. Information and consultation in the scope defined by the Information and Consultation Directive is a must. This means that all countries — old as well as new Member States — are in search of best practices and thereby embedded in a mutual learning process. Variety will prevail. But the 'spirit of cooperation' as contained in all three recent Directives will be the underlying paradigm and thereby an important characteristic of the European social model to be developed. As already indicated above, however, it is still quite unclear what this 'spirit of cooperation' means in legal terms.

Whether and in what way the Community's input will have direct economic implications is an open question. The example of the European Company Directive may illustrate this problem. In view of the solution which was chosen at the last moment due to Spanish pressure, it might become attractive for German companies to merge with companies of countries where so far no pattern of workers' participation in company boards exist and establish the company's seat there. This could lead to a gradual erosion of the institutional pattern of German-style workers' participation in company boards. Whether this is only a theoretical or a practical possibility is difficult to say. There might also be another scenario. Due to the maintenance rule in the European Company Directive, it might be difficult for German companies to find partners for mergers in other countries. Again, it is difficult to say whether this is a realistic assumption. It is pretty clear, however, that the maintenance rule in the European Company Directive will have another important impact. There will always be negotiations on whether to maintain existing standards or to establish something else. The advantages and disadvantages of existing patterns thereby will become the core of the debate. The 'pros and cons' of workers' participation in company boards will be more in the limelight in the future than ever before. This may also put pressure on existing schemes in different countries, as, for example, on the traditional German pattern. It may well be that such schemes will be reconstructed to serve better the purposes of a global age. How such schemes might look in the future is an open question. Seen from this angle, the Directive can be understood as a stimulus for the re-opening of an intensive debate on corporate governance in the European context where all the well-known concepts are to be reconsidered and rebalanced: stakeholders' value versus shareholders' value, industrial peace versus industrial conflict, cooperation versus adversarial patterns.

In essence, the Euopean Company Directive could provoke a new debate on the specific European culture of industrial relations.

All the Directives sketched above have, of course, their weaknesses; they are unnecessarily complicated, not always consistent and above all very vague in their terminology. The European Company Directive as well as the Information and Consultation Directive have been watered down during the legislative process: the result is a 'lowest common denominator'. However, in assessing the importance of these measures for the future of industrial relations in the EU these deficiencies should not be overstated. The decisive element is the fact that these instruments, taken as a whole, force all actors involved — trade unions and workers' representatives, employers' associations, employers and employees — to discuss and reflect on the potential of employees' information and consultation, and in the case of the European Company Directive, even on workers' participation in company boards.

Of course, at the present moment the Community instruments on the European company and on the national framework for information and consultation have not yet been implemented in reality. As far as the European company is concerned, it remains an open question to what extent it will become actual practice. However, the experience with the EWC Directive is an optimistic sign. As far as the Information and Consultation Directive is concerned, there will not be much chance to escape. The fact that some countries enjoy a longer transition period does not affect this evaluation.

As already indicated, the Community's approach is no longer focusing on introducing specific institutional patterns but simply on stimulating and initiating procedures for the promotion of the idea of employees' involvement in management's decision-making. This strategy is based on the assumption that workers' involvement in management's decision-making is favourable not only for employees but also for companies' economic performance. There are significant advantages for the legitimacy of management's decision-making, for elimination of conflicts, for increasing productivity, for improving employees' motivation and — last not least — for better management.

The decisive point in the end, of course, will be whether this pattern of industrial relations — based on partnership and cooperation — will prevail in the climate of global competition. Nobody can predict how, for example, international capital markets will react. It may well be that in an effort to promote shareholder value in a short-term perspective, investors might consider workers' participation to be an obstacle. However, if the insight grows that long-term stakeholder values are more important than short-term shareholder values, the European pattern of workers' participation might be considered to be a model also for other regions of the world. Which of these perspectives will guide the actors is an open question. It also may be that in the course of the negotiations initiated by these Directives, institutional arrangements will be created which make workers' participation attractive for those who today are still sceptical. And it also may be that the intensity of the discussion on the function of workers' participation will make it easier for the European actors to convince the actors elsewhere of the advantages of such a system. In short and to make the point: there are many options. It is impossible to predict which of them will govern the future.

12

The Future of Labour Law: Is There a Role for International Labour Standards?

BREEN CREIGHTON*

INTRODUCTION

IN HIS 2002 Sinzheimer Lecture, Bob Hepple identified a number of roads that might be used to achieve the equality of capability that he believes ought to be the goal of labour law in the twenty-first century.[1] Among these were 'strengthening social provisions in regional economic treaties, promoting a "race to the top" through corporate codes and the dissemination of best practices, empowering local actors and revitalising and enforcing international labour standards.' It is the last of these roads that constitutes the principal focus of this chapter.

Hepple clearly recognises that the existing system of setting and enforcing international labour standards (ILS) is in need of 'revitalisation.' I fully share that view. Indeed, this chapter proceeds from the assumption that the traditional system is in a state of crisis of such magnitude as to raise serious questions about its future role and relevance.

This assumption will be tested by first looking briefly at the traditional system of standard-setting and supervision. This is followed by a more detailed consideration of the origins and nature of the current crisis, and by a consideration of what can and should be done to ensure that ILS play a constructive role in the future of labour law.

---

* I wish to thank Alice Bryant for her research assistance in the preparation of this chapter.
[1] Equality of capability in this context means 'the substantive freedoms that individuals need in order to survive and prosper, including freedom to pursue education and training and a career of their own choosing, freedom of association and freedom to participate in economic and political decision-making that affects their lives as well as the capacity to obtain decent work': B Hepple, 'Labour Law, Inequality and Global Trade' Sinzheimer Lecture (2002), 14.

THE TRADITIONAL SYSTEM

A key element in the rationale for the establishment of the ILO was the perception that workers needed to be protected against the adverse effects of international competition. This required that nation states should not be allowed to obtain an unfair competitive advantage by tolerating the maintenance of abusive labour conditions within their territory. This could most effectively be achieved by the setting, promotion and enforcement of ILS.[2]

Article 41 of the original ILO Constitution provided detailed guidance for these standard-setting activities, by articulating a series of 'methods and principles' of 'special and urgent importance.' They included: recognition that labour should not be regarded merely as a commodity or article of commerce; the right of association for all lawful purposes; the payment of a wage adequate to maintain a reasonable standard of life; the adoption of an eight-hour day or 48-hour week; a weekly rest of at least 24 hours; the abolition of child labour; the principle that men and women should receive equal remuneration for work of equal value; and the establishment of a system of inspection to ensure the 'enforcement of the laws and regulations for the protection of the employed.'

These 'methods and principles' are now reflected in the Preamble to the Constitution, and clearly informed the early standard-setting activities of the ILO. For example, the first Convention adopted at the first session of the International Labour Conference (ILC) required adherence to the principle of the eight-hour day, 48-hour week.[3] At the same Session, the ILC adopted a Convention to prevent the employment of children under 14 in 'industrial undertakings,' together with Conventions restricting night work for women and young persons, the establishment of free public employment agencies and maternity protection.

Most of the other Conventions and Recommendations that were adopted prior to 1939 reflected similar concerns. Human rights issues received scant attention at this time. The sole exceptions were the Right of Association (Agriculture) Convention 1921 (No 11) and Forced Labour Convention 1930 (No 29).

---

[2] See D Morse, *The Origin of the ILO and its Role in the International Community* (Ithaca, NY, Cornell University Press, 1969), 57, cited in E Cordova 'Some reflections on the Overproduction of International Labour Standards' (1993) 14 *Comp Lab Law J* 138 at p 142; T. Ramm, 'The New Ordering of Labour Law 1918–45' in B Hepple (ed), *The Making of Labour Law in Europe* (London, Mansell, 1986) 279–84; P O'Higgins, 'The Interaction of the ILO, the Council of Europe and European Labour Standards' in B Hepple (ed), *Social and Labour Rights in a Global Context* (Cambridge, Cambridge University Press, 2002), 55–56; S Engerman, 'The History and Political Economy of International Labour Standards' in K Basu, H Horn, L Roman and J Shapiro (eds), *International Labour Standards* (Oxford, Blackwell, 2003) 37–39, 60–62.

[3] Hours of Work (Industry) Convention 1919 (No 1).

The situation changed quite dramatically after 1945. First, the two pivotal freedom of association Conventions (Nos 87 and 98) were adopted in 1948 and 1949. The principle of equal remuneration for equal work received formal recognition in the Equal Remuneration Convention 1951 (No 100). Convention 105 made further provision concerning forced labour, and the Discrimination (Employment and Occupation) Convention (No 111) was adopted in 1958. The deeply-flawed Minimum Age Convention 1973 (No 138) constituted the first comprehensive attempt to abolish child labour,[4] whilst the persistence of abusive child labour led to the adoption of the Worst Forms of Child Labour Convention (No 182) in 1999.

Read together, these eight instruments constitute the core ILO human rights standards, and form the basis of the Declaration of Fundamental Rights and Principles which was adopted by the ILC in 1998 (1998 Declaration).[5] These issues aside, standard-setting in the post-war period has concentrated mainly upon the needs of specific occupational groups; occupational health and safety; social security and conditions of work.[6] Many of the pre-war standards, and indeed some adopted after 1945, were highly prescriptive in character. More recently, there has been increasing reliance upon promotional standards, which set certain objectives, but leave it to Member States to decide how best to achieve that objective within the policy framework set out in the Convention and/or an accompanying Recommendation.[7]

Article 19(5)(b) of the Constitution obliges Member States to draw all newly adopted Conventions to the attention of the 'competent authorities' 'for the enactment of legislation or other action,' whilst Article 19(5)(c) requires Member States to inform the Director-General of the measures taken in accordance with paragraph (b), and of the action taken by the competent authorities.

These provisions clearly proceed from the assumption that the appropriate response to the adoption of a new Convention is ratification. However, there is no formal obligation to ratify, and the only obligation that rests upon Member States that have chosen not to ratify is to 'report … at appropriate intervals as requested by the Governing Body,

---

[4] The Convention adopts a highly prescriptive approach to the issue of child labour. It is difficult for either developed or developing countries to establish compliance. See further B Creighton, 'Combating Child Labour: The Role of International Labour Standards' (1997) 18 *Comp Lab Law J* 362.
[5] Convention No 182 was adopted the year after the Declaration, but is treated as part of it.
[6] See I Donoso Rubio, 'Economic Limits on International Regulation: A Case Study of ILO Standard-Setting' (1998) 24 *Queens' Law Journal* 189, at 202–7 for an overview of this activity.
[7] See, eg, Workers with Family Responsibilities Convention 1981(No 156), and Recommendation No 165.

the position of its law and practice in regard to the matters dealt with in the Convention ... and stating the difficulties which prevent or delay the ratification of such Convention.'[8] Recommendations are not open to ratification, but are otherwise subject to the same reporting requirements as Conventions.[9]

Ratifying States must 'take such action as may be necessary to make effective the provisions of the Convention.'[10] Failure to do so puts the defaulting State in breach of its obligations in international law. Amongst other things, this means that they may be subject to the representation and complaint procedures set out in Articles 24 and 26 of the Constitution.[11]

Article 22 of the Constitution requires ratifying States to make an annual report to the International Labour Office 'on the measures which it has taken to give effect to the provisions of Conventions to which it is a party.'[12] This report must be made available to representatives of employers and workers in the Member State. Article 23(1) requires the Director-General to lay summaries of all reports provided under Articles 19 and 22 before the next meeting of the ILC. In practice, this function is delegated to the CEACR.

The CEACR was established in 1927 on the basis of a resolution of the ILC. It presently consists of 20 distinguished jurists, and meets once a year for approximately three weeks. In that time it is meant to examine reports on all ratified Conventions that have been submitted over the previous year, together with reports on unratified Conventions (and Recommendations) that have been requested under Article 19.

Where the CEACR has concerns about the effect given to a ratified Convention it can direct an Observation to the Member State concerned, setting out the Committee's views on the matter, and requesting a response from that Member. Alternatively, it may conduct a dialogue with the Member State through a series of Direct Requests. These are generally used to deal with relatively minor issues or to initiate a dialogue that may later be elevated to the level of an Observation.

The Report of the CEACR is used as the basis for discussion at the ILC Committee on the Application of Conventions and Recommendations. This is an extremely important part of the ILO's supervisory machinery, whereby

---

[8] Article 19(5)(e). This is part of the constitutional basis for the General Surveys which are conducted by the Committee of Experts on the Application of Conventions and Recommendations (CEACR) each year into the effect given to ILS dealing with a particular topic.

[9] Article 19(6).

[10] Article 19(5)(d).

[11] See further N Valticos and G von Potobsky, *International Labour Law* (Deventer, Kluwer, 1995) 290–94.

[12] In practice reports are not required on an annual basis, but rather on a cycle which requires reports at either two-yearly or five-yearly intervals.

Member States that have breached ratified Conventions can be called to the bar of international public opinion to give an account of themselves. Debate in the Committee can be lively and contentious, especially where a Member State stands to be singled out for mention in a 'Special Paragraph' in the Committee's Report to the ILC.[13]

The Reports of the CEACR are an invaluable source on the interpretation of Conventions and Recommendations. However, they do not constitute formal determinations as to the matters with which they deal. According to Article 37 of the Constitution, the interpretation of ILS is the province of the International Court of Justice (ICJ). In the absence of any reference to the ICJ since the 1930s,[14] and in light of the continuing failure of the Governing Body to establish a tribunal under Article 37(2),[15] the Observations and General Surveys of the CEACR constitute the most authoritative source available as to the meaning and effect of ILS.

WHAT HAS GONE WRONG?

Quantity and Quality of Standards

By June 2003 the ILC had adopted a total of 379 formal standard-setting instruments (185 Conventions and 194 Recommendations). Each of these contains a significant number of substantive standards.[16] In addition, the Constitution and the Declaration of Philadelphia, expressly or impliedly impose significant obligations upon Member States by virtue of the fact of membership.[17] On top of that, there are innumerable resolutions, declarations and determinations that have been adopted under the auspices of the ILO over the years. These do not impose formal obligations upon Member States, but still set norms by reference to which the behaviour of the international community can be measured.

This proliferation of standards has caused some observers to suggest that there are too many standards, and that they are too often of questionable quality and relevance. For example, Cordova warned that the proliferation

---

[13] See further V Leary, 'Lessons from the Experience of the International Labour Organisation' in P Alston (ed), *The United Nations and Human Rights: A Critical Appraisal* (Oxford, Clarendon Press, 1991) 598–602.

[14] See Valticos and von Potobsky, above n 11, 67.

[15] This enables the establishment of 'a tribunal for the expeditious determination of any dispute or question relating to the interpretation of a Convention which may be referred thereto by the Governing Body or in accordance with the terms of the Convention.'

[16] Cordova, above n 2, at 146 estimated that the 171 Conventions that had been adopted up to 1990 contained a total of 2,100 substantive labour standards, whilst the 180 Recommendations contained a further 2,500 substantive standards.

[17] This includes the obligation to respect the Principles of Freedom of Association (PFA), and the other principles embodied in the 1998 Declaration.

of standards was 'reaching critical proportions and may soon bring about detrimental effects to the ILO and its Member States' and that 'such excessive proliferation of standards may lead to serious imbalances in the world socioeconomic order, thus defeating the very purpose that originally inspired the adoption of labour standards.'[18] He also deprecated the increasing recourse to Conventions of a 'promotional or procedural nature', and the apparent tendency to see the ILO 'as the framer of the whole social and labor policy of Member States.'[19] Cordova clearly favoured a reversion to what he saw as the founders' intent that the 'standard-setting function be characterised by concrete labor standards, or "precise norms." '[20]

On another view, the proliferation of ILS should be seen as counterproductive only if the standards that are adopted do not meet a real need and/or they do not make meaningful provision in relation to the issues with which they deal. Of course, the concept of 'need' inevitably depends upon the observer's perception of the proper role of labour standards: if that role is seen in terms of protecting fundamental rights at work, then the adoption of the core standards in the 1998 Declaration might indeed seem largely to have exhausted the proper scope for standard-setting. However, if the role of standards is seen in terms of facilitating equality of capability as defined by Hepple, then the legitimate territory of standard-setting manifestly would not be exhausted by the adoption of the core human rights standards. However, even on the most generous view of facilitating equality of capability, it seems inherently unlikely that there is an objective need for 379 formal instruments, containing in excess of 5,000 specific standards.

It must be acknowledged that there is a continuing need for new standards to take account of changing circumstances, including the emergence of new forms of work relationships and changing community expectations. Even allowing that, it could reasonably be expected that there would be a significant slowing in the rate of adoption of new instruments over time. Until recently, that had not happened. For example, between 1919 and 1943, the ILO adopted a total of 67 Conventions and 66 Recommendations at rates of 2.68 and 2.64 respectively per session. Between 1944 and 1968 it adopted 61 Conventions and 66 Recommendations, at rates of 3.05 and 2.44 per session. The pace slowed somewhat over the next 25 years, with 46 Conventions and 49 Recommendations at rates of 1.9 and 1.96 per session. There has been a further slowing over the last decade, with only 11 Conventions and 13 Recommendations at rates of 1.1 and 1.3 per session since 1993.

---

[18] Cordova, above n 2, at 138.
[19] *Ibid* at 139–40.
[20] See also Rubio, above n 6, at 209–10 but cf N Valticos, 'The Future Prospects for International Labour Standards' (1979) 118 *Int Lab Rev* 679.

As indicated, concerns have been expressed about the quality, as well as the quantity of standard-setting. As with 'need,' 'quality' is a subjective concept. But in general terms it can be measured by reference to whether a given standard makes provision that moves beyond existing standards and has the capacity to confer some discernible benefit upon those whose interests it is meant to protect or promote. On that basis, few recent standards could be said to have made any significant qualitative contribution to the corpus of ILS. Many simply call for the application of existing standards to specific occupational groups.[21] In other instances they are simply devoid of substance, or are so qualified as to have little operative effect.[22] On the other hand, Convention 182 clearly struck a chord with Member States, and by June 2003 had attracted 138 ratifications.

Leaving aside concerns about the quality and quantity of recent standards, it must also be recognised that many of the older standards are obsolescent, if not obsolete. This is borne out by the fact that the ILO lists some 27 Conventions as having been 'shelved or withdrawn.' This means that they are no longer promoted, and that ratifying States are not required to report on the effect given to them. However, they remain on the international statute book, and theoretically remain binding upon ratifying States unless denounced. There have been attempts to update a number of standards in recent years through the use of protocols,[23] but there is still the problem that adherence to a protocol requires a separate act of accession. A constitutional amendment was adopted in 1997 to facilitate the abrogation of obsolete Conventions, but this has not yet received sufficient ratifications to become operative.[24] Absent such amendment, denunciation remains the only way to escape the effect of obsolete Conventions.[25]

---

[21] See, eg, the Part Time Work Convention 1994 (No 175) and Home Work Convention 1996 (No 177). As at June 2003 these instruments had attracted 10 and four ratifications respectively.

[22] See, eg, the Working Conditions (Hotels and Restaurants) Convention 1991 (No 172) and Private Employment Agencies Convention 1997 (No 181). As at June 2003 each had attracted 13 ratifications.

[23] See, eg, the 1996 Protocol to the Merchant Shipping (Minimum Standards) Convention 1976 (No 147) and the 2002 Protocol to the Occupational Safety and Health Convention 1981 (No 155).

[24] See S Cooney 'Testing Times for the ILO: Institutional Reform for the New International Political Economy' (1999), 20 *Comp Lab Law & Pol J* 365–80, who also notes that amendments in 1986 relating to the anomalous position of 'Members of chief industrial importance' (Articles 7(3) and 36) have not yet received sufficient ratifications to become operative.

[25] See K Widdows, 'The Denunciation of International Labour Conventions' (1984) 33 *International and Comparative Law Quarterly* 1052; see also ILO, *Abrogation or Extinguishment of International Labour Conventions* (Governing Body Paper GB.265/LILS/WP/PRS/2, Geneva, ILO, 1996).

Ratification and Compliance

Ratification levels provide a rough guide to the practical impact of Conventions. Here again there is cause for concern about the health of the system. In particular, it is clear that Member States are increasingly reluctant to ratify newly-adopted Conventions. For example, the average number of ratifications for each of the 34 Conventions adopted since 1978 is 20.1. If Convention 182 is excluded, the rate drops to 16.05.

Ratification is only one indicator of the state of health of the standard-setting process. In many respects the more important factor is the level of compliance with those Conventions that are ratified. Here again, the picture is bleak.

During the Cold War era, many governments ratified Conventions that either had no practical relevance to them, or in relation to which they had no realistic prospect of establishing and maintaining compliance. They did this to gain kudos by being seen to have a 'better' ratification record than countries of a different ideological persuasion.[26] They often did this confident in the knowledge that there was little prospect of independent scrutiny of their compliance record, given that employer and employee organisations in authoritarian countries were unlikely to be in a position to express an independent view as to the effect given to any particular Convention, with the consequence that the supervisory bodies were almost entirely reliant upon the government itself for information on compliance. This practice of 'trophy ratification' appears to be less prevalent now than was formerly the case, although even a cursory reading of the ratification lists shows that it has not entirely disappeared.

More disturbing in current circumstances is the fact that very many countries that have ratified Conventions simply do not honour their reporting obligations, or having done so, are found to be in breach of the obligations incurred by ratification. Furthermore, many of the most serious areas of non-compliance relate to the core standards in the 1998 Declaration. For example, in 2003 the CEACR directed Observations to 88 Member States in respect of at least one area of non-compliance with Convention No 87, and a further 36 in relation to Convention No 98. This was in addition to 49 Direct Requests in relation to Convention No 87, and 18 in relation to Covention No 98. Furthermore, a significant proportion of these breaches related to developed countries that were the traditional mainstays of the system of standard-setting and supervision.[27]

---

[26] See Cordova, above n 2, at 155–56.

[27] For an analysis of OECD countries' compliance record in relation to Conventions Nos 87 and 98 see B Creighton, 'Freedom of Association' in R Blanpain and C Engels (eds), *Comparative Labour Law and Industrial Relations in Industrialised Market Economies* (8th edn, The Hague, Kluwer, 2004) 239–50. See also K Ewing, *Britain and the ILO* (London, Institute for Employment

It seems reasonable to suppose that the levels of non-compliance recorded in the Reports of the CEACR, and of the Governing Body's Committee on Freedom of Association (CFA), significantly understate the extent of non-compliance with ratified Conventions. This reflects the fact that the entire system of supervision is in a state of profound crisis. This is compounded of a number of factors:

(1) The existing machinery cannot cope with the volume of material generated by ratifying States. For example, in 1927 the eight members of the CEACR had responsibility for examining 180 reports.[28] Seventy-six years later, the Committee's 20 members had to examine 1,772 Article 22 reports and 141 Article 19 reports. Self-evidently, it would not be possible to undertake a thorough review of this volume of material in the time available.

(2) In practice, the greater part of the work of the CEACR is performed by the Office, with the members of the Committee providing their imprimatur to the work of the Secretariat. That is not necessarily a problem in itself. However, it becomes one in consequence of the chronic under-resourcing of the Office. For example, the Freedom of Association Branch of the ILS Department has a staff equivalent to eight permanent officials. In preparing the 2003 Report of the CEACR this staff had to draft 137 Observations and 93 Direct Requests. The Branch also constitutes the Secretariat for the CFA, which currently has 105 active cases, and 104 that are subject to follow-up. Manifestly, a Secretariat of this size cannot be expected to develop a level of understanding of the national legal systems of the 157 countries that have ratified either or both of Conventions Nos 87 and 98 to ensure that the CEACR and the CFA are adequately informed of the state of compliance with these Conventions in each Member State. Even a Secretariat many times the present size could not realistically be expected to do so.

Rights, 1994) (United Kingdom); B Creighton, 'The ILO and the Protection of Freedom of Association in the United Kingdom' in K Ewing C Gearty and B Hepple (eds), *Human Rights and Labour Law: Essays for Paul O'Higgins* (London, Mansell, 1994) (United Kingdom); S Mills, 'The International Labour Organisation, the United Kingdom and Freedom of Association: An Annual Cycle of Condemnation' [1997] *European Human Rights Law Review* 35 (United Kingdom); B Creighton, 'The ILO and Protection of Fundamental Human Rights in Australia' (1998) 22 *U Melb LR* 239 (Australia); T Novitz, 'Freedom of Association and "Fairness at Work": An Assessment of the Impact and Relevance of ILO Convention No. 87 on its Fiftieth Birthday' (1998) 27 *ILJ* 169 (United Kingdom); B Burkett, J Craig and S Gallagher, 'Canada and the ILO: Freedom of Association Since 1982' (2003) 10 *Canadian Labour and Employment Law Journal* 231 (Canada).

[28] ILO (2002) Report of the Committee of Experts on the Application of Conventions and Recommendations ILC, 90th Session, Report III (Part 1A) (Geneva, ILO, 2002).

(3)   Many ratifying states do not furnish Article 22 and Article 19 reports when due.[29] In some cases this is indicative of a lack of commitment. More often it reflects the fact that many developing countries simply do not have the resources to collect the requisite information (even assuming that it is available), and then to put it into the form required by bureaucrats in far-away Geneva. Similarly, trade unions and employer organisations in many countries do not have the resources and/or inclination rigorously to scrutinise the Reports prepared by their governments, and then to provide their comments to the Office.

Globalisation and Other Challenges

Globalisation and Trade Liberalisation

The challenges to both national and international labour law posed by globalisation of the world economy, and the debate on whether access to liberalised trading regimes should be linked to adherence to core labour standards, have generated an extensive literature.[30] It is not necessary to rehearse these debates here. However, it is necessary to recognise that they have profound implications for the future of ILS, and indeed of the ILO as a whole.

It will be recalled that part of the rationale for the adoption of ILS was to try to ensure that nation states did not obtain an unfair competitive advantage in the international marketplace by tolerating abusive labour conditions. This logic was always flawed by reason of the fact that, under the voluntarist model enshrined in the ILO Constitution, the only countries where ILS took labour out of competition were those who elected to ratify, and implement, those standards. In other words, recalcitrant Member States could retain their unfair advantage simply by not ratifying. Furthermore, there has always been a tension between preventing unfair competition

---

[29] Eg, only 65.1 per cent of the Article 22 reports, and 55.29 per cent of the Article 19 reports, requested for the 91st session were received by the due date.

[30] See, eg, the essays collected in W Sengenberger and D Campbell (eds), *International Labour Standards and Economic Interdependence* (Geneva, IILS, 1994) and W Sengenberger and D Campbell (eds), *Creating Economic Opportunities: The Role of Labour Standards in Industrial Restructuring* (Geneva, IILS, 1994). See also H Arthurs, 'Reinventing Labor Law for the Global Economy: The Benjamin Aaron Lecture' (2001) 22 *Berkeley Journal of Employment and Labor Law* 272; B Hepple, 'Enforcement: The Law and Politics of Cooperation and Compliance' in Hepple, *Social and Labour Rights in a Global Context*, above n 2, at 14–15; R Staiger, 'A Role for the WTO' in Basu et al, above n 2; N Singh, 'The Impact of International Labour Standards: A Survey of Economic Theory' in *ibid*; C Summers, 'Free Trade v Labor Rights/Human Rights: Doubts, Definitions, Difficulties' in R Blanpain and M Weiss (eds), *Changing Industrial Relations and the Modernisation of Labour Law* (The Hague, Kluwer, 2003).

through maintenance of abusive labour practices and a recognition that some countries could compete effectively in the marketplace only because of their lower labour costs: the so-called comparative advantage. It must be acknowledged that lower labour costs are not necessarily indicative of abusive labour practices, but in many instances this must indeed be the case.

This issue has bedevilled the system from the outset. The Constitution itself recognised the need to 'have due regard to those countries in which climatic conditions, the imperfect development of industrial organisation, or other special circumstances make the industrial conditions substantially different' and to make such modifications, if any, that were considered necessary 'to meet the case of such countries.'[31] This reasoning was reflected in many early Conventions.[32] But the fact remains that there is a circularity about the notion that ILS are meant to be of universal application and to take labour out of international trade but that at the same time they should formally (or informally) recognise the need to protect the comparative advantage of developing countries, even where that comparative advantage is based upon what would elsewhere be regarded as abusive labour practices.

This dilemma has assumed a special significance in the context of trade liberalisation. There are some who would argue that access to liberalised trade regimes should be conditional upon adherence to 'core' labour standards, whilst others would oppose any such linkage on the ground that this is simply a colourable device to protect industry in the developed world. Some accommodation between these extremes was reached at the World Summit for Social Development in Copenhagen in 1995 and at the Ministerial Conference of the WTO in Singapore in 1996. In both instances, the role of the ILO as the guardian of labour standards was formally endorsed.[33]

No doubt, some of those who support the separation of trade and labour issues are motivated by a cynical desire to push the matter to one side by syphoning it off to what is perceived to be a marginal institution such as the ILO. Equally clearly, many who support the separation do so out of a genuine concern that a linkage of trade and labour standards would operate to the disadvantage of developing countries, even though this proposition receives little support from the empirical evidence.[34] On either view, and despite the apparent vote of confidence by the international community in

---

[31] ILO Constitution, Art 19(3).

[32] Eg, Arts 9–13 of Convention 1 made special provision for the application of the Convention to Japan, British India, China, Persia, Siam, Greece and Romania.

[33] See ILO, *The ILO, Standard Setting and Globalisation*, Report of the Director-General to the 85th Session of the ILC (Geneva, ILO, 1997), 2, 12–14.

[34] See OECD, *Trade, Employment and Labour Standards: A Study of Core Workers' Rights in International Trade* (Paris, OECD, 1996); OECD, *International Trade and Core*

the Copenhagen and Singapore Declarations, the ILO has not addressed these issues in a coherent or effective manner.

For example, adoption of the 1998 Declaration was made possible only by the inclusion of a provision which expressly stipulated that it could not be used for purposes of trade protection, or to deprive Member States of their comparative advantage. Simply stated: the trade/labour standards nexus was placed in the 'too hard' basket.

The ILO's shortcomings in the context of globalisation and trade liberal-isation are further illustrated by its consistent failure to address one of the key factors in the comparative advantage debate: the power of transna-tional corporations (TNCs), and in particular their capacity to direct invest-ment from countries that adhere to relatively high labour standards to countries that do not. At first blush this would appear to be an issue that was ideally suited to the adoption and supervision of appropriately framed ILS.[35] Instead, the ILO has adopted only the manifestly inadequate Tripartite Declaration of Principles Concerning Multinational Enterprises and Social Policy of 1977.[36] This is largely devoid of substance, and entirely lacks an effective supervisory mechanism. It is of small comfort that the ILO shares its shortcomings in this area with the OECD.[37]

The End of the Cold War

With the end of the Cold War the factors that impelled the practice of trophy ratification no longer operated. This has had a number of significant conse-quences both for standard-setting and for supervision. On one hand, the disintegration of the Soviet Union and the break-up of Czechoslovakia and Yugoslavia generated additional ratifications as newly independent entities became party to various Conventions in their own right.[38] On the other hand, there was no longer an (express or implied) consensus that supported the adoption of new standards as a means of exerting economic, political or moral pressure on 'the other side.' Similarly, Western govern-ments and (especially) employer organisations became increasingly uncom-fortable with the jurisprudence concerning the right to strike and with the priority accorded to the collective regulation of terms and conditions of

Labour Standards (Paris, OECD, 2000); B Hepple, 'New Approaches to International Labour Regulation' (1997) 26 *ILJ* 353, at 356; W Sengenberger, 'Economic Law or Labour Law? Issues of International Labour Standards and Development,' paper presented at ILO seminar, *'Future Challenges and Opportunities to Enhance the Relevance of International Labour Standards'*, Geneva, 23–24 May 2002, 18–20.

[35] See O'Higgins, above n 2, at 69.
[36] See further Hepple, above n 30, at 240–41.
[37] *Ibid*; see also O'Higgins, above n 2, at 65–66.
[38] It appears that 500 of the 750 ratifications recorded between 1992 and 1996 reflected confirmations by new member states of instruments that had previously applied to their territory: ILO, above n 33, at 36.

employment by the CFA and the CEACR, both of which they had supported in the Cold War context.[39] These changes of attitude reflect, and have been fuelled by, the ascendancy of neo-liberalism in the English-speaking democracies and in the major international financial institutions.

The Ascendancy of Neo-liberalism

Neo-liberal economic orthodoxy is hostile to any kind of interference with the operation of market forces.[40] Not surprisingly, therefore, neo-liberal governments in developed countries have not been keen to support the adoption or implementation of labour standards either in their own countries, or in the developing countries where they do business. They have, however, supported the adoption of standards that are intended to increase labour market 'flexibility', often at the expense of entrenched worker rights.[41]

Pursuit of a neo-liberal agenda has caused some governments to withdraw from active participation in the activities of the ILO as a whole,[42] thereby serving further to impoverish its standard-setting and supervisory functions and to marginalise it as an influence on the evolution of international labour law.[43]

Competing Sources of Standards

Traditionally, the ILO has been the principal source of international labour law. However, it is facing increasingly significant competition from regional trade groupings (notably the European Union)[44] and from bilateral trade arrangements.[45]

---

[39] See Creighton, 'The ILO and the Internationalisation of Australian Labour Law', (1995) 11 *Int Journ Comp Lab Law C Ind Rels* 199–208.

[40] For a helpful overview see S Deakin and F Wilkinson, 'Rights vs. Efficiency? The Economic Case for Transnational Labour Standards' (1994) 23 *ILJ* 289. For an interesting rebuttal of neo-liberal arguments against international labour standards, see Sengenberger, above n 34.

[41] See, eg, the Night Work Convention 1990 (No 171); Part-Time Work Convention 1994 (No 175); and Private Employment Agencies Convention 1997 (No 181). See further L Vosko, 'Legitimizing the Triangular Employment Relationship: Emerging International Labour Standards from a Comparative Perspective' (1997) 19 *Comp Lab Law and Policy J* 43; J Murray, 'The Sound of One Hand Clapping? The "Ratcheting Labour Standards" Proposal and International Labour Law' (2001) 14 *Aus J of Lab Law* 306, at 314.

[42] Eg, the present Australian government has greatly reduced Australian participation in the ILO, including relinquishing membership of the Governing Body: see B Creighton and A Stewart, *Labour Law: An Introduction* (3rd edn, Sydney, Federation Press, 2001) 56–57.

[43] Cf Murray, above n 41, at 316: 'the forces of globalisation and neo-liberalism have, paradoxically, strengthened the ILO's regulatory regime' — albeit 'not in terms of providing it with binding powers of enforcement.'

[44] See, eg, E Mazuyer, 'Labor Regulation in the North American Free Trade Area: A Study on the North American Agreement on Labor Cooperation' (2001) 22 *Comp Lab Law and Policy J* 239.

[45] See, eg, L Compa and J Vogt, 'Labor Rights in the Generalised System of Preferences: A 20-Year Review' (2001) 22 *Comp Lab Law and Policy J* 199.

The emergence of the EU as a source of international labour law is especially significant: first, because it is a source not just of international labour law, but of supranational labour law that can be enforced both through domestic courts and tribunals and through Community institutions. This inevitably means that traditional ILO standards and procedures are of reduced relevance to Member States of the EU, and to the social partners in those Member States. This has served further to impoverish the ILO's standard-setting and supervisory functions since it is the democracies of Western Europe that have traditionally been the key drivers of the ILO system.

On a more positive note, the EU has actively pursued the possibility of ILO membership,[46] which suggests that the ILO is seen to have a continuing relevance in the context of European integration. Moreover, Continental countries have continued to ratify newly adopted Conventions and actively to participate in the activities of the Governing Body and the ILC. Most importantly, the fact that European labour law is primarily focused upon individual employment rights, and is ambivalent about issues such as freedom of association and the right to engage in collective bargaining,[47] means that ILO standards on these issues are of real and continuing relevance to EU Member States.[48]

An Organisation in Crisis

Most of the pressures discussed above are external to the ILO, but some are self-imposed, whilst others are the product of the structure of the ILO itself. Among the self-imposed pressures is the existence of an excessively compartmentalised and overly hierarchical bureaucracy of somewhat uneven ability. They also include the fact that some employer and worker representatives make little positive contribution to the work of the ILO, and often remain as members of the Governing Body and/or as delegates to ILC until well past their 'use-by' date. This problem is compounded by declining levels of union membership and declining employer interest in the ILO, which have the effect that there are fewer competent individuals with the time and commitment to make a significant contribution to the work of the ILO.

Ironically, the structural problems include one of the most distinctive characteristics of the ILO — its tripartite structure whereby 'representatives of workers and employers, enjoying equal status with those of governments, join with them in free discussion and democratic decision.'[49] Tripartism as

---

[46] See O'Higgins, above n 2 at 62.
[47] See M Weiss, 'The Politics of the EU Charter of Fundamental Rights' in B Hepple (ed), *Social and Labour Rights in a Global Context* (Cambridge, Cambridge University Press, 2002).
[48] See, eg, *Wilson and National Union of Journalists v United Kingdom* [2002] IRLR 568, and K Ewing, 'The Implications of Wilson and Palmer' (2003) 32 *ILJ* 1.
[49] Declaration of Philadelphia, Art I(d).

enshrined in the Constitution had an obvious logic in 1919, when most Member States were industrialised economies characterised by large workplaces and relatively high and/or growing levels of union membership. Nowadays, most Member States are developing countries, large workplaces are increasingly rare, and union membership is in decline almost everywhere. This inevitably raises questions about the appropriateness of the existing basis for worker representation in the ILO. The changing structure of the global economy also raises not dissimilar questions about the continuing basis for employer representation. That said, tripartism in its traditional form still has much to commend it, and should not lightly be discarded. However, it must also be recognised that the continuing relevance of the existing structure needs to be reconsidered in light of the contextual changes noted in this chapter.[50]

RESPONDING TO THE CRISIS

Concentrating on Core Standards

The crisis in standard-setting and supervision has not gone unrecognised. One response has been to try to concentrate on core competencies. This led to the adoption of the 1998 Declaration.[51] Essentially, this involved all Member States formally committing themselves to implementation of the principles enshrined in the core human rights Conventions, a duty that is said to derive from the fact of ILO membership, and not from ratification

This is the basis upon which member states have traditionally been required to observe the PFA. However, the 1998 Declaration does not contain any complaints mechanism analogous to the CFA. Instead, Member States are required to provide an annual report on the core Conventions which they have not ratified. This is clearly intended to encourage ratification and indeed appears to have enjoyed a measure of success in this regard.[52]

Welcome as increased ratification of core standards may be, it is important to keep the matter in perspective. It does, for example, seem somewhat paradoxical to impose additional reporting requirements upon Member States when the onerous character of those requirements is a

---

[50] See further Cooney, above n 24, at 370-73.

[51] See further H Kellerson, 'The ILO Declaration of 1998 on Fundamental Principles and Rights: A Challenge for the Future' (1998) 137 *Int Lab Rev* 223; B Langille, 'The ILO and the New Economy: Recent Developments' (1999) 15 *IJCLLIR* 229; J Bellace, 'The ILO Declaration of Fundamental Principles and Rights at Work' (2001) 17 *IJCLLIR* 269. For background see ILO, above n 33, and the comment thereon in A Frazer and C Nyland, 'In Search of a Middle Way: the ILO, Standard-setting and Globalisation' (1997) 10 *Aus J Lab Law* 280.

[52] Ratification figures for the core documentations since 1998 are: no 87=22; no 98=13; no 29=19; no 105=31; no 100=27; no 111=31; no 138=72; and no 182=144.

significant contributor to failure to ratify in the first place. A complaints procedure similar to the CFA might help to address some of these difficulties. However, it seems clear that had the 1998 Declaration included any such process, it would not have been adopted.[53]

Furthermore, important as the principles enshrined in the core human rights Conventions may be, it does not necessarily follow that they should be regarded as constituting the 'core' of international labour law as a whole. In particular,[54] there is much to be said for the view that protection against work-related injury and disease or access to a fair wage are just as fundamental as the right of national trade union centres to send representatives to the ILC, or even to engage in collective bargaining.[55]

The likely efficacy of concentrating on core standards and competencies must also be questioned in light of the persistent refusal of governments in certain developed countries to honour their obligations under these core Conventions. This is exemplified by the continuing failure of the governments of Australia, Canada and the United Kingdom to bring their law and practice into line with ILO standards on freedom of association.[56] This does not provide a positive role model for developing countries, and indeed such cynical disregard for core principles can only serve further to marginalise both core and non-core standards. The same is true for the continuing failure of the USA to ratify either Convention No 87 or No 98.

The focus on core Conventions also leaves unresolved the question of what can or should be done in relation to non-core standards.[57] On one view, respect for the core principles should provide a basis for adoption and implementation of non-core standards. That is, respect for core principles can help create a social and economic environment where Member States can realistically look to adherence to non-core standards in relation to issues such as social security, termination of employment or occupational

[53] See, eg, F Maupain, 'International Labour Organisation Recommendations and Similar Instruments' in D Sheldon (ed) *Commitment and Compliance: The role of non-binding norms in the International Legal System* (Oxford University Press: Oxford, 2000) at 387–88.

[54] See Hepple, above n 34, at 359; Engerman, above n 2, at 11; Summers, above n 30, at 385–87. S Cleveland, 'Why International Labour Standards?,' paper presented at ILO seminar, above n 34, at 19, notes that consideration was given to the inclusion of both occupational health and safety and a fair minimum wage in the 1998 Declaration, but that they were excluded at the insistence of the Employer Group.

[55] Convention 87, Art 5 and Convention 98, Art 4, respectively. Interestingly, at its 91st session the ILC committed the ILO to a number of significant initiatives in relation to occupational health and safety: see ILO standards-related activities in the area of occupational safety and health, ILC, 91st Session, Report VI (Geneva, ILO, 2003). Report of the Committee on Occupational Safety and Health ILC, 91st Session, Provisional Record 22 (Geneva, ILO, 2003).

[56] See the sources cited above n 27.

[57] See further P Alston and J Heenan, 'The Role of International Labour Standards Within the Free Trade Debate: The Need to Return to Fundamentals,' paper presented at ILO seminar, above n 34.

health and safety. This logic is not without its attractions, but clearly there is a real risk that the emphasis on the so-called core standards will serve further to marginalise non-core instruments.

A New Approach to Standard-Setting?

An obvious response to criticisms concerning the proliferation of ILS would be to adopt fewer of them. As noted earlier, that does indeed appear to be happening. Furthermore, several of the more recent instruments appear to have more substance than some of those adopted during the 1980s and early 1990s.

It is also interesting to note the increased use of Recommendations. In the early days of the ILO the ILC frequently adopted free-standing Recommendations that dealt with issues that were not considered suitable for treatment by means of a Convention.[58] They were also used to complement the obligations set out in Conventions, for example by providing guidance as to ways in which Member States could give effect to the obligations incurred by ratification. The use of free-standing Recommendations became much less common in the 1970s, although the practice never died out entirely.[59]

In his Report to the 85th session the Director-General argued strongly for increased use of Recommendations for standard-setting.[60] Among other things, he suggested that this would help minimise the damage to the prestige of the ILO and to the credibility of the standard-setting process in consequence of the poor rates of ratification of recent Conventions.[61] He also argued that it would help avoid the difficulties associated with the 'blocking' effect of adoption of Conventions due to the difficulty of removing them from the international statute book, and the restrictive procedures relating to denunciation.

The arguments for and against the use of Recommendations rather than Conventions are finely balanced. Manifestly, Conventions enjoy a higher status than Recommendations in international law, and as such constitute a more authoritative affirmation of principle. On the other hand, it must be recognised that some Recommendations have had a significant influence upon national law and practice in certain countries,

---

[58] For example the first session of the ILC adopted six Recommendations, five of which were free-standing, and one of which complemented a Convention.

[59] See ILO, above n 33, at 49, which notes that autonomous Recommendations constituted 55 per cent of the instruments adopted between 1951 and 1971, but only 7 per cent of instruments adopted between 1971 and 1983.

[60] *Ibid* at 49–58. To similar effect, see ILO, *Defending Values, Promoting Change, Report of the Director-General to the 81st Session of the ILC* (Geneva, ILO, 1994).

[61] See Maupain, above n 53, at 373.

despite their ostensibly lesser status. This is exemplified by the influence of the Termination of Employment Recommendation 1963 upon the unfair dismissal provisions of the *Industrial Relations Act* 1971 (United Kingdom).[62] Furthermore, the adoption of Recommendations is subject to the same consultative and deliberative processes as Conventions, so that their authoritativeness does not suffer by comparison in that respect.[63]

In his 1997 Report, the Director-General emphasised that increased reliance upon Recommendations should be accompanied by revived use of the requirement to report on the effect given to Recommendations under Article 19(6)(d). This may indeed have merit. But it is important to bear in mind that Member States can be required to report on the effect given to unratified Conventions in essentially the same way as in relation to Recommendations. [64]

The idea that there should be greater reliance upon Recommendations as a source of ILS is often accompanied by suggestions that there should be greater reliance upon other forms of 'soft law' such as codes of practice, guidelines and 'social labelling' programmes. Some observers see considerable potential in these options, especially if they are enforced through the internal markets of TNCs, and provided they incorporate core ILO principles, including those relating to freedom of association and collective bargaining.[65] They cannot, however, be regarded as substitutes for properly drawn and effectively supervised ILS.

A New Approach to Supervision?

It was suggested earlier that the problems that beset the supervisory process can be attributed to a number of factors, including lack of resources and the fact that the supervisory bodies are simply trying to do the impossible. However, with goodwill and commitment on the part of governments and the social partners, there may be some capacity to develop new procedures that could provide a more effective means of securing adherence to at least the core standards (whatever they may be), without the necessity for cumbersome and time-consuming constitutional amendment.

---

[62] This Recommendation helped pave the way for the adoption of the Termination of Employment Convention 1982 (No 158), and accompanying Recommendation 166. See further Maupain, above n 53, at 377–79.

[63] *Ibid* at 373–74.

[64] Constitution, Art 19(5)(e)

[65] See, eg, J Murray, 'Corporate Codes of Conduct and Labour Standards' in R Kyloh (ed), *Mastering the Challenge of Globalisation* (Geneva, ILO, 1998); B Hepple, 'A Race to the Top? International Investment Guidelines and Corporate Codes of Conduct' (1999) 20 *Comp Lab Law and Policy J* 347.

One possibility would be to adopt a complaints mechanism similar to the CFA in respect of core principles. This proposition has been aired on a number of occasions over the years, but has not received sufficient support to come to fruition. The fact that the 1998 Declaration appears to have been adopted only on condition that it did not encompass any such procedure does not provide cause for optimism for the future.

A further possibility might centre upon an expansion and streamlining of the representation process in Article 24. This would, of course, be available only in relation to ratified Conventions, but could nevertheless provide a basis for dealing with 'complaints' concerning alleged breaches of ratified Conventions without the need to fall back on the more formal complaints procedures in Article 26. Indeed, to some extent this potential is already being realised, as evidenced by the marked increase in the use of representation procedures in recent years.[66] There may also be a useful role for a tribunal established in reliance upon Article 37(2), at least for purposes of interpreting Conventions.[67]

More proactive use of the constitutional provisions relating to reporting on the effect given to unratified Conventions and to Recommendations could also play a positive role in a reinvigorated supervisory process, although it is important to take account of the resource implications of such initiatives both for the Office and for Member States.

The CEACR manifestly cannot do what it is presently supposed to do. However, that does not mean that it could not play a positive role in the future, perhaps on the basis of a more narrowly defined remit, and with a focus on major issues of policy and principle rather than legal and administrative minutiae, as too often appears to be the case at present. It is certainly necessary to abandon the pretences that underpin the present system lest its failures inflict irreparable damage upon the entire system.

Addressing the Organisational Crisis

In principle, it ought to be possible to address the intra-organisational issues noted earlier by means of executive action. There have been

---

[66] For example in its 2001 Report (*Report of the Committee of Experts on the Application of Conventions and Recommendations*, ILC, 89th Session, Report III (Part IA) (Geneva, ILO, 2001)) the CEACR noted (at 16–17) that in 2000 three representations had been declared receivable, three had been the subject of tripartite committee reports and five were pending. In 2001 (see *Report of the Committee of Experts on the Application of Conventions and Recommendations*, ILC, 90th Session, Report III (Part IA) (Geneva, ILO, 2001) 20–21) three representations were declared receivable, five were subject to report and one was withdrawn. In 2002 (see *Report of the Committee of Experts on the Application of Conventions and Recommendations*, ILC, 91st Session, Report III (Part IA) (Geneva, ILO, 2001) 14) two were declared receivable.

[67] See above n 15 and accompanying text.

numerous attempts to do so in the past. All have foundered in the face of resistance (active and passive) from staff; intervention by governments and employer and worker groups to protect 'their' interests; and loss of will on the part of successive Directors-General. The fact remains that these issues must be addressed in a rigorous manner if the ILO is to play a significant role in the future of labour law.

The structural problems identified by observers such as Cooney are even more intractable. This is because some of the difficulties are embedded in the structure of the ILO itself. This is a source of particular difficulty in light of the fact that the procedures for amending the Constitution are such as to make any change, let alone radical change, exceedingly difficult to achieve.

That said, there is much that could be achieved without formal constitutional amendment. For example, the employer and worker groups could ensure that they elect as members of the Governing Body only individuals with the talent and energy to make a positive contribution to the work of the ILO. There would also be merit in imposing limits on the number of terms that individuals can serve on the Governing Body.

The ILO also needs to adopt a more inclusive approach to groups and interests who are not formally represented within the existing institutional structure. This is necessary in recognition that organisations of workers can no longer credibly claim to represent the interests of all workers, that the self-employed are now a sufficiently large sector of the workforce to merit recognition in their own right, that 'employers' are not a homogenous group, and above all, that the 'informal sector' plays a major role in the economies of many Member States. Absent constitutional amendment, such interests could not be given formal voting rights at the ILC or membership of the Governing Body, unless included in national delegations to the ILC or elected as members of the Governing Body as part of the employers or workers groups. However, they could and should be given rights of audience and a role in policy formation in relation to matters that affect them.[68]

CONCLUSION

On the basis of the foregoing, it is clearly possible that ILS could make a positive contribution to the future of labour law in both developed and developing economies. However, even leaving aside the issue of political commitment, for this to happen there needs to be a much clearer understanding of the role for labour law in the new order, and of the appropriate role for ILS in that order.

---

[68] This has not gone unrecognised, both in theory and in practice: see, eg, ILO, above n 33, at 27–32. However, there is still a long way to go before the issues raised by Cooney, above n 24, at 386, 389–93, could be said adequately to have been addressed.

In the final analysis, that new role may not be radically different from the traditional role of taking labour out of competition and preventing unfair competitive advantage through exploitative labour practices. However, that cannot be achieved through the medium the ILO system as it presently stands. There have been some positive developments in recent years, including the adoption of the 1998 Declaration, the focus on the concept of 'decent work' as an objective of policy,[69] and what appears to be a more selective approach to the adoption of new standards. However, the fact remains that the challenges associated with reform of the supervisory process and of the structure of the ILO are formidable in the extreme. Recognising that the problems exist is a positive start, but self-evidently is not sufficient in itself. There is indeed a hard road to travel if ILS are to make a meaningful contribution to the promotion of equality of capability and to the future of labour law.

---

[69] According to the Director-General's Report to the 1999 Conference this means 'decent and productive work, in conditions of freedom, equity, security and human dignity.' See *Decent Work*, Report of the Director-General to the 85th Session of the ILC (Geneva, ILO, 1999). See also ILO, *Reducing the Decent Work Deficit: A Global Challenge* (Geneva, ILO, 2001); Hepple, above n 1, at 12–13; R Owens, 'Decent Work for the Contingent Workforce in the New Economy' (2002) 15 *Aus J Lab Law* 209, at 217–18, 233–34.

13

Beyond Borrowing and Bending: Labour Market Regulation and the Future of Labour Law in Southern Africa

EVANCE KALULA*

Had I been present at the creation I would have given some useful hints for the better ordering of the Universe. (Alphonso X, the Learned, 1252–84, King of Spain).

INTRODUCTION

AFRICA CONTINUES TO be marginal in global developments. Few remember that it was not always this way. There was a time, at the height of the decolonisation process, when many observers thought they were 'present at the creation.' Then came along Rene Dumont, the French agronomist, who bluntly told the world, not least Africans themselves, that the so-called development decade of the 1960s was no more than a 'false start in Africa.'[1]

Dumont's message was direct, the priorities set were wrong. No new societies would come about until more attention was paid to the basics.

Although there have been many factors at play which have led to Africa's declining fortunes, most of what has happened in Africa seems to bear out

---

* I am indebted to Clive Thompson for the inspiration of part of this title, see his 'Borrowing and Bending: The Developing of South Africa's Unfair Labour Practice Jurisprudence' in R Blanpain and M Weiss (eds), *The Changing Face of Labour Law and Industrial Relations: Liber Amicorum for Clyde W Summers* (Baden Baden, Nomos, 1993) 109–32. The term 'Southern Africa' here refers to the countries comprising the Southern African Development Community (ie Angola, Botswana, Lesotho, Malawi, Mauritius, Mozambique, Namibia, South Africa, Swaziland, Tanzania, the Seychelles, Zambia and Zimbabwe).
[1] Rene Dumont, *False Start in Africa* (London, Earthscan Publications Ltd, 1966).

Rene Dumont's views. Africa continues to be on the margins of a globalising world. Since the beginning of the 1990s, however, culminating in the 'miracle' of 1994 in South Africa, there has been some glimmer of hope that the founding of the Southern Africa Development Community (SADC) might create a momentum for development through the process of regional integration.

How realistic is such optimism and to what extent does it affect labour law? This chapter is an attempt to examine some of the issues facing the development of labour law, particularly labour markets regulation and social policy. I shall reflect in general terms and in an eclectic manner on the link between labour markets and social protection, the role of the courts and the implementation of labour policy. In essence, my argument is that given the nature of societies and countries in Southern Africa, the future of labour law will depend on going beyond 'borrowing and bending' and the legacy of 'imposed law'[2] which have characterised much of labour law in the region. The future of labour law will depend on taking social-economic realities, apparent in the high levels of poverty and other manifestations of under-development, into account.

LEGACY AND CONTEXT

Cecil John Rhodes, the British imperialist adventurer and visionary, conceived of an African continent on which *Pax Britannica* would reign supreme.[3] While Rhodes' ideal of British colonial Africa was never entirely a reality, British domination of Southern Africa endured for almost a hundred years. During the period, British rule fostered many social and economic links in the sub-continent, ranging from migrant labour, mining and transportation systems to customs unions, to mention but a few. It is the irony of history that as the integration agenda appears to take hold, the essence of the Rhodian dream should appear to be resurrected in some of its major respects.

The changed political dispensation in South Africa has offered the prospect of closer political and economic relations among states in the sub-continent, outstanding conflict and other 'local difficulties' notwithstanding. The process of what appears to be a transition, albeit likely to be a long one, to integration has obvious implications for the future of labour law and policy. As was expected, migrant labour and movements of capital have increased within the region. The uneven state of development, particularly

---

[2] On the concept of imposed law, see themes explored in Sandra B Burman and Barbara E Harrell-Bond (eds), *The Imposition of Law* (London, Academic Press, 1979).

[3] For a sense of the Rhodian dream, see Stanlake Samkange's fictional but historically-based account in *On Trial for My Country* (London, Heinemann, 1967).

but not only between South Africa and the rest, is already leading to complex problems as countries seek to gain competitive advantage.

The situation is compounded by high levels of unemployment, poverty and deprivation in most parts of the region. It has been suggested that Southern Africa is in African terms one of the most promising regions with good economic potential. With a total population of 200 million (important in markets terms) and a combined GDP of about US$190 billion, the region has the potential to develop.[4] However, the fact that 40 per cent of the population live in abject poverty, with high levels of unemployment and under-employment, means that a growth rate of around 7 per cent per annum would be required to tackle deprivation effectively. The total combined growth rate has averaged around 1.5 per cent for the last decade.

The bleak outlook is compounded by the impact of the widespread HIV/AIDS pandemic which has tended to reduce the already relatively low levels of skilled labour. About 15 million people are infected with HIV in Southern Africa. This figure accounts for 51 per cent of infections in Africa, and 37 per cent in global terms. In 2001, 10 million people died of HIV/AIDS.[5] Apart from the resultant crises in health-care, the epidemic has led to high numbers of orphans and child-led households. In the event, the region is in fact one of the poorest in the world. In considering the future of labour law in Southern Africa, therefore, the historical legacy and current context are important.

LABOUR STANDARDS AND HARMONISATION OF LABOUR LAW

The current systems of labour law in the SADC region have been largely influenced by international labour standards. Even before independence when 'imposed law' in the form of received law was the norm, there was creeping ILO influence on labour legislation. At independence, the influence of international labour standards became more widespread with increased ratification but not necessarily effective implementation of international labour Conventions.

In the wake of South Africa's democratic transformation, renewed interest was generated by the ILO fact-finding mission in 1992.[6] The interest in international labour standards has been reinforced in recent years. As part

---

[4] MP Olivier, ER Kalula and LJ van Rensburg, 'Social Protection, Poverty Alleviation and Social Security in the SADC Region: The Need for a Coordinated Paradigm' paper presented at the Third African Regional Congress of the International Industrial Relations Association, Stellenbosch, South Africa, 2002.

[5] Report by President Benjamin Mkapa, SADC Chairman, *The Guardian (Tanzania)*, 28 August 2003.

[6] *Prelude to Change: Report of the Fact-Finding and Conciliation Commission Concerning the Republic of South Africa* (Geneva, ILO, 1992).

of the ILO renewal in the face of globalisation, the focus has changed to core labour standards, about eight Conventions being regarded as providing fundamental human rights important to labour law. The SADC Employment and Labour Sector has embraced the approach of core standards as a basis of heightening commitment to both good governance and human rights in the region. All member countries are now expected to ratify the core ILO Conventions.[7] Attempts are also being made to improve the implementation of such standards.[8]

The ratification and implementation of international labour standards is linked to the debate concerning the quest for harmonisation of labour law as a necessary part of the process of regional integration. The case for harmonisation of labour standards in Southern Africa has been well articulated.[9]

In the SADC context, harmonisation is taken to be the process of striving for common elements in the labour law systems of the member states. It also means the notion of 'minimum requirements', particularly in the context of the ILO's Declaration on Fundamental Principles at Work 1998, and core labour standards. Coupled with these is coordination of policies to enhance employment and growth while respecting labour rights. Seen this way, there are therefore similarities with the approach in the European Union in spite of the different conditions obtaining.

It has been argued that the process of integration needs to be underpinned by the harmonisation of labour law regimes to overcome obstacles to economic integration and help speed it up. The multiplicity of labour laws and industrial relations practices within the SADC region poses many problems in attempts at economic transformation. Transnational companies, for instance, find it difficult to develop effective regional industrial relations policies and are compelled to duplicate structures and personnel in jurisdictions in which they do business. Labour mobility is affected by varying obligations encountered and lack of uniform rights in various jurisdictions.[10] On labour's side, trade unions are not able to develop effective

---

[7] Freedom of Association and Collective Bargaining Conventions 1948 (No 87) and 1949 (No 98), Forced Labour Convention 1930 (No 29) and 1957 (No 105), Non-discrimination Convention 1951 (No 100) and 1958 (No 111) and Child Labour Convention 1973 (No 138) and 1999 (No 182).

[8] See Article 50 of the draft SADC Charter of Fundamental Social Rights 2001. The Charter was recently adopted by the SADC Summit.

[9] D Woolfrey, 'Harmonisation of Southern Africa's Labour Laws in the Context of Regional Integration' (1991) 12 *Industrial Law Journal* (South Africa) (Part 4-6) 709; see also M Clarke, T Feys and ER Kalula, *Labour Standards and Regional Integration in Southern Africa: Prospects for Harmonisation*, Development and Labour Monographs no 2/99 (University of Cape Town, 1999)

[10] For a survey of some such legal obstacles to trade union activities in the SADC region, see ER Kalula 'Labour Law and Trade Union Rights in Southern Africa: Problems and Prospects'. paper presented to conference on Labour Law and Trade Union Rights in Southern Africa, Manzini, Swaziland, 9–12 November 1992.

links in the face of different laws and practices that at best restrict their activities and in many cases prohibit transnational organisation.[11]

The strongest argument in favour of harmonisation of labour laws and standards however (equally relevant to business and labour) is that it is the best preventive mechanism against the phenomenon of 'social dumping,' the temptation for countries to reduce or do away with social protection to reduce labour costs to gain competitive advantage.[12] Where the prospect might be the removal of tariff barriers and free mobility of capital in the form of investment, 'social dumping' becomes a real problem. Harmonisation of labour standards, particularly labour laws, is therefore seen as an effective antidote to deal with unfair competition.[13]

There are, of course, various ways of harmonising labour standards. To a large extent it all depends on the form of integration which develops. In the case of Southern Africa, integration is still at its infant stage with hardly any viable institutions in place. Given the uneven nature of labour markets, ILO standards provide a meaningful basis of approximation. Although the current approach which emphasizes core standards is rather a 'minimalist' approach, it provides a viable basis on which to develop common thresholds in keeping with the ILO's Declaration of Fundamental Principles and Rights at Work of 1998.[14]

The future of labour law in Southern Africa has to take account of, and will be influenced by, current efforts towards harmonisation.

LABOUR MARKETS AND REGULATION IN SOUTHERN AFRICA

The nature of labour markets in Southern Africa is important to the understanding of the regulation in place and its shortcomings. In this section, I briefly consider the character of the labour markets and the process of current efforts at labour law reform. Current labour law reform efforts are mainly concerned with improving labour market regulation by developing better legislative frameworks and institutions.

It is necessary from the outset to define the terms 'regulation' and 'labour law.' I have been attracted by and borrowed from a recent work on law and

---

[11] *Ibid.*

[12] See, eg, HG Mosley 'The Social Dimension of European Integration' (1990/1992) 129 *International Labour Review* 147; A Byre, EC Social Policy and 1992 (Deventer, Kluwer, 1992).

[13] Woolfrey, above n 9.

[14] See B Hepple, 'New Approaches to International Labour Regulation' (1997)26 *ILJ* 358; on the ILO's vision of attempting to reconcile liberalisation and labour standards, see *Defending Values, Promoting Change*, Director-General's Report to the 81st Session of the International Labour Conference (1994).

market regulation in East Asia.[15] Drawing on the work of others, it takes regulation to mean 'a range of uses, from rules promulgated by the state to all mechanisms of social control, by whomsoever exercised.'[16] Equally borrowed from these works is the term 'labour law' which goes beyond the mere scope of the employment relationship to embrace 'broader labour market dimensions' such as the protection of the unemployed.[17] This broader approach is important in understanding labour markets in Southern Africa and how they are regulated. Labour markets in Southern Africa are characterised by high levels of under-employment and underemployment. The vast majority of workers are in the informal sector.[18]

Just as in East Asia and many other developing countries, systems of labour law in the SADC region fundamentally reflect norms developed in Western countries, particularly the United Kingdom and in more recent years, North America. Apart from 'imposed law' that was inherited at independence, there has been conscious 'borrowing and bending.'[19] Since the beginning of the 1990s, labour law reform has proceeded at breath-taking pace. A 'new labour law' has been emerging in different jurisdictions of the region.[20] In many countries, far-reaching changes, in some cases fundamental changes, have been made to labour legislation and practice. South Africa is the obvious case in point with changes made to its labour law regime from 1995 which have continued to the present time.[21] South Africa is, however, not the only country affected. Significant changes have taken place in most countries of the region. Major changes have taken place and are taking place in such countries as Lesotho (1992 and 2002), Namibia (1992 and pending), Swaziland (1998), Zambia (1993 and pending), Botswana (1992 and pending), Tanzania and Zanzibar (underway) and Zimbabwe.[22]

Such changes, made with ILO encouragement and assistance in many cases, have been varied but they have common features. Many have sought

---

[15] S Cooney, T Lindsay, R Mitchell and Y Zhu (eds), *Law and Market Regulation in East Asia* (London, Routledge, 2002).
[16] *Ibid.*
[17] *Ibid.*
[18] G Mhone and ER Kalula, *Report of a Study on the Formulation of Policy Objectives, Priorities and Strategies for the SADC Employment and Labour Sector* (SADC Secretariat, 2001).
[19] On 'the imposition of law' and 'borrowing and bending,' see Burman and Harrell-Bond, above n 2 and C Thompson, 'Borrowing and Bending: The Development of South Africa's Unfair Labour Practice Jurisprudence' (1998) *Journal of Comparative Labor Law and Industrial Relations* 183. A revised version of the article was published as part of R Blanpain and M Weiss (eds), *The Changing Face of Labour Law and Industrial Relations: Liber Amicorum for Clyde W Summers* (Baden Baden, Nomos, 1993).
[20] ER Kalula, 'To Borrow and Bend: The Challenge of Comparative Labour Law in Southern Africa' (1993) *African Society of Comparative and International Law*, Proc 5, 345.
[21] The following legislation, among others, has been enacted: Labour Relations Act 1995 (as recently amended); Basic Conditions of Employment Act 1997; Employment Equity Act 1998; Skills Development Act, 1998.
[22] See, among others, ER Kalula (ed), *Labour Relations in Southern Africa* (Johannesburg, Friedrich Ebert Stiftung, 1993); ER Kalula and L Madhuku, *Public Sector Labour Relations in*

to bring labour legislation into line with fundamental international labour standards. Thus they have been concerned with the enhancement of freedom of association, elimination of child labour and discrimination, and the introduction of dispute resolution procedures which enhance social dialogue.[23]

One fundamental feature reveals the 'transplant' nature of these new labour laws. They have all been concerned with the regulation of formal labour markets to the exclusion of 'irregular' workers, particularly those in the informal sector.[24] The focus of emerging new systems of labour market regulation remains the formal employment sector. To the extent that vulnerable workers are targeted at all, they are limited categories with the vast majority left out. Thus, the increasing number of atypical workers bordering on unemployment and self-employment, home workers, casual and part-time workers, do not have the benefit of the new protection, such as it is.[25]

The problems of labour legislation and institutional arrangements of labour market regulation also extend to the lack of effective monitoring and enforcement. The South African experience is instructive in this respect. Labour legislation has, for instance, been largely decriminalised. Attempts have also been made to integrate inspectorate and compliance services on the one hand, and advisory services on the other.[26]

These attempts, intended to enhance monitoring and enforcement, have not worked well at all. The process continues to be slow with insufficient resources and lack of capacity. In the case of agricultural and domestic sectors, problems of access to workplaces, which apparently were overlooked in devising the regulation, are a major obstacle.[27]

The situation in many other SADC countries is considerably worse. In most countries, the tasks of monitoring and enforcement are undertaken by the labour inspectorates. As various ILO Reports have indicated over the years, such inspectorates have inadequate personnel and are badly trained, if at all.[28] They have no capacity to be proactive, and in many cases cannot even react. In the event, regulation is either non-existent or ineffective.

Southern Africa (Cape Town, Institute of Development and Labour Law, University of Cape Town, 1997).

[23] Mhone and Kalula, above n 18.

[24] *Ibid.*

[25] ER Kalula, 'National Legislation and Institutional Arrangements: Glimpses from Southern Africa' paper presented at Regulatory Frameworks in the Global Economy, Knowledge Network Meeting, ILO World Commission on the Social Dimension of Globalization, Geneva, ILO, 21–22 November 2002.

[26] *Ibid.*

[27] *Ibid.*

[28] See, eg, *Report by the ILO Multidisciplinary* Advisory Team *for Southern Africa* to the Annual Conference of the SADC Employment and Labour Sector, Maputo, Mozambique, 2000.

The situation concerning export processing zones (EPZs) is another area of great inadequacy in terms of labour market regulation. A number of countries are known to formally host EPZs, for instance Mauritius, Namibia and Zimbabwe. A few others, for example Lesotho and Swaziland, in effect have EPZs without formally acknowledging them. Although EPZs in a number of countries are formally covered by labour legislation, for example in Mozambique, Namibia (except for strikes and lock-outs) and Zimbabwe, labour laws are hardly implemented. The tendency is to ignore the application of labour legislation in EPZs.[29] Besides, no account is taken of particular gender characteristics of some of the EPZs, especially those in the clothing and textile sector. In the result, facets of discrimination in employment are widespread.[30]

HUMAN RIGHTS AND SOCIAL PROTECTION INTERFACE

With increasing emphasis on good governance, both by development aid donors and within the Southern African Development Community itself, the link between labour law on the one hand, and human rights and social protection on the other, has become important. Given the historical context of Southern Africa, such a link is particularly important. In many countries, the struggle for equality and improvement in labour conditions was in reality a quest for the better protection of human rights.

There is a clear apparent commitment to human rights in formal terms. As highlighted above, SADC's adoption of ILO core standards for ratification and implementation is one such instance. There are also other indications of formal policy on commitment to human rights. Many countries have ratified not only core ILO labour standards but other international instruments relevant to labour and social policy such as the International Covenant on Economic, Social and Cultural Rights and the African Charter on Human and Peoples' Rights.[31] Internal SADC efforts also show a commitment to human rights. These include the adoption of a draft Protocol on

---

[29] H Jauch, D Keet and L Pretorius, *Export Processing Zones in Southern Africa: Economic, Social and Political Implications*, Development and Labour Monographs 2/96 (University of Cape Town, 1996) vol 2.

[30] *Ibid.*

[31] Angola has ratified all the core Conventions except those specified, that is, 87, 138 and 182; Botswana has ratified all of them; the Democratic Republic of Congo has ratified three: 98, 29 and 100; Lesotho has ratified all the core Conventions except 105, 138 and 182; Mauritius has ratified four: 98, 29, 105 and 138; Mozambique has ratified three: 29, 138 and 182; Namibia has ratified two: 87 and 98; the Seychelles has ratified all of them; South Africa has ratified all of them; Tanzania has ratified all except three: 87, 100 and 111; Zambia has ratified all of them; Zimbabwe has ratified all but two: 87 and 182.

Freedom of Movement of Persons[33] and the Charter of Fundamental Social Rights.[34]

The Charter is particularly interesting from both human rights and social protection perspectives. It is conceived as a tool in market regulation underpinning the need for social protection, in particular of workers and other vulnerable groups. The Charter takes its lead from the SADC Treaty itself, particularly Article 5, which has, among others, some of the most significant objectives, the alleviation of poverty, achievement of development and growth and the social inclusion of disadvantaged and vulnerable groups.[35] Article 10 of the Charter provides

> SADC Member States shall create an enabling environment such that every worker in the SADC region shall have a right to adequate social protection and shall, regardless of status and the type of employment, enjoy adequate social security benefits. Persons who have been unable either to enter or re-enter the labour market and have no means of subsistence shall be able to receive sufficient resources and social assistance.

The Charter also places particular emphasis on equal treatment (in terms of equal opportunities for men and women) and requires countries to take reasonable measures to enable workers to reconcile their occupational and family obligations.[36] It gives priority to the protection of vulnerable groups such as people with disabilities, the elderly and young people.[37] The Charter conceives of implementation at both national and regional levels, requiring the submission of regular reports and discussion in tripartite policy structures.[38] Significantly, it requires member states to ratify and implement core Conventions as contained in the ILO Declaration on Fundamental Principles and Rights at Work of 1998.[39]

It is interesting that there is now apparent willingness on the part of the World Bank to accept considerations of social protection for vulnerable groups in the Bank's dealings with developing countries.[40] However, in spite of the apparent normative guidelines at the regional level, and in at

---

[33] Draft Protocol on the Facilitation of Persons in Southern African Development Community, reproduced at www/queens.ca/samp/migdocs/protocol.htm

[34] *SADC Employment and Labour Sector Report 1999* (ELS.MSP/2004/4.2.5, final version 2001).

[35] Olivier *et al*, above n 4, at 14.

[36] Charter, Art 6(c).

[37] *Ibid*, Arts 7 and 8.

[38] *Ibid*, Art 16(1).

[39] *Ibid*, Art 5.

[40] For the apparent change, see, eg, R Holzman (Director of Social Protection, Human Development Network at the Bank), 'Risk and Vulnerability: The Forward Looking Role of Social Protection in a Globalising World in E Dowler and P Mosely (eds), *Poverty and Social Exclusion in the North and South* (London and New York, Routledge, 2002).

least one country's constitutional entrenchment, no attempt has as yet been made in practice in the SADC region to link labour market regulation to human rights and social protection.[41]

One notable exception is the area of HIV/AIDS. Countries in the region have in the main adopted ILO and SADC Codes on HIV/AIDS which focus on workplaces.[42] In addition, many of them now have detailed policy and practical measures which focus on the prevention and impact of the pandemic generally and in the workplace, especially in terms of occupational health and safety.[43]

THE ROLE OF THE COURTS

Most of the jurisdictions in Southern Africa are common law ones, either English or Roman-Dutch common law.[44] The Roman-Dutch common law jurisdictions have largely been influenced by Anglo-American jurisprudence in labour law.[45] In many areas of the development of the law, therefore, courts have played a leading role. In labour law, however, with the exception of South Africa, the role of the courts has not been that significant.

In a perceptive piece, Clive Thompson sketched the transformation of South African labour law through a process he called 'borrowing and bending.'[46] The process by which the jurisprudence was developed was an interesting one. It essentially arose out of the unintended consequences of the then South African apartheid regime's attempts at 'social engineering' and 'public relations' conceived to convince the international community that the system was not as repressive as its detractors made it out to be, that progress was being made to eliminate discrimination and other unacceptable practices. The findings of the Wienhahn Commission[47] in the 1970s resulted in the establishment of the Industrial Court in 1979. The court, in effect an administrative tribunal, akin to England's employment tribunal system, was accorded an ill-defined unfair labour practice jurisdiction. The court was in the main presided over by 'safe appointments', men of conservative disposition in the mainstream of the political establishment at the time. However, responding to pressure from the then emerging militant

---

[41] The South African Constitution entrenches social protection, in particular the right to social security, see S 27.
[42] Olivier *et al*, above n 4, at 13.
[43] *Ibid.*
[44] The exceptions are mainly those countries which were not former British colonies: Angola, Democratic Republic of Congo and Mozambique.
[45] The Roman-Dutch common law jurisdictions being Botswana, Lesotho, Namibia, South Africa, Swaziland and Zimbabwe.
[46] Thompson, above n 19.
[47] Later published as the Wiehahn Report (Johannesburg, Lex Patria Publications, 1982).

trade union movement, and prodded on by a group of then young radical lawyers, the court came to shape one of the most progressive labour law jurisprudence which has endured in many respects.[48] The new 'labour law' was very much along the lines of the prescriptions of international labour standards. Even though there was an appeal from the Industrial Court to the Labour Appeal Court (consisting of High Court Judges), its decisions were upheld in many cases.

Although the jurisprudence of the court was rather mixed and inconsistent in some respects, it was unassailable in some major aspects. Its enduring influence on South African labour law has been such that when the Cheadle Committee came to draft the current collective labour law, the Labour Relations Act 1995, it was a codification of the court's jurisprudence in some key areas. Such codification was so apparent that one of the major textbooks on labour law came to refer to the Act as 'continuity and change.'[49]

In an attempt to overcome the inconsistencies and lack of authority of the Industrial Court, a real court system in the labour courts (consisting of a Labour Court of High Court standing and the Labour Appeal Court) was created. It is a great disappointment that the labour courts, particularly the Labour Appeal Court, do not seem to have attained those objectives. Courts seem to have lost sight of the fact that labour law is not as decisive in labour relations as it is presumed to be in other areas of regulation. They tend to place too much emphasis on the contract of employment at the expense of the need to protect parties in the employment relationship, particularly the employees. Their approach is contrary to the apparent intention of the legislature.[50]

If the role of the South African courts has been disappointing, courts elsewhere in the region have fared far worse. In almost all countries of the region, industrial courts (operating as administrative tribunals) are in existence, with the exception of Namibia where magistrate courts double up as district labour courts. Unlike the South African experience of the Industrial Court, labour courts in the region have been rather timid. They have acted as no more than dispute resolution mechanisms with almost exclusive focus on the contract of employment. With the occasional exception of the labour courts in Lesotho and Zambia, where attempts have been to interpret their briefs more broadly in keeping with ILO ideals, courts in the region have

---

[48] Thompson has recounted the influence of such labour lawyers and teachers who included Martin Brassey, Halton Cheadle, John Brand, Dennis Davis, Charles Nupen, Paul Pretorius, Edwin Cameron, not to mention Clive Thompson himself, above n 19, at 184.

[49] D du Toit *et al*, *The Labour Relations Act 1995* 1st ed, (Durban, Butterworths, 1996) ch 1.

[50] It would appear that the current proposed amendment restructuring the courts is partially a recognition of some of the shortcomings of the labour courts as currently constituted. See the Superior Courts Bill: http://www.pmg.org.za/bills/030728superior.htm).

not been adventurous.[51] Where labour courts have tried to be adventurous, as in the case of Zambia, they have been reigned in by the High Court exercising its review jurisdiction.[52]

BEYOND BORROWING AND BENDING

In addition to the received law, the bulk of labour law in Southern African countries has been derived by 'borrowing and bending.'[53] In so doing, not a lot of the borrowed law has been adapted to the imperatives of under-developed polities and labour markets.

In the absence of any concrete linkages to reflect the development agenda of SADC countries in which social protection and poverty alleviation should be imperative, there are major shortcomings in the current labour market regulation. The above eclectic survey by implication suggests that the current labour market regulation and the institutions designed to implement it are not focusing on the needs of the vast majority in the labour markets of Southern Africa: the under-employed, under-employed and those in non-wageemployment. The informal sector, in particular, unaccounted for in formal terms, should not as such be ignored.

It is all very well to talk of linkages. What kind of linkages can realistically be forged? It is widely assumed, in a globalising world, that there is a need to reform labour market regulation in keeping with global developments, to encourage competitive production of goods and services. It is also intended to attract investment. These attempts focus on the formal labour market sector. The informal sector is seen as irrelevant.

To seek the heightening of the social dimension of labour law is not to deny the relevancy of the traditional labour market regulation such as ordinary labour law jurisprudence on which labour rights and obligations depend. The fact remains that in countries where the majority of workers are outside the formal labour market, innovative approaches to regulation ought to be considered and adopted. It may well result in dual market regulation but there need not be any disjuncture.

There are already indications of some accommodation of both approaches. At least three constitutional jurisdictions in the region (Lesotho, Namibia and

---

[51] *Ibid.*

[52] See, eg *Jospeh Kalomo v Reunited Engineering Co* [1999] ZILR 75.

[53] As former Belgian, British and Portuguese colonial possessions, the basis of all countries' labour law, as with other parts of the legal systems, was received. In some respects, the reception consciously continued after colonial rule. For instance, the Zambian British Acts Extension Act 1965 created an automatic adoption framework for British legislation as it was passed in the United Kingdom. In many other countries 'borrowing and bending' has proceeded in various guises and degrees.

South Africa) contemplate realisable social rights.[54] As pointed out elsewhere in this chapter, both the SADC founding treaty and the Charter of Fundamental Social Rights point to the need for social justice as a pillar of SADC policy. The emergence of what has been called 'surrogate corporatism,' coupled with the desire for democratic governance, reinforces the need for a socially conscious labour market regulation. This is most apparent in South Africa where a statutory framework for social dialogue with structured capacity to contribute to social and labour policy, clearly indicates the potential to link labour market regulation to social policy ideals. In South Africa, a statutory body, the National Economic Development and Labour Council (NEDLAC) was set up under a 1994 Act.[55] NEDLAC comprises four chambers: Trade and Industry; Public Finance and Monetary Policy; Labour Market; and Development. There is equal tripartite (government, business and labour) representation in each chamber. Significantly, all legislation relating to labour, economic and development policy has to be considered by NEDLAC and consensus sought before it is presented to Parliament. A lot of interest has been shown by other SADC countries in the NEDLAC structure. Already, instances of social dialogue are apparent in at least three countries in their efforts to reform labour law, particularly dispute resolution law.[56]

As Dennis Davis and others have argued, social rights are not an agenda of the past.[57] I would add that, in spite of a globalising world that expects countries to adapt and respond to new imperatives, the future of labour law in Southern Africa depends on going beyond 'borrowing and bending,' to embrace the realities of deprivation and social needs.

[54] The South African Constitution is particularly forthright in this respect: see ss 26–29, and in particular, s 23 relating to fair labour practices.
[55] National Economic, Development and Labour Council Act (35 of 1994).
[56] Lesotho and Swaziland have already set up similar social dialogue and joint decision-making bodies in respect of dispute resolution. Botswana and Namibia have similar legislation in the pipeline.
[57] DM Davis, P Macklem and G Mundlak, 'Social Rights, Social Citizenship, and Transformative Constitutionalism: A Comparative Assessment' in Joanne Conaghan *et al* (eds), *Labour Law in an Era of Globalization: Transformative Practices and Possibilities* (Oxford, Oxford University Press, 2002) 534.

14

The End of Labour Law as We Have Known It?

T O BEGIN WITH, I should tell you that the areas of labour law that I shall be concerned with here have already received the attention of two distinguished scholars.[1]

We now live in a globalised world in which there exists one solitary superpower and very many powerful multi-national enterprises, without any strong countervailing forces. It is possible, I suppose, to see globalisation as a largely benign force, as was done in a recent TUC publication on globalisation.[2] Reading it was rather like reading a version of the story of *Little Red Riding Hood* without any mention of the Wolf.

The USA is clearly determined to exercise a dominant role, culturally, economically and politically, disregarding where necessary any prior legal restraints and to ensure that no countervailing power emerges internationally. Michael Meacher, former Environment Minister in the British government, said recently: 'The biggest single geopolitical issue today is the over-weening power of the US in a unipolar world and the problem of how it should be

*I should like to thank the following people, who have no shared responsibility for the views expressed here, for the help I have received in the preparation of this chapter: Monica Evans, International Labour Office, London; Professor Keith Ewing; Dave Feichert, Brussels Office, TUC; Professor Bob Hepple; Dr Sonia McKay; Professor Gillian Morris; Professor Niall O'Higgins; David Wills, Squire Law Library, Cambridge; and Peter Zawada, Squire Law Library, Cambridge.

[1] Lord Wedderburn, 'Common Law, Global Law' in Bob Hepple (ed), *Social and Labour Rights in a Global Context: International and Comparative Perspectives* (Cambridge, Cambridge University Press, 2002) 19–54; Bob Hepple, *Labour Law, Inequality and Global Trade* (Amsterdam, Hugo Sinzheimer Intitute, 2002), and Bob Hepple, *Labour Laws and Global Trade,* (Oxford, Hart Publishing, 2004).

[2] *Globalisation: Myths and Realities* (London, Trades Union Congress, 2002). A more balanced critique of globalisation can be found in Martin Khor, *Rethinking Globalization: Critical Issues and Policy Choices* (London, Zed Books, 2001). This book was first published by the United Nations Conference on Trade and Development as *UNCTAD* Discussion Paper no 147 (April 2000). UNCTAD is a notably free-thinking UN agency. For a critical review of the TUC publication, see Steve French (2003) 10(2) *International Union Rights* 32.

handled by all other nations'[3] Will Hutton, Chief Executive of the Work Foundation and former editor-in-chief of the *Observer*, has recently written[4]: 'If the rest of the world is not careful, our future will be to accept globalisation almost entirely on American conservative terms and around American conservative pre-occupations.'

My starting point is to ask the question: how did the state of labour law, both internationally and at the national level, at the end of the twentieth century come about? In my view, the answer is that national and international labour law are the results of a balance of power, primarily between organised labour and organised capital, mediated by governments. The fear of social revolution has always been a major factor in the achievement of this balance of power. Professor Richard Falk has expressed a similar view:

> Crudely put, the humanization of industrial capitalism since the mid-nineteenth century must be understood predominantly as an outcome of struggle, centring upon the emergence in civil society of a robust labour movement increasingly influenced by radical thought, especially by the Marxist critique of capitalist exploitation combined with revolutionary optimism about the socialist future of humanity.[5]

What has been achieved by workers over the past centuries has largely been as a result of long and sometimes bloody conflict. As some states became more democratic, overt violence became less significant. But overt violence and violent repression continues to play a major role in the struggle for reasonable labour standards in many countries of the world today, such as Colombia.[6] Countervailing power, real or perceived, has played a vital role in bringing about a reasonable level of labour standards. The changes over recent years include the demise of the Soviet Union, whose implicit threat of social revolution was one of the moving factors in the establishment of the International Labour Organisation. While the Soviet Union existed, it was possible for states to enjoy some degree of independence of the West and of the Soviet Union by playing off one side against the other. There are even examples of interesting developments in labour law occurring in non-aligned states, independent of the major powers, such as a degree of worker-management in the Federal Republic of Yugoslavia. Recently, the Prime Minister of Malaysia lamented the

---

[3] *Guardian*, Supplement, 21 June 2003 (London).
[4] *The World We're In* (London, Abacus, 2003) 443.
[5] Richard Falk, 'On the Political Relevance of Global Civil Society' in John H Dunning (ed), *Making Globalization Good: The Moral Challenges of Global Capitalism* (Oxford, Oxford University Press, 2003) 280–300.
[6] See the annual publication, *Survey of Violations of Trade Union Rights* (Brussels, International Confederation of Free Trade Unions).

demise of communism, which he abominates, because the existence of the Soviet Union in the past had created for Third World countries a limited freedom of action to resist pressure from one camp or the other.

The existence of the Soviet Union even had some beneficial impacts on capitalism. The distinguished British historian, Eric Hobsbawm, pithily summarised the results of the interaction between capitalism and the Soviet Union:[7]

> It is one of the ironies of this strange [twentieth] century that the most lasting results of the October [1917] revolution [in Russia], whose object was the global overthrow of capitalism, was to save its antagonist, both in war and in peace ... by providing it with the incentive — fear — to reform itself after the Second World War; and, by establishing popularity of economic planning, furnishing it with some of the procedures for its reform.

The weakening of trade union power is another important feature of recent developments. This is due to many reasons. The concentration of large numbers of workers in single places, shipyards, mines, etc, has ceased to be a major feature of working class organisation. An increase in the service and financial sectors and other occupations such as tele-selling, which have no tradition of solidarity or union organisation, is significant. Also important is the welcome entry into the labour force of groups of workers such as women, immigrants, etc, which likewise have no tradition of organisation. Again, the rising affluence of many workers in the advanced industrial countries has weakened their sense of identity with less well-off groups in the community, and encouraged an apparent community of interest with the better-off.[8] It was the recognition of the declining significance of the traditional industrial working class that has led to the rise of new political configurations such as New Labour.

The USA is committed to an extreme form of economic liberalism which threatens to erode nationally and internationally existing labour standards, except where it may serve the economic interests of the USA to invoke minimum legal standards to protect those same economic interests. We have the apparent paradox of the USA insisting, through various devices, upon its trading partners complying with core international labour standards as a price they must pay for the privilege of trading with

---

[7] Interview in the *Guardian*, 15 October 1994 (London).

[8] For a discussion of union power and changes in the labour force see Eric Hobsbawm, *Age of Extremes: The Short Twentieth Century 1914–1991* (London, Michael Joseph, 1994) 266–67, 302–13 and 415. See also, for the unevenness of these developments, Kim Moody, *Workers in a Lean World: Unions in the International Economy* (London, Verso, 1997), Ch 9. This book also contains an important account of the reaction of trade unions and trade unionists to globalisation.

the USA. The motivation for this practice, which is of long standing, is not to advance the interests of foreign workers so much as to protect the interests of American workers. Under the heading of 'international fair labour standards,' minimum labour standards have been added to many American trade laws and agreements, including the Caribbean Basin Economic Recovery Act 1998, the Generalised System of Preferences, recent free trade agreements such as the North American Free Trade Area and various bilateral free trade agreements.[9] A recent example is the Singapore Free Trade Agreement. Article 17.1 ('Statement of Shared Commitment') provides:

> The Parties reaffirm their obligations as members of the International Labour Organisation and their commitments under the ILO Declaration on Fundamental Principles and Rights at Work and its Follow-up. Each Party shall strive to ensure that such labor principles and the internationally recognised labor rights set forth in Article 17.7 are recognized and protected by domestic law.

Article 17.2 provides inter alia:

> The Parties recognize that it is inappropriate to encourage trade and *investment* by weakening or reducing the protections afforded in domestic labor laws.

These provisions are of a kind commonly utilised in American fair trade agreements. They require some comment. Article 17.7 enumerating the minimum labour standards follows the formula used in the ILO Declaration on Fundamental Principles and Rights at Work but adds to them 'acceptable conditions of work with respect to minimum wages, hours of work, and occupational safety and health.' This is a welcome addition but it is doubtful whether it goes as far as the principle 'labour is not a commodity' as embodied in the Philadelphia Declaration 1944.[10] It is doubtful, also, whether the additional words embody the detailed safety standards laid down in the relevant international labour Conventions. The second departure from the ILO Declaration is that labour standards are not only not to be used for 'protectionist trade purposes' but also to prevent the weakening of minimum labour standards to encourage investment.

---

[9] For a discussion, see R Michael Gadbaw and Michael T Medwig, 'Multinational Enterprises and International Labor Standards: Which Way for Development Jobs?' in Lance A Compa and Stephen F Diamond (ed), *Human Rights, Labor, and International Trade* (Philadelphia, University of Pennsylvania Press, 1996) 141–62.

[10] P O'Higgins, 'Labour is not a Commodity' : An Irish Contribution to International Labour Law' (1997) 26 *Industrial Law Journal* 225.

The imposition of such conditions on American trading partners is not always welcome. Recently, Australia has objected. The former Australian Trade Minister, Peter Cook, said recently:[11]

> Australia has resisted mixing labour standards with trade negotiations in the past, and the US approach to this free trade deal [with Australia] involves them for the first time. The weird feature of this agreement is that a conservative administration in Washington is seeking to impose ILO core labour standards on a conservative administration in Canberra.

The USA at the end of 2002 had ratified only 14 ILO Conventions. These included the Abolition of Forced Labour Convention 1957 (No 105) (ratified 1991); the Tripartite Consultation (International Labour Standards) Convention 1976 (No 144) (ratified 1988), and the Worst Forms of Child Labour Convention 1999 (No 182) (ratified 1999). The USA has not ratified the Freedom of Association and Protection of the Right to Organise Convention 1948 (No 87) and the Right to Organise and Collective Bargaining Convention 1949 (No 98), although these latter two Conventions are part of the core international labour standards binding upon all states, as embodied in the ILO's Declaration on Fundamental Principles and Rights at Work and its Follow-up.[12] Non-compliance with these two Conventions has been a matter for discussion and criticism in the Report of Human Rights Watch in 2001.[13]

The relationship between the USA and the International Labour Organisation has been long and fractious. The USA has long been sceptical, if not contemptuous, of involvement in international organisations such as the United Nations and its specialised agencies. This, in part, has been due to a lack of widespread popular knowledge of the significance and role of these organisations. In the case of the ILO, difficulties arose shortly after the Second World War because of the membership of the Soviet Union in that organisation. In 1970, the USA suspended payments of its membership dues to the ILO because the Director-General of the ILO (Dr CW Jenks) had appointed a Soviet national to the prestigious post of an Assistant Director-General. Despite widespread opposition in the State Department and among American diplomats, the USA withheld payment of its dues.[14]

---

[11] *The Australian*, 1 May 2003 (Sydney).

[12] International Labour Office Geneva, 1998. The text of the Declaration may also be found in KD Ewing and Tom Sibley, *International Trade Union Rights for the New Millenium* (London, Institute of Employment Rights, 2001) 60–63.

[13] *Unfair Advantage: Workers' Freedom of Association in the United States under International Human Rights Standards* (Washington, Human Rights Watch, 2000). There is an important discussion of this report by many contributors in the *British Journal of Industrial Relations* in the years 2001 and 2002.

[14] Stephen M Schwebel, 'The United States Assaults the ILO' (1971) 65 *American Journal of International Law* 136.

Ultimately, however, arrears of dues were paid off by 1976. Apart from the appointment of a Soviet national there were other background reasons for the withholding of the American subscription, in particular, the accusation of the application of double standards by the ILO. In 1977, the USA withdrew from membership of the ILO. On this occasion, the reasons were:

(1)   double standards : the alleged failure of the ILO to condemn violations of labour standards in communist countries while criticising the behaviour of some democratic countries;

(2)   lack of due process : the condemnation of the conduct as regards labour standards by some states without first conducting a formal investigation of the facts;

(3)   tripartitism : the participation as workers' delegates of people from trade unions in communist countries who were not seen to be clearly independent of their governments, and

(4)   politicisation : the raising of issues, seen by the USA as being purely political, in respect of American conduct over the war in Vietnam and of Israeli treatment of Arab workers.[15]

After three years' absence, the USA returned to membership of the ILO in 1980. The account given above illustrates the deliberate and overt use by the USA of its economic power, paying as it does one-quarter of the annual income of the ILO, to seek to influence the conduct of the ILO. Other states, too, from time to time where they are significant contributors to the ILO income, have subjected the ILO to implicit threats of suspension of payment of dues.

Evidence of continuing uncertainty of the US administration's attitude towards the ILO may be found in an article entitled 'ILO's affrontery' by Arnold Beichman in *The Washington Times* of the 18 June 2003. Arnold Beichman, a Hoover Institution research fellow, is a columnist for *The Washington Times*. Mr Beichman writes that there is a problem with the ILO:

> The U.N. International Labor Organisation, winner of the 1946 Nobel peace prize, was founded in 1919. It is the only surviving major creation of the Treaty of Versailles that brought the League of Nations into being, and it became the first specialized agency of the U.N. in 1946. Its self-described mandate is to promote social justice and internationally recognized human and labor rights.
>
> Ok, enough history. So what's the problem?
>
> The problem is that like so many U.N. institutions, the ILO is in the process of betraying its mandate as it did in the days when the Soviet Union and its satellites dominated the politics of the ILO. This time, the betrayal is the work of the Organization of the Islamic Conference. More below.

---

[15] For a very good discussion of USA/ILO relations, see Walter Galenson, *The International Labour Organisation: An American View* (Madison, University of Wisconsin Press, 1981).

The ILO, headquartered in Geneva, is endowed with two sacred writs: Convention No. 87, which among its articles says 'workers and employers are guaranteed the right to establish and ... to join organizations of their own choosing.'

Convention No. 98 protects workers against anti-union discrimination and encourages collective bargaining. These rights are respected in democratic countries and flouted in communist or theocratic countries. There are no genuine free-trade unions in one-party states anymore than there are strikes or collective bargaining.

Nevertheless, the Soviet Union and Communist China were not only ILO members but they dominated the organization's proceedings as the 56-member Arab and Muslim OIC does today.

Conditions in those days got so bad that in 1975 George Meany, the then AFL-CIO president, withdrew the American labor delegates from the ILO. Meany's action forced the U.S. government to withdraw as well and to stop dues payments to the ILO, which represented a loss of one-quarter of the ILO budget. The AFL-CIO returned to the ILO when it reformed itself. With Muslim-Arab power now in the ascendant, it is time to consider another withdrawal, assuming that the ILO is reformable.

For what the Arab-Muslim-dominated ILO has this month organized in the annual International Labor Conference is the setting up, according to the National Post, a special critical session focused entirely on Israel for alleged mistreatment of Palestinian workers within Israel and the so-called occupied territories. This is politicization of a U.N. agency where some of the worst violators of human and labor rights are members, notably Communist China. This politicization has now been carried to an extreme by a group of countries where few, if any, free trade unions exist. And, of course, there are no special ILO sessions on labor conditions in, say, Saudi Arabia or Syria or Iran. Few Arab countries have free, independent trade unions. But in the ILO as in the U.N. General Assembly Israel is the culprit. Always.

Even worse is how the ILO ignores the plight of women workers in Arab and Muslim countries. ILO resolutions demand elimination of discrimination in the workplace but the percentage of women workers in these countries are among the smallest internationally in the low 'teens compared with Israel, where women comprised in 2000 almost half the workforce, according to ILO figures.

Following the 1975 AFL-CIO withdrawal from the ILO, then Secretary of State Henry Kissinger wrote:'The ILO Conference for some years now has shown an appallingly selective concern in the applications of the ILO's basic conventions on freedom of association and forced labor. It pursues the violations of human rights in some member states. It grants immunity from such citation to others. This seriously undermines the credibility of the ILO's support of freedom of association, which is central to its tripartite structure, and strengthens the proposition that these human rights are not universally applicable, but rather are subject to different interpretations for states with different political systems.'

Should free trade unions participate in the ILO? Is it time for free trade unions to walk out once more, and not participate in a mass hypocrisy called the International Labor Conference?

Why not?

(Copyright © 2003 News World Communications, Inc. Reprinted with permission of *The Washington Times*.)

It is not known how far Mr Beichman's views have been adopted by the current US administration, but they are shared by an increasing number of American neoconservatives disillusioned as they are with the United Nations and all its works. It should be noted that Mr Beichman complains of the role of the ILO concerning itself with the situation of workers in the occupied Arab territories. This is not the result of domination of the ILO by Arabs and Muslims. There is no such domination. But it is the result of the basic principle of the ILO that peace is dependent on social justice. Nonetheless, the ILO's concern with the situation of Arab workers echoes the complaint that the ILO was biased in the past against Israel and which was one of the complaints which led the USA to cease to be a member of the ILO in 1977. There have been a number of reports as appendices to the annual *Reports of the ILO Director-General to the International Labour Conferences*, concerned with the position of Arab workers in the occupied territories.[16]

We need now to consider what the attitude of the current US administration is towards international labour standards. The prospect is not encouraging At one stroke of a pen, President Bush deprived 170,000 public servants on their transfer to the Department of Inland Security of all rights to union membership, collective bargaining and civil service protection. The US Department of Homeland Security has taken the view that any interruption of work on the docks would be treated as a threat to national security and that the government was prepared to deploy the military to replace striking workers. 'According to a principle elaborated by the US Defence Secretary, Donald Rumsfeld, in the war against terrorism, all commercial cargo, not only goods directly intended for military use, would be considered to have a military importance.' US trade unions have been subject to increasing administrative burdens to record all expense over $2,000 incurred in organising workers. While under the current US Budget funds have been cut for the policing of health and safety laws, child labour regulations, and violations of the minimum wage, expenditure has been dramatically increased for the auditing and investigation of trade unions.[17]

---

[16] Eg *Report of the Director-General to the International Labour Conference, 85th Session 1997, The ILO, Standard Setting and Globalization* (Geneva, International Labour Office, 1997) App. For another view of the problem of Arab workers, see Guy Mundlak, 'Power-breaking or Power-entrenching Law? The Regulation of Palestinian Workers in Israel' (1999) 20 *Comparative Labor Law and Policy Journal* 569.

[17] This paragraph is based upon Rick Fantasia and Kim Boss, 'US: State of the Unions,' *Le Monde diplomatique*, June 2003 (Paris).

The USA appears to be in some difficulty over its compliance with Convention for the Abolition of Forced Labour Convention 1957 (No 105), which, as we have seen, it has ratified. Criticism from the International Confederation of Free Trade Unions has centred on widely varying conditions of employment in prison industries in different states, as well as alleging forced labour of migrant workers. The relevant ILO body commenting on the latter has said in 2002:[18]

> Some of the employment in territories under the control of the USA Government amounts to forced labour. Since the 1980s the USA Commonwealth of the Northern Mariana Islands has developed a garment industry based on the ability of these islands to ship products duty free and without quotas to the USA. This status, together with local control of wage and immigration laws, has had the practical effect of introducing a system of indentured servitude into the territory. Local authorities permit foreign-owned companies to recruit thousands of foreign workers, mainly young women from Thailand, China, the Philippines and Bangladesh. These workers are recruited by private agencies that demand exorbitant fees from these workers. Fees are either paid in advance or are deducted from pay in an arrangement that requires the workers to remain in the employ of the same manufacturer who in turn has a relationship with the recruiting agency.
>
> In addition to the abuse of fee-charging, these foreign workers are routinely required to sign employment contracts where they agree to refrain from asking for wage increases, seeking other work and from joining a union. The workers are informed that contract violations will result in dismissal as well as deportation and that the workers concerned must pay the travel expenses to return to their home country.
>
> Many similar conditions are faced by migrant domestic workers coming to the USA under the 400 various applicable employer-related visa schemes. These workers are often victims of physical abuse, face severe restriction on their freedom of movement, and work under conditions tantamount to slavery.
>
> Many migrant domestic workers are paid far less than the minimum wage, and, under the terms of their visa, face deportation for leaving their employer to escape from these oppressive conditions.
>
> There are grounds for serious concern about commercial production by prisoners in the United States and about practices amounting to forced labour by exploited migrant workers (mainly women) in United States dependent territories, and immigrant domestic workers in the United States.

There is no indication that the USA intends to remedy this situation with regard to the use of forced labour.

It should be noted that trading partners of the USA are only able to invoke the provision relating to labour standards in trade agreements if the failure to

---

[18] *International Labour Conference, Committee of Experts on the Application of Conventions and Recommendations* (Individual Observations) 2002.

comply with labour standards affects trade between the two countries. Thus, the use of forced labour in the USA to produce goods could not be invoked unless the goods produced were exported from the USA to its trading partner.

Sadly, the attitude of the UK government towards international and national labour standards is lacking in certain respects. Before the 1997 election, Tony Blair said:[19]

> It was claimed ... that employers will not be able to dismiss people on strike. Untrue. That employees will get full employment rights from their first day. Wrong. Let me state the position clearly, so that no one is in any doubt. The essential elements of the trade union legislation of the 1980s will remain. There will be no return to secondary action, flying pickets, strikes without ballots, the closed shop and all the rest. The changes that we do propose would leave British law the most restrictive on trade unions in the western world. ... As for union recognition, we have rejected the TUC proposals, which were for wider rights of representation.

There have been many improvements in British labour since 1997, but it would be difficult to identify any one of them as being the result of trade union pressure. Such pressure as there has been to improve the collective rights of workers have failed. The improvements in labour law since 1997 are either a hangover from the policy of 'Old Labour' (pre-1997), or as a result of obligations imposed upon the United Kingdom as a result of its obligations as a member of the EU. Where the United Kingdom has been faced with reforms emanating from the EU, it has often opposed them, and when they were adopted as part of European law has implemented them in a niggardly and dilatory way.[20]

As regards the United Kingdom's obligation to respect international labour standards as laid down by the ILO or under the provisions of the Council of Europe's Social Charter, the United Kingdom has remained steadfastly and shamelessly for many years in breach of its obligations in the area of the collective rights of workers, particularly as regards the right to minimum notice and the right to strike. For several decades the United Kingdom's failure to provide workers with adequate periods of notice has been recorded in the

---

[19] As quoted in John Hendy, *Union Rights and Wrongs: The Reform of Britain's Anti-union Laws* (London, Institute of Employment Rights, 2001) 15.

[20] Richard Corbett, *Fairness at Work: Labour — Leader or Laggard in Europe?* (Leeds, Richard Corbett, 2002).

[21] See Lenia Samuel, *Fundamental Social Rights: Case law of the European Social Charter* (2nd edn, Strasbourg, Council of Europe Publishing, 2002) 94–100 (notice periods); 150–70 (right to strike).

[22] See, eg, *Report of the Committee of Experts on the Application of Conventions and Recommendations, International Labour Conference*, 78th Session 1991, Report III (Part 4A) 217–23. See, more generally, KD Ewing (ed), *Employment Rights at Work: Reviewing the Employment Relations Act 1999* (London, Institute of Employment Rights, 2001) ch 4.

case law of the Council of Europe's Social Charter. The United Kingdom's failure to implement its obligations to recognise the right to strike has been the subject of comment over many years by the supervisory organs of the Social Charter[21] and of the International Labour Organisation.[22]

The latest example of the United Kingdom's intransigence and its refusal to recognise proper minimum labour standards over notice periods and the right to strike is the United Kingdom's obdurate refusal to allow the Charter of Fundamental Rights in the draft Constitution of the European Union to be given legal force.[23] The significance of the government's opposition to the Bill of Rights provisions in the proposed European Constitution is not in reality an opposition to these provisions being legally obligatory, but it is opposition to their enforcement by the European Court of Justice. These rights, as embodied in relevant ILO Conventions and the Council of Europe's Social Charter, are already legally obligatory but the machinery for their enforcement currently lacks teeth. Their embodiment in the proposed Constitution would guarantee an effective judicial machinery for their enforcement.

The International Labour Organisation itself has been changing in its policies as a result of globalisation. On the whole, it has tended to emphasise the possible benefits of globalisation. It has deliberately reduced the emphasis on the elaboration of new international labour Conventions and given preference to the adoption of Recommendations which are, of course, guidelines rather than legally obligatory. The ILO has also recognised the importance of non-state actors in the preservation of international labour standards. This recognises the growing importance of the role of non-governmental organisations (NGOs) in promoting the implementation of international labour standards.[24]

Where is the countervailing power to the USA and the multi-national corporations to come from? As regards state countervailing power, there is no immediate prospect of the emergence of such a state. Divisions in the European Union between those states who wish to ally themselves with the interests of the USA, such as Britain, Spain and Italy, as well as the 'new Europe,' comprising the recent new members of the EU, on the one hand, and on the other hand countries like France, which seek to encourage an independent role for the EU, will ensure for the moment that the European Union, will not become that countervailing force. It is not insignificant that the recent new membership in the EU of countries in Eastern Europe has been accompanied by a lowering of labour standards in those countries.[25]

---

[23] *The European Convention*, Brussels, 27 May 2003 (Document CONV 725) vol II, Title IV: Solidarity, eg Art II-28: 'Workers and Employers ... have ... the right ... in cases of conflicts of interest, to take collective action to defend their interests, including strike action.'
[24] See Report of the Director-General, above n 16.
[25] Stefan Clauwaert, Wiebke Duvel and Isabelle Schomann (ed), *The Community Social Aquis in Labour Law in the CEECS and Beyond: Fighting Deregulation, Conference Report, 11/12 October 2002 Brussels* (Brussels, European Trade Union Institute, 2003).

If countervailing power to balance the power of the USA and of multi-national enterprises is not likely to come from a state or states, where else is it to be found? Can it be found in international organisations such as the ILO? The reality is that the financial dependence of the ILO on continuing American membership will ensure that this will not happen. Could trade unions, including the international trade Secretariats,[26] come to represent countervailing power? For trade unions, there are several problems. They would need to have the ability to engage in transnational collective bargaining and, above all, in international solidarity action across frontiers. The national legislation of many states tends to operate in a way to inhibit cross-frontier collaborative strike action.[27] The European Union itself, where the EU gives preference to the interests of trade as against the right to strike where international trade is concerned, will also operate as a barrier to international solidarity action.[28] Can international trade Secretariats, the International Confederation of Free Trade Unions and other similar bodies make a contribution to countervailing power? There is already small but significantly growing evidence that such bodies are engaging in transnational collective bargaining, contributing to pressure for the 'enforcement' of corporate 'fair trade' codes and corporate social responsibility.[29] Declining union membership in advanced industrial countries will tend to lessen the possibility of union power coming to represent international countervailing power. One of the problems facing movements to protect labour standards is that the international organisations that they may seek to influence, such as the World Bank, the International Monetary Fund and the World Trade Organisation, suffer from a serious democratic deficit in their constitutions.[30] Can the increasingly influential non-governmental organisations represent countervailing power? The dependence of some NGOs upon state financial support renders this less likely. In the United Kingdom,. the Institute of Employment Rights has published *A Charter of*

---

[26] It is understood that the misleading term 'international trade Secretariats' used to describe international trade union bodies such as the Public Services International is being replaced by the new term 'global union federations.' See (2003) 2/03 *Focus on the Public Services* 14.

[27] Paul Germanotta, *Protecting Worker Solidarity Action: A Critique of International Labour Law* (London, Institute of Employment Rights, 2002).

[28] See Lord Wedderburn, above n 1, 44–45.

[29] For an interesting example of cooperation between an NGO and a trade union, *see Workers' Rights in the Global Economy: The Need for a Social Clause* (Dublin, Trocaire (The Catholic Agency for World Development) Services Industrial Professional Technical Union (SIPTU), 1997).

[30] See *Trade Justice: A Campaign Handbook* (London, Trade Justice Movement, 2002). On the World Trade Organisation in particular, see Martin Kor *et al*, *WTO and Global Trading System: Development Impacts and Reform Proposals* (London, Zed Books, 2003), and Fatoumata Jawara and Aileen Kwa, *Behind the Scenes at the WTO: The Real World of International Trade Negotiations* (London, Zed Books, 2003). See also Richard Peet (ed), *Unholy Trinity: The IMF, World Bank and WTO* (London, Zed Books, 2003).

Workers' Rights[31] based upon international labour standards as well as reforms needed to readjust the statutory balance of power between workers and employers.

There is, however, a growing movement represented by the meetings of the World Social Forum at Porto Alegre, which suggests that an effective countervailing power may emerge. Represented at Porto Alegre were groups like Oxfam, Corpwatch and Global Exchange, Attac (France), the International Rivers Network, the Congress of South African Trade Unions and other unions, World Forum on Education, academics, and activists concerned with the relief of debt in the Third World, the protection of the environment, consumers, anti-global and anti-capitalist groups, indigenous local movements like the Zapatistas, which together may come to develop a sufficiently solid common front to become an adequate countervailing power, at least in particular communities and nations. Programmes were presented at the World Social Forum to control transnational corporations and to promote labour standards nationally and internationally as a more effective opposition to globalisation.[32]

To put it in perhaps old-fashioned terms, the balance of power between Labour and Capital arrived at in the course of the twentieth century has now been changed to the benefit of Capital as a result of the growing influence of economic liberalism represented in its most powerful form by the USA. There is, however, a growing movement of opposition which has not yet achieved the ability significantly to readjust the balance in favour of Labour.

---

[31] KD Ewing and John Hendy (ed), *A Charter of Workers'* Rights (London, Institute of Employment Rights, 2002).
[32] William F Fisher and Thomas Ponniah (ed), *Another World is Possible: Popular Alternatives to Globalization at the World Social Forum* (London, Zed Books, 2003).

Bibliography of the Writings of Professor Sir Bob Hepple QC, FBA*

BOOKS

RACE, *Jobs and the Law in Britain* (London, Allen Lane/Penguin Press, 1968). Second edn Law and Society Series, (Harmondsworth, Penguin, 1970) 342 pp.

Individual Employment Law (with P O'HIGGINS) (London, Sweet and Maxwell, 1971). Second edn, *sub nom Employment Law* (1975). Third edn (1979) (sole author). Fourth edn (1981) (sole author) 430 pp.

Public Employee Trade Unionism in the United Kingdom: The Legal Framework (with P O'HIGGINS) (Ann Arbor, Institute of Labor and Industrial Relations, University of Michigan, 1971) (sole author of Part II, chs 1–3, pp 39–93, ch V, pp 105–57, Part III, pp 163–210).

Laws Against Strikes (with O KAHN-FREUND) (London, Fabian Society, 1972) (sole author chs 4–8, pp 18–52).

A Bibliography of the Literature on British and Irish Labour Law (with P O'HIGGINS and J M NEESON) (London, Mansell, 1975) 331 pp.

Labour Law in Great Britain and Ireland: A Companion Volume to the Bibliography of the Literature on British and Irish Labour Law to 1978 (with J HEPPLE, P O'HIGGINS, P STIRLING) (London, Sweet and Maxwell, 1981) 131 pp.

Equal Pay and Industrial Tribunals (with digest of cases by SONIA MACKAY AND GILLIAN S MORRIS) (London, Sweet and Maxwell, 1984) 66 pp.

The Making of Labour Law in Europe: A Comparative Study of Nine Countries up to 1945 (London, Mansell, 1986) 412 pp (editor, and author of 'Introduction' pp1–30, ch 3 'Welfare Legislation and Wage Labour,' pp 114–53, and Appendices pp 301–59).

Labour Law and Industrial Relations in Great Britain (with S FREDMAN) (Deventer, Kluwer, 1977). A revised version of the monograph on 'Great Britain' in *International Encyclopaedia for Labour Law and Industrial Relations* (R Blanpain (ed)) (Deventer, Kluwer, 1977); revised edn (1980); revised edn (with S Fredman) (1986) 295 pp; revised edn (with S Fredman) (1992); revised edn (with S Fredman and G Truter) (2002) 313 pp.

---

* Shorter articles, case notes, notes on legislation, working papers and conference papers are not included in this bibliography.

Tort: Cases and Materials (with MH MATTHEWS) (London, Butterworths, 1974). Second edn (1980). Third edn (1985). Fourth edn (1991) 956 pp. Fifth edn (with D HOWARTH AND J A O'SULLIVAN) (2001) 1151 pp.

Foundations of the Law of Tort (with G WILLIAMS) (London, Butterworths, London, 1976). Second edn (1984) 230 pp. Japanese and Italian translations have been published.

Working Time: A New Legal Framework? Employment Paper no 3 (London, Institute for Public Policy Research, 1991) 32 pp.

Discrimination: The Limits of Law (editor with E SZYSZCZAK and contributor) (London, Mansell, 1992) 481 pp.

European Social Dialogue: Alibi or Opportunity? (London, Institute of Employment Rights, 1993) 54 pp.

Human Rights and Labour Law: Essays for Paul O'Higgins (editor with K D EWING and C A GEARTY and contributor) (London, Mansell, 1994) 367 pp.

Fundamental Social Rights: Proposals for the European Union (with R BLANPAIN, S SCIARRA and M WEISS) (Leuven, Peeters, 1996) 22 pp. German translation (*KritV* 78, Heft4/1995).

Equality: A New Framework: Report of the Independent Review of the Enforcement of UK Anti-Discrimination Legislation (with M COUSSEY and T CHOUDHURY) (Oxford, Hart Publishing, 2000) xiv + 147 pp.

Tackling Religious Discrimination: Practical Implications for Policy-Makers and Legislators (with T CHOUDHURY) (London, Home Office, Research, Development and Statistics Directorate, 2001) 74 pp.

Social and Labour Rights in a Global Context: International and Comparative Perspectives (editor and contributor) (Cambridge, Cambridge University Press, 2002) 273 pp.

Labour Law, Inequality and Global Trade (Amsterdam, Hugo Sinzheimer Institute, 2002) 35 pp.

Rights at Work, Discussion Paper DP/147/2003 (Geneva, International Institute for Labour Studies, 2003) 28 pp.

CONTRIBUTIONS TO EDITED BOOKS

'Economic and Racial Legislation' in HR HAHLO and E KAHN (eds), *The British Commonwealth: The Development of its Law and Constitutions, vol 5. The Union of South Africa* (London, Stevens, 1960) 760–813.

'Employment' in S ABBOTT (ed), *Prevention of Racial Discrimination in Britain* (London, Oxford University Press, 1971) ch 6, 155–74.

'Liability and Protection' in the title 'Administrative Law' in *Halsbury's Laws of England* (4th edn, London, Butterworths, 1973) vol 1, s 5, paras 188–300.

'Great Britain' in JJ Loewenberg (ed), *Compulsory Arbitration: An International Comparison* (Lexington, Mass, DC Heath and Company, 1976) ch 3, 83–115.

'The Temporary Worker' comparative report in W ALBEDA, R BLANPAIN and GMJ VELDKAMP (eds), *Temporary Work in Modern Society: A Comparative Study* Netherlands, Kluwer, 1978) 493–511.

'Great Britain' (with BW NAPIER) in W ALBEDA, R BLANPAIN and GMJ VELDKAMP (eds), *Temporary Work in Modern Society: A Comparative Study* (Netherlands, Kluwer, 1978) 186–226.

'Conflict of Laws on Employment Relations within the EEC', in K LIPSTEIN (ed), *Harmonisation of Private International Law by the EEC* (London, Institute of Advanced Legal Studies, 1978) 39–49.

'Work Discipline and the Law' in *Dysciplina Pracy* (Wroclaw, University of Wroclaw, 1978) 85–100.

'The Freedom of the Worker to Organise in the UK' in *The Freedom of the Worker to Organise* (Heidelberg, Max Planck Institute, 1980) 1001–56.

'Trade, Labour and Employment' (with JW CRONIN) in Lord Evershed (ed), *Atkin's Encyclopaedia of Court Forms in Civil Proceedings* (2nd edn London, Butterworths, 1979), vol 38, 245–436. Third edn (with JOHN BOWERS) (1986) 109–340.

'A Functional Approach to Dismissal Laws' in F GAMILLSCHEG, BA HEPPLE, J DE GIVY and JM VERDIER (eds), *In Memoriam Sir Otto Kahn-Freund* (Munich, CH Beck, 1980) 477–91.

'Individual Labour Law' in GS BAIN (ed), *Industrial Relations in Britain* (Oxford, Basil Blackwell, 1983) 393–417.

'Security of Employment' in R BLANPAIN (ed), *Comparative Labour Law and Industrial Relations* (Deventer, Kluwer, 1982). Second edn (1985). Third edn *sub nom* 'Flexibility and Security of Employment' (1987). Fourth edn (1990) 167–95. Fifth edn (R Blanpain and C Engels (eds)) (1993) 255–80. Sixth edn (1998) 277–303.

'European Labour Law: The European Communities' in R BLANPAIN (ed), *Comparative Labour Law and Industrial Relations*. Fourth edn (Deventer, Kluwer, 1990) 293–316. Fifth edn (R BLANPAIN and C ENGELS (eds)) (1993) 143–66.

'Labour Law and Public Employees in Britain' in LORD WEDDERBURN and WT MURPHY (eds), *Labour Law and the Community: Perspectives for the 1980s* (London, Institute for Advanced Legal Studies, 1983), 67–83.

'Harmonisation of Labour Law in the European Communities' in J ADAMS (ed), *Essays for Clive Schmitthoff* (Abingdon, Professional Books, 1983) 14–28.

'Unfair Dismissals Legislation in Great Britain' in J STIEBER and J BLACKBURN (eds), *Protecting Unorganised Employees Against Unjust Discharge* (East Lansing, Michigan State University, 1983) 135–46.

'Tort' in Jane Allen (ed), *All England Law Reports Annual Review* (London, Butterworths, 1983–1990). 1982, 297–312; 1983, 327–42; 1984, 288–96; 1985, 294–311; 1986, 309–20; 1987, 284–301; 1988, 321–35; 1989, 329–41.

'Dictionary of Labour Relations Law' in BA HEPPLE and P O'HIGGINS (eds), *Encyclopedia of Labour Relations Law* (London, Sweet & Maxwell, 1985) vol I, 1001–148.

'Practice and procedure' in *Sex Discrimination and Equal Pay* (London, College of Law, 1984) 29–43.

'The Scope and Function of the English Law of Tort' in WE BUTLER and VN KUDRIATSEV (eds), *Comparative Law and the Legal System: Historical and Socio-Legal Perspectives* (New York, Oceana Publications, 1985). Russian translation (Moscow, 1985).

'Lord Donovan' in LORD BLAKE (ed), *Dictionary of National Biography Supplement 1971–80* (Oxford, Oxford University Press, 1986); revised in *New Dictionary of National Biography* (forthcoming).

'The Monitoring of Labour Legislation' (with W BROWN), Foreword to P FOSH and CR LITTLER (eds), *Industrial Relations and the Law in the 1980s* (Aldershot, Gower, 1986) ix–xv.

'Some Problems of Comparing Socialist and Capitalist Systems of Labour Law' in WE BUTLER, BA HEPPLE and AC NEAL (eds), *Comparative Labour Law: Anglo-Soviet Perspectives* (Aldershot, Gower, 1987) 22–28. Russian translation (Moscow, 1987).

'Great Britain' in MG ROOD (ed), *Fifty Years of Labour Law and Social Security* (Deventer, Kluwer, 1986) 101–20.

'The Judicial Process in Claims for Equal Pay and Equal Treatment in the UK' in C MCCRUDDEN (ed), *Women, Employment and European Equality Law* (London, Eclipse, 1988) 143–60.

'Deregulation and the Rule of Law: An English View' in MAP BOVENS, W DERKSEN and WJ WITTEVEEN (eds), *Rechtstaat en Sturing* (Zwolle, WEJ Tjeenk Willink, 1987), 161–70.

'United Kingdom' in R BLANPAIN and E KOHLER (eds), *Legal and Contractual Limitations to Working Time in the European Community Member States* (Deventer, Kluwer, 1988) ch 11, 419–44. Second edn (with C HAKIM) (J ROJOT, R BLANPAIN and E KOHLER (eds)) (Deventer, Kluwer, 1996) 659–93.

'The Role of Trade Unions in Hiring and Dismissal' in WE BUTLER, BA HEPPLE and RW RIDEOUT (eds), *The Right to Work under English and Soviet Law* (Leicester, International Journal of Comparative Labour Law and Industrial Relations, 1988) 209–12.

'Some Problems of Comparison of Socialist and Capitalist Systems of Labour Law' in H LEWANDOWSKI (ed), *Studia Z Prawa Pracy* (dedicated to Professor Waclaw Szubert) (Warsaw Lodz, Panstowe Wysawnictwo Naukowe, 1988) 79–85.

'Part 1A: Sources and Institutions' (chs 1–7) and 'Part 1B: Restatement' (Divisions A–E.) in BA HEPPLE and P O'HIGGINS (eds), *Encyclopedia of Labour Relations Law* (London, Sweet and Maxwell, 1988–90) (Releases 98 (11 October 1988) to 104 13 April 1990) 120 pp, 248 pp and 20 pp respectively. (Note: as General Editor responsible for the design of the whole Restatement and Commentary, but author only of those sections indicated here. Some of the sections by other contributors are based on the earlier *Individual Employment Law* above.)

'Labour Law and the New Work Force' in A GLADSTONE *et al* (eds), *Labour Relations in a Changing Environment* (Berlin, Walter de Gruyter, 1991) 287–96.

'The Fall and Rise of Unfair Dismissal' in Lord McCarthy (ed), *Legal Intervention in Industrial Relations* (Oxford, Blackwell, 1992) 79–102.

'Have 25 Years of the Race Relations Acts Been a Failure?' in BA HEPPLE and E SZYSZCZAK (eds), *Discrimination: The Limits of Law* (London, Mansell 1992) 19–34.

'The Integration of Contract and Tort' in PETER BIRKS (ed), *Examining the Law Syllabus: The Core* (Oxford, Oxford University Press, 1992) 54–57.

'United Kingdom' in R BLANPAIN (ed), *Temporary Work and Labour Law of the European Community and Member States* (Deventer, Kluwer, 1993) 227–46.

'Trade Unions and Democracy in Transitional Societies: Reflections on Russia and South Africa' in KD EWING, C GEARTY and BA HEPPLE (eds), *Human Rights and Labour Law: Essays for Paul O'Higgins* (London, Mansell, 1994) 56–75.

'Equality: A Global Labour Standard' in W SENGENBERGER and D CAMPBELL (eds), *International Labour Standards and Economic Interdependence* (Geneva, International Institute for Labour Studies, 1994) 123–32.

'The ILO: Reinventing Tripartism and Universal Labour Standards' in ILO (ed), *Visions for the Future of Social Justice: Essays on the Occasion of the ILO's 75th Anniversary* (Geneva, ILO, 1994) 133–36.

'Tort Law in the Contract State', in P BIRKS (ed), *The Frontiers of Liability* (Oxford, Oxford University Press, 1994) vol 2, 71–82.

'Some Concluding Reflections' in P BIRKS (ed), *Reviewing Legal Education* (Oxford, Oxford University Press, 1994) 109–12.

'Great Britain' in R BLANPAIN and T HANAMI (eds), *Employment Security: Law and Practice* (Leuven, Peeters, 1994) 159–69.

'Freedom to Form and Join or Not Join Trade Unions' in Council of Europe (ed), *Freedom of Association* (London, Nijhoff, 1994) 161–74.

'The Development of Fundamental Social Rights in European Labour Law' in AC NEAL and S FOYN (eds), *Developing the Social Dimension of the Enlarged European Union* (Oslo, Scandanvian University Press, 1995) 23–34.

'Equality and Discrimination' in PL Davies, A LYON-CAEN, S SCIARRA AND S SIMITIS (eds), *European Community Labour Law: Principles and Perspectives* (Oxford, Clarendon Press, 1996) 237–59.

'Economic Efficiency and Social Rights', in R BLANPAIN (ed), *Law in Motion* (Deventer, Kluwer Law International, 1996) 868–79.

'The Principle of Equal Treatment in Article 119 and the Possibilities for Reform' in A DASHWOOD and S O'LEARY (eds), *The Principle of Equal Treatment in EC Law* (London, Sweet and Maxwell, 1997) 137–152.

'The Protection of Acquired Rights' in *Ongelijkheidscompensatie als roode draad in het recht: Liber Amicorum voor Prof. MG ROOD* (Leiden, University of Leiden, 1997) 311–20.

'Negligence: The Search for Coherence' in MDA FREEMAN (ed), *Law and Opinion in the Twentieth-Century: Current Legal Problems*, (Oxford, Oxford University Press, 1997) vol 50, 69–94.

'The Impact on Labour Law' in BS MARKESINIS (ed), *The Impact of the Human Rights Bill on English Law* (Oxford, Oxford University Press, 1998) 53–84.

'Towards a European Social Constitution' in C ENGELS and M WEISS (eds), *Labour Law and Industrial Relations at the Turn of the Century, Liber Amicorum for Professor Roger Blanpain* (The Hague, Kluwer Law International, 1998) 291–304.

'United Kingdom' in European Commission Directorate General for Employment, Industrial Relations and Social Affairs, *The Regulation of Working Conditions in the Member States of the European Union* (Luxembourg, Office for Official Publications of the European Communities, 1998) 235–46.

'Labour Regulation in Internationalised Markets' in S PICCIOTTO and R MAYNE (eds), *Regulating International Business* (Basingstoke, Macmillan Press, 1999) 183–202.

'The Historical Development of Collective Labour Law: Comparative Reflections' in M VAN DER LINDEN and R PRICE (eds), *The Rise and Development of Collective Labour Law* (Bern, Peter Lang, 2000) 415–36.

'Freedom of Expression and the Problem of Harassment' in J BEATSON and Y CRIPPS (eds), *Freedom of Expression and Freedom of Information* (Oxford, Oxford University Press, 2000) 177–96.

'The Principles of Subsidiarity and Proportionality in Community Social and Employment Law' in D O'KEEFE (ed), *Judicial Review in European Union Law: Liber Amicorum for Lord Slynn of Hadley,* (London, Kluwer Law International, 2000) vol 1, 639–50.

'Supporting Collective Bargaining: Some Comparative Reflections' in B TOWERS and W BROWN (eds), *Employment Relations in Britain: 25 Years of the Advisory Conciliation and Arbitration Service* (Oxford, Blackwell, 2000) 153–61.

'Workplace Regulation and Benefits' in American Bar Association and West Group, *Common Law, Common Values, Common Rights* (San Francisco, American Bar Association, 2000) 231–38.

'Enforcement: The Law and Politics of Cooperation and Compliance' in B HEPPLE (ed) *Social and Labour Rights in a Global Context: International and Comparative Perspectives* (Cambridge, Cambridge University Press, 2002) 238–57.

'Mapping International Labor Disputes: An Overview' in International Bureau of the Permanent Court of Arbitration (ed), *Labor Law Beyond Borders: ADR and the Internationalization of Labor Dispute Settlement* (The Hague, Kluwer Law International, 2003) 35–49.

'Age Discrimination in Employment: Implementing the Framework Directive 2000/78/EC' in S FREDMAN and S SPENCER, *Age as an Equality Issue: Legal and Policy Perspectives* (Oxford, Hart Publishing, 2003) 71–96.

JOURNAL ARTICLES

'The British Race Relations Acts, 1965 and 1968' (1969) 19 *University of Toronto Law Journal* 248–57.

'Labour Law' (with P O'HIGGINS) *Annual Survey of Commonwealth Law* 1968, 1969, 1970, 1971, 1972, 1973, 1974, 1975.

'Intention to Create Legal Relations' (1970) *Cambridge Law Journal* 122–37.

'Ethnic Minorities at Work' (1968) X(1) *Race* 17–30.

'The Future Protection of Migrant Workers' (1971) 1 *New Community* 47–51.

'Aliens and Administrative Justice: The Dutschke Case' (1971) 33 *Modern Law Review* 501–19.

'Union Responsibility for Shop Stewards' (1972) *Industrial Law Journal* 197–211.

'Drafting Employment Terms' (with P O'HIGGINS) (1972) 36 *Conveyancer* 77.

'The Effect of Community Law on Employment Rights' (1975) *Poly Law Review* 50–57.

'Workers' Rights in Mergers and Takeovers: The EEC Proposals' (1976) 5 *Industrial Law Journal* 197–210.

'Community Measures for the Protection of Workers Against Dismissal' (1977) 14 *Common Market Law Review* 489–500.

'Temporary Workers and the Law' (with BW NAPIER) (1978) 7 *Industrial Law Journal* 84–99.

'Lock-outs in Great Britain' (1980) (January/February) 33 *Recht der Arbeit* 25–32.

'Job Security: Some Comparative Reflections' (1980) 11 *Bulletin of Comparative Labour Relations* 231–49.

'Job Security and Industrial Relations in the United Kingdom' (1980) 11 *Bulletin of Comparative Labour Relations* 211–30.

'Tasks for Labour Law Research' (with WA BROWN) (1981) 1 *Legal Studies* 56–57. Polish translation in *Poznanie Prawy Pracy* (Wroclaw, 1981) 45–58.

'The British Employment Act 1980' (1981) (May/June) 34 *Recht der Arbeit* 164–69.

'A Right to Work?' (1981) 10 *Industrial Law Journal* 65–83. Japanese translation published 1982; Italian translation published 1983.

'The Transfer of Undertakings (Protection of Employment) Regulations' (1982) 11 *Industrial Law Journal* 29–40.

'Judging Equal Rights' (1983) 36 *Current Legal Problems* 71–90.

'The Development of Legislation on Temporary Work Since 1978: A Comparative Report' (1983) 22 *Cahiers* (International Institute for Temporary Work) 182–97.

'Equality and Prohibition of Discrimination in Great Britain' (1985) 14 *Bulletin of Comparative Labour Relations* 117–30.

'Job Security: A Legal Myth?' (1985) 4 *Journal of the Irish Society for Labour Law* 1–20.

'Do We Need the Contract of Employment?' (1986) 36 *King's Counsel* 11–31.

'Restructuring Employment Rights' (1986) 15 *Industrial Law Journal* 69–83.

'Westland Affair: What About the Workers?' (1986) 39 *Current Legal Problems* 259–68.

'The Crisis in EEC Labour Law' (1987) 16 *Industrial Law Journal* 77–87.

'Aspects of Flexibility in Labour Law' (1987) I *Zeitschrift fur auslandisches und internationales Arbeits — und Sozialrecht* 280–86.

'The Role of Neutrals in the Resolution of Shop Floor Disputes: The United Kingdom', (1987) *Comparative Labor Law Journal* 198–211 (with SIR J WOOD and TL JOHNSTON).

'The Race Relations Acts and the Process of Change' (1986) XIV *New Community* 32–39.

'Labour Courts: Some Comparative Perspectives' (1988) 41 *Current Legal Problems* 169–96.

'The Harmonisation of Labour Law in the EEC: A British perspective' (1989) (November/December) 42 *Recht der Arbeit* 348–52.

'Flexibility and Wages' (1990) 19 *Bulletin of Comparative Labour Relations* 189–206.

'EEC Labour Law in the United Kingdom: A New Approach' (1990) 18 *Industrial Law Journal* 129–43 (with A Byre)

'Discrimination and Equality of Opportunity: Northern Irish Lessons' (1990) 10 *Oxford Journal of Legal Studies* 408–21.

'The Role of Trade Unions in a Democratic Society' (1990) 11 *[South African] Industrial Law Journal* 645–54.

'Social Rights in the European Economic Community: A British Perspective' (1991) 11 *Comparative Labor Law Journal* 425–40.

'Tort' (1992) 45(I) *Current Legal Problems* 151–71 (with R O'DAIR).

'Tort' (1993) 46(I) *Current Legal Problems* 128–54 (with R O'DAIR).

'The Regulation of Working Conditions in the United Kingdom' (1994) Supplement 5/93 *Social Europe* 221–34.

'Strikes and Lock-outs in the United Kingdom' (1994) 29 *Bulletin of Comparative Labour Relations* 181–98.

'Social Values and European Law' (1995) 48(2) *Current Legal Problems* 39–61.

'The Future of Labour Law' (1995) 24 *Industrial Law Journal* 303–22.

'The Renewal of the Liberal Law Degree' (1996) 55 *Cambridge Law Journal* 470–87.

'European Rules on Dismissal Law?' (1997) 18 *Comparative Labor Law Journal* 204–28.

'New Approaches to International Labour Regulations' (1997) 26 *Industrial Law Journal* 353–66.

'Glanville Williams: Civil Obligations' (1997) 56 *Cambridge Law Journal* 440–45.

'Equality and Economic Efficiency' (1997) 18 *[South African] Industrial Law Journal* 598–608.

'Human Rights and Employment Law' (1998) 8 *Amicus Curiae* 19–23.

'Pension Rights in Business Transfers' (1998) 27 *Industrial Law Journal* 309–24 (co-author K MUMGAARD).

'Can Collective Labour Law Transplants Work?' The South African Example' (1999) 20 *[South African] Industrial Law Journal* 1–12.

'Employee Loyalty in English Law' (1999) 20 *Comparative Labor Law and Policy Journal* 205–24.

'A Race to the Top? International Investment Guidelines and Corporate Codes of Conduct' (1999) 20 *Comparative Labor Law and Policy Journal* 347–63.

'Indirect Discrimination: Interpreting *Seymour-Smith*' (1999) 58 *Cambridge Law Journal* 399–412 (co-author C BARNARD).

'Human Rights and the Contract of Employment,' *Employment Lawyers' Association 2000 Annual Lecture* (London, Employment Lawyers' Association, 2000) 20 pp.

'Substantive Equality' (2000) 59 *Cambridge Law Journal* 562–85 (co-author C BARNARD).

'Equality and Empowerment for Decent Work' (2001) 140 *International Labour Review* 5–18 (also in French and Spanish translations).

'The Employment Act 2002 and the Crisis of Individual Employment Rights' (2002) 31 *Industrial Law Journal* 245–69 (co-author GILLIAN S MORRIS).

'Race and Law in Fortress Europe' (2004) 67 *Modern Law Review* 1–15.

EDITORSHIPS

1969–71   Editor, *Bulletin of the Industrial Law Society.*
1972–77   Founding Editor, *Industrial Law Journal.*
1972–89   Joint General Editor (with Paul O'Higgins), *Encyclopedia of Labour Relations Law* (from 1990 consultant Editor and contributor) (from 1992 retitled *Sweet & Maxwell's Encyclopedia of Employment Law*).
1973–76   Note editor and editorial committee, *Cambridge Law Journal.*
1975–92   Joint General Editor (with Paul O'HIGGINS), *Studies in Labour and Social Law*
    (series of books published by Mansell)
1979–   Chief Editor, vol XV *(Labour Law), International Encyclopedia of Comparative Law* (Max-Planck Institute, Hamburg).
1989–92   Co-editor, *Current Legal Problems.*

Editorial Boards

Comparative Labor Law and Policy Journal (University of Illinois, USA); *International Journal of Comparative Labour Law and Industrial Relations* (Kluwer) (until 1999); *Industrial Law Journal* (OUP for Industrial Law Society); *Equal Opportunities Review* (IRS Publications); *Current Legal Problems* (OUP); *Cambridge Law Journal* (CUP); *British Journal of Industrial Relations* (Blackwell)(until 1999); *International Journal of Discrimination and the Law* (ABA); *Industrial Relations Journal* (Blackwell).

OTHER WORK IN THE PUBLIC DOMAIN

The Position of Coloured Workers in British Industry, Report commissioned by National Committee for Commonwealth Immigrants (London, National Committee for Commonwealth Immigrants, 1967) 50 pp.
Industrial Tribunals, Report by JUSTICE (Chairman of Committee) (London, JUSTICE, 1987) 72 pp.
The Application of EEC Labour Law in the United Kingdom (with A Byre), Report commissioned by the Directorate-General for Employment and Social Affairs of the Commission of the EC (Brussels, European Commission, 1988), 158 pp.
The Regulation of Working Conditions in the Member States of the European Communities: United Kingdom Report, Report commissioned by the Directorate-General for Employment and Social Affairs of the Commission of the EC (Brussels, European Commission, 1989) 231 pp.

Memorandum on the relevance of the Council of Europe Social Charter to the inquiry into Community accession to the European Convention on Human Rights, to Select Committee on the European Communities, House of Lords, Session 1992–93; Third Report, *Human Rights Re-examined*, HL Paper 10 (London, HMSO,) 41–47.

Memorandum and evidence on the revision of the Acquired Rights Directive 77/187/EC, to the Select Committee on the European Communities, House of Lords, Session 1995–96.

First Report on Legal Education and Training, Report for the Lord Chancellor's Advisory Committee on Legal Education and Conduct (April 1996) 171 pp (principal draftsman).

The Legal Consequences of Cross-Border Transfers of Undertakings within the European Union, Report for the European Commission DG-V (Brussels, European Commission, 1998) 45 pp.

The Transfer of Rights in Supplementary Pension Schemes in the Event of Transfers of Undertakings, Report for the European Commission DG-V (Brussels, European Commission, 1998) 75 pp. (assisted by Karen Mumgaard).

Invited memorandum on the revision of the Acquired Rights Directive to the House of Lords Select Committee on the European Communities, Session 1997–98, 22nd Report, HL Paper 98 (with Professor PL Davies).

Employment, UNCTAD series on issues in international investment agreements, (New York and Geneva, United Nations Conference on Trade and Development, 2000) 48 pp (principal draftsman).

Invited evidence on EU proposals to combat discrimination to the House of Lords Select Committee on the European Union, Session 1999–2000, 9th Report, HL Paper 68, pp 129–38.

The Future of Multi-Ethnic Britain, Report for Runnymede Trust Commission on the Future of Multi-Ethnic Britain. (the Parekh Report) (London, Profile Books, 2000) (principal draftsman of ch 19, 'Legislation and Enforcement').

Genetics and Human Behaviour: The ethical Context (Chair of Working Group)(London, Nuffield Council on Bioethics, 2002) 220 pp.

Index